The Trinitarian Dimension of John Wesley's Theology

ELMER M. COLYER

WIPF & STOCK · Eugene, Oregon

Wipf and Stock Publishers
199 W 8th Ave, Suite 3
Eugene, OR 97401

The Trinitarian Dimension of John Wesley's Theology
By Colyer, Elmer M.

Softcover ISBN-13: 979-8-3852-7673-8
Hardcover ISBN-13: 979-8-3852-7674-5
eBook ISBN-13: 979-8-3852-7675-2
Publication date 2/17/2026
Previously published by New Room Books, 2019

This edition is a scanned facsimile of the original edition published in 2019.

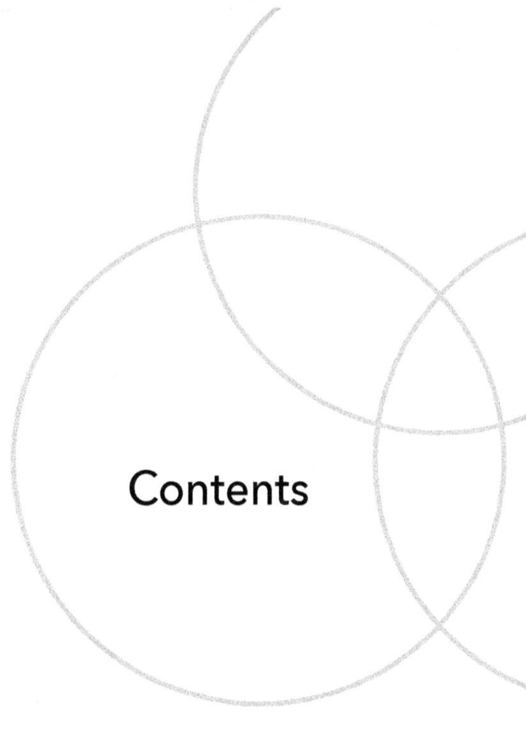

Contents

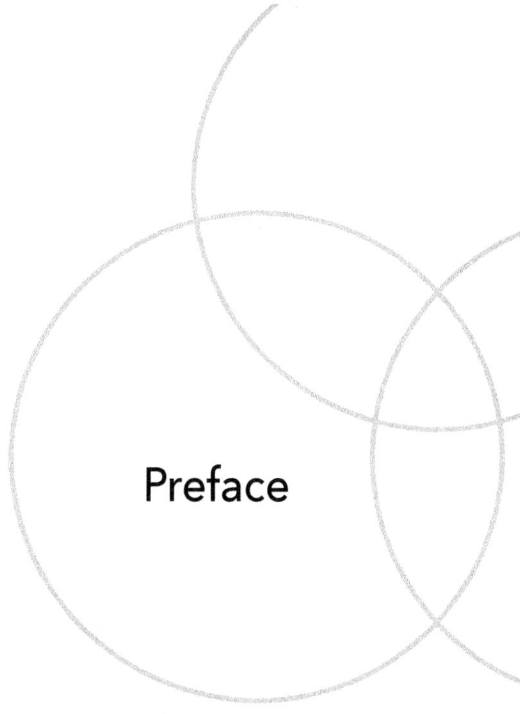

Preface

After my first encounter with John Wesley as a seminarian many years ago, I never thought I would write a book on his theology. In fact, I considered his thought unworthy of further investigation, since, like others, I viewed Wesley as the leader of a renewal movement who had little to contribute to theological reflection. I was both amused and chagrined when, at the beginning of my teaching career at the University of Dubuque Theological Seminary (UDTS), the dean asked me to offer courses that took me deeply into Wesley's theology.

While studying Wesley in order to teach his theology to seminarians, I was astonished at how theologically astute and pastorally wise he had become in the decade since I had read him in my seminary days. A PhD program in theology had deepened and widened my encounter with theology throughout the history of Christian faith, so I could now hear, in many places in Wesley's writing, reverberations of theological voices from the early church. I rediscovered what Albert Outler and many others had learned and shared about Wesley being a serious theologian who has something to say to today's church.

The idea of this monograph came as a surprise to me. Studying, teaching, and writing about Wesley's theology, especially the Trinitarian dimension of his work, became a joyful endeavor of discovery in which I have been theologically, pastorally, and personally enriched. What has been particularly gratifying is that a whole generation of United Methodist seminarians, as well as my colleagues here at UDTS, share my enthusiasm for Wesley as I recount what I have learned from him.

I dedicate the book to my United Methodist colleagues at UDTS, Tom Albin, Russ May, Phil Jamieson, Les Longden, Matt Schlimm, and Stephanie Schlimm, and to my many United Methodist students over the past twenty-five years.

I am grateful to the various scholars who read parts or all of the manuscript and provided innumerable criticisms and suggestions that improved the book. I also want to thank my student research assistants, Greg Schimpf, Cindy Marino, Travis Stevick, Corrie Aukema-Cieslukowski, Adam Penn, Gail Ray, and Robby Higgins, who helped me with all manner of mundane tasks from tracking down references to acquiring scholarly articles during the research and writing of this book. Thanks to everyone who helped move this project from an idea to a completed manuscript. Dr. M. Kathryn Armistead, publisher for New Room Books at The United Methodist General Board of Higher Education and Ministry, deserves special recognition for her enthusiasm for this book, matched only by her kindness throughout the process of getting the manuscript into print.

Christmas 2017

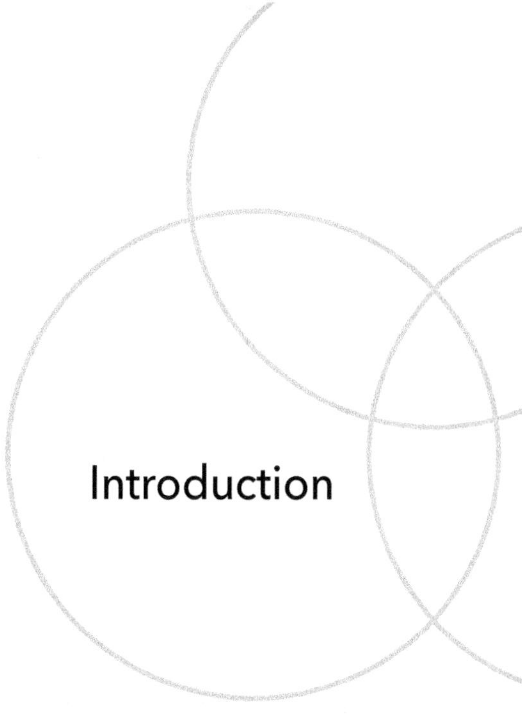

Introduction

One of the curious facts evident to anyone who spends time examining the secondary literature on John Wesley's theology is how little has been written about the Trinitarian dimension of his thought compared with how much has been published on other aspects of his theology.

With notable exceptions, the secondary literature on Wesley's theology often struggles to integrate Wesley's doctrine of the Trinity into an overarching account of his theology and fails to note the Trinitarian dimension when dealing with his soteriology and ecclesiology. Nearly all of the scholars who have written on Wesley's doctrine of the Trinity grant the importance of the Trinity in his theology. The Trinitarian dimension of Wesley's theology is far more pervasive than is evident in much of the secondary literature. Documenting the pervasive Trinitarian dimension of Wesley's theology is the goal of this monograph.

The first chapter situates Wesley's doctrine of the Trinity within the Trinitarian controversies in England in the seventeenth and eighteenth centuries. What is noteworthy is that precisely during the period when many intellectuals in the British Isles questioned the doctrine of the Trinity, John and Charles Wesley injected a robust Trinitarian dimension back into Christian faith, thought, worship, and life in early Methodism.

For over a century, heated debate about the Trinity inundated Britain in wave after wave of deep and bitter controversy, leading to preferment for some, marginalization for others, and, for one critic of the Trinity, death. Moreover, these Trinitarian controversies were part of a profound rupture of consensus about the foundations and limits of human knowledge, what constitutes a viable organization of society and government, and the place of the church in the midst of it all. The quarrel was part of far-reaching social turmoil and transition that birthed modern Western culture.

For readers who are interested in how those Trinitarian debates were part of the wider turmoil and transition, I have included substantial discussions of this historical background in the footnotes for chapter 1, as well as references to primary sources and secondary literature on the subject. Including this information in the notes keeps the central nerve of narrative recounting the Trinitarian controversies uncluttered by this additional material.

I have benefited greatly from the secondary sources dealing with various aspects of the Trinitarian controversies. Chapter 1 summarizes these Trinitarian debates from the inroads of Socinianism in the early seventeenth century through the arguments that rendered the doctrine of the Trinity unintelligible and irrelevant and finally led to the founding of the first independent and openly Unitarian congregation in England in 1774 by Theophilus Lindsey and Joseph Priestley.

These debates cast considerable light on Wesley's understanding of the Trinity and the Trinitarian dimension of his theology. What becomes clear is that the Wesley brothers' Trinitarian vision of Christian faith offered an alternative to the arid speculative accounts of the Trinity published by those who sought to defend the doctrine and in the process detached the doctrine of the Trinity from vibrant Christian faith and life. John and Charles reclaimed the doctrine of the Trinity and the Trinitarian dimension of vital Christian faith and practice. In so doing, the Wesley brothers adopted a participatory, evangelical, doxological, economic approach to the Trinity similar to what we find in the origins of Trinitarian doctrine and piety in the early church, an approach quite unlike what we see in the publications of those who sought to defend the doctrine of the Trinity in the late seventeenth and eighteenth centuries.

The final section of chapter 1 examines Wesley's sermon "On the Trinity" in light of the Trinitarian controversies, revealing just how different Wesley's vision of the Trinity and the Trinitarian character of Christian faith are when compared to the defenders whose writing profoundly damaged the doctrine and rendered it irrelevant. What Wesley said about the Trinity and its inescapable connection with the essence of the gospel raises the question of whether Wesley's summaries of the gospel in his publications bear the Trinitarian imprint his sermon on the Trinity suggests.

Chapter 2 begins by pointing out that, apart from a spate of articles on the Trinity in Wesley's theology and several discussions of the Trinity in chapters of books on Wesley's theology that include scattered insightful comments, not much has been written about the Trinitarian dimension in Wesley's theology. The rest of the chapter identifies, documents, and explains the pervasive, participatory, economic Trinitarian depictions of the essence of Christian faith or the vital religion throughout Wesley's publications from the spring of 1738 to the end of his career. These Trinitarian summaries of the gospel bear a striking similarity to what Wesley said about the doctrine of the Trinity in his sermon "On the Trinity," examined in chapter 1.

By the end of chapter 2, it becomes clear that this economic Trinitarian summary of the essence of Christian faith is actually Wesley's characteristic way of conceptualizing vital religion after 1738. Those who read my book will find it difficult not to see and identify these Trinitarian summaries when they read Wesley again.

Although we do not find Trinitarian summaries of the gospel in Wesley's publications prior to 1738, it is clear that he affirmed the doctrine of the Trinity before that crucial year. This begs the question, What happened in 1738 that caused Wesley to define vital religion in participatory Trinitarian terms? The final section of chapter 2 poses and documents an answer to this question.

If Wesley saw a Trinitarian dimension in the essence of the gospel, was his entire *ordo salutis* Trinitarian as well? Chapter 3 shows that there is a participatory, economic Trinitarian dimension in the entire fabric or pattern of salvation from beginning to end.

The first section of chapter 3 provides a brief summary of Wesley's struggle to make theological sense of his Christian faith and life within the Holy Living Tradition that profoundly influenced him from 1724 to 1738. The next section demonstrates that Wesley had a robust Trinitarian understanding of grace, not a predominately pneumatological account, as some scholars have argued. The rest of the chapter documents how Wesley often incorporated a Trinitarian dimension in his discussions of various aspects of the order of salvation, and at times in areas we would never expect, as in his reading the Trinitarian dimension back into the Genesis account of Creation and the Fall of humanity.

Since there is a Trinitarian dimension in the essence of the gospel and throughout the *ordo salutis* in Wesley's theology, one would expect to him to develop a parallel Trinitarian account of the church. This leads to the content of chapter 4, Wesley's Trinitarian vision of the church.

The first section of chapter 4 deals with some of the accounts of Wesley's ecclesiology found in secondary literature that characterize his vision of the church as functionalist, or essentially practical and primarily a means of grace. An examination follows of Wesley's sermon "Of the Church," written late in life and reflecting Wesley's mature position. This sermon reveals a profound Trinitarian understanding of the *esse* of the church similar to, and inextricably interconnected with, Wesley's Trinitarian soteriology, discussed in chapters 2 and 3.

A careful reading of this sermon makes clear that Wesley's vision of the essence of the church is unlike the Anglican Church and the Anabaptist tradition within which some scholars try to locate Wesley's ecclesiology. The same understanding of the *esse* of the church, including the Trinitarian dimension, can be found elsewhere in Wesley's writings. Even more intriguing is that Wesley's sermon "On Schism," written soon after his sermon "Of the Church," reveals an account of this unpleasant subject that parallels his discussion of the essence of the church. Schism is an unraveling of the Trinitarian essence of the church.

Chapter 4 provides a close reading of places in Wesley's writing where he construes the church in functionalist terms as a means of grace and demonstrates that Wesley was not speaking of the essence of the church but rather of the right functioning (*bene esse*) of the church in its institutional embodiment with its various structures and ministries. The key to unlocking Wesley's reflection on the *esse* of the church in relation to its *bene esse* is found in his sermon "On Zeal," one of the places where Wesley defined the church in functionalist categories. As soon as the social and ecclesial character of love and the holy tempers comes into view in the sermon "On Zeal," the consistency of Wesley's Trinitarian vision of salvation and the essence of the church becomes clear. The essence of salvation and the essence of the church are, in the end, different dimensions of a single reality within Wesley's participatory, economic Trinitarian understanding of Christian faith. The chapter provides a different spin on Wesley's often-quoted statement that Christianity is a social religion and to turn it into a solitary religion is to destroy it. Chapter 4 concludes with a discussion of the Trinitarian dimension in Wesley's account of the sacraments and the means of grace.

Did Wesley's Trinitarian vision of Christian faith actually get embodied in the life, community, worship, and ministry of the early Methodist movement? Here early Methodism is particularly interesting as the communal character of the early Methodist practices of discipleship and ministry embodies and reflects Wesley's Trinitarian participatory understanding of soteriology and ecclesiology. Chapter 5 describes how the practices, forms of community, and ministries in early Methodism both embody this Trinitarian communion at the heart of Wesley's soteriology and ecclesiology, as well as mediate it to others.

One of the fascinating things about Wesley's ecclesiology is his selection of texts when he dealt with the essence of the church (Ephesians 4) and when he provided an example of what a real Christian community should look like (Acts 2 and 4). The first section of chapter 5 identifies and discusses Wesley's appeal to Acts 2 and 4 as the dawning of a gospel day and a proper Christian church. The second section reveals that Wesley interpreted the rise of Methodism in light of Acts 2 and 4 and the gospel day and church bound up with it.

The main body of chapter 5 documents and explains the Trinitarian dimension in Wesley's accounts of the various forms of community and ministry that developed in early Methodism. Together, this material solidifies the pervasiveness and significance of the Trinitarian dimension of Wesley's ecclesiology and soteriology.

The conclusion draws the various strands of the individual chapters together in a summary of the Trinitarian dimension of Wesley's theology. This book is not a sequential argument or series of arguments; rather, the chapters identify, document, explain, and describe the Trinitarian dimension found in various themes in Wesley's theology across a wide spectrum of Wesley's publications from 1738 to the end of his life. The persuasiveness of this reading of Wesley is holistic in the way all the chapters together illumine the Trinitarian dimension of Wesley's theology.

While the primary intention of this work is to present a Trinitarian reading of Wesley's theology and to allow the Trinitarian dimension of Wesley's theology to be heard, I hope the book will also encourage appropriation and extension of Wesley's Trinitarian insights. To this end of engaging Wesley's insights, the postscript notes that these insights suggest a more comprehensive Trinitarian expression of Wesleyan/Methodist Christian faith than we have seen to date. The postscript also points out some unresolved problems in Wesley's theology, including his depiction of the moral law in Christological incarnational categories and the lack of a Trinitarian dimension in his discussions of God's attributes and the divine providence. There are better alternative ways forward while still building on Wesley's Trinitarian insights.

My hope is that this fresh reading of the Trinitarian dimension of Wesley's work will not only contribute to our understanding of the Trinitarian character of Wesley's theology and early Methodism but will also reinvigorate Trinitarian theological reflection and ecclesial vision and practice in our own day within the Wesleyan/Methodist tradition and beyond.

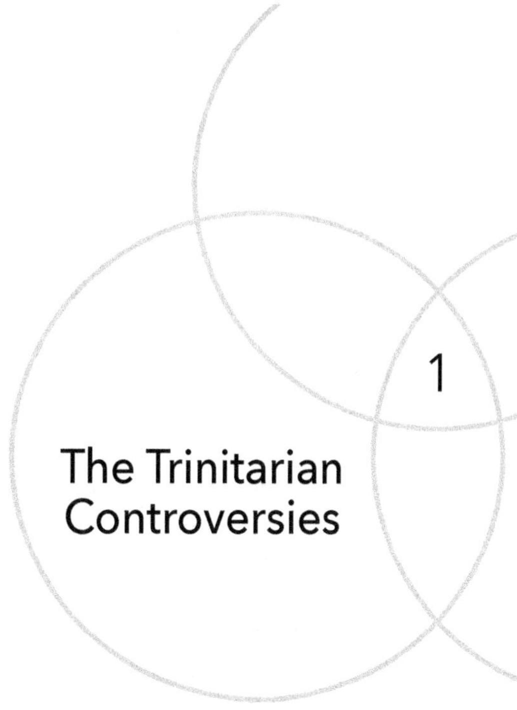

1

The Trinitarian Controversies

Introduction

In his sermon "On the Trinity," John Wesley states that the Trinity is at the heart of vital Christian faith. The sermon also reveals Wesley's awareness of the way the Trinitarian controversies in England in the seventeenth and eighteenth centuries damaged the doctrine of the Trinity. According to Wesley, it was the doctrine's defenders who "above all other persons hurt the cause which they intended to promote."[1]

This chapter examines the attacks upon the doctrine of the Trinity and the responses on the part of those who sought to defend it. The chapter indicates how the assaults on the doctrine of the Trinity arose within a wider matrix of intellectual, social, and religious upheaval. It also shows how the defenders of the Trinity damaged the doctrine by disconnecting the Trinity from the economic activity of the Triune God in the gospel, a strategy that turned the Trinity into a complex intellectual artifact unintelligible to most laypersons and irrelevant to their Christian faith, life, and worship.

The chapter (1) reveals the kinds of Trinitarian theology and defenses of the doctrine of the Trinity that Wesley saw as part of the problem, and (2) intimates the different approach to the Trinity and the Trinitarian dimension of Christian faith found in Wesley's sermons and his other publications. The

---

1 *The Works of John Wesley*, ed. Albert C. Outler, vol. 1–4 *Sermons* (Nashville: Abingdon Press, 1984–87), 2:377.

main body of the chapter provides a historical and theological context within which to read and evaluate Wesley's contribution to the resurgence and revival of Trinitarian Christian faith, thought, life, piety, worship, community, and discipleship. The final section of the chapter returns to Wesley's sermon "On the Trinity" and examines it in light of the Trinitarian controversies in England. This section leads into the discussion of the Trinitarian dimension of Wesley's theology developed in the remaining chapters of the book.

Various secondary sources have been immensely helpful in sorting through the Trinitarian controversies discussed in this chapter. The following works have been particularly beneficial: William Babcock, "The Changing of the Christian God: The Doctrine of the Trinity in the Seventeenth Century"; Philip Dixon, *Nice and Hot Disputes: The Doctrine of the Trinity in the Seventeenth Century*; William C. Placher, *The Domestication of Transcendence: How Modern Thinking about God Went Wrong*; and Jason Vickers, *Invocation and Assent: The Making and Remaking of Trinitarian Theology.*[2] This chapter summarizes Dixon's account of the Trinitarian controversies, adding material from primary and secondary sources.[3] Dixon's narrative ends with the exchange between Samuel Clarke and Daniel Waterland in the first quarter of the eighteenth century. The chapter's final section discusses what

2 See William Babcock, "The Changing of the Christian God: The Doctrine of the Trinity in the Seventeenth Century," *Interpretation* 45 (1991): 133–36; Philip Dixon, *Nice and Hot Disputes: The Doctrine of the Trinity in the Seventeenth Century* (London: T & T Clark, 2003), 34–66; William C. Placher, *The Domestication of Transcendence: How Modern Thinking about God Went Wrong* (Louisville: Westminster/John Knox, 1996); and Jason Vickers, *Invocation and Assent: The Making and Remaking of Trinitarian Theology* (Grand Rapids, MI: Eerdmans, 2008). See also Jason Vickers's important chapter "Charles Wesley and the Revival of the Doctrine of the Trinity: A Methodist Contribution to Modern Theology," in *Charles Wesley: Life, Literature & Legacy*, ed. Kenneth G. C. Newport and Ted A. Campbell (Peterborough, England: Epworth, 2007). Vickers is one of the scholars who have written on the Trinitarian character of Charles Wesley's theology, noting that Charles wanted to retrieve the Trinitarian dimension of Christian faith and life in eighteenth-century England. Vickers also sees the uniqueness of Charles Wesley's approach, which stands in sharp contrast to the Trinitarian defenders throughout the controversies over the Trinity in the seventeenth and eighteenth centuries in England.

3 Where possible, I have consulted the primary sources to deepen my understanding of the Trinitarian controversies so crucial to the intellectual history of the British Isles during the seventeenth and eighteenth centuries. In the footnotes for this chapter, I provide the references to the secondary sources and primary sources so that readers do not have to cross-reference the secondary source to retrieve the primary source references for quotations and information.

happens after the contributions of Clarke and Waterland from the 1730s to 1774, when Theophilus Lindsey and Joseph Priestley established the first openly Unitarian Congregation in England.

I. The 1640s and 1650s: The Beginning of the Trinitarian Controversy in England

1. Political and Religious Instability

The Elizabethan balance and its *via media*, or middle way, between Roman Catholicism and the more radical views of the Puritans among other Protestants was shattered in the turbulent 1640s. Oliver Cromwell (1599–1658) and the army of the predominately Puritan Parliament executed Charles I in 1649 and ended the monarchy and the Church of England for a time. The English Civil War plunged the British Isles into a period of chaos and confusion.[4]

4 The complex history of the English Reformation from the time of King Henry VIII (1491–1547) to Elizabeth I (1533–1603) resulted in a Church of England characterized by the *via media*. This "Elizabethan settlement" included the Act of Supremacy (1559), which declared Elizabeth to be head of state and church, as well as the Act of Uniformity (1559), which required the use of the Book of Common Prayer in churches and demanded that clergy and other officials affirm the doctrinal statements found in the Thirty-Nine Articles of Religion, including the doctrine of the Trinity. The Book of Homilies, provided substantially by Thomas Cranmer (1489–1556), supplied an expanded exposition of the theological legacy of the Church of England.

However, the Elizabethan settlement remained a "middle way" always caught between the still-present Roman Catholics on the one side and the Puritans, among other Protestants, concerned to complete the unfinished Reformation of England. There were protests on the part of the Puritans and Roman Catholics and controversies in the 1570s and 1580s that threatened the middle way of the Church of England. By the beginning of the seventeenth century, Richard Hooker, in his classic *Of the Laws of Ecclesiastical Polity* (1595), outlined and defended the *via media* of the Elizabethan Settlement.

Although Hooker sought to ameliorate the conflicts with the Puritans and Catholics, it was not long before tensions resurfaced. The movement of King James I (1566–1625) and his son, Charles I (1600–1649), toward Roman Catholicism could not but elicit antagonism and resistance on the part of the Puritans and other Protestants who saw the need for further conformity of the church's belief and practice to the simple teachings of scripture in order to complete the Reformation, an idea that recurs throughout the Trinitarian controversies. It is no coincidence that it was precisely during the tumultuous 1640s and 1650s that anti-Trinitarian ideas found pervasive expression in England.

Oliver Cromwell's victory provided a religious freedom of sorts, but it also led to a proliferation of various religious groups, including Presbyterians, Baptists,

Religious disputes played a crucial role in the turmoil and disorder that engulfed church and state. In turn, the civil anarchy created a context in which heterodox religious doctrine and practice developed nearly unchecked because of the breakdown of censorship.[5] Tracts streamed from presses no longer regulated. The result of the disruption of censorship in the 1640s to 1660, as Philip Dixon noted, was that "dogma, moral teaching and the interpretation of scripture was examined, questioned and rejected as never before."[6]

It is during these chaotic decades that we find the root issues around which the future conflicts over the doctrine of the Trinity from the 1690s will revolve, including the role of reason, the nature of language, the place of tradition, the need for toleration, the interpretation of the Bible, and the meaning of the term "person" in relation to God.[7] Many of the themes in the controversies from the 1690s through the 1770s were already present in the debates in the 1640s and 1650s.

Thomas Edwards (1599–1647), a convinced Puritan and Presbyterian known for his temper and vitriolic diatribe, wrote a treatise in 1646 entitled

---

Congregationalists, and Quakers, among others. The whole period came to be viewed as a time of religious fanaticism, and it instilled a deep mistrust, if not outright fear, of zealous religiosity among the English. See Richard Heitzenrater's splendid overview of this history from the Reformation to the beginning of the eighteenth century in his book *Wesley and the People Called Methodist* (Nashville: Abingdon, 1995), 2–17. See also Henry D. Rack, *Reasonable Enthusiast: John Wesley and the Rise of Methodism*, 2nd ed. (Nashville: Abingdon, 1992), 1–42.

5 See Christopher Hill, *The World Turned Upside Down* (London: Temple Smith, 1972); John Morrill, *The Nature of the English Revolution* (London: Longman, 1993); Nigel Smith, *Literature and Revolution in England 1640–1660* (New Haven: Yale University Press, 1994); and Dixon, *Hot Disputes*.

The dynamics of "theory reception" are always influenced by sociological factors, like the relaxation of censorship that allows for the questioning of what had been communally normative ideas, theories, or doctrines. "Theory reception" refers to that complex nonlinear social process of exploring, evaluating, and appropriating ideas, theories, or doctrines, while also criticizing, rejecting, and marginalizing other rival ideas, theories, or doctrines. See Alister McGrath's account of "theory reception" in Alister McGrath, *A Scientific Theology,* 3 vols. (Grand Rapids: Eerdmans, 2001–3), vol. 3, *Theory,* 213–36.

The whole history of the Trinitarian controversies can be viewed as an example of the messy process of theory reception. In the end, the historic doctrine of the Trinity was not "received" but rather rejected by many intellectuals not only in England but throughout Western culture in the seventeenth, eighteenth, and nineteenth centuries.

6 Dixon, *Hot Disputes*, 34.

7 Ibid., 35.

Gangraena, against various errors preached by radical sects that developed in the early 1640s in London and elsewhere in the chaotic context of the Civil War. He railed against the "swarms . . . of all sorts of illiterate mechanick Preachers, yea of women and Boy Preachers . . . for we instead of a reformation, are grown from one extreme to another, . . . from Popish innovations . . . to damnable heresies, horrid blasphemies, Libertinisme and fearful anarchy."[8] What is especially revealing in Edwards's list of errors are those related to the doctrine of the Trinity, for they provide a summary of many of the major themes at the center of the later Trinitarian debates:

> 8. That right reason is the rule of Faith, and that we are to believe the scriptures, and the Doctrine of the Trinity, Incarnation, Resurrection, so far as we see them agreeable to reason, and no further.
>
> 24. That in the unity of the God-head there is not a trinity of Persons, but the Doctrine of the Trinity, believed and professed in the Church of God, is a Popish tradition and a doctrine of Rome.
>
> 25. There are not three distinct persons in the Divine essence, but only three offices; the Father, Son, and holy Ghost are not three persons, but offices.
>
> 26. That there is but one Person in the Divine nature.[9]

One of the chief sources behind the anti-Trinitarian teaching in the tumultuous 1640s and 1650s was Socinianism, whose ideas spread to England from the continent. The other source arose in England out of an unfortunate combining of post-Reformation biblical primitivism, with its desire to "complete" the Reformation, and the growing rationalism in intellectuals like Francis Bacon, René Descartes, and John Locke. The combination of these

---

8 Thomas Edwards, *Gangraena* (London, 1646), from "The Epistle Dedicatory," unpaginated, qtd. in Dixon, *Hot Disputes*, 36.

9 Edwards, *Gangraena*, 19, 21, qtd. in Dixon, *Hot Disputes*, 37. Edwards was not alone in his estimations. Ephraim Pagitt, a royalist-turned-Presbyterian, identifies four groups who rejected the Trinity in his work *Heresiography*. Some Anabaptists believed that "Christ is not true God." The "Familialists" thought it "ridiculous" to say that Father, Son, and Spirit are each God because in so doing "they should affirme to be three Gods." Socinians reject that Christ is truly God and deny any scriptural basis for the Trinity. The fourth group of "Antitrinitarians," or new Arians, "deny the Trinity of Persons" and do not believe that Christ and the Spirit are of the divine essence (Ephraim Pagitt, *Heresiography*, 2nd ed. [London, 1645], 12, 86, 125, 154). See also Dixon, *Hot Disputes*, 38–39.

two streams of thought led to the idea that the meaning of scripture is rendered by reason alone without appeal to the church fathers, tradition, or the Spirit.[10] Socinianism reflects these motifs as well.

2. Socinian Inroads in England

Socinianism had its source in northern Italian Renaissance humanism and individualism, particularly Faustus Socinus (actually Sozzini) (1539–1604).[11] Socinianism, with its Renaissance humanist background, viewed scripture interpreted by human reason to be the sole source of its teaching. When the interpretation of a text of scripture was in question, it is reason, not the church, tradition, or the Holy Spirit, that properly renders its meaning.

Socinianism ruled out belief in Christ's deity and the doctrine of the Trinity as unreasonable, indeed unintelligible, and also unscriptural. In fact, it also observed that the very terms "Trinity" and "three persons," used in reference to God, are not found in scripture but represent the intrusion of popish innovations into Christian faith. Socinianism viewed itself as simply the full culmination of the Reformation impulse left incomplete by the magisterial Reformers. This Socinian attack on the Trinity as both unscriptural and unreasonable made its way to the British Isles when the Racovian Catechism was translated into Latin and arrived in England as early as 1609.[12]

By the 1640s, Socinianism was viewed as a growing threat in England. In 1647, Paul Best (1590–1657), a friend of John Milton, encountered Socinian views while traveling in Poland and became a convinced anti-Trinitarian. Best

10 Dixon, *Hot Disputes*, 39, 53.

11 Because of his radical views, Socinus was forced to leave his homeland, migrating first to Basel and then to Poland, where the ruler, Sigismund II, provided a safe haven for dissidents fleeing persecution. There in Rakow, Socinus's views evolved, and he promoted them through the founding of a college (Dixon, *Hot Disputes*, 39–40). See also H. John MacLachlan, *Socinianism in Seventeenth Century England* (Oxford: Oxford University Press, 1951) for an in-depth discussion of Socinus and Socinianism.

12 Dixon, *Hot Disputes*, 39–41. It was at the Socinian college in Rakow in 1605 that the infamous "Racovian Catechism" came into being, providing a summary of Socinian doctrine. Since the term "person" refers to an individual intelligent essence (*essentia individua intelligem*), God can only be one person. For the Socinians, Trinitarian Christians can be saved, but Trinitarian belief is dangerous because it confuses God's unity and is a stumbling block to the conversion of those outside Christian faith who cannot understand why Christians believe in three Gods. Socinian monotheism views Christ as a human mediator between God and humanity and the Spirit as the personification of God's activity in history (*Catechesis ecclesiarum quae in regno Poloniae* [Racoviae, 1609], 32, 41–42, summarized in Dixon, *Hot Disputes*, 40–41).

published his *Mysteries Discovered*, an open attack on the doctrine of the Trinity, which was written while he was imprisoned for blasphemy.[13]

Yet, even more moderate figures, like John Fry (1609–1657), who claimed to be orthodox, found themselves profoundly troubled by the use of "three persons" in reference to God. In a clearly orthodox statement, Fry, in the late 1640s, affirmed "that the Father is God, the Son is God, and the Holy Ghost is God, and that these three are equally God . . . and yet there are not three Gods but one God." Nevertheless, he objected to the use of the term "person" because he wondered "how it can be demonstrated, that there can be three distinct persons, or subsistencies in one entire being."[14] For Fry, to speak of three persons in reference to God is unscriptural, misleading, irrational, and in danger of tritheism.

Socinianism created suspicion about the doctrine of the Trinity in England in the 1640s and 1650s. It led some, like Best, straight into anti-Trinitarianism. But Socinianism, with its biblicism and appeal to reason, generated questions about the appropriateness of the accepted language used to articulate the doctrine of the Trinity even among those who considered themselves to be orthodox. This is especially true of the terms "Trinity" and "person," terms that end up at the center of the Trinitarian controversies from the 1690s into the eighteenth century, and terms Wesley said he used without scruple, even though they are not in scripture.

3. John Biddle, English Unitarianism, and Further Developments

John Biddle (1615–1662), father of the English Unitarians, appears to be the first person on English soil to assert that God is "one person." Biddle was the most significant anti-Trinitarian writer prior to the 1690s. His influence was immense, and his works were republished in the early 1690s, when the Trinitarian controversies flared up and engulfed much of the intellectual landscape in England.[15]

Like the Socinians, Biddle praised Luther and Calvin "for the pains they took in cleansing our Religion from sundry idolatrous Pollutions of the

---

13 Dixon, *Hot Disputes*, 43–44. According to Best, to speak of "three persons" implies three individuals and thus three gods. Following the Socinian attack on the Trinity, Best appealed to scripture interpreted by reason and viewed the Trinity as a corruption that crept into the church in the third century (ibid., 44–45).

14 John Fry, *The Accuser Shamd* (London, 1648), 15, 21–23, qtd. in Dixon, *Hot Disputes*, 45–46.

15 Dixon, *Hot Disputes*, 49.

Romane Anti-Christ, yet are the dregs still left behinde."[16] Chief among the dregs was the doctrine of the Trinity, which for Biddle was "a baffle on the simplicity of scripture."[17]

Biddle was imprisoned numerous times for his dissident views, and his critique of the doctrine of the Trinity in the late 1640s reveals what became a familiar intellectual path: (1) the doctrine of the Trinity is not found in scripture, and there is no biblical basis for the technical terms used to explicate the doctrine; (2) contested biblical interpretation is resolved not by appeal to tradition or the church but by human reason alone; and (3) the designation " three persons" is inappropriate when utilized in reference to God for it indicates three separate deities.[18]

Biddle defines a person as "an intellectual substance compleat" (*suppositum intelligens*).[19] This understanding of person can be traced back to Boethius and his infamous definition of a person as *naturae rationabilis individua substantia*, an individual substance of the rational nature. Boethius's way of understanding person repeatedly created problems for conceptualizing the Trinity throughout the seventeenth and into the eighteenth century, as will become clear as this chapter unfolds.

In 1648, the Draconic Ordinance was passed with its proposed strict punishment for those critical of the doctrine of the Trinity. Orthodox defenders, like John Owen, Francis Cheynell, and Nicholas Estwick, wrote works designed to counter the writings of the Socinians and Biddle. These defenders tried to (1) refute the charges of irrationality and tritheism; (2) demonstrate that the term "person" could bear a Trinitarian interpretation; and (3) develop the biblical basis for the doctrine of the Trinity.[20]

The growing rationalism of the era shifted the understanding of language in ways that made talk about God as Triune appear either baffling or absurd. Instead of seeing knowledge of the Trinitarian persons arising out of one's participation in the gospel, where one comes to know the love of God the Father through the grace of Christ in the fellowship of the Spirit,

---

16 John Biddle, *A Confession of Faith Touching the Holy Trinity, According to the Scripture* (London, 1648), 2–3. See Dixon, *Hot Disputes*, 52.

17 John Biddle, *A Twofold Catechism* (London: 1654), preface qtd. in Dixon, *Hot Disputes*, 53.

18 Dixon, *Hot Disputes*, 49–53.

19 Dixon provides Biddle's definition of "person" (ibid., 51).

20 See Francis Cheynell, *The Divine Triunity of the Father, Son and Holy Spirit* (London, 1650); John Owen, *Vindicae evangelicae* (Oxford, 1656); and Nicholas Estwick, *Mr. Biddle's Confession of Faith Touching the Holy Trinity* (London, 1656), all referenced in Dixon, *Hot Disputes*, 55–65.

and allowing that content to inform one's understanding of the Triune God, including how one conceives of "person" when predicated of God, critics and defenders alike focused on current philosophical and cultural understandings of "person" and then tried to show how these concepts of person led to either tritheism or how they could bear a Trinitarian exposition. This shift in the grounding of the meaning of Trinitarian discourse from our participation in the Trinitarian gospel to current philosophical conceptions of "person" doomed orthodox defenses of the doctrine of the Trinity before the defenders ever put their pens to paper. By accepting the contemporary philosophical assumptions around language and the meaning of "person" in particular, the Trinitarian defenders appeared to be less than successful, and that fact fueled the growth of anti-Trinitarian sentiment, a point that recurs again and again in the Trinitarian controversies that follow.[21]

---

21 William Babcock was one of the first scholars to see the importance of the Trinitarian debates of seventeenth-century England for the marginalization of the doctrine of the Trinity in modern Western culture. His 1991 article "A Changing of the Christian God: The Doctrine of the Trinity in the Seventeenth Century" paved the way for several other scholarly forays into the fate of the doctrine of the Trinity in the period (see Babcock, "Changing of the Christian God," 134ff.).

It is also to Babcock's credit that he sees the marginalization of the doctrine of the Trinity as bound up with a much larger "shift in sensibilities that led much of Western Christianity to a tacit changing of its God." Babcock suggests that "there took place, in one strand of seventeenth-century English culture, a monumental and ultimately successful struggle to recast the language of learned discourse and that one outcome of the struggle was to drain the language of Trinitarian doctrine, at least as then current, of its meaning" (ibid., 135).

This shift in sensibility in Western culture beginning in the seventeenth and eighteenth centuries was much larger than simply a recasting of the language of learned discourse, as Babcock notes. The rise and success of modern natural science, advances in philosophy, the dawning of the Enlightenment, with its confidence in human reason to solve the riddles and problems of human life, all involved questioning many assumptions inherited from the premodern world beyond simply recasting language in the seventeenth and eighteenth centuries.

This shift in sensibility raises the highly contentious question of when and why modern culture arises. As William Placher correctly notes, "The beginning for the modern era has been dated everywhere from the origin of the Renaissance to the French Revolution" (see Placher, *Domestication*, 1ff.).

Placher maintains that it was in the seventeenth century that intellectuals became much more confident in the powers of human reason to understand God and the world. At the same time, they also restricted what constitutes a valid argument for, and valid articulation of, Christian faith. Intellectuals applied the same restriction in many fields of human discourse. Placher astutely notes just how traumatic the

II. The 1660s to 1680s: Developments after the Restoration

The Civil War left its mark on the rest of the seventeenth century and led to the subsequent quest for stability. With the "restoration" of Charles II to the

---

seventeenth century was for Western culture, with the Thirty Years' War bloodying the landscape and killing a third of Germany's population, civil war fragmenting England, plagues ravaging various countries, and severe depressions sapping economic health in various cultures. Placher argues, "In such a context, the modern appeal to reason, rigorously defined, can appear less a matter of confident optimism than a kind of desperation" (Placher, *Domestication*, 5).

For a masterful charting of the current scholarly debate and lack of consensus about when the modern era comes into being in England, particularly in relation to the social and cultural context of Wesley and early Methodism, see Jeremy Gregory, "The Long Eighteenth Century," in *The Cambridge Companion to John Wesley*, ed. Randy L. Maddox and Jason E. Vickers (Cambridge: Cambridge University Press, 2010), 14–16, 23–25.

The older position emphasized that the eighteenth century is when the modernizing of England took place. This view dominated historiography in the nineteenth and most of the twentieth centuries. See, for example, Roy Porter, *English Society in the Eighteenth Century* (London: Allen Lane, 1982). This modernizing thesis profoundly influenced the way scholars read Wesley as reviving vibrant Christian faith in his day, standing against the culture, and resisting the secularizing and modernizing tendencies of his context.

Yet a growing number of historians contest this view of England in the eighteenth century and see Wesley's context primarily in terms of continuity rather than rupture and the dawning of modern English culture. J. C. D. Clark, in his monumental study *English Society, 1688–1832: Ideology, Social Structure and Political Practice during the Ancient Regime,* argues for a complete rejection of the modernizing account of eighteenth-century England. Clark maintains that the power of the Anglican Church in political and social life created a situation in which radicalism in politics could be developed only in relation to heterodoxy in theology, including anti-Trinitarian sentiment. This radicalism in politics and theology was held in check by the effective hegemony of the Anglican Church throughout the eighteenth century. See also Clark's recent restatement of his understanding of the eighteenth-century context in relation to Wesley and early Methodism, "The Eighteenth-Century Context," in *The Oxford Handbook of Methodist Studies,* ed. William J. Abraham and James E. Kirby (Oxford: Oxford University Press, 2009), 3–29.

Clark's thesis has faced challenges from various quarters by those who remain convinced that modernity was taking hold in English society in the eighteenth century. Clark also sees too close a link between political radicalism and heterodoxy in theology, particularly anti-Trinitarianism of various kinds (Arian, Socinian, or Unitarian). In the 1750s, 1760s, and 1770s, there is a closer link between Socinian and

throne and the Church of England to its place as the national church, the virtues of stability and legitimate hierarchy gained ascendency once again.[22]

Unitarian criticism of the Trinity and radical politics in some of the key protagonists. But Dixon, among others, has noted that there is no "straight-forward corollary between religious and political radicalism" in the late seventeenth and on into the eighteenth centuries. An attack on the Trinity is not always an attack on the established civil order of "Church-King-Parliament" (Dixon, *Hot Disputes*, 2, 174). Already in the seventeenth century, John Donne (1572–1631) argued that "the Trinitarian God was a model for a pluralist state" (David Nichols, "Divine Analogy: The Theological Politics of John Donne," *Political Studies* 32 [1984]: 580, qtd. in Dixon, *Hot Disputes*, 1).

We do not need to resolve the issues for our purposes, though Jeremy Gregory is surely correct in his judgment that these "binary polarities" of "traditional" and "modernizing" accounts of "the eighteenth century in Britain/England are rather misleading. We need a more complicated and nuanced account" (Gregory, "Long Eighteenth Century," in *Cambridge Companion*, 23).

22 British Parliament invited Charles II (1630–1685) to the throne in 1660, reestablishing both the monarchy and the Church of England. This transition, of course, did not mean that everyone's mind had changed about the need for further reformation of the Church of England. The seeds of anti-Trinitarian sentiment sown in the 1640s and 1650s were still present in a growing minority within England, awaiting germination and expression when conditions were more favorable (see Heitzenrater, *Wesley and the People*, 14–15).

The whole situation was further complicated by the fact that Charles II had Roman Catholic tendencies. These became public. With Charles's death in 1685 and the ascension of James II (1633–1701), the situation worsened, as James II openly professed his Roman sympathies and appointed Roman Catholic dons at Oxford and Cambridge Universities, as well as Catholics to offices in the state and army (see Rack, *Reasonable Enthusiast*, 39).

In the end, Parliament decided to curtail the move toward Rome in this line of monarchs by inviting James's Protestant daughter, Mary (1662–1694), to the throne, with her husband, Prince William of Orange (1650–1702), as king. It was a "bloodless revolution" in 1688 as James wisely fled to France rather than challenge William and Mary's army. Those leaders in the church who supported James (the Jacobites) and could not sign the oath to the new king and queen under the Act of Supremacy lost their positions in the church and in the government (nonjurors) (see Heitzenrater, *Wesley and the People*, 14–15).

All of the religious and related political turmoil in the second half of the seventeenth century posed a profound problem for the Church of England around its stance toward the undeniable religious diversity that the Act of Conformity simply could not erase. Another group developed within the Church of England for whom orthodox doctrine and liturgical conformity were far less important than tolerance (the latitudinarians). This loosely connected group stressed a simplified Christian faith that downplayed the more mysterious doctrines (the Trinity and the

In 1662, the Act of Uniformity required "unfeigned consent and assent" to both the Thirty-Nine Articles of Religion (including the doctrine of the Trinity) as the standard of true doctrine and the Anglican Book of Common Prayer (with its Trinitarian liturgy and classical Trinitarian creeds) as the only legitimate form of worship. This act led to more than 1,700 "nonconformist" clergy refusing to assent and losing their appointments, including the financial and other benefits associated with them.[23]

In 1662, a licensing act reintroduced censorship of printed materials by the church and universities to help enforce the Act of Uniformity. But conformity ended up being an ideal impossible to enforce. So the questioning of the Anglican Church, its practices and its official doctrine, continued both in private and in print throughout the 1660s to 1680s. The doctrine of the Trinity was on the short list of ultimate beliefs probed, criticized, and denounced by more than a few, including intellectuals like John Milton and Thomas Hobbes.

1. John Milton

John Milton (1608–1674) is an example of the growing dissatisfaction with the doctrine of the Trinity. While Milton in his earlier years was orthodox in his beliefs, later in life he moved away from a Trinitarian perspective toward a position similar to that of Arius, the infamous critic of the Trinity in the third and fourth centuries of the early church. Many of the themes from the 1640s and 1650s appear in Milton's work *A Treatise on Christian Doctrine*, discovered in 1825 in Latin manuscript.[24]

Milton found little scriptural warrant for the Trinity, except for the Johannine Comma (1 John 5:7), which Milton saw as the main text supporting the Trinitarian error. He asserted that "on the authority of this text, almost

---

Incarnation) and emphasized the use of reason in religious matters and morality as the central content of the gospel. The mainstream of Anglican leadership suspected this group of being anemic toward, if not opposed to, the doctrine of the Trinity as well as the Incarnation (see Rack, *Reasonable Enthusiast*, 39).

As will become clear later in this chapter, there were latitudinarians who wanted to revise, and in cases reject, the doctrine of the Trinity, but they were not always inclined to admit it publicly out of fear of recrimination. Open denial of the Trinity could be a dangerous act in the second half of the seventeenth and first half of the eighteenth centuries in England.

23 John Spurr, *The Restoration Church of England* (London: Yale University Press, 1991), 43ff. See also Dixon, *Hot Disputes*, 66–67, 98–99, for a helpful summary of these transitions.

24 Dixon, *Hot Disputes*, 101–2.

exclusively, . . . the whole doctrine of the Trinity has been hastily adopted."[25] Like others at the end of the seventeenth century, Milton questioned the authenticity of the text. Since there is little scriptural warrant for the doctrine of the Trinity beyond the Johannine Comma, the Trinity, like transubstantiation, turned out to be a corruption introduced by the Roman Catholic Church.

Milton called for both a return to the true and clear sense of scripture as the only rule of faith, and also a commitment to complete the yet-unfinished Reformation of the church. Unlike the Socinians, but similar to Biddle, Milton saw that the Father, Son, and Spirit can be called "persons" according to scripture. What he did not find in the Bible is their equality and consubstantiality.

Thus, he ended with a subordination of the Son, as the first of Creation, to the Father, who alone is supreme. He rejected the idea that the Son is "of the same being" with the Father. The Spirit ended up subordinate to both.[26] This kind of Arian subordinationism reappeared in many later anti-Trinitarians, like Samuel Clarke. However, unlike Milton, whose anti-Trinitarian sentiments came to light only posthumously, Clarke and the others championed their views publicly and got themselves into trouble in the process.

2. Thomas Hobbes

There is still significant scholarly debate as to whether Thomas Hobbes (1588–1679) was an outright atheist or merely a believer with rather eccentric beliefs concerning the Trinity.[27] What is significant about Hobbes for the

---

25 John Milton, *A Treatise on Christian Doctrine*, trans. Charles R. Summers (Cambridge: Cambridge University Press, 1825), 171. See Dixon, *Hot Disputes*, 104.

26 Ibid., 87, 161, 166. See Dixon's insightful treatment of Milton in Dixon, *Hot Disputes*, 101–4.

27 Dixon, *Hot Disputes*, 99–100. On the one end of the interpretive spectrum is Leo Strauss, who sees Hobbes as a subversive atheist, a purposefully esoteric writer, whose subtle and deliberate ambiguities are simply part of his plot to unravel Christian faith, including the doctrine of the Trinity (Leo Strauss, *The Political Philosophy of Hobbes* [Oxford: Clarendon, 1936], esp. chap. 5). See also Dixon, *Hot Disputes*, 66–97, for an insightful treatment of Hobbes.

At the other end of the spectrum is Aloysius P. Martinich, who views Hobbes as "a sincere, and relatively orthodox, Christian," though clearly Sabellian in his views on the Trinity (Aloysius P. Martinich, *The Two Gods of the* Leviathan [Cambridge: Cambridge University Press, 1992], 1, 205). Of course, if Hobbes is Sabellian, he can hardly be considered a basically orthodox Christian. See also Martinich's more recent work on Hobbes, *Thomas Hobbes* (London: Macmillan, 1997).

Dixon argues persuasively that Hobbes is best understood as an eccentric Christian, reinterpreting the Trinity using a non-Boethian definition of person. However,

purpose of this book is that he is one of the first thinkers in the later seventeenth century to self-consciously shift his understanding of the concept of "person" and then utilize it to reinterpret the doctrine of the Trinity.

This shift in his understanding of person arose out of his discontent with the Aristotelian natural philosophy and Scholastic method he had encountered in his student days in Magdalen Hall, Oxford, including the Aristotelian understanding of language in general and "person" in particular. It is a discontent found in Bacon, Descartes, Newton, and Locke. Listen to Hobbes's pointed criticism:

> There is yet another fault in the Discourses of some men; which may also be numbred amongst the sorts of Madnesse; namely, that abuse of words. . . . When men speak such words, as put together, have in them no signification at all . . . as the Schoole-men [do]. . . . See if he can translate any one chapter concerning any difficult point; as the Trinity; the Deity; the nature of Christ; . . . etc. into any of the moderne tongues, so as to make the same intelligible. . . . When men write whole volumes of such stuffe, are they not Mad, or intend to make others so?[28]

Hobbes's sentiments reflect those of Bacon: the ill-formed Scholastic Aristotelian language he learned at Oxford was both artificial and incapable of fostering genuine knowledge of the world or of formulating a political agenda, let alone rendering intelligible the doctrine of the Trinity.[29]

---

one is hard-pressed to find a single orthodox contemporary of Hobbes who shares Dixon's sentiments. I see Hobbes as most likely a very idiosyncratic believer or one of the most clever and deliberate esoteric anti-Christian writers of the modern era.

28 Thomas Hobbes, *Leviathan*, introd. A. D. Lindsay (New York: Dutton, 1950), chap. 8. See Dixon, *Hot Disputes*, 71. Hobbes attacked the Scholastic Aristotelianism of Francisco Suárez by name. See Placher, *Domestication*, 74–82, for a helpful discussion of the significance of Suárez.

29 Bacon wanted nothing less than "a total reconstruction of the sciences, arts and all human knowledge, raised upon the proper foundations" (Francis Bacon, *The New Organon and Related Writings*, ed. Fulton H. Anderson [Indianapolis: Bobbs-Merrill,1960], 3). See also Babcock, "Changing of the Christian God," 136. This quotation reveals the profound sense of discontent with the accepted forms of human thought and culture, and signals just how far-reaching a change Bacon, among others, had in mind.

Bacon was quite aware of the social construction of language and its thick association with forms of life and vested interests, and the way in which the human mind can impose those forms, concepts, or ideas on what it seeks to know so that the act of knowing deforms the knowledge that results. Language could be ill-formed, according to Bacon, "confused and overhastily abstracted from facts," and then

Hobbes radically departed from the accepted forms of scholarly expression current in the second half of the seventeenth century. Hobbes's

---

lodged in "the vulgar" masses as "idols and false notions which are now in possession of the human understanding" and "so beset men's minds that truth can hardly find entrance." Bacon insightfully noted, "Men believe that their reason governs words; but it is also true that words react on the understanding" (Bacon, *The New Organon*, 41, 49, 56, 47). See also Babcock, "Changing of the Christian God," 136.

Even more troubling for Bacon than the confusion of the "vulgar" masses was the learned discourse of Aristotelian natural philosophy he first encountered in Cambridge during his years as a student, for the Aristotelians, in a far more learned way, also forced reality to fit their "decisions and axioms" instead of allowing experience to shape their concepts and theories (Bacon, *The New Organon*, 61). See also Babcock, "Changing of the Christian God," 136–37. This Aristotelian tradition lodged in the educational system in England was, in fact, profoundly mistaken and part of the problem. Hobbes and Locke, among others, all saw this Aristotelian tradition as a major impediment.

Bacon realized that there had to be a more adequate way to integrate form in the sciences, arts, and all of human knowledge. Bacon's alternative was to focus "upon experience and the facts of nature" and utilize his famous "method of induction" to develop concepts and theories in strict conformity to what the human subject seeks to know (Bacon, *The New Organon*, 61, 11). See also Babcock, "Changing of the Christian God," 137. Babcock maintains that Bacon argued for "an abandonment of theory in favor of a patient and attentive dwelling 'upon experience and the facts of nature'" so as to accumulate data from which to form ideas and recast discourse via induction (ibid.).

But this is an oversimplification of Bacon's views. Bacon actually argued against "empiricists" who "like ants, only heap up and use what they accumulate." He was equally critical of rationalists or "dogmatists" who "like spiders, spin webs out of their own resources." Bacon saw that there had to be a much profounder interaction, coordination, or integration between the empirical and theoretical components in human knowing, which he likens to a "bee" that "gathers material from the flowers of the garden and the field, and digests it by its own faculties. . . . We have good reason, therefore, to derive hope from a closer and purer alliance of the faculties (the experimental and rational) than has yet been attempted" (Francis Bacon, *Novum organum scientiarum* [London: John Brill, 1620], 1:102). See McGrath, *Scientific Theology*, vol. 3, *Theory*, 1, especially pages 10–14, for a more judicious account of Bacon's defense of the importance of theory. Although Bacon's method of induction is clearly inadequate to the "closer and purer alliance" between the empirical and theoretical elements that have to be coordinated or integrated in human knowing, at least he clearly saw the problem and the issues at stake.

Already in Bacon we see a radical questioning of the received framework of thought and culture, including the ill-formed language of Scholastic Aristotelian philosophy and how that language is actually an impediment to genuine knowledge. This criticism by Bacon and others of language, its artificiality, and its inability

new way of thinking and speaking, along with his vitriolic anticlericalism, created near-universal rejection of his views by orthodox Trinitarian scholars and Anglican leaders, among others.[30]

When Hobbes deployed his concept of "person," it was not the doctrine of the Trinity that was his real concern. Rather, in the forefront of his mind was his political agenda of developing the idea of an absolute sovereign whose actions are authorized by his subjects since the sovereign acts on their behalf.[31] Hobbes rejected the static Boethian definition of person (an individual substance of a rational nature) assumed by most intellectuals in his day and developed a more dynamic concept of person, one centered on action and the person as actor. Hobbes found intimations of this kind of conception of "person" in Cicero.[32]

This dynamic view of person as actor led to Hobbes's distinction between a "naturall" person and an "artificiall" person. For Hobbes, a person is one

---

to foster efficacious epistemic activity created deep problems for the doctrine of the Trinity in the second half of the seventeenth into the eighteenth century. The received language, the very concepts used in explicating the doctrine of the Trinity, including "substance," "nature," and "person," were all called into question and redefined by various thinkers, including Hobbes and Locke, as will become clear by the end of this chapter.

The other move we see already in Bacon is the modern turn to the subjective pole of the knowing relation and the attempt to map the inner processes of human perception and cognition that lead to genuine knowledge. The goal is to render the conditions of indubitable knowledge entirely explicit (foundationalism), a quest that ends in skepticism rather than absolutely certain knowledge. See Elmer M. Colyer, "The Integration of Form in Theology," in *How to Read T. F. Torrance: Understanding His Trinitarian and Scientific Theology* (Downers Grove, IL: InterVarsity, 2001), chap. 9, for an account of this modern turn to the subject, from Descartes through Kant, and then how Einstein, Polanyi, and Torrance all attempt to move toward a non-foundationalist critical realist epistemology. The chapter also discusses the nature of doctrine and the doctrine of the Trinity in the theology of Thomas F. Torrance. See also Elmer M. Colyer, *The Nature of Doctrine in T. F. Torrance's Theology* (Eugene, OR: Wipf and Stock, 2001) for a fuller account of the debate around the nature of doctrine that developed since George Lindbeck published his important work *The Nature of Doctrine* (Philadelphia: Westminster, 1984).

30 Dixon, *Hot Disputes*, 70–73, 95–97. By the end of Hobbes's life, "Hobbism" had become a slur of the most disparaging variety (ibid., 96).

31 Ibid., 74–75.

32 In *Leviathan*, chap. 16, Hobbes quotes Cicero's famous maxim: "*Unus sustineo tres Personas; Mei, Adversarii, & Judicis,*" (I bear three Persons: my own, my Adversaries, and the Judges) (Cicero, *De oratore* 2:102; emphasis mine; see Dixon, *Hot Disputes*, 75).

whose words or actions either are her own or represent the words of another. For example, the press secretary for the White House does not speak or act on her own behalf but rather communicates on behalf of the president.

Hobbes said that when one's words or actions "are considered as his owne, then he is called a *Naturall Person*: And when considered as representing the words or actions of an other, then he is a *Feigned* or *Artificiall Person*."[33] When the Sovereign speaks or acts on behalf of the subjects, which Hobbes also called "personation," the Sovereign is an "actor" or an "artificiall" person whose actions are authorized by the subjects.[34] While this understanding of "person" may have served his political agenda, it rendered Hobbes's account of the doctrine of the Trinity problematic.

According to Hobbes: "The true God may be Personated. As he was; first, by *Moses*. . . . Secondly, by the Son of man, his own Son our Blessed Saviour *Jesus Christ*. . . . And thirdly, by the *Holy Ghost* . . . speaking, and working in the Apostles."[35] Later, in chapter 42 of the *Leviathan*, in the section entitled "Of Ecclesiastical Power," Hobbes further developed his Trinitarian reflection on the basis of this concept of "person":

> But a Person, (as I have shewn before, chapt. 13 [actually 16]) is he that is Represented, as often as he is Represented; and therefore God, who has been Represented (that is, Personated) thrice, may properly enough be said to be three Persons; though neither the word Person, nor Trinity be ascribed to him in the Bible. . . . To conclude, the doctrine of the Trinity, as far as can be gathered directly from the scripture, is in substance this; that God who is always One and the same, was the Person Represented by Moses [the Father]; the Person represented by his Son Incarnate; and the Person Represented by the Apostles [the Spirit].[36]

Hobbes's understanding of the Trinity was controversial. Although he employed an understanding of "person" different from the reigning Boethian definition, Hobbes's concept was still hopelessly individualist.[37] Given

---

33 Hobbes, *Leviathan*, chap. 16.

34 Dixon, *Hot Disputes*, 74–75. This idea that the actions of the sovereign are "authorized" by the subjects when the sovereign acts on their behalf is rooted in Hobbes's notion that there is a "foundational covenant" between sovereign and subjects, a clever device on Hobbes's part serving his political agenda.

35 Hobbes, *Leviathan*, chap. 16; my emphasis.

36 Ibid., chap. 42.

37 Atomistic conceptions of reality arising in natural science, due to Newton among others, profoundly influenced other areas of thought. The Cartesian "I," who doubts everything in order to arrive at certainty, is also an atomistic individual. Hobbes

Hobbes's understanding of "person," his only real alternative for understanding the Trinity is that God is one person who is "personated" or "represented" three times.

Attacks upon Hobbes's eccentric Trinitarian talk were swift, merciless, and sustained. Even Hobbes's friends were chagrined by what he had said about the doctrine. Alexander Ross (1591–1654) labeled Hobbes's account "a strange wheemsie concerning the blessed Trinity," for there is no reason why God could not be personated in additional ways and lead to many more than three persons.[38]

John Bramhall (1594–1663), archbishop of Armagh, was Hobbes's most bitter and prolonged critic. Bramhall focused on Hobbes's understanding of "person," for it seemed to generate a purely historical distinction between the three persons where one and the same God gets personated or represented by Moses (the Father), by Christ (the Son), and by the Apostles (the Spirit), rather than there being eternal persons within God's own life as God. Was there any real existence of the second and third persons of the Trinity beyond simply representation or personation in the Son and the Spirit in history?[39]

---

extended this atomistic individualism into the political and social realm. He understood social relations as self-contained individual persons exerting themselves and acting on others by external constraint or acting on behalf of others (personation) without there being "real" relations between them that are in any way constitutive of their being as persons (Dixon, *Hot Disputes*, 94–95).

38 Dixon, *Hot Disputes*, 78–79. In 1663, William Lucy (1597–1677), bishop of St. David, echoed the profound concerns of many others that Hobbes was an absolutely dangerous man, who had "spoken very dangerously of the blessed Trinity." According to Lucy, Hobbes was so hazardous to the faith that there was "no man ever writing so destructively of the principles of Christianity" (ibid., 79–80).

39 Ibid., 81. Hobbes had a strong apophatic sense of the limitations of human understanding of God and held a very dim view of natural theology, maintaining that there is no natural knowledge of God beyond the fact that God exists. Scripture alone provides knowledge of God. In addition, theological language is primarily doxological in character. When people say God is "Infinite, Omnipotent, and Eternall . . . or if they give him such a title, it is not *Dogmatically*, with intention to make the Divine Nature understood; but *Piously* to honour him with attributes, of significations, as remote as they can be from the grossenesse of Bodies Visible" (Hobbes, *Leviathan*, chap. 12, qtd. in Dixon, *Hot Disputes*, 74). See also Dixon, *Hot Disputes*, 71–74.

This apophaticism, of course, raises questions about just what we can know about the Trinity given Hobbes's statements about the sheer limitation of our knowledge of God. Do these distinctions rooted in these personations in history really tell us anything about God when everything we say about God is simply to piously honor God rather than make a dogmatic assertion?

Even the Cambridge Platonists saw Hobbes as a threat, though more for his atomistic materialism than his eccentric doctrine of the Trinity. In addition, Ralph Cudworth (1617–1688) and the Platonists were greatly disturbed by the rancorous character of the debates, especially the use of politics and violence to win the day. Cudworth noted, "I persuade my self, that no man shall ever be kept out of heaven, for not comprehending mysteries that were beyond the reach of his shallow understanding."[40] This sentiment would soon find its way into the minds of many, particularly in the aftermath of the Trinitarian debates in the 1690s and early 1700s.

For Hobbes, the idea that one and the same God was personated three times or had three identities seemed less of a problem and a far more palatable way to integrate what he saw in scripture. Like so many others in the

---

It was nearly ten years before Hobbes read Bramhall's book, yet the hostility between them and the rather nasty character of the bishop's critique led Hobbes to write a reply, something he seldom did. Hobbes granted that he had not stated the doctrine of the Trinity with the care it deserved, so the bishop correctly saw that the king could be personated by as many constables as there are in the kingdom.

It is precisely here that Hobbes noted that there are differences between the use of person and personating with reference to kings and to God: the king and the constables are not of the same substance, whereas the persons in the Godhead are (Dixon, *Hot Disputes*, 82). Hobbes significantly qualified and amended his way of speaking about the Trinity: "God, in his own person . . . created the world . . . the same God, in the person of his Son God and man, redeemed the same world . . . the same God, in the person of the Holy Ghost, sanctified the . . . Church. Is not this a clear proof that it is no contradiction to say that God is three persons and one substance? (Thomas Hobbes, *An Answer to a Book Published by Dr. Bramhall* in *The English Works of Thomas Hobbes,* ed. Sir William Molesworth [London: 1839–45], 4:316–17, qtd. in Dixon, *Hot Disputes*, 82).

In addition, Hobbes issued a Latin edition of *Leviathan* in 1668 and substantially altered it in light of the overwhelming flood of criticism lodged especially against his understanding of "person." The controversial passages in chapter 42 were omitted so that there is nothing about Moses or the Apostles "personating" God. Hobbes also included a long appendix dealing with the Nicene Creed, heresy, and attacks on his book. Hobbes ended by emphasizing that the words "person" and "Trinity" are neither used in the Nicene Creed nor found in scripture. They do not solve the mystery of the Trinity, and nothing should be said unless it is rooted in scripture (Dixon, *Hot Disputes*, 84–85).

All of Hobbes's revisions and additions did little to pacify the outrage of orthodox defenders of the doctrine of the Trinity. His enemies decided not simply to respond in print, but to act in Parliament. A bill was introduced in 1666 to combat heresy, and Hobbes was the apparent target (Dixon, *Hot Disputes*, 85).

40 Qtd. ibid., 90.

second half of the seventeenth century, Hobbes was wary of the implicit tritheism that existed in the Boethian account of a person as an individual substance of a rational nature. When applied to the Trinity, the Boethian concept of person seemed to assert that there are three individual intelligible substances in the Godhead, and thus tritheism.[41] But was Hobbes sincere, or was everything he said simply part of his grand scheme to undermine the Trinity and all of Christian faith in a deliberate esoteric manner?

What is clear is that nearly everyone rejected Hobbes's account of the doctrine of the Trinity. This may have blinded Hobbes's critics to how profoundly he influenced their own theological responses, as well as the responses of others in the future. In the words of Samuel Mintz, "The critics were satisfied that they had cut Hobbes down to size; in fact they had yielded, slowly and imperceptibly, but also very surely, to the force of his rationalist method."[42] Particularly fateful for the 1690s was that Hobbes deployed a different concept of "person" to articulate the doctrine of the Trinity. At no point do orthodox defenders of the Trinity follow Hobbes more unwittingly and with such devastating consequences.

Throughout the 1670s and 1680s, anti-Trinitarian conviction was on the rise. Ecclesial anxiety over atheism, Arianism, and Socinianism increased throughout these decades. One gets the sense of a growing volatility around the doctrine of the Trinity during this era and of anticipation of an event that would bring it all into a full-blown crisis.

3. *Stephen Nye*

James II wanted more freedom for his Roman Catholic friends, so he emphasized greater toleration during his short reign from 1685 through 1688, including relaxing the censorship of the press. The result, however, was not simply greater freedom for Roman Catholics but also liberty to promote more radical anti-Trinitarian views.[43] In 1687, Stephen Nye (1648–1719), a graduate of Cambridge and rector in Hertfordshire, published his *A Brief*

41 While Hobbes's exposition of the doctrine of the Trinity was problematic and sounded Sabellian in character, he can be read as simply trying to restate the doctrine of the Trinity in an era when the Scholastic way of articulating the doctrine had broken down. In this reading of Hobbes, he employed a concept of "person" that he believed was more efficacious for explicating what scripture has to say about the Economic Trinity.

42 Samuel I. Mintz, *The Hunting of Leviathan* (Cambridge: Cambridge University Press, 1962), 149–50. See also Dixon, *Hot Disputes*, 96.

43 Dixon, *Hot Disputes*, 105.

History of the Unitarians.[44] Thomas Firmin (1632–1697), philanthropist and successful businessman, funded the publication of Nye's work, as well as other anti-Trinitarian books and tracts.[45]

Nye's *Brief History* was not really a history at all but a bitter attack on the doctrine of the Trinity. Nye followed the same line as many critics of the doctrine earlier in the century: scripture is clear; God is one Person, not three; and the Father alone is divine and eternal. The Son is a messenger from God, and the Spirit is merely the personification of God's power.[46] Thus, the doctrine of the Trinity is "absurd, and contrary both to Reason and to itself, and therefore not only false, but *impossible*." The Trinity is really "an error in counting."[47]

In another important controversial tract, *Brief Notes on the Creed of St. Athanasius*, Nye attacked the Nicene Creed. The Book of Common Prayer stated that the Creed was to be recited twelve times a year. There had been a proposal to make the recital of the Athanasian Creed optional because Mary and William of Orange fostered a more tolerant and inclusive religious climate. But the High Church Tories scuttled the proposal at a Convocation, and this elicited Nye's attack.[48]

Nye and his two works played a central role in the launching of the full-blown Trinitarian controversies of the 1690s. During these years, the ongoing dissatisfaction burst forth in systematic and open attack upon the doctrine of the Trinity. However, it was the shattering of the unity within the Orthodox camp and the bitter infighting among those who affirmed the Trinity that distinguish the 1690s as the real beginning of the Trinitarian controversies. The Act of Toleration passed in 1689, combined with allowing the licensing requirements for presses to expire between 1693 and 1695, and both furthered the volatility of the atmosphere.[49] The stage was now set for the Trinitarian controversies that follow.

---

44 [Stephen Nye], *A Brief History of the Unitarians. Called Socinians in Four Letters Written to a Friend* (n.p., 1687). See also Dixon, *Hot Disputes*, 105–6.

45 As a young man, Firmin had encountered Biddle, who won him over to anti-Trinitarian convictions. Firmin repeatedly provided financial support for those who attacked the Trinity in the second half of the seventeenth century (Dixon, *Hot Disputes*, 107).

46 Ibid., 106.

47 [Nye], *A Brief History*, 24, 25. See Dixon, *Hot Disputes*, 106.

48 Dixon, *Hot Disputes*, 108.

49 Roland N. Stromberg, *Religious Liberalism in Eighteenth-Century England* (London: Oxford University Press, 1954), 6. I am indebted to a former student, Cindy Marino, for calling my attention to Stromberg's work.

III. The 1690s: The Trinitarian Debate Explodes, and the Orthodox Consensus Shatters

1. The Bury Affair

Indicative of the heat generated by the Trinitarian controversies of the 1690s is the infamous incident involving Arthur Bury, rector of Exeter College, Oxford, and author of *The Naked Gospel.* Bury argued for a simple gospel message—repent and believe! He saw the Trinity as a corruption that undermined Christian faith: "Whether Mahomet, or Christian Doctors have more corrupted the Gospel, it is not so plain by the light of scripture, as it is by that of Experience. . . . For when by nice and hot disputes (especially concerning the Second and Third Persons of the Trinity) the minds of the whole people had been long confounded, . . . the scandal was encreased."[50] It was not so much that Bury simply wanted to dismiss the doctrine of the Trinity, but rather that he saw theological speculation, and especially controversy, as antithetical to the simple gospel and undermining of faith.

The result was swift. Jonathan Trelawnet, the bishop of Exeter, was summoned to expel Bury from his house and from the college. There were additional issues involved including lax administration of the college and alleged immorality with women employed to perform housekeeping duties. The bishop was barricaded out of the chapel, though in the end Bury was deposed for bribery, heresy, and incontinence.[51] An Oxford Convocation met on August 19, 1690, condemned Bury's book "to the glory of the blessed Trinity and the honour of Oxford," and then burned the book itself in the university quadrangle.[52] The scandal received national attention and led to the publication of a number of pamphlets on both sides of the debate.[53]

---

50 [Arthur Bury], *The Naked Gospel* (n.p.: 1690), "The Preface" and 9. Bury also argued that "reason is no less the Word of God than is the scripture" (ibid., 17). See Dixon, *Hot Disputes*, 108–9.

51 See John Redwood, *Reason, Ridicule and Religion: The Age of Enlightenment in England 1660–1750* (London: Thames and Hudson, 1976), 156–59, for a vivid chronicling of these events.

52 Dixon, *Hot Disputes*, 109.

53 Redwood, *Reason, Ridicule and Religion*, 159–62. Several years later, after the debates disclosed the sheer depth of acrimonious rhetoric and ridicule on the part of so many of the participants, including the orthodox defenders, Bury was further stunned by the "extraordinary heat" of the controversy and asserted that "the Tartars manage their wars with less cruelty than the clergy" (see [Arthur Bury], *The Judgement of a Disinterested Person Concerning the Controversy about the B. Trinity* [London, 1696], 61). See Dixon, *Hot Disputes*, 133, for fuller treatment of Bury. In

2. William Sherlock

Yet, it was not so much the Bury affair as it was Stephen Nye and the republication of his *A Brief History of the Unitarians* in 1690 that launched the Trinitarian controversies of the 1690s.[54] Nye's work drew William Sherlock (1641–1707), dean of St. Paul's in London, into the debate. Sherlock's work, in turn, shattered the unity within the orthodox Trinitarian camp.[55]

Sherlock defended his attack on Nye, arguing that Nye's *Brief History* had to be addressed because Nye's errors were the talk of every coffee-house in England, a comment revealing the public character of the controversy.[56] In the midst of this kind of growing criticism of the doctrine of the Trinity, Sherlock argued that "our business is to prove it, and explain it and vindicate it."[57] Sherlock's concerns were utterly real: the doctrine of the Trinity was being effectively marginalized for many in England as the Trinitarian debates unfolded. What is ironic is that Sherlock's own injudicious defense did more harm to the doctrine than those who attacked it.

Sherlock addressed Nye's criticisms of the Trinity and argued that the Trinity is not only Scriptural but is also plain and intelligible.[58] Sherlock's attempt to demonstrate this intelligibility involved his appeal to a new

---

the 1690s, the vitriolic character of these "nice and hot disputes" about the Trinity undermined the credibility and the significance of the doctrine.

54 Here Redwood and Placher (who follows Redwood) place far too much stress on the impact of the Bury affair for launching the controversies of the 1690s, probably because of its drama, and not enough emphasis on the impact of Stephen Nye (Dixon, *Hot Disputes*, 109–10).

55 The very title indicated that Nye was the real threat and therefore Sherlock's target: William Sherlock, *A Vindication of the Doctrine of the Holy and Ever Blessed Trinity and the Incarnation of the Son of God. Occasioned by the Brief Notes on the Creed of St. Athanasius, and the Brief History of the Unitarians, or Socinians, as Containing an Answer to both* (London, 1690).

56 It is clear that Sherlock was aware and alarmed that the attacks upon the Trinity had spread beyond the scholarly realm and had begun to affect a much broader audience. Sherlock feared that Nye's works would negatively impact the faith and lives of the faithful in the Church of England.

57 William Sherlock, *An Apology for Writing against Socinians* (London, 1693), 29. See Dixon, *Hot Disputes*, 122.

58 Indeed, he noted in his introduction that "the writing of this work has given me clearer and more distinct Notions of this Great Mystery, than I had before" (Sherlock, *A Vindication,* 2). See Dixon, *Hot Disputes*, 112.

concept of person as "self-consciousness," once again breaking with the Boethian definition, as Hobbes had done in previous decades.[59]

Armed with this understanding of person, Sherlock characterized the Trinity as three centers of self-consciousness unified via their mutual consciousness of each other: "Each Divine Person has a Self-consciousness of its own . . . Whereby he knows and feels himself to be the Father, and not the Son, nor the Holy Ghost" and vice versa. Yet each of the persons "do by an internal sensation . . . feel each other in themselves."[60] It is this mutual consciousness that unites the three in a union that is not simply moral but so essential that there is one will and one power, and even the thoughts of each belong to the others. Sherlock identified this unity of mutual consciousness with the patristic concept of *perichoresis.*[61]

One cannot but see a glaring implicit tritheism in Sherlock's exposition, despite his affirmation designed to assure his readers of his orthodoxy.[62] Sherlock's critics, both the anti-Trinitarians and those within the Trinitarian camp, were less than convinced. The fundamental issue was that Sherlock's reconceptualized vision of person as self-consciousness was still hopelessly individualist. An essentially individualist concept of person, developed outside of Trinitarian discourse, cannot readily bear the relational depth inherent in a Trinitarian understanding of divine persons. Sherlock's conception generated tritheistic connotations when utilized to explicate the doctrine of the Trinity.

Furthermore, Sherlock's apparent intimate knowledge of the inner life and consciousness of the Trinitarian persons had a twofold effect of horrifying many of the other orthodox defenders of the Trinity and providing new ground for criticizing the Trinity by those who opposed the doctrine. Sherlock's book also focused the dispute more narrowly on the meaning and use of the term "person" in the Trinitarian debates that followed.[63]

---

59 Placher, *Domestication*, 175–76; Babcock, "Changing of the Christian God," 141–42. It was actually a renegade Cambridge Platonist, John Turner, who first injected the idea of self-consciousness into Trinitarian discourse on the nature of the divine persons and their relations (see Dixon, *Hot Disputes*, 110–11).

60 Sherlock, *A Vindication*, 67, 56. See also Placher, *Domestication*, 175–76; Babcock, "Changing of the Christian God," 142–43; and Dixon, *Hot Disputes*, 112–13.

61 Sherlock, *A Vindication*, 48–50, 55–57. See Dixon, *Hot Disputes*, 112–14.

62 Sherlock even asserted, "We must allow each Person to be a God, but each distinct Person is not a distinct God" (Sherlock, *A Vindication*, 98, 100, 130–36). See also Placher, *Domestication*, 175–76; Babcock, "Changing of the Christian God," 142–43; and Dixon, *Hot Disputes*, 113–14.

63 Dixon, *Hot Disputes*, 114–15.

Sherlock's work generated a flood of pamphlets from the pens of various Unitarians, a number of them collected and published under the title *The Faith of One God*, also popularly called the "Unitarian Tracts," and paid for once again by Thomas Firmin, who gave them away free.[64] Nye reentered the fray and counterattacked on the two points where Sherlock was most vulnerable: (1) his novel, even eccentric, explanation for which there is no precedence either in scripture or in tradition; and (2) his notion of mutual self-consciousness utilized to secure the unity of the Trinity. Nye pointed out that even if each person of the Trinity is conscious of, and at one with, the will, thought, and action of the others, each of the three is not aware of the other two in the same way.[65] There is no substantial unity to be found in this account of the relations between the numerically three divine persons as self-consciousness.

3. John Wallis and Robert South

Orthodox defenders of the Trinity responded to Sherlock's presumptuous familiarity with the consciousness of the intra-Trinitarian life and dangerously tritheistic explanation of the doctrine of the Trinity with shock and consternation.[66] John Wallis (1616–1703), a distinguished professor of mathematics at the University of Oxford, and Robert South, canon of Christ Church Cathedral, Oxford, both attacked Sherlock and his novel explication of the doctrine.

Wallis and South wrote from within the earlier Scholastic account of the Trinity using the traditional language of "nature," "essence," "substance," etc. Both rightly recognized that the Triune God cannot be fully captured by human thought and speech and that human language has to undergo shifts in meaning when it is applied to God.[67] But this line of argumentation, reflecting an older vision of language, indeed of life, did not gain much traction in the emerging new world of thought associated with Bacon, Hobbes, Locke, and others, with its emphasis on clear and distinct ideas and the

64 *The Faith of the One God* (London, 1691). See Dixon, *Hot Disputes*, 114–15.

65 [Stephen Nye], *The Acts of Great Athanasius with Notes, by Way of Illustration, on His Creed* (n.p., 1690), republished in *The Faith of the One God*, 4–5, 11–12, 20, 26. See also Dixon, *Hot Disputes*, 115.

66 Dixon, *Hot Disputes*, 112–25.

67 In the words of Wallis, the word person "doth not agree to them [the Trinitarian persons] exactly in the same sense in which it is commonly used amongst men; . . . nor doth any Word, when applyed to God, signifie just the same as when applyed to men" (John Wallis, "Letter I," in *Theological Discourses: Concerning VIII Letters and III Sermons Concerning the Blessed Trinity* [London, 1692], 10). See also Dixon, *Hot Disputes*, 117.

power of human reason to master mysteries. Indeed, the very idea of "mystery," so much a part of the great tradition of the church, began to be viewed as a hindrance to religion that dishonors God.

Although Wallis wanted to deflect attention away from Sherlock toward a more traditional way of talking about the Trinity, he got himself into trouble by employing his own inadequate ways of thinking and speaking about the doctrine. Stressing the importance of analogy, Wallis introduced what was to become the infamous and unfortunate "trinitarian cube": as a cube has three equal dimensions that are necessary to the very existence of a cube, so the Trinity comprises three persons who only together constitute the one God.[68] Drawing upon Augustine's warnings about the use of "person" with reference to God, Wallace foolishly spoke of "three somewhats" in God that are conventionally or metaphorically called "persons."[69]

The real problem is that this kind of defense detaches the "doctrine" of the Trinity from the actual Trinitarian persons and their activity in the gospel even though this Trinitarian presence and activity are the source of the doctrine itself and provide all of the content of what one can know about the intra-Trinitarian life. The defenders, without ever realizing it, accepted the assumptions about language, about reality, about what theology is, about the use of reason, etc., held by those who attacked the doctrine. In the process, the defenders lost sight of how the doctrine of the Trinity arose in the early church and continues to arise out God's Trinitarian self-revelation and self-communication in the gospel, something Wesley saw ever so clearly, retrieved, and injected into early Methodism.

As a result of accepting these assumptions, the defenders detached the doctrine of the Trinity from its true ground and in the process (1) lost the doctrine's true content, and (2) defended the doctrine in ways that rendered the Trinity obscure and insignificant to Christian faith and practice. In light of the defenses of the Trinity on the part of Sherlock and Wallis, we can begin to understand Wesley's lack of enthusiasm for "philosophical illustrations" of the Trinity and his rather negative judgment concerning the defenders who did more damage to the doctrine than those who attacked it.

The infelicitous attempts on the part of Trinitarian defenders, like South and Wallis, to provide a better account of the Trinity than that of Sherlock

---

68 Wallis noted that all analogies are inadequate but this one was extraordinarily deficient (Wallis, "Letter I," in *Theological Discourses*, 11–13). See Dixon, *Hot Disputes*, 117–18.

69 Wallis, "Letter III," in *Theological Discourses*, 40, 62. See Dixon, *Hot Disputes*, 118–19.

elicited even greater ridicule on the part of the anti-Trinitarians. One anonymous tract scorned Wallis for inviting the faithful to "love God the Father, who is the length of the Cube, with all their Hearts."[70] Stephen Nye reentered the debate yet again with his usual shrewd satire on "Dr. W's Three New Nothings," for to call the Trinitarian persons "somewhats" is effectively to view them as "nothings," since we are left entirely in the dark as to what they are.[71]

These kinds of attacks provide ample evidence for Redwood's astute observation that it was "the age of ridicule which did far more harm to the Christian defences than did the onslaught of reason and nature."[72] Ridicule engenders cynicism, and this is precisely what took place through the course of the Trinitarian controversies in the 1690s, though the less-than-helpful defenses of the Trinity deserve some of the scorn they received from those who rightly understood their problematic character.

Furthermore, while those who attacked the Trinity were far more adept at deploying ridicule and derision, some of the orthodoxy defenders used it as well. This is especially evident in the rancorous venom of South, who disliked Sherlock personally and sought to discredit Sherlock's account of the Trinity as inadequate, erroneous, and ultimately heretical. In 1695, South went beyond critique, formally charged Sherlock with heresy, and called upon the universities to censure Sherlock. Oxford University did just that in October 1695. In a related decree, on November 25, the university declared Sherlock's language about the Trinity "false, impious, and heretical," "contrary to . . . the publicly received doctrine of the Church of England."[73]

4. Stephen Nye, Matthew Tindal, and the Deepening Crisis

It was the obvious disagreement among those attempting to defend the Trinity that helped undermine the doctrine by making it appear incoherent, precarious, and something less than the "universally" affirmed faith of the Church through the ages. Stephen Nye jumped at the chance to expose the disunity of the Trinitarian camp.

---

70 Qtd. in Dixon, *Hot Disputes*, 118.

71 [Stephen Nye], *Observations on the Four Letters of Dr. John Wallis Concerning the Trinity and the Creed of Athanasius* (n.p.: n.d.), republished in *The Faith of One God*, 4–5, 8. See Dixon, *Hot Disputes*, 119–20.

72 Redwood, *Reason, Ridicule and Religion*, 14. Note that Dixon's citation is incorrect (see Dixon, *Hot Disputes*, 118n46).

73 *An Account of the Decree of the University of Oxford against Some Heretical Tenets* (Oxford, 1695). See Dixon, *Hot Disputes*, 132–33. Joseph Bingham preached a sermon defending Sherlock. The university pounced on Bingham, forcing him to resign his fellowship at University College (ibid., 133).

Nye's work is another example of the sheer power of ridicule and derision. He satirized Wallis's views of a "Ciceronian Trinity" for being so effectively Sabellian that even some of the anti-Trinitarians call themselves "Wallisians." Sherlock's "Cartesian Trinity" of three infinite minds in "Mutual-Consciousness maketh them to be a Consult or Council . . . but by no means one Numerical God."[74] After dispatching with Cudworth's "Platonic Trinity" and South's "Trinity of Aristotle," Nye criticized the "Mystical Trinity" of "the mob," those who say that the Trinity is a mystery simply to be accepted rather than explained: "They deny all Explications: we must say therefore 'tis Samaritanism for . . . they worship they know not what."[75] At the end of the day, what was clear to Nye was that such differences of explanation, indeed "civil war" among Trinitarians, simply revealed that "the Trinitarian Faith is at best but precarious, uncertain, and doubtful."[76]

Matthew Tindal (1655–1733), one of the leading deists, echoed Nye's judgment about the sheer differences in how the defenders of the Trinity understand the meaning of person: "There is nothing . . . more unaccountable and absurd, than their jangling and wrangling about the meaning of the word *Person*."[77] Tindal saw political implications in a Trinitarian source of creation and culture: "I wonder under what Form of Government the Trinitarians reckon that of the Universe! Monarchy it cannot be, because there is in that but one Person that is Supream, but here are Three, each of whom is Supream."[78] Tindal also had no place for mystery because it is what we do know of God, "not what we do not know, that makes us honour him. . . . [T]he less there is of mystery in Religion, the brighter and clearer it appears."[79]

Tracts, pamphlets, and books flowed from various presses fanning the flames of the Trinitarian controversy in the early to mid-1690s. By 1696, Anglican authorities had seen quite enough and were deeply concerned about the damage the debate was having upon the church. Thomas Tenison,

---

74 Stephen Nye, *Considerations on the Explications of the Doctrine of the Trinity by Dr. Wallis, Dr. Sherlock, Dr. S___th [sic], Dr. Cudworth and Mr. Hooker; and also of the Account given by those who say, the Trinity is an Unconceivable and Inexplicable Mystery* (n.p., 1693), 7–9, 10–12. See Dixon, *Hot Disputes*, 126–27.

75 Nye, *Considerations*, 32. See Dixon, *Hot Disputes*, 127–29.

76 Nye, *Considerations*, 7. See Dixon, *Hot Disputes*, 129.

77 [William Tindal], *A Letter to the Reverend Clergy of both Universities*, 5. See Dixon, *Hot Disputes*, 130.

78 [William Tindal], *A Letter to the Reverend Clergy of both Universities*, 26. See Dixon, *Hot Disputes*, 130.

79 [William Tindal], *A Letter to the Reverend Clergy of both Universities*, 35. See Dixon, *Hot Disputes*, 131.

archbishop of Canterbury, encouraged King William to intervene. On February 3, 1696, from the king came *Directions to our Arch-Bishops and Bishops for the Preserving of Unity in the Church, and the Purity of Christian Faith, Concerning the Holy Trinity.*[80]

The document rightly noted and warned of the damage done to the doctrine of the Trinity by the differences in terminology and explication. It also demanded that the fierce and acrimonious character of the debate cease and that argumentation utilize expressions "commonly used" and avoid "new terms."[81] Finally, the document was given teeth through the Blasphemy Act of 1698, promising three years of prison for anyone convicted of anti-Trinitarian sentiment.[82]

In Scotland, the Scottish Parliament had passed its own Act Against Blasphemy in 1695, with even harsher consequences. In 1696, Thomas Aikenhead, a nineteen-year-old medical student at the University of Edinburgh, made the mistake of scorning the Trinity, suggesting that speaking about God being three and one is as unbelievable as talking about a square circle. It might have been youthful imprudence or maybe personal conviction, but the result was that Aikenhead was found guilty on Christmas Eve, 1696. The Kirk enforced the full extent of the Act Against Blasphemy and hanged the youth at Gallowlee on January 8, 1697, the last execution for heresy in the British Isles.[83]

Yet even the king's *Directions to our Arch-Bishops and Bishops* and the two Blasphemy Acts did little to contain the controversy. The persecutions and the death of Aikenhead simply galvanized anti-Trinitarian convictions, hardened the lines of debate, and horrified many persons who remembered the turbulent 1640s and 1650s and realized there was something profoundly wrong with the bigoted zeal manifest in the whole course of the

80 Dixon, *Hot Disputes,* 131–34.

81 *Directions to Our Arch-Bishops and Bishops for the Preserving of Unity in the Church, and the Purity of Christian Faith, Concerning the Holy Trinity* (London, 1695). See Dixon, *Hot Disputes,* 134.

82 Dixon, *Hot Disputes,* 134.

83 See Robert E. Florida, "British Law and Socinianism in the Seventeenth and Eighteenth Centuries," in *Socinianism and Its Role in the Culture of XVIth to XVIIIth Centuries,* ed. Lech Szczucji (Warsaw: PNW, 1983). See also Michael Hunter, "'Aikenhead the Atheist': The Context and Consequences of Articulate Irreligion in the Late Seventeenth Century," in *Atheism from the Reformation to the Enlightenment,* ed. Michael Hunter and David Wotton (Oxford: Oxford University Press, 1992). Dixon provides a summary account of the incident in *Hot Disputes,* 134–35.

Trinitarian controversies of the 1690s. This provided significant impetus for those longing for greater toleration and religious latitude of belief.

In addition to the level of sheer venom and rancor, what is especially notable and disconcerting about all of these works published in the 1690s, as Dixon astutely observes, is the wholesale loss of any vital soteriological or ecclesiological import of the doctrine of the Trinity: "Knowledge of the Trinity is conceived in extrinsicist terms as a piece of information rather than a lived experience of faith."[84] The emphasis on clear and distinct ideas, when coupled with a rather atomistic and literalist approach to scripture, called into question the biblical basis of the Trinity, for the doctrine originally arose, and continues to find its origin, not via deduction and induction from particular biblical texts treated like disconnected data. Rather, as Wesley noted in his sermon "On the Trinity," the doctrine of the Trinity is bound up with "vital religion" and is implicitly there in our evangelical and doxological encounter with the gospel where we come to know the love of God the Father through the grace of our Lord Jesus Christ in the communion of the Holy Spirit on the basis of scripture, as we will see at the end of this chapter.

Indeed, we realize that what we have come to know cannot be fully grasped, articulated, and rendered entirely explicit. We can *apprehend* something of the love of God and the Triune God of love through Christ and in the Spirit, but we cannot fully *comprehend* it. Mystery in relation to the Triune God of the gospel is not pure unintelligibility but rather the encounter with, and participation in, something so replete with meaning, content, and significance that it cannot be fully grasped or comprehended. If we cannot even describe adequately the aroma and flavor of a cup of coffee within the confines of our language and concepts, how much less well can we capture the glory and grace of the Triune God in our encounter with the gospel?

Insofar as the defenders of the doctrine of the Trinity accepted the assumptions that the doctrine arose by induction or deduction from individual biblical texts and needed to be "a clear and distinct idea," one that can be "proved," "explained," and "vindicated" using the kinds of methods we have noted in this period of England's intellectual history, the Trinity was doomed by presupposition before the course of the debate worked itself out in the explicit demise of the doctrine in history.

The overall result of these Trinitarian controversies, which came to such an astonishing acrimonious head in the 1690s, was a growing sense that the doctrine of the Trinity was an esoteric belief at best, a subject fraught with danger, certainly not a doctrine that was clear and intelligible to the

---

84 Dixon, *Hot Disputes*, 137.

average person on the street and, therefore, not a doctrine integral to salvation, to the church, or to the ongoing Christian life. By the beginning of the eighteenth century, there was a growing sense that even if the doctrine of the Trinity could be rationally defended, it was too complex to be among the items necessary for salvation. Thus, a chasm developed between the *doctrine* of the Trinity understood in terms of a rationally defensible explication of how God can be three and one, and the *faith* of ordinary Christians, a chasm that should not exist and simply did not exist in Wesley's approach to the Trinity.[85]

5. John Locke and Bishop Stillingfleet

The passing of Blasphemy Acts and the hanging of Aikenhead horrified John Locke (1632–1704), who was an influential defender of religious toleration. Locke, a philosopher, an amateur scientist, and a friend and counsel to various political figures, wrote on nearly every controversial or popular topic of the day. His ideas greatly accelerated the intellectual changes taking place in England in the final quarter of the seventeenth century.[86]

What is rather intriguing about Locke is his virtual silence regarding the doctrine of the Trinity. While deeply concerned with religious issues, including defending Christian faith against deism in his *The Reasonableness of Christianity*, Locke never wrote on the Trinity in any of his published works. This silence is all the more stunning in light of the pervasive character of the controversies over the Trinity in the 1690s.[87] This all changed when Edward Stillingfleet (1635–1699), bishop of Worchester, entered the

---

85 As Babcock, Placher, and Dixon all note, by the end of the 1690s, the doctrine of the Trinity was no longer the central and vibrant reality of Christian faith, the vital and indispensable Christian doctrine of, but rather an intellectual puzzle on the periphery of Christian faith and life and a problem for theology. What is so disturbing about the controversies, as Wesley noted in his sermon "On the Trinity," is that it was the defenders of the doctrine (like incautious and idiosyncratic Sherlock, rather boring Wallis with his infelicitous and singularly unhelpful analogies like the "trinitarian cube," and caustic and scurrilous South, whose vituperative venom was both uncharitable and unbecoming to anyone claiming to be Christian) who did the greatest damage to the doctrine of the Trinity. In reading their works one cannot help but wonder, even if they were correct, what do these accounts of the Trinity—how the three can be one and the one three—have to do with anything that really matters?

86 Babcock, "Changing of the Christian God," 137–39, 142–46; Dixon, *Hot Disputes*, 137–38, 148–54.

87 John Locke, *The Reasonableness of Christianity* (Bristol: Thoemmes, 1697). See also Dixon, *Hot Disputes*, 138–39.

Trinitarian debate in 1697 and dragged Locke into the controversy by arguing that others had used Locke's "new way of ideas" to undermine the doctrine of the Trinity.[88]

Locke shared Bacon's and Hobbes's deep mistrust of the received framework of thought and also envisioned a restructuring of the sciences, arts, and all human knowledge upon a proper foundation of rightly formulated ideas.[89] Locke also read Descartes during his student days at Oxford and was profoundly influenced by Descartes's quest for epistemic certainty and the necessity of developing "clear and distinct" or "determinate" ideas to that end.[90]

---

88 Dixon, *Hot Disputes*, 139; Babcock, "The Changing," 142–46.

89 See note 29 above in this chapter for more on Bacon.

90 René Descartes (1596–1650), like Bacon, encountered Scholastic Aristotelian philosophy, that of Francisco Suárez (1548–1617) in particular, during his education at the Jesuit school (Le Flèche) in Paris (see Placher, *Domestication*, 74–76, 80–81). Descartes's search for absolute certainty as a foundation upon which to build scientific knowledge is well known. At the beginning of his *Meditations on First Philosophy*, he said: "From my earliest years, I have accepted many false opinions as true, and that what I concluded from such badly assured premises could not but be highly doubtful and uncertain. From the time that I first recognized that if I wished to have any firm and constant knowledge in the sciences, I would have to undertake, once and for all, to set aside all the opinions which I had previously accepted among my beliefs and start again from the very beginning" (René Descartes, *Meditations on First Philosophy*, in *Discourse on Method and Meditations*, trans. Laurence L. Lafleur [New York: Macmillan, 1960], 75). See also Placher, *Domestication*, 80.

After demolishing various beliefs via his methodological doubt, Descartes arrived at the one thing he could not doubt: his own self-conscious existence as a thinking subject. Even if he was in error or deceived, Descartes thought it is still "I" who am in error or deceived. So "after examining all things with care, I must finally conclude and maintain that this proposition: *I am, I exist*, is necessarily true every time that I pronounce it or conceive it in my mind" (Descartes, *Meditations*, trans. Lafleur, 82). See Placher, *Domestication*, 80–81.

As Placher correctly notes, this starting point enabled Descartes to develop a general principle that was to play a significant role in the Trinitarian controversies: "Therefore it seems to me that I can already establish as a general principle that everything which we conceive very clearly and very distinctly is wholly true" (Descartes, *Meditations*, trans. Lafleur, 92). See Placher, *Domestication*, 81. By analyzing the idea of his own existence as a thinking subject, it seemed absolutely clear to Descartes that this was beyond doubt and trustworthy. This led him to believe that by carefully analyzing concepts, breaking them down into clear and distinct ideas, he could arrive at other truths equally as certain.

The upshot was that Descartes believed he had found a way to secure the existence of God. By carefully analyzing the idea of God, he concluded that nothing

Thus, Locke was one of a number of leading intellectuals advocating a new method in science and philosophy of breaking down concepts into their constitutive simple ideas that could be directly correlated with sense experience. The goal of his *Essay Concerning Human Understanding* was to restore a direct link between the mind and reality, between (scientific) concepts and sense experience or the data/facts of nature. All of one's ideas come either from one's senses (the simple idea of "heat" that one senses

---

could account for the reality of (or have enough reality to cause) this clear and distinct idea, other than God: "These attributes [infinite, eternal, immutable, etc.] are such that—they are so great and so eminent—that the more attentively I consider them, the less I can persuade myself that I could have derived them from my own nature. And consequently we must necessarily conclude . . . that God necessarily exists" (Descartes, *Meditations*, trans. Lafleur, 101). See Placher, *Domestication*, 82. Because such a God would not deceive us, Descartes argued that when we appropriately use the perceptual and cognitive faculties God gave us, we will not be deceived. This enabled Descartes to secure the existence of the world and a whole lot more. See Placher's helpful discussion of all of this in Placher, *Domestication*, 81–85.

Of course, the question this immediately raises in relation to God (and particularly the Trinity) is whether it is possible for finite human beings to develop or possess a clear and distinct idea of God (or the Trinity). Here the mainstream of Christian tradition always said that while we can apprehend an infinite God, we cannot comprehend an infinite God. The same is true of the Trinity. This qualification of human knowledge of God led to what has been called the "Cartesian paradox" in which Descartes both admitted that (1) "the idea of the infinite, if it is to be a true idea, cannot be grasped at all"; and yet (2) the whole scheme of scientific knowledge rested on the assured clear and distinct idea of God, an idea that necessarily includes God's existence (Placher, *Domestication*, 83).

We see here in Descartes the flowering of the modern turn to the human subject. It was Descartes's dualism between the human subject over against the material world of nature, which scientific endeavor seeks to know, that led to the notion of "representative perception" in which sense data or subjective representations mediate between the independent immaterial human mind and the material world that the human knower accesses via the senses. While Descartes argued that God would not deceive us and has provided us with dependable perceptual and cognitive faculties, many were not convinced. Are the sense data or subjective representations really indicative of properties in nature or merely epiphenomena that enable the mind to render nature intelligible? The trend was toward analyzing the mental processes and consciousness of the human subject with the goal of providing a secure delineation (foundation) of how the immaterial mind is able to arrive at genuine knowledge of the material world through the sense data or representations that mediate between the immaterial mind of the subject and the material object of knowledge. We see many of these points in Locke as well.

from a fire or the "green" of grass that one sees in a field) or from one's mental life through introspection (the "awareness" that one is thinking, reasoning, willing while writing a letter). Locke said that this mental "awareness" is similar to one's five senses by which one perceives external objects "and might properly be called internal sense."[91]

This empiricist epistemology, with its passive account of perception and its vision of reason as constructing concepts in a complicated and at times ambiguous manner, proved to be fatal to more than a few complex concepts. Locke was particularly suspicious of those who use "words without clear and distinct *ideas*, or which is worse, signs without anything signified." Here the chief offenders were his Oxford Aristotelian teachers whom he calls "the great mintmasters of these kinds of terms, I mean the schoolmen and metaphysicians."[92]

---

91 John Locke, *An Essay Concerning Human Understanding*, ed. John W. Yolton, complete ed. (London: J. M. Dent and Sons, 1978), 2.1.4. Locke's goal in his monumental work was to "inquire into the original, certainty, and extent of human knowledge, together with the grounds and degrees of belief, opinion, and assent" (Locke, *Human Understanding*, 1.introduction.2).

He rejected the Platonic conception of innate ideas, arguing that the mind is a *tabula rasa*. All our knowledge comes either from experience (sensation via the senses) or reflection (D. J. O'Connor, "Locke," in *A Critical History of Western Philosophy*, ed. O'Connor [New York: Free Press, 1985], 213).

92 Locke, *Human Understanding* 3.10.2. See also Babcock, "Changing of the Christian God," 137. Locke accused these thinkers of "extending their inquiries beyond their capacities, and letting their thoughts wander into those depths where they can find no sure footing . . . never coming to any clear resolution . . . only to continue and increase their doubts and confirm them . . . in perfect skepticism" (Locke, *Human Understanding*, I.Introduction.7).

The solution to these kinds of problems, according to Locke, was through a critical delineation of the cognitive procedures by which we develop and formulate our ideas. No matter how complex an idea or line of thinking might be, Locke thought that it ultimately can be broken down by tracing it back to its source in these simple ideas. "All those sublime thoughts, which tower above the clouds . . . take their rise and footing here: . . . it stirs not one jot beyond those *ideas* which *sense* or *reflection* have offered to its contemplation" (ibid., 2.1.24). See also O'Connor, "Locke," 205; and Babcock, "Changing of the Christian God," 137.

These simple ideas rooted in the senses or reflection are combined in various ways to develop our most complex ideas of material objects (a computer), complex ideas of imaginary realities (Harry Potter and Hogwarts School of Wizardry), and even our moral and religious ideas (justice and God). So if we can unpack, analyze, and isolate the simple ideas that are constitutive of our complex concepts, we can make our concepts determinate, clear, and distinct, and therefore also certain, as we

It was Locke's deconstruction of the complex concepts of the "great mintmasters," particularly substance or nature, which got him into trouble with Stillingfleet.[93] The bishop believed that the doctrine of the Trinity was

---

trace complex concepts back to simple ideas and their sources. See Locke's second book of *An Essay Concerning Human Understanding* for his account of ideas, and the third book for his understanding of words or language.

Notice how much Locke's account of the combining of simple ideas with determinate sources into complex concepts parallels the Newtonian atomistic account of the material universe. As complex compounds can be broken down into particular combinations of atoms and molecules, so can our most complicated concepts and lines of thought be traced back to their source in simple ideas. Unless, of course, the complex ideas are confused or simply wrong and in the end turn out to be virtually empty of content and therefore incapable of explaining anything at all (see O'Connor, "Locke," 207–9, 213, 215–16). See also Babcock, "Changing of the Christian God," 137–38.

As Babcock astutely points out, Locke's way of ideas was in part designed precisely to dismantle the Aristotelian discourse he encountered in school at Oxford. In Locke's mind, Aristotelian talk of "essence" and "substance" is a prime example of mintmasters making up of terms that have no determinate meaning and signify nothing at all. Talking about essence and substance as that which makes something what it is ends up being a perverse impediment to the scientific investigation of things in terms of their chemical composition or atomic structure that Locke saw Isaac Newton and Robert Boyle pursuing with astonishing success, for they provided *real* explanations of how the world functions (see Babcock, "Changing of the Christian God," 137–38). So it is no coincidence that Locke turned his attention to the idea of "substance" or "essence" for the express purpose of dismantling it.

93 Babcock, "Changing of the Christian God," 137–39; Dixon, *Hot Disputes*, 138–40. Locke radically departed from the Boethian tradition in his understanding of "person." Like a number of others, Locke saw personal identity lodged not in an individual substance of a rational nature but in self-consciousness. A person according to Locke is "a thinking intelligent Being, that has reason and reflection, and can consider itself as itself, the same thinking thing, in different times and places; which it does only by that Consciousness which is inseparable from thinking . . . consciousness always accompanies thinking, and 'tis that, that makes everyone to be, what he calls *self*" (Locke, *Human Understanding*, 2:27.9). See Dixon, *Hot Disputes*, 141. This definition of person, as self-consciousness, is similar to the one used by Sherlock to explicate the doctrine of the Trinity with disastrous consequences, as noted earlier in this chapter.

The tensions that develop between Stillingfleet and Locke were rooted in Boethius's understanding of person. Boethius developed his definition of person as the individual substance of a rational nature (*naturae rationabilis individua substantia*) to help explicate Chalcedonian Christology with its understanding of Jesus Christ as one person in two natures.

bound up with rightly understanding the very concepts Locke destroyed in his *Essay Concerning Human Understanding*.

As a noted and influential bishop, Stillingfleet was deeply troubled by the course of the Trinitarian controversies in the 1690s and their negative effective on the state of the Anglican Church. In 1697, the bishop published his *Discourse in Vindication of the Doctrine of the Trinity* in a masterful attempt to address the problems created by the controversies.[94] Stillingfleet was by far the greatest intellect among active bishops, and his work is a classic both in terms of the depth and breadth of scholarship and its more charitable tone as compared to the vitriolic character of so many of the published works of the period.

Stillingfleet hoped to accomplish three goals with his work: First, he wanted to show that the Trinitarians were not as hopelessly divided as some seemed to think, so the preface to his work stressed the unity that existed between the Trinitarians, despite the differences found in their explanations and illustrations of the doctrine.[95] Second, he wanted to defend the Trin-

---

What was fateful, as Babcock astutely points out, was that medieval theologians transferred Boethius's definition of "person" to Trinitarian discourse. The problem, then, was that the Triune God is one being or substance (*substantia*) and three persons (*personae*). But since a person is an individual *substance*, we are now faced with a conundrum: God is one substance and three individual substances at the same time (Babcock, "Changing of the Christian God," 141–42). Bishop Stillingfleet and many others in England in the second half of the seventeenth century utilized this Boethian concept of person and the Aristotelian notions of nature and substance to explain the doctrine of the Trinity. But the Boethian definition of person turns the doctrine of the Trinity into a mathematical puzzle, for God is both one substance and three individual substances simultaneously. In the end, this was the real point of attack on the part of many of the anti-Trinitarians, from the Socinians and Biddle in the 1640s and 1650s to the new Arians, Sabellians, and Unitarians of various sorts in the 1690s.

94 Edward Stillingfleet, *A Discourse in Vindication of the Doctrine of the Trinity: With an Answer to the late Socinian Objections against it from the Scripture, Antiquity, and Reason and a Preface Concerning the Different Explications of the Trinity, and the Tendency of the Present Socinian Controversie* (London, 1697).

95 In the preface, Stillingfleet made a key distinction between an article of faith and the way it is explicated or explained. This enabled him to argue that the defenders were not, in fact, hopelessly divided as Nye and other antagonists contended. While it is clear that Bishop Stillingfleet thought Sherlock's exposition of the Trinity was mistaken, he did not explicitly condemn Sherlock and his work. Despite the differences in expression, the Trinitarian defenders agree that there are three distinct persons in the Godhead that inhere in the one being or substance of God in a manner that does not undermine the unity of God. This divine essence or substance

ity against various attacks by those who wanted to dismantle the doctrine. Thus, the body of his *Vindication* countered the Socinian criticism that the Trinity lacks scriptural grounding, involves contradictions, and is ultimately a mystery offensive to reason, since the doctrine demands belief in an article of faith that cannot be understood.[96] And third, he wanted to provide his own reasonable account of the doctrine of the Trinity. This final point is what brought Stillingfleet into conflict with Locke.

In chapter 10 of his book, Bishop Stillingfleet turned his attention to John Toland (1670–1722) and his work *Christianity not Mysterious*, published the previous year. Toland argued that reason had saved him from the superstitions of his Catholic upbringing and that "Reason is the only Foundation of all Certitude. . . . [T]here is nothing in the Gospel contrary to Reason, nor above it; and that no Christian Doctrine can properly be call'd a Mystery."[97] We cannot be expected to believe anything of which we cannot form an idea, for faith is rational assent to what is intelligible, a conception of faith radically different from Wesley's understanding. For Wesley, faith is inextricably bound up with our encounter with the Trinitarian persons in the gospel and therefore implicitly Trinitarian from beginning to end, even before that implicit Trinitarian content comes to explicit articulation.

It was precisely at this point that Stillingfleet saw the hand of Locke, since Toland believed that there is no clear idea of "substance," and it was

---

can be communicated from the Father to the Son and Spirit while remaining one and the same (Stillingfleet, *Vindication*, Introduction). See also Dixon, *Hot Disputes*, 144–46.

96 Babcock, "Changing of the Christian God," 142–43; Dixon, *Hot Disputes*, 143–44. Dixon includes a lengthy and astute analysis of Stillingfleet's work (see ibid., 143–48).

In the main body of the work, Stillingfleet spends four chapters showing that the Unitarians cannot trace their lineage back behind the "corruptions" of Chalcedon and Nicea to the "true" faith and correct interpretation of scripture found among the early Christians. The chapters that follow argue that the Trinitarian vision of God did not involve contradiction and was in fact the natural development of the Trinitarian convictions implicit in Christian faith from the beginning (Stillingfleet, *Vindication*, chaps. 1–4, 5–9). See also Dixon, *Hot Disputes*, 146–48.

97 John Toland, *Christianity Not Mysterious* (London, 1702), 6. See Dixon, *Hot Disputes*, 149. This forced Stillingfleet into a ticklish situation of having to defend the legitimate use of mystery in theology, while at the same time explaining why Christians are not obliged to believe other mysteries like the Roman Catholic doctrine of transubstantiation. Both Catholics and Unitarians utilized this "all-or-nothing" apologetic against Protestant defenders of the Trinity (Dixon, *Hot Disputes*, 148–49).

Locke who had dismantled "substance" in his *Essay Concerning Human Understanding.* The bishop was absolutely clear that "all our Notions of the Doctrine of the Trinity depend upon the right understanding" of "the *Distinction* between *Nature* [substance] and *Person*," for "unless we have clear and distinct apprehensions concerning *Nature* and *Person*, and the grounds of *Identity* and *Distinction*," we cannot render the doctrine of the Trinity intelligible.[98]

According to Stillingfleet, certainty comes not from a clear and distinct idea of substance, essence, or nature but from the evidence provided by reason that these ideas are true or correspond to reality. Substance is that which underlies accidents (individual things that exist) and makes them what they are. It is this "substratum" and "essence" (or nature) that enables one to sort individual things into common groups (dogs or oak trees, for example). If there were no substance or essence, the grouping of things together under a common category would be purely arbitrary.[99]

The bishop affirmed the "real" rather than "nominal" character of "nature" (substance) as that which makes a particular "to be what it is."[100] With regard to human beings, it is a real human "nature" (substance/essence) present in every human person that makes such a person identifiable as a human being rather than a monkey. Human beings share a real common substance or nature.

Locke saw things rather differently. For Locke, "substance" or "essence" meant a common set of characteristics (distinct or simple ideas) that make up a general idea like "dog" or "flower," which one (or the culture one inhabits) has constructed to classify things together to better organize experience of the world and enable discourse.[101] These general ideas have no "real" existence: there is no "essence" or "nature" (substance) that makes a dog

---

98 Stillingfleet, *Vindication*, 252. See Babcock, "Changing of the Christian God," 143. Notice that Stillingfleet had accepted Locke's terms of the debate: "clear and distinct ideas." The bishop acknowledged that Locke's ideas were "borrowed to serve other purposes." Yet Locke's ideas still provided support to those, like Toland, who attacked the doctrine of the Trinity (Stillingfleet, *Vindication*, 503). See Dixon, *Hot Disputes*, 149–51.

99 Stillingfleet, *Vindication*, 504–11. See Dixon, *Hot Disputes*, 151.

100 Stillingfleet, *Vindication*, 234. See also Babcock, "Changing of the Christian God," 143–44; Dixon, *Hot Disputes*, 145–48.

101 O'Connor, "Locke," 216–17. See also Babcock, "Changing of the Christian God," 138–39.

a dog: "dog" is simply a culturally constructed way of organizing experience and making discourse possible.[102]

102 In Locke's atomistic view of reality, all that exists are particular things. So the complex idea of a "dog" is merely a combination of simple ideas (four legs, a tail, barks, etc.) that are common characteristics of a particular set of animals: there is no "essence" or "nature" that makes a dog a dog, and not a cat. It is simply a culturally agreed-upon artifact that designates a set of characteristics. These general or complex ideas enable communication, as it would be entirely impossible to have a specific name for every single particular animal, let alone for everyone to have the same set of names. If pressed, Locke thought that this complex general idea "dog" could be analyzed and broken down into the many distinct and simple ideas that are constitutive of it.

In Locke's words: "Words become general by being made signs of general *ideas* and *ideas* become general by separating them from the circumstances of time and place and any other ideas that may determine them to be this or that particular existence. By this way of abstraction they are made more capable of representing more individuals than one; each of which having in it a conformity to that abstract *idea* (as we call it), of that sort" (Locke, *Human Understanding*, 3.3.6). See also O'Connor, "Locke," 216.

However, when we go a step further and construct the idea of "substance" or "essence" to refer to something real that accounts for the common characteristics that makes a dog a dog, as if the general word "dog" and general idea "dog" refer to "something" real that all dogs possess, Locke thinks we have become "mintmasters" making up words with no reference. These general ideas like "dog" or "horse" or "flower," according to Locke, are "nominal": they merely refer to common characteristics among a set of particular things that enable us to organize them under a general idea and general word. To speak of the "substance" or "essence" of something is simply a confusion; it is an idea devoid of content, possessing no explanatory power whatsoever (O'Connor, "Locke," 207–9, 213, 215–16). See also Babcock, "Changing of the Christian God," 137–38.

There are deep problems with Locke's account of language, including his understanding of complex words and the complex ideas they intend. These problems were rooted in his atomistic understanding of reality and language. When combined with his representative perception, in which sensory awareness is mediated to the immaterial mind through the senses, there is already a gap opening up between the impression the material world has upon the human knower through the senses and that world as it is in itself. We really never know anything about the world as it exists apart from the simple ideas (sensory data) impressed upon the immaterial mind via the senses. This is why Locke ended with a purely nominal account of complex ideas, like "dog" or "flower." What is ironic is that Locke wanted to develop a secure account of human knowing that would shore up the advance of natural science, but his work actually contributed to the radical questioning of natural science, as became clear in Hume's critique of Newton.

Stillingfleet also defended the Scholastic understanding of person. "Person" is what allows us to distinguish between individuals who share a common human nature. This common human nature has a unique "subsistence" in every particular individual human "person"; otherwise, human persons with the same nature would be identical. In other words, this unique or distinct "*manner of subsistence*" makes Peter, Peter (Peter's unique personhood) rather than James or John and "is in one Individual, and is not Communicable to another."[103] Thus, for Stillingfleet, "a *Person* is a compleat intelligent Substance, with a peculiar manner of Subsistence."[104]

This means that each human person seems to require a distinct substance because that substance has to "subsist" in a unique manner to account for differences between persons. But then, for Stillingfleet, substance accounts for both what makes every person a human (and thus what is common to all human beings) and also what distinguishes one person from another, if the unique subsistence of that substance accounts for the differences between individual persons.

When such a definition is applied to the doctrine of the Trinity, it leads directly to tritheism: three persons each with a unique subsisting substance. Stillingfleet believed that he could escape this problem by arguing that because of God's necessary existence and divine perfection, this difference in substance (the manner of its subsistence in particular human persons) did

---

In the end, Locke's epistemology is hopelessly flawed, for its account of human knowing fails to take into account the fact that reality is not made up atomistically of discrete particulars known via perception and resulting simple ideas. Realities are what they are because of the constitutive *relations* between them. In addition, human knowledge of realities in their interrelations requires a more complex, holistic, and integrative epistemological approach than Locke realized. Indeed, forms of human knowing that isolate particulars in this atomistic fashion do violence to the relations that make them what they are. Whether we are dealing with an electromagnetic field or relativity theory, or with the *relations* of love between the Trinitarian persons within the one Being-as-Communion that God is, these realities are what they are because of their *relations*, and they have to be grasped and articulated in a far more complex integrative and holistic manner than Locke's atomistic account of ideas and human knowing allows. The doctrine of the Trinity would never and could never arise on Lockean epistemic soil. Nor could Maxwell's or Einstein's influential theories that changed the course of natural science have developed on the basis of Locke's theory of knowledge (see Colyer, *How to Read*, chap. 9).

103 Stillingfleet, *Vindication*, 260, but see also 252–62. See also Babcock, "Changing of the Christian God," 143–44; and Dixon, *Hot Disputes*, 145–48.

104 Stillingfleet, *Vindication*, 511. See Dixon, *Hot Disputes*, 153.

not apply. Divine substance is not like finite substance and therefore does not rule out a real distinction between persons within one substance.[105] Bishop Stillingfleet believed that he had provided a reasonable account that rendered the doctrine of the Trinity intelligible.

Locke did not like being drawn into the debate. Coming under attack by a distinguished, influential, and learned bishop like Stillingfleet could easily endanger Locke's reputation and career. Locke was shocked and especially alarmed that of all his works, it was *An Essay Concerning Human Understanding* that had come under the bishop's critique, a book he publicly owned and had not expected to be linked to the Trinitarian controversies.

In response, Locke said he would retract anything that implied opposition to the Trinity or any other doctrine found in the Bible. Locke then proceeded to skillfully dismantle the bishop's carefully constructed notion of nature or substance. How could nature or substance be both common to every individual and yet, at the same time, due to the unique "manner of subsistence" of this nature in each individual, account for the distinction between individuals? This is less than a clear and reasonable account of substance or nature. In Locke's words: "I cannot understand these words, that the common nature of man is in Peter; for . . . whatever exists in Peter, is particular: but the common nature of a man, is the general nature of man. . . . [I]t confounds my understanding to make a general a particular."[106] Locke shrewdly pointed out the ambiguity in Stillingfleet's notion of nature or substance in relation to persons, showing that it cannot be simultaneously both the principle of commonality and of differentiation. Locke had little problem showing that Stillingfleet's notion of substance was in fact far from "clear and distinct."

Locke did not shy away from driving his point home with more than a touch of irony and ridicule: "I humbly crave leave to represent to your lordship, that if want of affording clear and distinct apprehensions concerning nature and person, make any book anti-Trinitarian, and, as such, fit to be writ against by your lordship; your lordship ought, in the opinion of a great many men, in the first place, to write against your own Vindication of the Doctrine of the Trinity."[107]

---

105 Stillingfleet, *Vindication*, 259–62. See also Babcock, "Changing of the Christian God," 143–44; and Dixon, *Hot Disputes*, 145–48.

106 John Locke, *The Works of John Locke* (London, 1823, repr., Aalen: Scientia Verlag, 1963), 4:96, cited in Babcock, "Changing of the Christian God," 144. See also Dixon, *Hot Disputes*, 150–62.

107 Locke, *Works*, 4:180, cited in Babcock, "Changing of the Christian God," 145. See also Dixon, *Hot Disputes*, 150–62. Dragged into a debate he had studiously

However, what is revealing is that, throughout his debate with Bishop Stillingfleet over several years, Locke never *affirmed* the doctrine of the Trinity.[108] Indeed, in his final letter to the bishop, Locke asserted: "My Lord . . . I do not remember that I ever read in it [the Bible] either of these propositions in these precise words, 'that there are three persons in one nature. . . .' When your Lordship shall show me a Bible wherein they are set down, I shall then think them a good instance of propositions offered me out of scripture . . . but I deny that these very propositions are in express words in my Bible."[109]

The debate between Locke and Stillingfleet continued for three years and finally ended with the bishop's untimely death in 1699. The whole exchange had nearly the opposite effect from what Stillingfleet had hoped: the exchange simply added to the growing distress about the viability of Trinitarian belief. Locke was certainly more convincing than Stillingfleet and often made the bishop's arguments appear silly.[110] In addition, Locke effectively undermined the concept of substance and also further shifted the notion of person away from the Boethian definition toward an understanding of person as agent or consciousness, neither of which are particularly capable of bearing a Trinitarian understanding.[111]

---

avoided, Locke stated that he had written nothing on the doctrine of the Trinity, that he believed the scriptures, that he accepted revelation, and even believed that there are mysteries in Christian faith (see Dixon, *Hot Disputes*, 155).

108 Locke was actually far less supportive of the Trinity than he wanted to appear. His notebooks from the 1690s contain a volume entitled, *Adversaria theologica*, with lists of biblical texts bearing upon the question of the Trinity. Under "*Non Trinitas*" are many texts, under "*Trinitas*" there are just two! (See Redwood, *Reason, Ridicule and Religion*, 162; and Placher, *Domestication*, 176.) See Dixon's account of the evidence supporting Locke's disenchantment with the doctrine of the Trinity in Dixon, *Hot Disputes,* 159–68.

Locke also complained that Stillingfleet had tarred him with guilt by association. In addition, Locke asserted that he had not attempted, in the bishop's words, "to discard substance out of the reasonable part of the world"; rather, he had simply pointed out various difficulties associated with the concept of substance (see Dixon, *Hot Disputes*, 154). Locke's understanding of "substance" bears similarity to Kant's infamous *ding-an-sich* (thing-in-itself): Locke did not deny "substance"; he simply said that we can know nothing of its nature, and wryly noted that his views were rather close to those of the bishop who seemed to be equally unclear as to what substance actually is.

109 John Locke in a letter to Bishop Stillingfleet as qtd, in Dixon, *Hot Disputes*, 158–59.

110 See Babcock, "Changing of the Christian God," 145–46.

111 A generation later, David Hume observed that "most philosophers seem inclined to think, that personal identity *arises* from consciousness" (David Hume, *A Treatise*

In reality, Stillingfleet's Scholastic understanding of substance and person were swept away by the profound transformation in the assumptions about language, about how we acquire and form ideas, and about the relationship between language/ideas and the things they signify, a transformation purposely precipitated by influential intellectuals like Bacon, Descartes, Hobbes, and Newton. Locke simply hastened the process. Stillingfleet's explication of the Trinity proved unpersuasive because it was inextricably linked to a worn-out Scholastic Aristotelian perspective. In addition, though Stillingfleet was a pious bishop, his book did little to reconnect the doctrine of the Trinity to vital Christian faith and life. Stillingfleet defended the intelligibility of the Trinity as concept or idea, but the content of the concept is detached from God's Trinitarian self-revelation and self-communication in the gospel that generated the doctrine of the Trinity in the early church and ever after, a point that Wesley demonstrated in his sermon "On the Trinity," as will be clear by the end of this chapter.

The one thing that Stillingfleet did accomplish was to draw Locke into the debate, and many other orthodox critiques of Locke's doctrinal beliefs followed. In the process, Locke's reputation was irreparably damaged in orthodox Christian circles.[112]

IV. The 1700s to 1740s: Samuel Clarke versus Daniel Waterland

1. A "Lull" before Another Storm

There was only a brief lull in the storm before yet another wave of controversy over the Trinity spread across the British Isles. The vitriolic character of the debates in the 1690s, including events like the censure of Sherlock at the end of 1695 and the hanging of Aikenhead in 1697, had several effects.

The latitudinarian camp grew considerably. Doctrinal concerns, particularly the technicalities of the doctrine of the Trinity, were viewed more and more as peripheral and insignificant compared to questions of morality and practical concerns relevant to living life. Books and tracts focused on what the Thirty-Nine Articles actually said and on explaining what the Act of Blasphemy really meant.[113]

of Human Nature, book I [Glasglow: Collins, 1962], 330). See Dixon, *Hot Disputes*, 169.

112 Dixon, *Hot Disputes*, 162ff.

113 Ibid., 170–71.

New problems arose, such as: Do persons with Unitarian inclinations belong in the Anglican Church, and what does the church do with sincere clergymen who cannot affirm the Thirty-Nine Articles or in good conscience use the Book of Common Prayer?[114] The irenic Daniel Allen, in his work *The Moderate Trinitarian*, argued that those who could not in good conscience affirm the deity of Christ should not be excommunicated.[115]

The volume of controversial works slowed to a trickle. Reticence to foment further controversy is evident in several other works published in the first decade of the eighteenth century. Erasmus Warren and Charles Leslie (1650–1722) both wrote superficial treatises in defense of the Trinity that did not really enter into the problems and issues raised by the controversies of the 1690s.[116] Even Stephen Nye, the anti-Trinitarian who played such a huge role in the controversies of the 1690s, moved closer to an orthodox Trinitarian position in his moderate work *The Doctrine of the Holy Trinity*, published in 1701.[117]

Yet, the questions and problems that surfaced during the 1690s had hardly been resolved. What is the real character of Protestantism? Is the Reformation complete? What is the role of reason in the interpretation of scripture? Is the Trinity really the Christian doctrine of God, or is it, like transubstantiation, a later Roman Catholic intrusion into biblical Christian faith and life? And what is the meaning of the term "person," particularly when applied to God/the Trinity?

2. *William Whiston*

In 1703, William Whiston (1667–1752) succeeded Sir Isaac Newton (1642–1727) as Lucasian Professor of Mathematics at Cambridge. A recent historian characterized Whiston as "an eccentric, a perennial Cambridge type, of immense and many-sided learning, combined with feeble judgment, and

114 Ibid.

115 Daniel Allen, *The Moderate Trinitarian* (London, 1699). See Dixon, *Hot Disputes*, 170.

116 Dixon, *Hot Disputes*, 174–76.

117 Stephen Nye, *The Doctrine of the Holy Trinity* (London: Bell, 1701). The work appeared under his own name, unlike his earlier works, which were all anonymous. While Nye's deep fear of tritheism was still evident, he at least tried to make sense of the doctrine of the Trinity, even if he ended up dangerously close to Sabellianism. Maybe Nye was simply worried about the fallout of Peter Allix exposing Nye as the author of the infamous *The Brief History of the Unitarians*, a work that fueled the controversies of the 1690s (Dixon, *Hot Disputes*, 171–74).

complete faith in his own opinions,"[118] character traits that were to get him into trouble. Like Newton, who, already in the 1670s, was convinced that the doctrine of the Trinity was a massive fraud, Whiston, based on his own research into the origins of the Trinity along with the Trinitarian controversies of the 1690s, believed that the Athanasian doctrine of the Trinity was a lamentable corruption of original Christian faith. Whiston's views were essentially Eusebian, a subordinationist heresy similar to Arianism.[119]

However, unlike his mentor, Newton,[120] Whiston published his views. Purposefully provocative, Whiston accused Athanasius of being a "knave and

---

118 Gordon Rupp, *Religion in England 1688–1791* (Oxford: Oxford University Press, 1986), 249.

119 Dixon, *Hot Disputes*, 181–82.

120 While Newton avoided the Trinitarian controversies publicly, he was an anti-Trinitarian. Newton's understanding of how we know, combined with his atomistic view of reality, could not but influence his understanding of God and other aspects of Christian faith, including his interpretation of scripture. An atomistic view of scripture and the idea that concepts (in this case, doctrines) are deduced from the Bible will never yield a robust doctrine of the Trinity, in a similar way that electromagnetic field theory or the theory of relativity cannot be deduced from phenomena/data or abstracted from observation in natural science (see Colyer, *How to Read*, 325–44, for a detailed analysis of Newton's epistemology and its fateful consequences for natural science).

In the 1670s, after a massive study of the New Testament and early church, Newton became convinced that the doctrine of the Trinity was a grievous mistake perpetrated in the fourth and fifth centuries with Athanasius as the key figure who corrupted the original apostolic faith that was actually Arian. For Newton, the Father alone was fully divine (see Placher, *Domestication*, 174–75; and Dixon, *Hot Disputes*, 180).

Furthermore, Newton in the end identified absolute time and space, independent of and within which all the events of the universe of space and time (and thus all of human history) takes place, with the Divine *Sensorium*. This created a vision of the universe as a vast but closed system that operates on the basis of immutable natural (cause-and-effect) laws independent of God. Any action of God in this closed system becomes an intrusion, a breach of the inexorable natural laws that govern all events.

Newton's closed cause-and-effect universe was also rather inhospitable to the traditional Christian understanding of the Incarnation and the Trinitarian doctrine of God. Newton's predilection for Arianism comported rather well with his scientific convictions about the universe. It is no coincidence that Newton's perspective paved the way for the God of deism.

Newton was the most brilliant physicist of his day. He was elected a Fellow of Trinity College in 1667. When it came time to renew his fellowship at Cambridge, he was trapped because to retain his position he had to be ordained in the Church

an ignoramus." Whiston also asserted that the Reformation would arrive at its full culmination only when the last relic of Roman Catholic popery, the doctrine of the Trinity, was excised from the articles of faith.[121] Whiston was not afraid to alter the liturgy of the Book of Common Prayer to reflect his eccentric theological views. The result was a wave of protest.

At a Convocation at Cambridge on October 31, 1710, Whiston was charged with heresy and deprived of his chair. His anti-Trinitarian publications were nearly censured and would have been if Queen Anne had given her Royal Assent. Whiston died a member of the General Baptists.[122]

Yet Whiston was not alone in his views that (1) the Reformation was incomplete, (2) scripture alone as interpreted by reason was the sole rule of faith, and (3) primitive Christian faith did not reflect the Athanasian doctrine of the Trinity. Whiston's friend Samuel Clarke was among those who shared these convictions, and it was Clarke's work on the Trinity that reignited the Trinitarian controversies, further shattering the relative peace of the early years of the eighteenth century.[123]

3. Samuel Clarke

Samuel Clarke (1675–1729) was a towering intellect. At Cambridge he encountered the "new science" and became friends with Newton. Clarke established his reputation as a leading theologian early on in his career.

---

of England and in the process profess faith in the Trinity. At the last moment a special royal exemption freed him from the requirement of ordination and its associated affirmation of the Trinity.

In the 1690s, Newton wrote two letters to John Locke expressing his conclusions about the nefarious Trinitarian corruption of true Arian Gospel by Athanasius, among others. Newton's plan was to have Jean LeClerc, a Dutch Remonstrant scholar and theologian, publish the letters anonymously. However, just before they went to press, Newton panicked, canceled the publication of the letters, and never commented on the doctrine of the Trinity publicly for the rest of his life.

Newton's reaction is a rather vivid commentary on how dangerous anti-Trinitarianism was at the dawn of the eighteenth century. The fate of William Whiston and Samuel Clarke, both followers of Newton, reveals that Newton's fears were well-founded. While Newton never published his anti-Trinitarian views, he profoundly influenced Whiston and Clarke, both of whom end up being rather un-Trinitarian (see Placher, *Domestication*, 174–75; and Dixon, *Hot Disputes*, 180).

121 Redwood, *Reason, Religion and Ridicule*, 204–5. See also Dixon, *Hot Disputes*, 180–81.

122 Dixon, *Hot Disputes,* 182.

123 Ibid., 182–83.

Many considered him to be the greatest metaphysician in England after Locke.[124]

After studying the various tracts and treatises associated with the controversies of the 1690s, Clarke published his work *The Scripture Doctrine of the Trinity* in 1712.[125] Clarke knew that his work would be controversial, so he purchased a house just in case he lost his position as rector of St. James's Church, Piccadilly, and needed a new place to live.[126]

The intent of the book is clear from the title. Indeed, we find in Clarke's introduction a well-worn path among anti-Trinitarians: the degenerative process away from the scriptural doctrine that had already begun at Nicea and that reached its culmination in medieval Scholasticism. Like Bacon, Descartes, Hobbes, and Locke, Clarke revealed his utter disdain for Aristotelian Scholasticism: "The Schoolmen . . . wrought great parts of their Divinity out of their own Brains, as Spiders do Cobwebs out of their own Bowels; starting a thousand Subtilties . . . that they . . . did themselves never thoroughly understand."[127]

The Reformers had attempted to retrieve genuine Christian faith found in scripture alone, but the process, according to Clarke, was still incomplete: Protestantism had not fully freed itself from unbiblical Scholasticizing tendencies. Following Locke and others, he rejected Aristotelian categories, like "nature," "substance," and "subsistence," used to explicate the Trinity and tried to return to scripture alone.

In order to complete the Reformation process, he argued that Protestants must rigorously apply the *sola scriptura* principle.[128] Clarke embraced an exceedingly narrow *sola scriptura* perspective, with no appeal to the tradition of the church. He read the Creeds in light of scripture, not vice versa.

---

124 Invited to give the famous Boyle Lectures in 1704 and 1705, Clarke presented a tour de force synthesis of the new science and theology (Dixon, *Hot Disputes*, 183; Placher, *Domestication*, 177).

125 Samuel Clarke, *The Works of Samuel Clarke*, 4 vols. (London, 1738). *The Scripture Doctrine of the Trinity* is found in volume 4, and all page references to that work are from volume 4 of the 1738 edition of Clarke's collected works.

126 Clarke was appointed rector at St. James's Piccadilly in 1709. The appointment indicated a very promising future in the Anglican Church, for the immediate predecessors at Piccadilly all went on to become bishops, including Tenison and Wake, both archbishops of Canterbury. A distinguished ecclesial career, however, never came to pass because Clarke got himself into deep trouble by entering the Trinitarian debate (Placher, *Domestication*, 177; Dixon, *Hot Disputes*, 183).

127 Clarke, *The Scripture Doctrine*, 147. See also Dixon, *Hot Disputes*, 187.

128 Dixon, *Hot Disputes*, 183–85.

Clarke also argued for the use of reason when interpreting the Bible, indeed for judging whether an article of faith was in fact found in scripture.[129]

In addition, Clarke had been profoundly influenced by Newton, Locke, and others not only in his view of scripture but also in his understanding of how concepts, theories, and doctrines are derived from scripture. Therefore, in part 1 of the work, Clarke isolated 1,251 texts from the New Testament relating to the Trinity and treated them like discrete and separate facts from which one can deduce or abstract concepts, theories, or doctrines. This process was very similar to Locke's new way of tracing ideas back to the sensory perceptions so that one can develop clear and distinct ideas that actually signify something. The implicit "atomism" in Clarke's view of biblical texts was not unlike Newton's atomistic view of nature, but it was unlike Wesley's understanding of scripture mediating the Trinitarian verities of the faith that we encounter and know by participation in the gospel, as we will see in chapters 2 and 3.[130]

This atomistic way of approaching scripture and its interpretation was not how the early Church and the Nicene theologians, who first articulated the doctrine of the Trinity, viewed scripture, grasped its meaning, and developed doctrines from scripture. Atomistically isolating texts and then trying to deduce or abstract doctrines from them will never yield a robust doctrine of the Trinity.[131] Despite Clarke's attempt to return to scripture alone, his vision of scripture and its interpretation was different from that of the early Church and the Reformers, and Clarke failed to realize how his flawed vision configured his results.

Nevertheless, Clarke's work was impressive and tightly argued. In his examination of the 1,251 texts, Clarke pointed out that "God" and "the Father" are used synonymously: "God in scripture-language, does not signify the Trinity, but the First Person of the Trinity."[132] Indeed, for Clarke, "The Word, God, in scripture, never signifies a complex Notion of more Persons

129 Ibid., 184–85.

130 Clarke's method of interpreting scripture is remarkably similar to Newton's understanding of natural science, deducing concepts from phenomena or abstracting theories from scientific observation.

131 The doctrine of the Trinity arises only out of a more integrative and holistic approach to scripture viewed as an organically interrelated canon in which we think about God in light of the conjoint witness of the whole fabric of scripture (see Colyer, *The Nature of Doctrine*, for a discussion of various current ways of viewing how doctrine arises in relation to scripture, especially the perspective of Thomas F. Torrance).

132 Clarke, *The Scripture Doctrine,* 191. See Dixon, *Hot Disputes*, 189.

(or Intelligent Agents) than One; but always means One Person only, viz. Either the Person of the Father singly, or the Person of the Son singly."[133]

The orthodox doctrine of the Trinity was not only unbiblical, according to Clarke, but also finally incomprehensible along similar lines that we have seen in others: God cannot be one "intelligent agent" and three "intelligent agents" at the same time. In response to his critics, Clarke, reminiscent of Locke's retort to Bishop Stillingfleet, asserted: "Your conclusion therefore, (if meant literally) one God IN Persons three, is a Language of which I understand not the terms. One Intelligent Agent in Three intelligent agents . . . are English words but have no English signification."[134] Clarke saw his scriptural doctrine of the Trinity as a middle ground between Socinianism (Sabellianism) and tritheism: the Son and the Spirit are persons subordinate to the one supreme God, the Father.[135]

Clarke's work sent shock waves through the Church of England, provoked a storm of protest, and cost him his ecclesial career. Edward Wells (1667–1727), rector of Cotesbach; Francis Gastrell (1662–1625), bishop

---

133 Clarke, *The Scripture Doctrine*, 155. See Dixon, *Hot Disputes*, 188.

134 Qtd. in Dixon, *Hot Disputes*, 193. Clarke was responding to a critique by Robert Mayo. Notice that Clarke's definition of a person as an "intelligent agent" was close to that of Locke and equally as individualist and incapable of a Trinitarian definition.

135 Clarke, *The Scripture Doctrine*, 122, 149, 191. See also Dixon, *Hot Disputes*, 186–90. However, the question that immediately arises is, What then is the precise relation of the Father to the Son and the Spirit? Clarke's emphasis on the monarchy of the Father pushed him toward subordinationism and the inequality of the Son and Spirit to the Father. The Father ends up as the "One Supreme Cause and Original of all Things" (Clarke, *The Scripture Doctrine*, 122). See also Dixon, *Hot Disputes*, 186–89.

This kind of emphasis on the monarchy of the person of the Father conflicts rather sharply with the position of many of the key Nicene theologians, like Athanasius, who said that the Son is begotten and the Spirit proceeds from the being of the Father, not the person of the Father.

Nevertheless, Clarke was probably not the Arian that many of his contemporaries accused him of being. Pfizenmaier argues that Clarke was a Eusebian, since Clarke appears to believe that Christ (and the Spirit) exists from all eternity in positions subordinate to the Father. The Son and Spirit are neither manifestations (Sabellianism) nor creatures (Arianism), but are in fact eternal persons, yet persons eternally subordinate to the one Supreme God, the Father. For a positive treatment of Clarke, and persuasive argument that Clarke was Eusebian, see Thomas Pfizenmaier, *The Trinitarian Theology of Dr. Samuel Clarke* (Leiden: Brill, 1997).

While Clarke said that he based his understanding solely on scripture and that he would refrain from all speculation about the immanent Trinity, we see that he inevitably made statements about the immanent Trinity.

of Chester; Thomas Bennett (d. 1728); and even Stephen Nye all attacked Clarke on various points.[136] Everyone was clear that Clarke's *The Scripture Doctrine of the Trinity* represented a radical departure from the orthodox doctrine of the Trinity.

Since Clarke was one of the most highly respected intellectuals of the day, Anglican Church officials viewed his work as all the more dangerous.[137] In 1714, the Lower House of Convocation attacked Clarke. The Anglican clergy appealed to the bishops to intervene in June. The bishops, in turn, requested an "Extract" of Clarke's work. Clarke provided the Lower House with a pointed defense by the end of June, but realizing how dangerous his situation had become, in early July he sent a more conciliatory paper to the bishops promising that he would neither preach nor write on the Trinity again.[138]

So the bishops decided not to press the matter further, whereas the Lower House was distraught and clearly wanted substantive action to be taken against Clarke. Relieved, Clarke sold the house he had purchased, but his ecclesial future was over. A few years later, a number of the bishops, including Wake, who had shielded Clarke from persecution, prevented Clarke from being elevated to bishop.[139]

4. Daniel Waterland

More than a few observers were scandalized by what they saw to be the un-Christian persecution of a wise and honorable man like Clarke. These

136 Dixon, *Hot Disputes*, 190–92.

137 Indeed, Daniel Whitby, a veteran Trinitarian theologian, had his orthodox convictions about the Trinity shattered by reading Clarke's book (Dixon, *Hot Disputes*, 195).

138 Placher, *Domestication*, 177–78; Dixon, *Hot Disputes*, 194–95.

139 Placher, *Domestication*, 177–78; Dixon, *Hot Disputes*, 194–95. In his *Lettres philosophiques* in 1734, Voltaire (1694–1778) recounts a story about Queen Anne's desire to make Clarke her archbishop of Canterbury. According to Voltaire's version of the event, Bishop Gibson of London had to inform her Majesty, "'Mr. Clarke is the wisest and most honorable man in the kingdom; he lacks only one thing.' 'What?' asked the Queen. 'He is not a Christian,'" the bishop responded (Voltaire, *Lettres philosophiques* [Oxford: Basil Blackwell, 1951)], letter 7, variant 129). English translations often omit the variant. See also Placher, *Domestication*, 164.

Of course, by the time Voltaire published the account, he assumed that everyone understood his joke: no respectable and informed person would consider the Trinity a belief of any real significance. But in the second decade of the eighteenth century, this was not a laughing matter to the orthodox Anglican bishops who in no way wanted someone like Clarke in their ranks.

events further contributed to the growing tandem latitudinarian distaste of theological speculation and of theological persecution. In addition, Clarke had enthusiastic supporters. It was one of them, John Jackson, who lured Daniel Waterland (1683–1740) into the fray.[140]

Waterland was easily Clarke's equal, and William van Mildert argues that "from the time that Waterland took the field, the reputation and authority of Dr. Clarke perceptibly declined."[141] Waterland had an impressive theological mind, plus a clear understanding of the doctrine of the Trinity and profound grasp of the early church.[142] The depth and breadth of Waterland's scholarship were masterful and made him a significant theological adversary. He entered the debate in 1719 with the publication of his work *A Vindication of Christ's Divinity*.[143]

Waterland quickly realized that much of Clarke's case rested on Clarke's contention that "God" is used in scripture primarily or "supremely" of the Father and that it was used of the Son in a lesser or "subordinate" sense. Waterland pointed out that the priority of the Father within the Godhead does not require the subordination or inferiority of the Son, and he demanded that Clarke and his followers provide evidence and arguments to support their position. This was a rather clever move by Waterland because it reversed the burden of proof, requiring Clarke to give arguments for his way of exegeting

140 Jackson had posed a number of questions to Waterland privately. Waterland answered them privately only to have Jackson publish their exchange without Waterland's knowledge or consent (Dixon, *Hot Disputes*, 195–97).

141 See William van Mildert's comment in his edition of Daniel Waterland, *The Works of the Rev. Daniel Waterland*, ed. van Mildert, 10 vols. (Oxford: Clarendon, 1983), 1:312, note a, cited in Dixon, *Hot Disputes*, 197. Waterland became the Regius Professor of Divinity at Cambridge University in 1717 and was master of Magdalene College from 1713 until his death in 1740.

142 In 1723, he published a stunning treatment of the origins, key theologians, and theological reflection behind the Athanasian Creed entitled *A Critical History of the Athanasian Creed* (Daniel Waterland, *A Critical History of the Athanasian Creed* [Cambridge, 1723]).

143 Daniel Waterland, *A Vindication of Christ's Divinity*, published in 1719, reprinted in Waterland, *Works*, vol. 1. All references to *A Vindication* are from vol. 1 of *Works*. Nearly half of the ten volumes of his collected works are devoted to the doctrine of the Trinity and the controversies around it. From 1719 until his death, Waterland, who was called "another Athanasius," defended the Trinity against the "new Arians," as he called them. Most of what Waterland had to say in his defense of the Trinity in his later writings was already in *A Vindication of Christ's Divinity* (Dixon, *Hot Disputes*, 196–97).

those texts. The Father "begetting" the Son does not imply the inferiority that Clarke assumed.[144]

In addition, Waterland pounced on Clarke's statement that "One Intelligent Agent in Three intelligent agents . . . are English words, but have no English signification," for it collapses the distinction between "being" and "person" in reference to the Trinity. Waterland astutely asked whether Clarke's "whole performance . . . be any thing more than a repetition of this assertion, that being and person are the same, or that there is no medium between Tritheism and Sabellianism? Which is removing the cause from scripture to natural reason."[145] Waterland pointed out that the church fathers repudiated the identification of "person" and "being." They are not interchangeable terms.[146]

Here Waterland was returning to Nicene patristic sources and breaking free of the Boethian understanding of person and all the problems it created for understanding and explicating the doctrine of the Trinity. In later works, Waterland made clear that it is not possible to start with a definition of person taken from human beings and apply it to God without radically shifting the meaning. Indeed, nowhere is this more true than in the perichoretic unity between the divine persons for which there is no human resemblance.[147]

Those who attempt to collapse person and being and say either (1) that God is one intelligent agent, the Father, and that the Son and Spirit are simply Sabellian modes or manifestations of the one Agent, or (2) that there are three intelligent agents but no real unity (tritheism), had not effectively argued their case. They had simply taken an understanding of identity between being and person applicable to human persons and assumed that it applied to God.

Waterland retorted that this is precisely what orthodox Trinitarian theology denies! The three persons are one God (one being), even if we do not know "how" they are so. Furthermore, Waterland noted that the opponents of the doctrine of the Trinity have not demonstrated that three persons cannot be one being with reference to God; they simply asserted it and then repeated it. What Waterland found particularly amusing was that the

---

144 Dixon, *Hot Disputes*, 197–98. See also Robert T. Holtby, *Daniel Waterland* (London: Charles Thurnam and Sons, 1966), 12–49, for an account of the controversy between Waterland and Clarke.

145 Waterland, *A Vindication*, 231. See Dixon, *Hot Disputes*, 198.

146 Waterland, *A Vindication*, 231–42. See Dixon, *Hot Disputes*, 198–99.

147 Waterland, *Works*, 2:83–85, 208–11. See also Dixon, *Hot Disputes*, 199–201.

language Clarke and his defenders used pushed them toward a polytheism of three Gods of progressively lesser deity.[148]

However, Waterland did not root the content of the terms "Trinity" and "person" in the gospel itself and our participation in it. So while Waterland effectively critiqued Clarke's position and defended the traditional doctrine of the Trinity, he did very little to reconnect the Trinity with vital Christian faith and life, as John and Charles Wesley did from 1738 on. In the end, despite his vigorous defense of the doctrine, Waterland contributed to the marginalization of the Trinity from vital Christian faith and practice.

There is no question that Waterland's work helped stem the tide of anti-Trinitarian publication, but political pressure by Anglican leaders and civil authorities played an important role as well. Few scholars or church leaders wanted to risk losing their positions or ruin promising careers, as happened to Whiston and Clarke, by openly espousing anti-Trinitarian sentiment.

Nevertheless, many thoughtful people, including some of the bishops, were sick of the controversies, and especially the un-Christian persecution of persons like the learned and honorable Clarke who sincerely held positions that fell outside orthodoxy. Despite the apparent intellectual victory of the orthodox doctrine of the Trinity, the very character of the debates, including the orthodox defenses, had turned the doctrine of the Trinity into a complicated, if not esoteric, belief. The doctrine may well be Christian, but it was clearly incomprehensible to all but the most gifted intellects, making contentiousness over the doctrine appear all the more uncharitable.[149] Waterland's work did not solve this problem.

Waterland's defense of the doctrine of the Trinity was impeccably orthodox and often extraordinarily insightful. But it was also spiritually arid. Aware of this loss of any practical significance or meaning of the Trinity, Waterland wrote his final work, *The Importance of the Doctrine of the Holy Trinity Asserted*, to address this consequence of the Trinitarian controversies.[150] The book comes across as an afterthought, an attempt to render the Trinity clear, practical, and scriptural after the life had been drained out of the doctrine in the course of the Trinitarian debates of which Waterland was so much a part. While still the official teaching of the Church of England, the practical

148 Dixon, *Hot Disputes*, 198–203.

149 Ibid., 205–6.

150 Daniel Waterland, *The Importance of the Doctrine of the Trinity Asserted* (1734), in *Works*, vol. 5. See Holtby, *Daniel Waterland*, 39–42; and Dixon, *Hot Disputes*, 205–6.

importance of the Trinity for Christian faith and life was now in dire need of defense.[151] Waterland's final work proved to be less than effective.

Underneath the relative public calm in the British Isles by the 1730s and 1740s, after the Trinitarian controversies in the 1710s and early 1720s, lay both continual and significant disenchantment with the doctrine of the Trinity even on the part of those who affirmed it. There were anti-Trinitarians within the Church of England who simply did not admit it out of fear of losing their ecclesial positions. The spirit of the age generated a new threat: those who denied the very existence of a personal God. Why be concerned about something as subtle as the Trinity, when the very idea of any God at all was under attack?[152]

The time was ripe for a retrieval of the participatory, economic Trinitarian Christian faith that came to expression in the early church among the theologians associated with Nicea, like Athanasius, among others.[153] John and Charles Wesley both discovered this kind of vibrant Trinitarian faith and life in 1738 and disseminated it in England among the Methodists for the remainder of their lives.

V. The 1750s to 1770s: Socinianism Revived, Independent Unitarianism Born

1. Ever-Present Anti-Trinitarian Sentiment

By the end of Waterland's life in the early 1740s, the doctrine of the Trinity had weathered the storms of controversy caused in no small part by the work of Samuel Clarke and his followers. Yet submerged anti-Trinitarian sentiment, very much present in England in the middle of the eighteenth century, broke out in yet another wave of controversy in the 1760s and 1770s. Only this time it was Socinianism and Unitarianism that generated the debate. At this point, Methodism had spread significantly across England and was a growing concern. The Methodists took note of the Trinitarian controversies.

Already in the 1750s, Edmund Law (1703–1787), master of Peterhouse beginning in 1754, and bishop of Carlisle in 1768, disseminated ideas from Samuel Clarke and was suspected of being "Socinian." When Law had the public disputation for his DD degree in 1749, some of the professors

---

151 Dixon, *Hot Disputes*, 205–7.

152 Ibid., 205–6.

153 See Thomas F. Torrance, *The Trinitarian Faith: The Evangelical Theology of the Ancient Catholic Church* (Edinburgh: T & T Clark, 1988), for an explication of the faith of the Nicene Fathers remarkably similar to that of John and Charles Wesley.

at Cambridge resisted granting him the degree because of his Socinian convictions.[154]

Law is an example of a small but growing number of leaders within the Anglican Church who were vocal advocates of anti-Trinitarian views. John Jones (1700–1770) and Theophilus Lindsey (1723–1808), among others, were part of this circle of leaders within Anglicanism who held heterodox views of the Trinity. So was Archdeacon Francis Blackburne (1705–1787), who had been deeply influenced by Locke and who played a crucial role in the Feathers Tavern Petition in the early 1770s.[155]

There was also a growing emphasis on toleration in England in the 1750s, generating various proposals to abolish subscription to the Anglican Articles (particularly those on the Trinity) and to the Book of Common Prayer on the part of clergy and those with positions in the universities. In 1766, Archdeacon Blackburne anonymously published his *Confessional*, which also argued for relaxing subscription to the Articles, liturgy, and creeds.[156] Echoing Clarke, Blackburne and others saw theological grounds for this move in the Protestant emphasis on *sola scriptura* and in the natural "rights" of Christians to judge for themselves in matters of conscience when interpreting scripture, an idea they also linked to the Reformation. Blackburne's work went through twenty editions between 1766 and 1770. The book led to a massive campaign to get rid of subscription and modify the Anglican Articles in a "modern" direction.[157] This campaign generated the infamous Feathers Tavern Petition discussed below.

It is no coincidence that William Jones (1726–1800) published his classic defense of the Trinity, *The Catholic Doctrine of the Trinity*, in 1756 as this new wave of anti-Trinitarian sentiment surfaced among Anglican leaders. The work ran through twelve editions by 1830.[158] The book is divided into four chapters entitled "The Divinity of Christ" (chapter 1), "The Divinity of the Holy Ghost" (chapter 2), "The Plurality and Trinity of Persons" (chapter 3), and "The Trinity in Unity" (chapter 4). Jones repeatedly mentioned Samuel Clarke and his book *The Scripture Doctrine of the Trinity*, revealing

154 Clark, *English Society*, 311–12.

155 Ibid., 312–13.

156 *The Confessional or, a full and free inquiry into the right, utility, edification, and success, of establishing systematical confessions of faith and doctrine in protestant churches* (London, 1766). See Rack, *Reasonable Enthusiast*, 461–62.

157 Rack, *Reasonable Enthusiast*, 462; Clark, *English Society*, 314.

158 William Jones, *The Catholic Doctrine of the Trinity* (Oxford, 1756). See Clark, *English Society*, 219.

the immense impact of Clarke on Anglicans, like Law, who utilized Clarke's work in the renewed battle against the Trinity.[159]

The third revised edition of Jones's work was issued in 1766, the same year that Blackburne published his *Confessional.* Jones's book was the inspiration for Charles Wesley's 1767 collection of hymns and poems about, and to, the Trinity, published the year after Blackburne called for the abolition of subscription to the Anglican Articles, liturgy, and creeds. This collection of hymns provided a way for the Methodists to express their Trinitarian faith that recaptured the Nicene theologians' conviction that the Trinity is more to be adored than theologically explored. Theological reflection on the Triune God of the gospel belongs in the context of worship, an element singularly missing throughout the Trinitarian controversies over the previous century. The "Advertisement" for Charles Wesley's hymns made this point explicit: "Such a mode [hymns] of treating it [the Trinity] is the best answer to those who represent it as a mere metaphysical speculation devoid of practical interest."[160] This doxological dimension was important for John Wesley, who noted that the one thing lacking in Jones's book was "application, lest it [the Trinity] should appear to be merely a speculative doctrine, which has no influence on our hearts and lives; but this is abundantly supplied by my brother's Hymns."[161]

The Wesley brothers were not only aware of the Trinitarian controversies but also cognizant that their own Trinitarian convictions represented a different perspective and approach, one that was closely connected to Christian faith, life, and worship. For John and Charles Wesley, the Trinity is deeply interconnected with "vital religion," and arid intellectual approaches to the doctrine were suspect.

In the 1760s and 1770s, the doctrine of the Trinity was at the center of yet another storm in eighteenth-century England. While not directly embroiled in the debates, John and Charles Wesley injected an alternative and vibrant way to be Trinitarian into the Methodist movement.

---

159 Jones, *Catholic Doctrine* (American Tract Society reprint), 80, 84, 104, 108, 119, 121.

160 Charles Wesley, *Hymns on the Trinity* (Bristol: Felix Farley, 1767), reprinted by the Charles Wesley Society in 1998 with a preface by S. T. Kimbrough Jr. and an introduction by Wilma J. Quantrille, xv. The Advertisement also notes, "The outbreak of Arianism in this country . . . called forth many . . . defenses of fundamental doctrines," Jones's *Catholic Doctrine* being one of them (ibid., xiv).

161 See Wesley's letter to Mary Bishop on April 17, 1776, in *The Works of John Wesley,* ed. Thomas Jackson, 14 vols., 3rd ed. (London: Wesleyan Methodist Book Room, 1872; reprint ed. Grand Rapids, MI: Baker Book House, 1986), 13:30–31.

2. John Wilkes

The infamous John Wilkes (1727–1797) is another example of a leader who outwardly conformed to the Church of England to be able to participate fully in public and political life but who did not hide his utter disdain for the doctrine of the Trinity. Wilkes freely used ridicule as a weapon against the doctrine.

J. C. D. Clark notes that the House of Lords in 1763 judged Wilkes's printed but unpublished works "An Essay on Woman" (actually a poem) and *Veni Creator* to be "a most scandalous, obscene, and impious libel; a gross profanation of many parts of the Holy scriptures; and a most wicked and blasphemous attempt to ridicule and vilify the person of our blessed Saviour."[162] Wilkes pointed out that he only printed, but had not published, the work, adding: "In my own closet I had a right to examine and even try by the keen edge of ridicule any opinions I pleased. If I laughed pretty freely at the glaring absurdities of the most monstrous creed which was ever attempted to be imposed on the credulity of Christians . . . [i]t was in private I laughed. I am not the first good Protestant who has amused himself with the egregious nonsense . . . of that strange, perplexed and perplexing mortal . . . Athanasius."[163]

Many of the themes found in past Trinitarian controversies in England were present in Wilkes's defense: the Trinitarian Athanasian and Nicene creeds were inventions imposed on the faithful; the doctrine of the Trinity is incompatible with reason and not found in scripture. Ridicule was an apt response to the incredulity and absurdity of orthodox Trinitarian doctrine.

3. The Feathers Tavern Petition and the Rise of Radical Unitarianism

By the early 1770s, the controversy bubbled over into overt action. Blackburne and his circle held a meeting in 1771 at the Feathers Tavern in London and drew up a petition to Parliament demanding the abolition of subscription to the Articles, liturgy, and creeds for Anglican clergy. Despite massive effort on the part of Blackburne and the other organizers, the petition received only around 250 signatures out of twelve thousand clergy. The petition was rejected in the Commons by a 217 to 71 vote in 1772, and then rejected again in 1773 and 1774.[164]

---

162 Qtd. in Clark, *English Society*, 309–10.

163 Qtd. ibid., 310.

164 Rack, *Reasonable Enthusiast*, 462; Clark, *English Society*, 314.

There was a parallel movement in the 1770s to abolish Dissenting subscription to the doctrinal portion of the Anglican Articles. The Act of Toleration (for those who did not conform to the Church of England) did not include anti-Trinitarian convictions. Dissenting ministers had to subscribe to the doctrinal section of the Anglican Articles. That subscription had never been universally enforced in England at any point in the eighteenth century. In 1779, it was abolished.[165]

The upshot of the rejection of the Feathers Tavern Petition was that a number of self-acknowledged anti-Trinitarians of primarily Socinian or Unitarian conviction left the Church of England, including Theophilus Lindsey (1723–1808) in 1773, John Jebb (1736–1786) in 1775, Robert Tyrwhitt (1735–1817) in 1777, and Gilbert Wakefield (1756–1801) in 1779.[166] Because Trinitarian Dissenters did not have the political, legal, and other resources that the Anglicans possessed, anti-Trinitarianism found easier inroads in Dissenting circles, particularly among the Presbyterians and General Baptists, who both moved rather easily to Arianism and then on to Socinianism or Unitarianism.[167]

By the early 1770s, there was a growing group in the ranks of Dissent with radical political views, as well as anti-Trinitarian convictions. This coterie could fit within a single coffeehouse in London, and they associated with one another in the "Club of Honest Whigs," a biweekly London gathering presided over for a time by Benjamin Franklin. There were many talented people in the group, including James Burgh (1714–1775), Richard Price (1733–1791), Joseph Priestley (1733–1804), and Ben Franklin (1706–1790). The religious expression of the movement centered in a Unitarian chapel opened by Theophilus Lindsey and Joseph Priestley, discussed in the next section.[168]

These Unitarian radicals united around three great causes: (1) anti-Trinitarian attack on all religious litmus tests, like subscription; (2) the independence of the Americas; and (3) parliamentary reforms rooted in a democratic vision, given definitive articulation by James Burgh in his three-volume *Political Disquisitions* (1774–75), where he stated that "all lawful authority, legislative, and executive, originates from the people."[169]

---

165 Rack, *Reasonable Enthusiast*, 462.

166 Ibid. See also Clark, *English Society*, 315.

167 Clark, *English Society*, 317.

168 Ibid., 320.

169 James Burgh, *Political Disquisitions: or, An Enquiry into Public Errors, Defects, and Abuses*, 3 vols. (London, 1774–75). Qtd. in Clark, *English Society*, 323.

Wesley opposed all three, and it is no coincidence that he preached and published his sermon "On the Trinity" in 1775, in the midst of this new flowering of anti-Trinitarianism in the aftermath of the Feathers Tavern controversy and in light of the public character of the radical Unitarian camp in the 1770s. This radical form of Unitarianism posed a far broader threat to the equilibrium of English society than had the anti-Trinitarians of the previous controversies from the 1690s through the 1740s.

4. Joseph Priestley and Independent Unitarianism

Joseph Priestley (1733–1804) did not contribute theologically to the debate about the Trinity beyond repeating earlier arguments against the doctrine. What makes Priestley important is that he played a key role in moving anti-Trinitarian sentiment outside of the Anglican Church, and even beyond religious Dissent, into Unitarianism as an independent movement. Priestley was born into an English Dissenting family and was a precocious child. Around 1749, because of a serious illness, Priestley began to question his Calvinist theological upbringing. He rejected the doctrine of election and embraced universal salvation.[170]

In 1752, he enrolled in the liberal Dissenting academy at Daventry; and, under the influence of David Hartley's materialist theory of the human mind, Priestley moved even further from his Calvinist heritage into a scientific rationalist form of Dissent. From this point onward, Priestley developed a life and worldview that combined theism, materialism, and determinism so that he could explain and defend the religious and moral dimensions of human life in a rationally and scientifically credible manner.[171] Priestley served as a pastor to two Dissenting congregations from 1755 to 1761,[172] and then as an educator at Warrington Academy from 1761 to 1767.[173]

---

170 Robert E. Schofield, *The Enlightenment of Joseph Priestley: A Study of His Life and Work from 1733 to 1773* (University Park: Pennsylvania State University Press, 1997), 1–29. Schofield added a second volume, *The Enlightenment of Joseph Priestley: A Study of His Life and Work from 1773 to 1804* (University Park: Pennsylvania State University Press, 2004). This two-volume set is the definitive work on Priestley.

171 Schofield, *Priestley* (1997), 28–57. This scientific rationalism led Priestley into "natural philosophy" (natural science). As an amateur scientist, Priestley conducted various electrical experiments. He wrote a history of electricity and developed a method for making soda water (ibid., 62ff.).

172 Ibid., 62–85.

173 Ibid., 89–160.

In 1767, Priestley moved to Leeds, where he became the pastor of the Mill Hill Chapel, one of the most outstanding Dissenting congregations in England. The congregation had been fragmented theologically and was losing members to the Methodist Society in Leeds. While in Leeds in 1769, Priestley became friends with Theophilus Lindsey, an Anglican clergyman, who by the early 1760s had moved from privately questioning the Trinity to publicly denouncing the doctrine.[174]

It was also during this period that Priestley published his influential three-volume *Institutes of Natural and Revealed Religion* (1772–74), a controversial work that attempted to reform Christian faith and restore it to its "pure," "primitive" form by applying the kinds of methods and mode of thinking of the emerging natural sciences and of comparative history to the Bible and early Christianity.[175] Priestley's *Institutes* appalled many readers because it openly denounced the deity of Christ and the doctrine of the Trinity. In fact, the Methodists in Leeds were so incensed over his ideas that they wrote a hymn petitioning God to "the Unitarian fiend expel /And chase his doctrine back to Hell."[176] Despite the consternation of the Methodists, among others, Priestley's *Institutes* became the standard doctrinal exposition for Unitarians in England.

Priestley's Anglican friend Lindsey was involved in the Feathers Tavern Petition. As a Dissenting minister, Priestley was in favor of the petition and deeply interested in the course of events associated with it. When the petition was rejected in 1772 and again in 1773, Lindsey resigned his living, openly embraced Unitarianism, and left the Anglican Church in November 1773. Lindsey moved to London, where soon he and Priestley moved in a bold new direction.[177]

Priestley found a better and more secure financial position in 1773, when Lord Shelburne invited him to oversee the education of Shelburne's

---

174 Ibid., 159–71. See J. D. Bowers, *Joseph Priestley and English Unitarianism in American* (University Park: Pennsylvania State University Press, 2007), 25–27.

175 Joseph Priestley, *Institutes of Natural and Revealed Religion* (London: Printed for J. Johnson), vol. 1, 1772; vol. 2, 1773; vol. 3, 1774. The section on the corruptions of primitive Christian faith became so large that it was published separately as a fourth volume, *Institutes, An History of the Corruptions of Christianity* in 1782) (see Schofield, *Priestley* [1997], 159–201).

176 Qtd. in Joe Jackson, *A World on Fire: A Heretic, an Aristocrat and the Race to Discover Oxygen* (New York: Viking, 2005), 102.

177 Bowers, *English Unitarianism*, 25–28; Schofield, *Priestley* (2004), 25–26.

children and serve as Shelburne's assistant.[178] The arrangement included freedom for Priestley to pursue his other interests.

In April 1774, Lindsey and Priestley established the first openly Unitarian congregation in England, the Essex Street Chapel, where more than two hundred gathered for Lindsey's dedicatory sermon, filling the building and flowing out into the street. Priestley was in attendance and had helped raise the money to fund and furnish the chapel.

Lindsey designed the worship service based on Samuel Clarke's revision of the Book of Common Prayer, with further Unitarian modifications suggested by Priestley. From 1774 on, Priestley spent considerable time in London. He attended worship services at the Essex Street Chapel nearly every Sunday, often preached there, and spent Sunday evenings with Lindsey.[179]

Together Priestley and Lindsey had a profound impact on the development of Unitarianism in England and beyond. In the words of J. D. Bowers, the formation of this Unitarian congregation on Essex Street in London was significant not simply because of

> the number of people in attendance, or the expressions of a unitarian-based theology, or even that dissenters had opened a chapel despite the prevailing legal and religious restrictions against doing so. Rather the event was notable for the simple fact that the doctrine of God's divine unity, unitarianism, had moved beyond its existence as a singular theological idea to become the cornerstone of an emergent denomination and the foundation of the developed theological system. . . . [W]hat they [Priestley and Lindsey] set out to accomplish eventually changed the course of religion on both sides of the Atlantic Ocean.[180]

Finally, anti-Trinitarian sentiment in England had come to a stunning crescendo in an independent socioreligious expression. The formation of this independent Unitarian congregation at the Essex Street Chapel exposed the level of damage done by the Trinitarian controversies examined in this chapter. A year later, in 1775, the Methodists in Cork asked John Wesley for a sermon on the Trinity.

In light of this 130-year history of debate concerning the doctrine of the Trinity, Wesley's sermon "On the Trinity" becomes all the more interesting, since it entailed such a different approach to the doctrine of the Trinity than we see in the course of these controversies. This sermon contains intimations

---

178 Schofield, *Priestley* (2004), 5–6, 25.

179 Bowers, *English Unitarianism*, 16–17, 25–29; Schofield, *Priestley* (2004), 25–28.

180 Bowers, *English Unitarianism*, 16.

of a Trinitarian vision of Christian faith, life, and community injected by the Wesley brothers into early Methodism, a vibrant alternative to the arid intellectual argumentation of the Trinitarian defenders throughout the Trinitarian controversies. The sermon reveals that Wesley was aware of the Trinitarian controversies, including the acrimonious character of the debates and that the defenders of the doctrine turned the Trinity into a complicated esoteric concept incomprehensible to the majority of Christians with little or no connection to vibrant Christian faith and life and too complex to be among items necessary for salvation.

The debates opened up a chasm between the *doctrine* of the Trinity understood as a rationally demonstrable account of the *how* God can be three and one, and the vital *faith* of ordinary Christians. Wesley realized that his vision of the Trinity and the Trinitarian dimension of Christian faith and life offered an alternative to the path taken by the doctrine's defenders, an alternative where there was no chasm between the Triune God of the gospel and vital Christian faith and life. His sermon "On the Trinity" points to a better way to be Trinitarian that John and Charles Wesley injected into the Methodist movement.[181]

VI. 1775: Wesley's "On the Trinity" Sermon

At the beginning of his sermon "On the Trinity," Wesley made it clear that while there may be "ten thousand mistakes which may consist with real religion" where we can think and let think, there are other truths that are crucial because they have "a close connection with vital religion." Wesley would neither call them "fundamental" nor enter into the "many warm disputes about the number of 'fundamentals.'"[182]

Nevertheless, Wesley unequivocally understood the Trinity as one of the truths with a vital connection to real religion: "Doubtless we may rank among these that contained in the words above cited: 'There are three that bear record in heaven, the Father, the Word, and the Holy Ghost: and these

181 See Jason Vickers, *Invocation and Assent*, esp. chap. 6; and Vickers, "Charles Wesley and the Revival of the Doctrine of the Trinity: A Methodist Contribution to Modern Theology," for an account of how Charles Wesley retrieved the Trinitarian vision of Christian faith and life in sharp contrast to the accounts of the Trinity by the doctrine's defenders, and mediated that vision to Methodism.

182 *Works*, 2:376. Wesley's comment about "warm disputes" over the number of "fundamental" truths may indicate a reason why he never provided his followers with a definitive list of the crucial doctrines bound up with vital religion.

three are one.' "[183] Wesley added that it is not "of importance to believe this or that *explication* of these words."[184] In fact, no "well-judging man would attempt to explain them [how the three are one] at all."[185]

As we have seen throughout Trinitarian controversies, explaining how the three could be one was precisely what the defenders of the doctrine tried to do. William Sherlock shattered the unity among the orthodox defenders of Trinity with his eccentric and presumptuous portrayal of the inner life of the Trinity as three centers of mutual self-consciousness. The defenses of Wallis, South, and Stillingfleet all operated within the older Aristotelian Scholastic perspective and were simply swept away by the new way of "clear and distinct ideas" represented by Bacon, Descartes, Hobbes, Newton, and Locke. Even Daniel Waterland, who successfully challenged Clark's attack on the Trinity, never reconnected the doctrine of the Trinity to "vital religion."

Against the Trinitarian defenders, Wesley sided with Jonathan Swift's (1667–1745) sermon "On the Trinity," where Swift objected to the whole stream of defenses in the seventeenth and eighteenth centuries designed to show that the doctrine of the Trinity was rationally demonstrable: "Herein [Swift] shows that all who endeavoured to explain it [the Trinity, how the three are one] at all have utterly lost their way; have above all other persons hurt the cause which they intended to promote."[186]

Swift's sermon reveals substantive knowledge of the Trinitarian controversies, including the appeal of the defenders to philosophic concepts of person that could bear a Trinitarian interpretation and the damage done to the doctrine of the Trinity and to Christian faith:

> This heresy [Arian denial of the Trinity] revived in the world about a hundred years ago, and continued ever since; . . . several divines, in order to answer the cavils of those adversaries to truth and morality, began to find out further explanations of this doctrine of the Trinity, by rules of philosophy; which have multiplied controversies to such a degree, as to

---

183 Ibid.

184 Ibid.

185 Ibid., 2:376–77.

186 Ibid., 2:377. Swift was an essayist and political pamphleteer, first a Whig and later a Tory. He earned his bachelor of arts and Doctor of Divinity degree from Trinity College, Dublin. He was dean of St. Patrick's in Dublin from 1713. His sermon "On the Trinity" was published in 1744 (see Albert Outler's note on Swift [ibid., 377]). See also Leo Damrosch, *Jonathan Swift: His Life & His World* (New Haven: Yale University Press, 2013); and Christopher Fox, ed., *Cambridge Companion to Jonathan Swift* (Cambridge: Cambridge University Press, 2003).

> beget scruples that have perplexed the minds of many sober Christians, who otherwise could never have entertained them.
>
> I must therefore bold affirm, that the method taken by many of those learned men to defend the doctrine of the Trinity was founded upon a mistake.[187]

Swift pointed out the various biblical texts that portray all three Trinitarian persons as God and others that affirm that God is one, concluding, "From these several texts it is plain, that God commands us to believe that there is a union and there is a distinction [between the three divine persons]; but what that union, or that distinction is, all mankind are equally ignorant, and must continue so, at least till the day of judgement."[188] What Swift did not do in his sermon was reconnect the Trinity with vital religion.

Wesley's appeal to Swift's sermon, at precisely where Swift took issue with the method of using a philosophic concept of person to provide a rationally demonstrable account of the *how* God can be three and one, reveals Wesley's awareness of the Trinitarian controversies and what was at stake. Wesley also realized how the debates opened up a chasm between the doctrine of the Trinity and the vital religion, the point that Swift did not address in his sermon. A few lines later, Wesley followed Swift and made a similar distinction between "the *substance* of the doctrine," which Wesley thought had a "close connection with vital religion," and the "philosophical *illustrations* of it [the doctrine of the Trinity]." Appealing to philosophical illustrations is precisely what the defenders of the doctrine did when they adopted a philosophic definition of "person" and tried to demonstrate that it could bear a Trinitarian interpretation as documented earlier in this chapter and as evident in Sherlock's Cartesian concept of person that shattered the unity among the orthodox defenders and in Stillingfleet's unsuccessful attempt to rehabilitate the older Aristotelian/Boethian model of substance and person that Locke skillfully dismantled.

Throughout his sermon "On the Trinity," Wesley distanced himself from these rationalist defenses that tried to explain how the three could be one.

---

187 Jonathan Swift, *Three Sermons* (1744), accessed through Wiki Source 11/14/2016. See https://en.wikisource.org/wiki/The_Works_of_the_Rev._Jonathan_Swift/Volume_10/A_Sermon_on_the_Trinity, [21].

188 Ibid., [22]. For Swift, it "is enough for any good Christian to believe on this great article, without ever inquiring further" (ibid., [23]). God calls faithful Christians to believe the "fact" of the Trinity, that God is three and one, that there is a union between the three persons and also a distinction between them, but nothing about the "manner" of the union and distinction.

Wesley's sermon encouraged his readers in Cork and elsewhere to do so as well. Yet at the same time Wesley affirmed in the strongest possible terms that the *substance* of the doctrine of the Trinity is crucial to Christian faith and life and is rooted in the heart of the gospel. Thus, Wesley provided the people of Cork and all the Methodists who would read his sermon with a different way to be Trinitarian.

As we have seen throughout this chapter, the way the Trinitarian defenders explicated the doctrine of the Trinity disconnected the Trinity from the participatory core of the gospel and from vital Christian faith, worship, and life. Wesley insisted "upon no explication at all," not even the best one he ever saw, the Athanasian Creed.[189] In fact, Wesley did "not insist upon anyone's using the words 'Trinity' or 'Person,'" both controverted terms at the center of the Trinitarian controversies. Wesley employed the terms without scruple but asserted that all one is required to believe and affirm is "the direct words unexplained, just as they lie in the text: 'There are three that bear record in heaven, the Father, the Word, and the Holy Ghost: and these three are one.'"[190]

At this point in the sermon, Wesley turned to one of the chief objections to the doctrine of the Trinity, which helped fuel the debate and pushed orthodox theologians into the rationalist mode of defense and proof: "We cannot believe what we cannot comprehend."[191] Repeatedly throughout the Trinitarian controversies was this refrain that people should not be coerced into believing mysteries that defy comprehension, for this is to fall prey to all manner of superstition and undermine integrity in matters of faith that are of ultimate importance. As we have seen throughout this chapter, defenders and critics of the Trinity nearly all believed that matters of faith must be

---

189 *Works,* 2:377.

190 Ibid., 2:377–78. When Wesley stated that there is nothing to say about *how* the three are one, we cannot but remember Stephen Nye's words, "Tis Samaritanism for . . . they worship they know not what" (*Considerations*, 32). See also Dixon, *Hot Disputes*, 127–29. A refusal to say anything at all about *how* the three are one can open up a gap *between* the three and the one. Such a gap can be dangerous because it allows the doctrine of the one God and the doctrine of the Trinity to drift apart in theological discourse and to develop without reference to one another, as happened repeatedly in the history of theology. We will return to this issue in the postscript of this monograph.

Wesley mistakenly argued for the authenticity of the so-called Johannine Comma, though that does not detract from his central point that scripture clearly bears witness to the *reality* or *substance* of the Trinity.

191 *Works*, 2:379.

amenable to human reason, could be defended by reason, and ought not to be believed if contrary to or beyond reason.[192] This was precisely the point of the debate between Stillingfleet and Locke. Locke demonstrated the ambiguity of Stillingfleet's notion of substance in relation to persons at the heart of the bishop's defense of the doctrine of the Trinity.

The bulk of Wesley's sermon, paragraphs 6–16 (out of a total of 18), challenged this central point of the Trinitarian controversies: the idea that people should not believe something they did not comprehend. Wesley retorted to this objection, "You do already believe many things which you cannot comprehend."[193] He then provided examples from everyday human life that illustrated and drove home his point. We need not examine them all; one will suffice to illustrate Wesley's intent.

Everyone believed in *light*, whether radiating from the sun or some other luminous source. Yet, Wesley noted, "You cannot comprehend either its nature or the manner wherein it flows."[194] This is still an issue in natural science today, for science has not yet found a way to reconcile the particulate and undulatory characteristics of light in a single unified theory. With a bit of irony, since it was a commonly used analogy for the Trinity, Wesley added: "Again: here are three candles, yet there is but one light. Explain this, and I will explain the Three-One God."[195]

After providing example after example of realities (facts) that his readers could neither deny nor comprehend, Wesley related his argument to the whole question of the Trinity. Wesley argued that "as strange as it may seem, in requiring you to believe . . . 'these three are one,' . . . the Bible does not require you to believe any mystery at all. . . . Now the mystery does not lie in the *fact* [*that* the three are one], but altogether in the *manner* [*how* the three are one]."[196] Wesley believed that scripture clearly witnesses to the *reality* of the Trinity without ever providing an explanation of *how* the three Trinitarian persons are one God: "The *manner, how* I do not comprehend; and I do not believe it. Now in this, in the *manner,* lies the mystery. . . . It is

192 Part of the problem was that both sides of the controversies accepted a problematic vision of reason, either one associated with Aristotelean Scholasticism (as in the case of Bishop Stillingfleet) or a conception of reason arising out of the new way of "clear and distinct ideas" promoted by Bacon, Descartes, Hobbes, Locke, and others. Neither account of reason proved helpful for understanding and explaining the doctrine of the Trinity.

193 Ibid.

194 Ibid., 2:380–81.

195 Ibid.

196 Ibid., 2:383.

no object of my faith; I believe just so much as God has revealed and no more."[197]

Whatever one thinks about the details of Wesley's argument, his central point has increasingly become an issue of consensus after the collapse of the modern foundationalist quest to render the conditions of indubitable knowledge entirely explicit. No human intellect, no matter how critical, operates outside of a fiduciary framework and a tacit dimension that include belief or faith in realities a person does not fully comprehend. This is every bit as true of the natural scientist or the critical skeptic as it is of people of religious faith. It is simply a facet of the finite human condition. Life forces people to sally forth in affirmation of, and faith in, realities they do not comprehend. This does not mean that all beliefs are equal or that it is impossible to make decisions between conflicting theories. That natural science has not yet developed a theory to reconcile light's particulate and undulatory characteristics does not mean that those characteristics are surreal. The inability to render a unified theory is an accurate response to what we currently apprehend about light but do not yet fully comprehend.[198]

At this point of his sermon, having rejected (1) the whole trajectory of "orthodox" defenses of "how" the three Trinitarian persons can be one as an effort in futility that profoundly harmed the Trinitarian cause, and (2) a central point underlying the debate, that people should only believe in realities they comprehend, Wesley turned his attention to the crucial character of the Trinity for Christian faith, as well as intimations of a another way to be Trinitarian.

With uncanny insight, Wesley asserted: "What God has been pleased to reveal upon this head is far from being a point of indifference, is a truth of the last importance. It enters into the very heart of Christianity; it lies at the root of all vital religion."[199] Here Wesley's noted Christian faith is Trinitarian to the core, indeed Trinitarian in the actual participatory evangelical and doxological relations entailed in the gospel itself out of which knowledge of the Triune God and salvation arise. In so doing, Wesley consciously closed

---

197 Ibid., 2:384. See *Works*, 1:101, where Wesley also states that we cannot know how the three are one.

198 See Colyer, *How to Read*, 322–74, for an account of the integration of form in human knowing from Descartes through Hume, Newton, Kant, Einstein, and Polanyi in relation to T. F. Torrance's account of the role of faith and the tacit dimension in the integration of form in natural science and in theology. See also Alister McGrath, *A Scientific Theology*, 3 vols., for an argument tracing this history in detail and arguing for a nonfoundationalist critical realism similar to that of Torrance.

199 *Works*, 2:384.

what the defenders had opened up, the chasm between the doctrine of the Trinity and the vital faith of ordinary Christians created by turning the Trinity into a complicated esoteric account of the how God can be three and one.

Wesley did not leave his readers in doubt about what he meant: "The thing which I here particularly mean is this: the knowledge of the Three-One God is interwoven with all true Christian faith, with all vital religion." Wesley here argued that whenever we encounter the grace of God, we are actually encountering the presence and activity of the Triune God:

> But I know not how anyone can be a Christian believer till "he hath" (as St. John speaks) "the witness in himself"; till "the Spirit of God witnesses with his spirit that he is a child of God"—that is, in effect, till God the Holy Ghost witnesses that God the Father has accepted him through the merits of God the Son—and having this witness he honours the Son and the blessed Spirit "even as he honours the Father."
>
> Not that every Christian believer *adverts* to this; perhaps at first not one in twenty; but if you ask any of them a few questions you will easily find it is implied in what he believes.
>
> Therefore I do not see how it is possible for any to have vital religion who denies that these three are one.[200]

Wesley boldly stated that Christian faith is intrinsically and aboriginally Trinitarian. The gospel itself and our most basic Christian participation in the gospel always involve the activity of all three persons of the Trinity. In another sermon, Wesley fleshed out what is involved:

> Happiness undoubtedly begins when we begin to know him [God] by the teaching of his own Spirit; when it pleases the Father to reveal his Son in our heart, so that we can humbly say, "My Lord and my God"; and when the Son is pleased to reveal his Father in us, "by the Spirit of adoption, crying in our hearts, Abba Father," bearing his testimony to our spirits, that we are children of God. Then it is that "the love of God" also "is shed abroad in our hearts." And according to the degree of our love is the degree of our happiness.[201]

According to Wesley, the persons of the Trinity mutually mediate one another to us: the Father reveals the Son, and the Son reveals the Father, while the Spirit is involved throughout. This is how we come to know the Triune God

---

200 Ibid., 2:385–86. Elsewhere Wesley said that "the root of all vital religion" is "our fellowship with the Father and with the Son" (*Works*, 3:147).

201 Ibid., 3:283.

as three-in-one and one-in-three or, as Wesley says elsewhere, "his Trinity in Unity and Unity in Trinity."[202] Our evangelical and doxological participation is rooted in the pattern of God the Father's reconciling activity through the incarnate Son, Jesus Christ, and his life, death, and resurrection, a reconciliation realized in Christians through the person and activity of the Holy Spirit ("The Holy Ghost witnesses that God the Father has accepted him through the merits of God the Son"). It is a pattern of personal presence and activity through which the Trinitarian persons reveal one another in Unity and Trinity.

This encounter with the Triune God in the gospel is *participatory*: via the Spirit we come to participate in the Love of God the Father through the grace of our Lord Jesus Christ. This participation is *evangelical*: it comes to us from the love of God the Father through the grace of Christ in the fellowship of the Spirit that sets us free. This participation is also *doxological*: we are set free to respond in Spirit in faith in, and in praise and worship of, the Son and the Spirit along with God the Father. In Wesley's words, "God the Holy Ghost witnesses that God the Father has accepted him [the Christian] through the merits of God the Son—and having this witness he [the Christian] honours the Son and the blessed Spirit 'even as he honours the Father,'" or acknowledges the fullness of deity in the Son and the Spirit in faith, thanksgiving, worship, and love for the patterned presence and activity of all three persons of the Trinity in vital Christian faith.[203]

Elsewhere, Wesley stated the same point about honoring the Son and the Spirit as one honors the Father, but made the breadth of the doxological response explicit: "We are to 'honour the Son even as we honour the Father.' We are to pay him the same worship as we pay to the Father. We are to love him with all our heart and soul; and to consecrate all we have and are, all

---

202 *Works*, 1:581.

203 *Works*, 2:385. The full content of my use of *evangelical, doxological,* and *participatory* to describe the character of the Trinitarian dimension of Wesley's theology will only become clear as each chapter documents and describes the character and content of the Trinitarian dimension in relation to various themes in Wesley's theology, including (1) his brief summaries of vital Christian faith found throughout his publication from 1738 to the end of his life, (2) the various aspects of the order of salvation, and (3) his understanding of the essence of the church. I am not reading a preconceived theologically rich and complex Trinitarian dimension into Wesley by using these terms. Rather, these terms are simply words used to indicate different aspects of the theologically rich Trinitarian dimension of Wesley's theology. The whole point of my book is to document and describe the character and content of this Trinitarian dimension in Wesley's publications. The terms "evangelical," "doxological," and "participatory" call attention to and describe the content of the Trinitarian dimension of Wesley's theology.

we think, speak, and do to the Three-One God, Father, Son and Spirit, world without end!"[204] In short, our participation in the gospel and the gospel itself are both rooted in the patterned activity of the economic Trinity.

Wesley maintained that this is a Trinitarian pattern that every Christian encounters and relives in coming to faith ("the Spirit of God witnesses with his Spirit that he is a child of God"), even if he or she is not explicitly aware of it ("not every Christian believer *adverts* to this"). This is an important point, since Wesley realized that what we come to know of the Triune God in our encounter with the gospel entails a tacit dimension of content that is genuine even if we are not focally aware of it at the time.

If you ask Christians about the core of their faith, Wesley thought this Trinitarian dimension quickly comes to the surface: the presence and activity of the economic Trinity is the vital transformative reality at the center of Christian faith and life. In Wesley's words, "God the Holy Ghost witnesses that God the Father has accepted him through the merits of God the Son."[205] Implicit in Wesley's appeal to the presence and activity of all three Trinitarian persons in the gospel and in our encounter with the gospel is that deep soteriological and doxological conviction concerning the divinity of Christ and the Holy Spirit found in the early church: only God can save, and only God is worthy of our worship. Without an affirmation of the full divinity of Christ and the Holy Spirit, their roles in salvation are called into question, and the church's worship of them degenerates into idolatry. This was Wesley's point about honoring the Son and the Spirit as a Christian honors the Father "when God the Holy Ghost witnesses that God the Father has accepted him [the Christian] through the merits of God the Son."[206]

It is this evangelical, doxological, and participatory, economic Trinitarian pattern that is characteristic of all that John Wesley had to say about the Trinity. The Trinity is central to Wesley's understanding of genuine Christian faith or "vital religion," and the Trinitarian dimension of Christian faith and life, including soteriology and ecclesiology, is pervasive throughout Wesley's publications. Yet it is a Trinitarian account of Christian faith remarkably different than what came from the pens of those who sought to explain and defend the doctrine throughout the Trinitarian controversies, and it is an account that closed the gap between the Trinity and vital Christian faith, worship, and life. Documenting, describing, and explaining the character and content of the Trinitarian dimension of Wesley's theology are the goals of the rest of this monograph.

---

204 *Works*, 4:106.
205 *Works*, 2:285.
206 Ibid.

2

Trinitarian Summaries and Sources

Introduction

The previous chapter examined John Wesley's sermon "On the Trinity" and placed it within the context of the controversies over the Trinity in England in the seventeenth and eighteenth centuries. Throughout the Trinitarian controversies, the defenders profoundly damaged the doctrine by disconnecting the Trinity from its matrix in the gospel. In sharp contrast, Wesley contended that the doctrine of the Trinity is interconnected with the very heart of vital Christian faith, as he made clear in his sermon "Knowledge of the Three-One God is interwoven with all true Christian faith, with all vital religion."[1] So if, when Wesley discussed knowledge of the three-one God, he did so in participatory, economic terms that link the Trinity with the essence of Christian faith or the core of the gospel, we should expect that when Wesley summarized the essence of Christian faith or vital religion, he would do so in Trinitarian categories similar to those in his sermon "On the Trinity." Did Wesley actually summarize the core of the gospel in Trinitarian terms? The answer is a resounding yes.

This chapter will show how pervasive the participatory, economic Trinitarian depictions of the essence of Christian faith are in Wesley's theology by documenting many of the Trinitarian summaries of vital religion in Wesley's

---

1 *The Works of John Wesley*, ed. Albert C. Outler, vols. 1–4, *Sermons* (Nashville: Abingdon, 1984–87), 2:385.

writings, as well as closely examining a number of those summaries. As will become clear, these Trinitarian characterizations of the gospel bear remarkable similarity to what Wesley said about the status of the Trinity in relation to "vital religion" in his sermon "On the Trinity." The chapter will also address the question concerning the source of Wesley's Trinitarian conceptualization of the essence of Christian faith. What is nearly as intriguing as the sheer number of economic Trinitarian summaries of Christian faith in Wesley's publications after 1738 is the dearth of Trinitarian summaries in his writings prior to 1738.

This chapter begins by noting how little has been written about the Trinitarian dimension of Wesley's theology in some of the prominent secondary literature on his theology. Part of my reason for writing this book is to provide an account of an aspect of Wesley's theology that has been noted in the secondary literature but is not adequately documented and described. The intent in the opening section of this chapter is not to criticize the work of other scholars but rather to show that there is more to add to the conversation. All of the scholars noted in the following section know that Wesley was Trinitarian and that there is a Trinitarian dimension to his theology.

I. The Trinitarian Dimension of Wesley's Theology in Secondary Literature

One of the curious discoveries in my initial research into Wesley's theology was how little has been written on Wesley's doctrine of the Trinity, save for a spate of articles.[2] There is also scant discussion of the Trinitarian dimension of Wesley's vision of Christian faith in some of the prominent books devoted to Wesley's theology.

An example of this is Kenneth Collins's work *The Scripture Way of Salvation: The Heart of John Wesley's Theology*.[3] Collins's outstanding book provides deep insights into Wesley's soteriology. Yet there is no substantive discussion of the Trinitarian dimension, not even a reference to the

---

2 A number of articles on Wesley's doctrine of the Trinity were published in the decade before I began my research on Wesley (see Seng-Kong Tan's article "The Doctrine of the Trinity in John Wesley's Prose and Poetic Works," *Journal for Christian Theological Research* 7 [2002], http://home.apu.edu/~ctrf/jctr). Tan's article has a bibliography listing other publications on Wesley's doctrine of the Trinity in the previous decade (see www.luthersem.edu/ctrf/JCTR/default.htm#7Volume7).

3 Kenneth J. Collins, *The Scripture Way of Salvation: The Heart of John Wesley's Theology* (Nashville: Abingdon, 1997). I intend my interaction with the secondary literature on Wesley theology to be representative, not exhaustive.

Trinitarian dimension of Wesley's understanding of salvation, despite the fact that Wesley understood salvation in economic Trinitarian terms. Collins does note, however, the Trinitarian dimension in a more recent book on Wesley's theology, as we will see later in this section.[4]

The chapter on Wesley's theology in Thomas Langford's book *Practical Divinity: Theology in the Wesleyan Tradition* provides another example. *Practical Divinity* is an excellent introduction to the Wesleyan theological history from Wesley up to the current day. It is the standard work that many United Methodist candidates for ordained ministry read in required courses on United Methodist doctrine. Similar to Collins's book, Langford's chapter on Wesley's theology focuses on the outworking of God's grace in human life rather than on the Trinitarian source and participatory character of grace.[5] The chapter contains no discussion of the Trinity, not even a robust reference to the Trinitarian character of Wesley's theology.[6]

An even more fascinating illustration of various issues around the Trinity in Wesley's theology is Randy Maddox's book *Responsible Grace: John Wesley's Practical Theology*. Maddox's work is extremely careful and

---

4 Collins's book mentions the three persons of the Trinity in relation to various themes of the order of salvation. The book references part of the key text in Wesley's sermon "On the Trinity": "But I know not how anyone can be a Christian believer till 'he hath' (as St. John speaks) 'the witness in himself'; till 'the Spirit of God witnesses with his spirit that he is a child of God'—that is, in effect, till God the Holy Ghost witnesses that God the Father has accepted him through the merits of God the Son—and having this witness he honours the Son and the blessed Spirit 'even as he honours the Father'" (see *Works*, 2:385; and Collins, *The Scripture Way of Salvation*, 142–43). However, Collins's appeal to this text was not to note the Trinitarian dimension of Wesley's soteriology but to document Wesley's strong affirmation that assurance is "necessary to the true Christian faith" (ibid., 142). I am aware of the various criticisms against using *ordo salutis* to designate Wesley's soteriology, but I find them unconvincing.

5 Thomas A. Langford, *Practical Divinity: Theology in the Wesleyan Tradition*, rev. ed. (Nashville: Abingdon, 1998). Langford's book is widely used in courses on United Methodist Doctrine required for ordination in the United Methodist Church.

6 There was been a tendency in American Methodism from the beginning to focus on the human pole of salvation and the benefits of grace and to neglect the Trinitarian source and goal of salvation. In addition, one whole stream of Methodist theology in the nineteenth and twentieth centuries viewed the Trinity as an embarrassing relic of premodern Christian faith that needed to be jettisoned. The doctrine of the one God has been far more prominent in American Methodism's intellectual history than the doctrine of the Trinity (see Elmer M. Colyer, "The Trinity," in *The Oxford Handbook of Methodist Studies*, ed. William J. Abraham and James E. Kirby [Oxford: Oxford University Press, 2009], 505–21).

comprehensive, one of the best studies of Wesley's theology to date. I have benefited immensely from the book and from Maddox's many articles on Wesley. Maddox's command of the primary and secondary literature is nothing short of astonishing. Yet the placement and brevity of his discussion of Wesley on the Trinity is puzzling.[7]

Responsible Grace has a chapter entitled "The God of Responsible Grace," but this is not where Maddox discussed the Trinity. He dealt with the doctrine of the Trinity in a final subsection of his chapter on the Holy Spirit. Wesley's emphasis on the Holy Spirit is the occasion for a discussion of the Trinity since Maddox correctly wanted to underscore the Trinitarian balance found in Wesley's theology.

Maddox provided an excellent discussion of Wesley's "routine" affirmation of the *filioque* clause. Maddox suggested that Wesley retained the Western tendency to first consider the one God (identified with the Father) and then deal with the distinctions between the three Trinitarian persons as a revelatory qualification of the one God. Maddox also acknowledged Wesley's emphasis on the personhood of each person of the Godhead in order to affirm the relational character of God's grace in its various dimensions. Throughout his discussion of the Trinity, Maddox stressed that Wesley's views resonate more with the Eastern than the Western theological perspective. In addition, Maddox noted that the Trinity, for Wesley, "enters into the very heart Christianity; it lies at the root of all vital religion." For Wesley, the doctrine of the Trinity "served implicitly as another 'grammar' of his theological convictions."[8]

Yet when Maddox described what this "grammar" entailed, he suggested that Wesley was warning against "practical unitarianism." Wesley intended to form his Methodist followers "in a truly Trinitarian balance" by distinguishing the Trinitarian persons "in terms their most defining work: creation/providence, redemption, and sanctification" and to encourage "reverence for the God of Holy Love . . . gratitude for the unmerited Divine Initiative in Christ . . . and responsiveness for the Presence of the Holy Spirit . . . [to] preserve such a Trinitarian balance as they proceed along the Way of Salvation."[9]

---

7 Randy L. Maddox, *Responsible Grace: John Wesley's Practical Theology* (Nashville: Kingwood Books, 1994). I have learned much from Maddox's various publications on Wesley's theology and the intellectual history of American Methodism.

8 Maddox, *Responsible Grace*, 137–40.

9 Ibid., 140. Part of the issue is that Maddox applied the "law of appropriations" to Wesley's theology and distinguished the persons of the Trinity "in terms of their most defining work": the Father in relation to creation/providence; the Son in relation to redemption; and the Spirit in relation to sanctification (ibid.). This may also

Here Maddox missed the key insight from Wesley's sermon "On the Trinity." Wesley described exactly what he meant in the quotation Maddox cited from Wesley's "On the Trinity" (the Trinity "enters into the heart of Christianity; it lies at the root of all vital religion"). A few lines later in his sermon, Wesley made a very different point than Maddox's account of Wesley warning against practical unitarianism:

---

be why Maddox organized his book with separate chapters on the Father, Son, and Spirit under the headings of "The God of Responsible Grace," "Christ—The Initiative of Responsible Grace," and "Holy Spirit—The Presence of Responsible Grace."

The law of appropriations arose in Latin or Western theology as a way to overcome the imbalance of approaching the doctrine of the Trinity first from the divine essence of the one God and only afterward treating the three persons. The law of appropriations permits certain attributes or activities of the whole Trinity to be assigned or "appropriated" to one of the Trinitarian persons as a way to reveal the distinctive character of that particular divine person. Since Maddox stressed that Wesley's Trinitarian theological inclinations are more Eastern than Western, I was surprised that Maddox utilized the law of appropriation when characterizing Wesley's theology.

While I do not deny that Wesley referred to God the Father as Creator, the Son as Redeemer, and the Spirit as Sanctifier on occasion, what is interesting is how seldom Wesley did so, and also how he occasionally mixed titles and applied Creator, Preserver, Governor, etc., for example, to Christ, as we will see later in chapter 3 (see *Works*, 3:90–94). Wesley's more characteristic way to identify the Trinitarian persons was on the basis of their economic coactivity in the gospel, a theological move that presupposes the doctrine of perichoresis (and its corollary concept of perichoretic coactivity), a doctrine that Maddox, among others, acknowledged as present in Wesley's theology (see Maddox, *Responsible Grace*, 138–40). See also Thomas F. Torrance, *The Christian Doctrine of God: One Being Three Persons* (Edinburgh: T & T Clark, 1998), 168–202, esp. 200–202, for an insightful account of the doctrine of perichoresis and a critique of the Western law of appropriations in light of it.

Maddox argued that Wesley "usually identified" the one God with the Father and then moved on to acknowledge the distinctions between the persons as a qualification of the one God. Then Maddox quoted Wesley's summary of beliefs in his "A Letter to a Roman Catholic": "This one God is Father of all things" (Maddox, *Responsible Grace*, 139). But Maddox did not provide the rest of the quotation, which continues this way: "that he is in a peculiar manner the Father of those whom he regenerates by his Spirit, whom he adopts in his Son as co-heirs with him and crowns with an eternal inheritance; but in a still higher sense, the Father of his only Son, whom he hath begotten from eternity" (John Wesley, "Letter to a Roman Catholic," in *John Wesley*, ed. A. C. Outler [New York: Oxford University Press, 1964], 494). For Wesley, to call God "Father" is not first and foremost to say something about God's relation to creation as Creator, and as such to first begin with the one

> The thing which I here particularly mean is this: the knowledge of the Three-One God is interwoven with all true Christian faith, with all vital religion. . . . I know not how anyone can be a Christian believer till "he hath" (as St. John speaks) "the witness in himself"; till "the Spirit of God witnesses with his spirit that he is a child of God"—that is, in effect, till God the Holy Ghost witnesses that God the Father has accepted him through the merits of God the Son—and having this witness he honours the Son and the blessed Spirit "even as he honours the Father."
>
> Not that every Christian believer *adverts* to this; perhaps at first not one in twenty; but if you ask any of them a few questions you will easily find it is implied in what he believes.

God before dealing with the Trinitarian persons. Rather, naming God "Father" in the highest sense is to say something about God's own being and life as God, about the inter-Trinitarian relation between the Father and the Son (and the Holy Spirit as well) revealed in the gospel that we come to know when we are adopted in Christ into the family of God via the Holy Spirit, as we saw in the discussion of Wesley's sermon "On the Trinity" at the end of chapter 1.

Wesley made this same point in his "Sermon on the Mount, VI," where he refers to, "Our *Father*—our Creator . . . Our *Father*—our Preserver . . . Above all, the Father of our Lord Jesus Christ, and of all who believe in him" (*Works*, 1:578). Part of the issue here is that "Father" is used of God in a twofold sense in the Bible and in this very quotation from Wesley: Father refers to the person of the Father, the first person of the Trinity; and Father refers to the God as almighty Father, the Creator and Lord of all. These two senses are not separate; rather, they refer to the distinction between the first person and the very being of the Triune God. Maddox noted this point (Maddox, *Responsible Grace*, 48). For Wesley, what defined the Father, Son, and Spirit and their relations to one another are the characteristics of their relations and activities in the gospel itself. The Father reveals the Son and the Son reveals the Father through the Spirit so that we come to know the three-one God as Trinity in Unity and Unity in Trinity through our encounter with the gospel as noted at the end of chapter 1. In Wesley's own words: "Happiness undoubtedly begins when we begin to know him [God] by the teaching of his own Spirit; when it pleases the Father to reveal his Son in our heart, so that we can humbly say, 'My Lord and my God'; and when the Son is pleased to reveal his Father in us, 'by the Spirit of adoption, crying in our hearts, Abba Father,' bearing his testimony to our spirits, that we are children of God. Then it is that 'the love of God' also 'is shed abroad in our hearts'" (*Works*, 3:283). This way of reading Wesley actually provides further evidence for Maddox's main point that Wesley's theology often resonates with Eastern Orthodoxy (I would say certain streams of Eastern Orthodoxy) more than the Western theological tradition, and it strengthens other points Maddox makes about the doctrine of the Trinity and its practical importance in Wesley's theology.

> Therefore I do not see how it is possible for any to have vital religion who denies that these three are one.[10]

There is nothing in this sermon to support the law of appropriations where the persons of the Trinity are distinguished by their most defining work: Father/Creator, Son/Redeemer, and Spirit/Sanctifier. Rather, Wesley stated that knowledge of the three-one God arises out of knowledge of Father, Son, and Spirit in their activities in the gospel itself as found in scripture. We know the Son through the Father, and the Father through the Son in the Spirit, who witnesses that the Father has accepted us through the merits of Christ and who sheds the love of the Father through the Son in our hearts in our participatory encounter with the Triune God in the gospel.

The robust Trinitarian dimension in Wesley's theology and his affirmation of the doctrine of the Trinity are more than another grammar to ensure that the early Methodists did not fall prey to practical unitarianism. For Wesley, the doctrine of the Trinity is embedded in the gospel itself and our most basic Christian participation in the gospel, which always involve the activity of all three persons of the Trinity, as noted at the end of chapter 1 in the discussion of Wesley's sermon "On the Trinity." Wesley closed the chasm between the doctrine of the Trinity and the vital faith and life of the Methodist followers in a different way than Maddox suggested in his appeal to the Trinity as a grammar to protect against practical unitarianism, and a way that raises questions about whether the law of appropriations was significant and characteristic of Wesley's theology.[11]

---

10 *Works*, 2:385.

11 While Maddox underscored the importance of the doctrine of the Trinity in Wesley's theology, Maddox did not identify the Trinitarian dimension of Wesley's theology or discuss the Trinitarian dimension in relation to Wesley's understanding of the way of salvation and the essence of the church. The purpose of this book is to identify, document, and describe the Trinitarian dimension in Wesley's theology, including the essence of Christian faith or vital religion, the entire *ordo salutis*, and the essence of the church.

It is important to note that in Maddox's documentation for his assertion that Wesley's characteristic way of distinguishing the Trinitarian persons was "in terms of their most defining work: creation/providence, redemption, and sanctification," only one of Maddox's references to Wesley's publications provides an unambiguous statement supporting the law of appropriations as characteristic of Wesley's theology. Wesley's "Sermon on the Mount, IX," in *Works* 4:649, ends with a clear example of Wesley using the law of appropriations (see Maddox, *Responsible Grace*, 322n166). In addition, although Wesley, in his sermon "On Perfection," referred to "God your Creator, your Redeemer, your Sanctifier," Wesley did not associate them

An additional example similar to Maddox, though with more attention to the Trinitarian dimension of Wesley's theology, is Ken Collins's more recent work *The Theology of John Wesley: Holy Love and the Shape of Grace*.[12] One does not have to read far into his book for it to become clear that Collins wrote it as a corrective to Maddox's interpretation of Wesley's theology.

The structure of Collins's book is strikingly similar to that of Maddox's, which surely is not coincidental. Like Maddox, Collins situates his discussion of the Trinity at the end of the chapter entitled "The Holy Spirit: The Presence of the God of Holy Love." Collins is as perceptive as Maddox concerning the importance of the Trinity, though Collins overstressed Wesley's affirmation of the filioque clause because of his ongoing attempt to portray Wesley as standing firmly in the Western tradition of Christian faith, contra Maddox's portrayal of Wesley as deeply influenced by the Eastern tradition.

If Wesley's affirmation of the filioque clause is symptomatic of a Western orientation in his understanding of the Trinity, it is curious that Wesley never does what so many Western theologians have loved to do from Augustine onward: assume the doctrine of the Trinity and then try to render how this Christian doctrine of God is intelligible by recourse to Trinitarian analogies. Indeed, this was precisely the approach of the Trinitarian defenders throughout the Trinitarian controversies examined in the previous chapter

with Father, Son, and Holy Spirit (see *Works*, 3:85). But Maddox's third documentation of Wesley's use of the law of appropriations, in Wesley's sermon "The Unity of the Divine Being," actually provides evidence against Maddox's claim. Here is what Wesley wrote: "He to whom this character belongs, and he alone, is a Christian. To him the one, eternal, omnipresent, all-perfect Spirit, is Alpha and Omega, the first and the last. Not his Creator only, but his Sustainer, his Preserver, his Governor; yea his Father, his Saviour, Sanctifier, and Comforter. This God is his God and his all (*Works*, 4:71). There is no association of the Father with Creator, the Son with Redeemer, and the Spirit with Sanctifier. Rather, Wesley ran through the list without any clear association of any one of these roles with a particular Trinitarian person. Wesley's text actually provides evidence of a much more flexible use of divine roles that is inconsistent with the law of appropriations utilized by the Western tradition and is again more in tune the Eastern tradition, a point that is in keeping with Maddox's many helpful arguments that Wesley's theology and doctrine of the Trinity most often reflect characteristics that resonate more with Eastern than with Western theological perspectives.

12 Kenneth J. Collins, *The Theology of John Wesley: Holy Love and the Shape of Grace* (Nashville: Abingdon, 2007).

that Wesley rejected in his sermon "On the Trinity." Nowhere does Wesley appeal to analogies to render the Trinity intelligible or defend it.[13]

Wesley's absolute silence is telling, save for his negative judgment on the use of analogies by the defenders of the Trinity throughout the Trinitarian controversies, as we saw in chapter 1. In sharp contrast, Wesley's approach to the Trinity was consistently participatory and economic, and it is more in keeping with the Nicene church fathers, as Jason Vickers astutely pointed out in relation to Charles Wesley,[14] though, if one knows where to look, this participatory and economic approach can be found in the West as well.

---

13 This is a point that neither Collins nor Maddox noted in their discussions of Wesley's doctrine of the Trinity.

14 See Jason Vickers's insightful book *Invocation and Assent: The Making and Remaking of Trinitarian Theology* (Grand Rapids, MI: Eerdmans, 2008); and Jason Vickers's important chapter "Charles Wesley and the Revival of the Doctrine of the Trinity: A Methodist Contribution to Modern Theology," in *Charles Wesley: Life, Literature & Legacy*, ed. Kenneth G. C. Newport and Ted A. Campbell (Peterborough, England: Epworth, 2007), 278–98.

The "Eastern tradition" is far from monolithic when it comes to the Trinity, particularly in relation to the monarchy of the Father. For example, Basil the Great and Gregory of Nyssa affirmed the *person* of the Father as the "origin" (*arche*) and "cause" (*aitia*) of the Son and the Spirit, though without beginning or separation. In contrast, Epiphanius and Athanasius did not try to ensure the unity of Godhead by linking it to the underived *person* of the Father but saw the Spirit proceeding "out of the Father through the Son," out of the same being (*ek tas autas ousios*), "out of the Godhead" (*ek tas autas Theotatos*), "Trinity in Unity, one Godhead of Father, Son and Holy Spirit" or from the *being* of the Father, not the *person* of the Father (see Thomas F. Torrance, *The Trinitarian Faith: The Evangelical Theology of the Ancient Catholic Church* [Edinburgh: T & T Clark, 1988], 302–40, esp. 325, 329, 331, 337).

We see resonances of this "Trinity in Unity," with its shared monarchy, in some of Charles Wesley's hymns where he wrote, "Jehovah is but One, Eternal God and true; The Father sent the Son, His Spirit sent Him too, the everlasting Spirit fill'd, And Jesus our salvation seal'd" (see Charles Wesley, *Hymns on the Trinity* [Bristol: William Pine, 1767; repr., Madison, NJ: Charles Wesley Society, 1998], 65–66). It seems that, for Charles, the Spirit, and not simply the Father, sends the Son, an intriguing theological idea.

Note also the way Charles begins with "Jehovah is but One, Eternal God and true" as the context for the Father and the Spirit sending the Son. It appears that this Nicene concept of "Trinity in Unity" (the final heading in Charles's *Hymns on the Trinity*) or perichoresis (the mutual indwelling of the three persons in and out of each other in God's own being and Trinitarian life and therefore the final unity of Godhead around "sending" and being "sent") clarifies and deepens the *monarchia* (monarchy) along Trinitarian lines as in the stream of Nicene theology found in Athanasius, Epiphanius, and others.

I am not taking sides in the debate between Maddox and Collins over whether Wesley is more "Eastern" or "Western" in his theological orientation. The point is simply that John Wesley's affirmation of the filioque clause does not demonstrate that his views of the Trinity and the Trinitarian dimension of Christian faith fall neatly into the Western tradition. John's and Charles's

---

Charles seems to be operating here with a concept of the perichoretic coactivity in which the Trinitarian persons always and everywhere act together in such a way that their activities coinhere and interpenetrate one another within the one being of God and in the economic activity of the Triune God in the gospel without compromising each divine person's distinctive mode of activity, in the same way that the incommunicable characteristics of the three persons in no way divide them but rather unite them in their differentiated oneness. There is a growing consensus that Charles and John both operate with a concept of perichoresis without explicitly using the term (see Maddox, *Responsible Grace*, 139, 322). The genesis of the concept of perichoretic coactivity and a shared *monarchia* seems to be found in one stream of Greek Patristic theology in Athanasius, Epiphanius, Cyril of Alexandria, and Gregory of Nazianzen, but *not* in Basil or Gregory of Nyssa, who both asserted the monarchy of the Father (see Torrance, *Christian Doctrine of God*, 168–202).

Charles's hymn continued by linking together the economic Trinity and the ontological Trinity: "Senders and Sent we praise, with equal thanks approve Th'economy of grace, The Triune God of love, And humbly prostrated before the One thrice holy God, adore!" Charles stated this connection between economic Trinity and ontological Trinity even more forcefully in two other hymns. In the first he wrote, "Come, Father, Son and Spirit, give Thy love, Thyself: and lo! I live Imparadised in Thee" (Charles, Wesley, *Hymns on the Trinity*, 114). The second comes from the 1780 *A Collection of Hymns for the Use of the People Called Methodists*: "Send us the Spirit of thy Son, to make the depths of Godhead known. To make us share the life divine" (see *The Works of John Wesley*, ed. Franz Hildebrant and Oliver A. Beckerlegge, vol. 7, *A Collection of Hymns for the Use of the People Called Methodists* (New York: Oxford University Press, 1983), 536.

Charles could not be more clear here that God's love *is* the very depths of the Trinitarian Godhead given to us in concrete redemptive activity ("give Thy love, –Thyself," "make the depths of Godhead known"). There is no dark inscrutable Godhead, no *deus absconditus,* no one God behind the back of the Father who we know through the Son and in the Holy Spirit who sent him too. This is, I believe, the Wesley brothers' ultimate theological ground for rejecting double predestination: How can there be an inscrutable double-predestinarian deity behind the depths of the Godhead revealed from the Father through the Son in the Spirit? The question that remains is why John Wesley did not apply a similar theological criticism to the doctrine of providence.

Throughout this discussion, I am not implying that Charles or John read Athanasius, Epiphanius, or other key Nicene theologians or knew about the subtle differences among the early Trinitarian theologians. Theological concepts are historically

writings betray a remarkable subtlety in their appropriation and use of various theological traditions.

Collins's discussion of the Trinity in Wesley also noted that Wesley's "usual way of referring to the Christian Godhead is basically descriptive, not systematic, a way that keeps close to the biblical idiom." Collins argued for "Wesley's preference for the raw, undeveloped biblical language in describing the Trinity," noting that Wesley did not insist on "adherence to the language of the later councils and theologians" or even the terms "Trinity" and "person" and often used the phrase "Three-One God."[15] In addition, Collins correctly noted that Wesley was reluctant to engage in the speculative questions of "how" the three could be one.

As should be clear from the discussion in chapter 1, however, it was not simply Wesley's desire to keep close to the raw biblical idiom that led to his unwillingness to be contentious around the terms "Trinity" and "person" and to his use of the phrase "Three-One God," as well as to his reluctance to engage the speculative questions of how the three are one. It was also his astute awareness of the bad examples of those defenders who were contentious over the terms "Trinity" and "person," who sought precisely to answer "how" the three are one, and who badly damaged the doctrine of the Trinity in the process.

Collins's other point regarding Wesley's "usual way of referring to the Christian Godhead," noting that it "is basically descriptive, not systematic," also needs to be challenged. Many Christian thinkers desire to "keep close to the biblical idiom." Yet, no one can approach the biblical idiom apart from a tradition, including its ultimate beliefs and forms of life, as Collins undoubtedly knows. The questions quickly become, What part of the biblical idiom does one keep close to, and how does one combine the particular parts of the biblical witness that one selects, and why? At this point there is often interesting theological development implicit, and at times explicit, in the way someone like Wesley employs biblical texts in general and in relation to the Triune God in particular. We will see this same issue of theological selection and synthesis of biblical texts in chapter 4 when we look at which part of the biblical witness Wesley utilizes when his focus shifts to the church. When Wesley appealed to "the raw, undeveloped biblical language" with reference

---

mediated in a far more complicated manner than direct encounter with particular texts. I am simply calling attention to some of the deep Trinitarian insights that we find in the Wesley brothers' writings and how these insights align better with certain strands of early Trinitarian theology.

15 Collins, *Theology of John Wesley*, 145.

to the church, it is not *loci classici* like Matthew 16:15–20 ("Upon this rock I will build my Church") or even 18:15–20 ("Wherever two or three are gathered together in my name, there am I"). Wesley most often appealed to Ephesians 4 and Acts 2 and 4. Wesley's selection, prioritizing, and synthesis of particular texts and biblical themes comes even more forcefully to the forefront in relation to his Trinitarian understanding of the "analogy of faith," including the way he read those Trinitarian convictions back into the Genesis account of Creation and the Fall, as we will see later in this chapter.

Even though Wesley did prefer the biblical idiom, as Collins correctly pointed out, Wesley's selection and handling of biblical idiom is undeniably theological. Wesley's sermons manifest a marvelously interwoven tapestry of biblical texts, images, phrases, and ideas. But his selection of them and how he interweaves them reveal a robust Trinitarian theology at work at times explicitly and at other times implicitly, both in relation to what parts of the Bible to which Wesley appealed in his discussions of various themes, and to the way he combined them, as will become clear throughout the rest of this chapter and the ones that follow.

There is another point where Collins is especially helpful, for he clearly sees that the three persons who constitute the Triune God are known through our actual participation in salvation. We know the "Three-One God," Collins correctly contends, in a "dynamic, personal, and participatory way" so that we will become "Transcripts of the Trinity," a wonderful quotation from Charles Wesley.[16] Yet, Collins's treatment of the Trinity amounts to fewer than six pages, and as in Maddox's work, his account of the Trinity ended up at the end of his discussion of the Holy Spirit, separated from the chapter dealing with the one God, as well as being insufficiently related to other themes in Wesley's theology.[17]

In summary, from reading some of the secondary literature on Wesley's theology, despite the deep insights from scholars like Maddox and Collins noted above, one might get the impression that the Trinitarian dimension of Wesley's theology is important but not all that prominent in Wesley's writings and thinking. There are a few notable exceptions like Geoffrey

---

16 Ibid., 146–49. See also *Works*, 7:88, Hymn # 7.

17 Part of the problem is that Wesley himself never developed his Trinitarian insights in detail in any one place in his publications, thereby forcing his interpreters to read all of Wesley's scattered comments and sort through the interconnections and implications of Wesley's convictions about the Trinity and the Trinitarian character of the Christian faith.

Wainwright and his articles "Why Wesley Was a Trinitarian,"[18] "Wesley's Trinitarian Hermeneutics,"[19] and "Trinitarian Theology and Wesleyan Holiness,"[20] which are among the best published discussions of Wesley on the Trinity and the Trinitarian dimension of his theology. Although Theodore Runyon's *The New Creation: John Wesley's Theology Today* devotes little discussion to the Trinity in Wesley's theology, Runyon does note the participatory, economic Trinitarian dimension of Wesley's theology and incorporates that Trinitarian dimension in helpful ways in several places in his work.[21]

The scholars who have written on Wesley's doctrine of the Trinity all grant Wesley's unequivocal affirmation of the Trinity and its significance as the Christian doctrine of God even when they struggle to integrate the doctrine of the Trinity into an overarching architectonic account of Wesley's theology, if they attempt this at all. As we will see in the rest of this chapter, Wesley not only affirmed the Trinity, but, after 1738, there is a Trinitarian dimension in his summaries of the gospel or the essence of Christian faith in his publications.

II. Trinitarian Summaries of True Christian Faith or Vital Religion

1. *"Letter to a Roman Catholic"*

When Wesley discussed the Trinity, he did so in relation to the center of Christian faith or vital religion: we come to know the love of God the Father *through* the grace of our Lord Jesus Christ, his life, death, resurrection, and ascension, *in* the communion of the Holy Spirit who unites us to Christ and

---

18 See Geoffrey Wainwright's insightful "Why Wesley Was a Trinitarian" in *Drew Gateway* 59, no. 2 (spring 1990): 26–43. Wainwright's article has been reprinted in Geoffrey Wainwright, *Methodists in Dialogue* (Nashville: Kingswood Books, 1995), 261–74.

19 Geoffrey Wainwright, "Wesley's Trinitarian Hermeneutics," *Wesleyan Theological Journal* 36, no.1 (spring 2001): 7–30.

20 Geoffrey Wainwright, "Trinitarian Theology and Wesleyan Holiness," in *Orthodoxy and Wesleyan Spirituality*, ed. S. T. Kimbrough Jr. (Crestwood, NY: St. Vladimir's Seminary Press, 2002), 59–80.

21 See Theodore Runyon's *The New Creation: John Wesley's Theology Today* (Nashville: Abingdon, 1998), 34–35, 54, 132, 241. Runyon's work is theologically deep and insightful. We share similarities in our reading of Wesley at several points, though Runyon's work notes the Trinitarian dimension in several areas of Wesley's theology but does not document and describe the Trinitarian dimension in depth and detail, as I do in the following chapters.

through Christ with the Father. The place we really come to know the Triune God is in the gospel itself as found in scripture, for the gospel is the Triune God personally active in history and in our lives for our salvation. That is where the content of our knowledge of the Triune God comes, according to Wesley. The rest of this chapter will document that Wesley summarized the essence of Christian faith in Trinitarian terms

The first Trinitarian summary of Christian faith that we will examine is found in Wesley's famous "Letter to a Roman Catholic," written in 1749 at the conclusion of his third trip to Dublin and the Methodist society there. The letter was published first as a tract that same year in Dublin, then reprinted in 1750, and reissued in a second edition in London in 1755.[22]

In the letter, Wesley acknowledged, with deep regret, the mistrust and ill will common between Protestants and Catholics. Wesley wanted to remove some of the ground of this bitterness by emphasizing what Protestants and Catholics believe in common. It is significant that he followed the basic trajectory of the Nicene Creed, repeating various phrases from it. In so doing, Wesley aligned himself with the most ecumenical and thoroughly Trinitarian creed in Christian history:

> As I am assured that there is an infinite and independent Being and that it is impossible there should be more than one, so I believe that this one God is the Father of all things, especially of angels and men; that he is in a peculiar manner the Father of those whom he regenerates by his Spirit, whom he adopts in his Son as co-heirs with him and crowns with an eternal inheritance; but in a still higher sense, the Father of his only Son, whom he hath begotten from eternity.
>
> I believe this Father . . . of his own goodness created heaven and earth, and all that is therein.
>
> I believe that Jesus of Nazareth was the Saviour of the world, the Messiah so long foretold; . . . I believe he is the proper, natural Son of God, God of God, very God of very God; and that he is the Lord of all, having absolute, supreme universal dominion over all things; but more peculiarly *our* Lord. . . .
>
> I believe the infinite and eternal Spirit of God, equal with the Father and the Son, to be not only perfectly holy in himself, but the immediate cause of all holiness in us: enlightening our understandings, rectifying our wills and affections, renewing our natures, uniting our persons to Christ, assuring us of the adoption of sons, leading us in our actions,

22 See Outler's introduction to "Letter" in Outler, ed., *Wesley*, 492.

> purifying and sanctifying our souls and bodies to a full and eternal enjoyment of God.
>
> I believe that Christ and his Apostles gathered unto himself a church . . . that this catholic (that is, universal) Church, extending to all nations and all ages, is holy in all its members, who have fellowship with God the Father, Son, and Holy Ghost.[23]

Wesley also affirmed that the Son of God was made human, "joining the human nature with the divine in one person," that he was conceived by the Holy Spirit and born of the "Blessed Virgin Mary," that he suffered and died on the cross under Pontius Pilate, that he rose again from the dead on the third day, ascended into heaven, and will come again to judge the living and the dead, all echoing the Nicene Creed.[24]

As in his sermon "On the Trinity," once again we find Wesley's Trinitarian talk embedded in a soteriological matrix, inherently bound up with our salvation and an economic approach in which the Trinitarian persons come into view through their activity in history on our behalf in the gospel. God is Father of those whom God regenerates by the Spirit, those whom God adopts in the Son as co-heirs with Christ. Jesus Christ is the Savior of the world, the proper Son of God, God of God, and our Lord. The infinite and eternal Spirit of God, equal with the Father and the Son, perfectly holy, is the immediate cause of all holiness in us, implying that the Father and the Son are also involved in the work of holiness in their own unique ways. For Wesley this Trinitarian activity extends throughout the *ordo salutis*, enlightening our understandings (prevenient grace), rectifying our wills and affections (convicting grace), renewing our natures, uniting our persons to Christ (justifying and regenerating grace), purifying and sanctifying our bodies to a full and eternal enjoyment of God (sanctifying and perfecting grace).

Wesley also made several important and interesting statements about the Trinitarian relations *ad intra*, within God's own Trinitarian eternal life as the Triune God. Though he did not explicitly address the question of "how" the three are one, what Wesley did say provides a different way to think about the Trinitarian relations *ad intra* than we saw through the Trinitarian controversies. The Spirit is infinite and eternal, equal with the Father and the Son. Jesus Christ is the proper natural Son of God, God of God, very God of very God. Most interesting of all is Wesley's statement that God's Fatherhood *in the highest sense* has nothing to do with God's relationship to us or the rest of creation but rather is an intra-Trinitarian relation. God is "in a

---

23 Ibid., 494–95.

24 Ibid.

still higher sense, the Father of his only Son, whom he hath begotten from eternity." All of these points were crucial to the development of the doctrine of the Trinity and the formulation of the Nicene Creed that enshrined this Trinitarian understanding of the Christian doctrine of God, but they are all dramatically different from the attempts by the defenders of the Trinity throughout the controversies to explain how the three are one using philosophical concepts of person that, in the end, could not bear a Trinitarian interpretation. It is unfortunate that Wesley did not pursue this line of Trinitarian reflection further.

Like the Nicene Creed itself, the very structure of Wesley's series of affirmations is Trinitarian. But, as in his sermon, his concern was not with an abstract concept of God, God as an all-knowing, all-powerful absolute solitary individual whom we know by some other kind of human intellectual argumentation that enables us to grasp God conceptually on our own apart from God's activity in the gospel. Rather, Wesley focused on the understanding of the Christian Triune God that arises in and out of the gospel itself within the faith, life, and worship of the church. Thus, Wesley related each section explicitly to soteriological concerns and provided intimations of a different way to be Trinitarian than the approaches used by the Trinitarian defenders examined in chapter 1. Wesley also effectively closed the chasm between the doctrine of the Trinity and the vital faith of ordinary Christians created by the defenders turning the Trinity into complicated esoteric account of the how God can be three and one.

In comparing the sermon "On the Trinity" and the "Letter to a Roman Catholic," it is interesting not only that Wesley saw the Trinity as bound up with our basic evangelical and doxological encounter with the gospel but also that when he discussed the creedal faith held in common by Protestants and Catholics, he did so in Trinitarian terms deeply connected with that same participatory encounter with the gospel. The gospel and our participation in it are thoroughly Trinitarian, and the doctrine of the Trinity arises out of soteriological soil since that doctrine is inextricably linked to the gospel and our encounter with it. This, I believe, is an important point and a defining characteristic of the Trinitarian theology of John Wesley (and Charles as well) that invites, if not requires, us to think of his understanding of the essence of Christian faith and all vital religion in the simultaneously participatory, soteriological, and economic Trinitarian terms so evident in his sermon "On the Trinity" and his "Letter to a Roman Catholic."

It is also illuminating that Wesley indicated that this economic Trinitarian activity extends throughout the *ordo salutis* and is likewise the defining characteristic of the "ecclesiality" of the church (those "who have fellowship with the Father, Son, and Holy Ghost") or that which makes the church the church, a point developed fully in chapter 4 of this book. Since the Trinitarian God *is* the God of the gospel, this is precisely what we would expect from Wesley.

What is of particular interest in this chapter is the consistency between what Wesley said about the Trinity being "interwoven with all true Christian faith, with all vital religion," and his summary of the ecumenical Christian faith shared by Protestants and Catholics in robust Trinitarian terms in his "Letter to a Roman Catholic." In light of this Trinitarian consistency, we should expect to find other participatory, economic Trinitarian summaries elsewhere in Wesley's publications.

2. "The New Birth"

One of the most profound and moving of these summaries of the center of Christian faith, following this same Trinitarian pattern that we saw in his sermon "On the Trinity" and in his "Letter to a Roman Catholic," is found in Wesley's famous sermon "The New Birth." What is also interesting about this sermon is that Wesley discussed the Fall of humanity in terms of loss of participation in the life of God.

At the beginning of that sermon Wesley noted that with the Fall, humanity "lost the life of God: he was separated from him in union with whom his spiritual life consisted. . . . The natural consequence of this is that everyone descended from him comes into the world spiritually dead, dead to God, wholly 'dead in sin'; entirely void of the life of God, void of the image of God, of all . . . 'righteousness and holiness.'"[25] Here Wesley established the theological context for his account of the new birth by providing the reason why we must be born again; the new birth reverses the three destructive consequences of the Fall: the loss of (1) the life of God, (2) the image of God, and (3) righteousness and holiness.

The second point of the sermon focused on the nature of the new birth. This restatement of the heart of the gospel that followed is vintage Wesley. He drew upon a profound, theologically driven assimilation of various scriptural texts and provided one of the most memorable Trinitarian summaries of vital religion found in all of his works:

> As soon as he is born of God there is a total change in all these particulars. The "eyes of his understanding are opened". . . he sees "the light of

25 *Works*, 2:189–90.

> the glory of God," his glorious love, "in the face of Jesus Christ." His ears being opened, he is now capable of hearing the inward voice of God, saying, "Be of good cheer, thy sins are forgiven thee": "Go and sin no more." . . . He "feels in his heart" (to use the language of our Church) "the mighty working of the Spirit of God.". . . He many times feels such a joy in God as is "unspeakable and full of glory." He feels "the love of God shed abroad in his heart by the Holy Ghost which is given unto him.". . . He is daily increasing in the knowledge of God, of Jesus Christ whom he hath sent. . . . And now he may properly be said *to live*: God having quickened him by his Spirit, he is alive to God through Jesus Christ. He lives a life . . . which "is hid with Christ in God." God is continually breathing, as it were, upon his soul, and his soul is breathing unto God. Grace is descending into his heart, and prayer and praise ascending to heaven. And by this intercourse between God and man, this fellowship with the Father and the Son, as by a kind of spiritual respiration, the life of God in the soul is sustained: and the child of God grows up, till he comes to "the full measure of the stature of Christ."
>
> From hence it manifestly appears what is the nature of the new birth. It is that great change which God works in the soul when he brings it into life. . . . It is the change wrought in the whole soul by the almighty Spirit of God when it is "created anew in Christ Jesus," when it is "renewed after the image of God," "in righteousness and true holiness."[26]

Notice the progression: (1) restoration into Trinitarian fellowship and life of God, (2) renewal in the image of God, and (3) recovery of righteousness and true holiness, the very three things lost in the Fall that Wesley pointed out earlier in the sermon, as noted above.

Wesley's summary provided a profound and winsome evangelical, doxological, participatory, and economic Trinitarian account of the very heart of the Christian faith. The statement epitomizes what I intend when I characterize his theology by these descriptors: evangelical, doxological, participatory, economic, and Trinitarian. The content of each of these descriptors of Wesley's theology comes progressively into view by carefully attending to what Wesley wrote, as documented throughout the chapters of this book. The love of God the Father flows to us through the grace of our Lord Jesus Christ in the communion of the Holy Spirit, reconciling us to God and awakening new life and faith in us so that in the communion of the Spirit we enter into fellowship with the Father through the Son and begin to live a life hidden

26 Ibid., 192–94.

with Christ in God. This is the evangelical movement of Trinitarian divine agency toward us in our salvation, freeing our human agency for free and full response.

We cannot but breathe prayer and praise in the Spirit back to God through Christ, who is our high priest at the right hand of the Father, the doxological movement of human agency interpenetrated by divine agency not simply in praise and thanksgiving but involving the entire range of human response in faith, love, hope, discipleship, service, etc., as we saw in chapter 1, which notes that Wesley said that "honoring" the three-one God included acknowledging the deity of the Son and Spirit along with the Father in worship, in love, and in all we think, speak, and do. Both movements are participatory. The Triune God's agency does not destroy human agency but frees it by, and for, participation in the Trinitarian life and activity of God. This activity of the Triune God is economic; it involves the activity of all three Trinitarian persons throughout the whole *oikonomia* or patterned interaction of the Trinitarian persons in the gospel as depicted by and embodied in scripture.

Wesley identified the evangelical and doxological movements (of grace descending into one's heart and of prayer and praise ascending to heaven) in clear Trinitarian terms of fellowship with the Father and the Son quickened by the Spirit, and he likened it to a kind of moment-by-moment participatory spiritual respiration (God is *continually* breathing and one's soul breathing back) that sustains the life of God in the soul until one grows up and reaches maturity in the faith. Wesley further deepened and explained this continual spiritual respiration in his sermon "The Great Privilege of those that Are Born of God":

> It immediately and necessarily implies the continual inspiration of God's Holy Spirit: God's breathing into the soul, and the soul's breathing back what it first receives from God; a continual action of God upon the soul, the re-action of the soul upon God; an unceasing presence of God, the loving, pardoning God, manifested to the heart, and perceived by faith [the evangelical movement]; an unceasing return of love, praise, and prayer, offering up all the thoughts of our hearts, all words of our tongues, all works of our hands, all our body, soul, and spirit, to be an holy sacrifice acceptable unto God in Christ Jesus [the doxological movement].[27]

This important point sheds light on Wesley's insight from his sermon "On the Trinity" that knowledge of the three-one God is interwoven with

27 *Works*, 1:442.

all vital religion, not simply the initial encounter with the Triune God in the gospel.

For Wesley, our knowledge of the three-one God comes from our participation in the gospel from the beginning of the Christian pilgrimage of faith through ongoing spiritual respiration with the Triune God to maturity in the faith, and even beyond this life to our eschatological destiny, as we will see in the next chapter. It is knowledge of the three-one God that is not simply information but a personal acquaintance that is soteriological, participatory, and transformative; the very life and fellowship of the Triune God is sustained in the soul.

Notice also the close connection between union and communion with the Triune God and the reestablishment of the image of God in humanity, along with righteousness and holiness. For Wesley, our utterly real union and communion with the Trinitarian God (bound up with the essence of the gospel) and our spiritual and moral life are inseparable. Notice also the astonishing tapestry of biblical texts referenced in Wesley's statement, but biblical texts combined in a very particular and profound theological manner, revealing Wesley's Trinitarian wisdom and commitments.

Statements like these selections from "The New Birth" and "Great Privilege" sermons begin to open up the spiritual and theological center of Wesley's vision of the Christian faith, including its profound Trinitarian dimension, a center around which much in Wesley's theology revolves, and a Trinitarian dimension that found its way into many of Wesley's accounts of the forms of life and ministry in early Methodism. Wesley sprinkled dozens of such summaries throughout his sermons and also in other publications after the spring of 1738.

In fact, when Wesley presented capsule summaries of the essence of the gospel or the very core of Christian faith or vital religion, he most often did so in characteristic Trinitarian terms.

3. "Original Sin" and "The End of Christ's Coming"

There are parallel accounts of the human dilemma and God's Trinitarian solution in two additional sermons. The first is Wesley's sermon entitled "Original Sin," published in 1759, the year before "The New Birth" sermon in the middle of Wesley's career, and included in his *Standard Sermons* right before "The New Birth" sermon. The second sermon, "The End of Christ's Coming," was published in 1781, in the final decade of Wesley's life. The sermons reveal remarkable consistency over many years in the way Wesley characterized the Trinitarian center of vital religion that restores humanity to the image of God.

Already in the 1740s, not only deists but also professed Christians were calling into question the Pauline understanding of the Fall and original sin. Wesley realized that this attack undermined the gospel as well. He entered the debate in 1757 by publishing his longest treatise, *The Doctrine of Original Sin: According to Scripture, Reason, and Experience.*[28] His sermon "Original Sin" is a summary of the first part of the treatise.

In part 1 of the sermon, Wesley chronicled the wickedness of fallen humanity according to his text in Genesis 6:5. Part 2 dealt with whether human beings "are the same now." Wesley responded that the fallen character of humanity in his day "is confirmed by daily experience," though "the natural man discerns it not." But when God opens our eyes, we see that we are atheists without God: We "are by nature 'altogether vanity'; that is, folly and ignorance, sin and wickedness. . . . We had by nature no knowledge of God, no acquaintance with him."[29]

At this point, Wesley qualified his rather dour view of general revelation and noted that as soon as we used our reason, we learned about God's "eternal power and godhead" from creation: "From things that are seen we inferred the existence of an eternal powerful being that is not seen." Wesley then made a clear distinction between the kind of rudimentary "acknowledgement" that God exists and the Trinitarian knowledge of God by participatory "acquaintance":

> But still, although we acknowledged his being, we had no acquaintance with him. As we know there is an emperor of China, whom yet we do not know, so we knew there was a King of all the earth; but yet we knew him not. Indeed we could not, by any of our natural faculties. By none of these could we attain knowledge of God. We could no more perceive him by our natural understanding than we could see him with our eyes. For "no one knoweth the Father but the Son, and he to whom the Son willeth to reveal him. And no one knoweth the Son but the Father, and he to whom the Father revealeth him." . . . Such is *natural* religion, abstracted from traditional, and from the influences of God's spirit![30]

This is a remarkable statement, for Wesley made it absolutely clear that to "really" know the Triune God of the gospel involves more than "information" about God gleaned from general revelation and worked up into natural theology. As Wesley stated it elsewhere, "'The Father revealed the Son' in our

28 See Outler's introduction to the "Original Sin" sermon in *Works*, 2:170–71.
29 Ibid., 2:176–77.
30 Ibid., 2:177.

hearts: 'and the Son revealed the Father' . . . 'and enlightened them with the knowledge of the glory of God in the face of Jesus Christ.'"[31] Christian knowledge of God involves participatory acquaintance with the Triune God in and through the gospel, where we come to know the Father through the Son and where the Son as the Father reveals the Son to us in the Spirit.

Wesley clearly placed limits on natural "knowledge" of God and differentiated it from participatory acquaintance of the Triune God in the gospel. The biblical text that Wesley quoted at the end of that passage is Matthew 11:27, a crucial text solidifying the Trinitarian convictions of the Nicene theologians.[32] Indeed, that whole citation from Wesley's "Original Sin" sermon is reminiscent of Athanasius's famous epigram: "It would be more godly and true to signify God from the Son and call him Father, than to name God from his works alone and call him Unoriginate."[33]

In his later sermon "The End of Christ's Coming," written in 1781, Wesley presented an equally dour view of humanity's ability to find God apart from Christ and the gospel: "Nature points out the disease; but nature shows us no remedy." The reason, Wesley noted, is that people "sought" the remedy "where it never was and never will be found, in themselves—in reason, in philosophy. Broken reeds! Bubbles! Smoke!" Wesley added, "So dim was the light of the wisest of men till 'life and immortality were brought to light by the gospel'; till 'the Son of God was manifested, to destroy the works of the devil.'"[34]

In part 2 of "The End of Christ's Coming," Wesley echoed what he said in the earlier sermon "Original Sin" (1759) about the Son of God coming to "destroy sin and its fruits." Wesley further developed this knowledge of God the Father that comes only through the Son and linked this theological idea to the early church, revealing his awareness of the Trinitarian convictions developing in the early church and coming to expression in statements like Athanasius's famous epigram: "He was manifest as the only-begotten Son

31 *Works*, 4:53. I am aware that Wesley dealt with general revelation in other places in his publications. So what he said here does not provide the full account of his thinking on general revelation. But nowhere does he repudiate this distinction between "acknowledgement" (awareness and/or information) via general revelation and "acquaintance" by participation in the gospel.

32 This appeal to Matthew 11:25–30 (especially 11:27) bears marked similarity to the use of this crucial text by the Nicene theologians (see T. F. Torrance, *Trinitarian Faith*, chapter 2, "Access to the Father," esp. 47–65).

33 Qtd. ibid., 49.

34 See *Works,* 2:472–73. Elsewhere, Wesley was more positive about human reason and general revelation.

of God, in glory equal with the Father. . . . Indeed it was the universal belief of the ancient church that God the Father none hath seen, nor can see; that from all eternity he hath dwelt in light unapproachable; and it is only in and by the Son of his love that he hath at any time revealed himself to his creatures."[35]

What is especially intriguing about the 1781 sermon "The End of Christ's Coming" is part 1. Here Wesley dealt with the Fall and its consequences in a way that parallels his account of the Fall in the earlier "Original Sin" sermon, but he inserted a Trinitarian description of humanity's relationship with God prior to the Fall that is not found in the earlier sermon. It is a description that goes well beyond the biblical text, and it reveals Wesley's Trinitarian theological commitments in the way he reads a robust Trinitarian dimension back into the Genesis narrative. Wesley began this account of humanity prior to the Fall by noting that God created humanity not only in the "natural" image of God (understanding, will, or affections, "which are only the will exerting itself in various directions," and a measure of liberty or free agency) but also in the "moral" image of God or "righteousness and true holiness."[36]

Wesley then defined this moral image as the proper exercise of the various faculties of the natural image toward "whatever was good." Finally, he placed the whole discussion in a participatory Trinitarian context: "In so doing (choosing the good), he was unspeakably happy, dwelling in God and God in him, having uninterrupted fellowship with the Father and the Son through the eternal Spirit; and the continual testimony of his conscience that all his ways were good and acceptable to God."[37] This quotation is remarkable and revealing because it is an integrative theological reading of scripture in which Wesley, despite being cautious about going beyond the biblical text, read what he learned of the Triune character of God and the character of God's participatory Trinitarian relation with us established and revealed in the gospel back into the Genesis narrative, back into God's relationship with humanity prior to the Fall, indeed, as we saw in his "Letter to a Roman Catholic," ultimately back into God's own Trinitarian life as God. This way of approaching and thinking the Trinitarian character of God is strikingly different than that of the Trinitarian defenders of the doctrine during the Trinitarian controversies.

---

35 See ibid., 2:478.

36 Ibid., 2:474–75.

37 Ibid., 2:475–76. Elsewhere Wesley read the Trinity back into Genesis 1:1: God's "Trinity in Unity and Unity in Trinity, are discovered to us in the very first line of the Written Word . . . literally 'the Gods created,' a plural noun joined with a verb of singular number" (*Works*, 1:581).

So we see that when Wesley described the Fall in the later 1781 "The End of Christ's Coming," the sermon showed uncanny theological consistency with what he had written in the earlier 1759 sermon "Original Sin" in terms of loss of participation in the life of God, then loss of spiritual life, and loss of the moral image of God. Yet in the later 1781 sermon, Wesley read the Triune character of God and participation in the Trinitarian life of God back into humanity's relation to God in the beginning before the Fall. He then described the Fall in terms of loss of this Trinitarian participatory vision of human life as the Triune God intended it. When the first human succumbed to temptation and sin, the 1781 sermon asserts, "The life of God was extinguished in his soul. The glory departed from him. He lost the whole moral image of God, righteousness and true holiness. He was unholy; he was unhappy; he was full of sin, full of guilt and tormenting fears."[38] It is precisely the Fall and its debilitating consequences that was the end of Christ's coming.

When Wesley dealt with the theme indicated in the 1781 sermon "The End of Christ's Coming," the undoing of the Fall and its consequences, he called it Christ's "grand manifestation" that culminates in the "glorious manifestation" when Christ suffered on the Cross, when he bore human sin, "having by that one oblation of himself once offered, and made a full, perfect, and sufficient sacrifice, oblation, and satisfaction for the sins of the whole world."[39] God the Father in and through Christ, the incarnate Son, overcame sin and its consequences.

According the Wesley, this glorious manifestation of Christ included further manifestations: Christ's "resurrection from the dead, his ascension into heaven, into the glory which he had before the world began" and also "his pouring out the Holy Ghost on the day of Pentecost . . . that the Lord God might dwell among, or in them."[40] For Wesley, there is no solution to the human dilemma apart from restoration to participation in the life and fellowship of the Trinitarian God, a solution that involves the economic activity of all three Trinitarian persons in the gospel.

So it is no coincidence that at precisely this point in his sermon "The End of Christ's Coming," Wesley carefully drew together (1) the activity of the Triune God in history in the life, death, resurrection, and ascension of Christ and the outpouring to the Holy Spirit at Pentecost that Wesley had just discussed in points 1–6 of part 2, with (2) the activity of the economic

38 Ibid., 2:477.
39 Ibid., 2:478–80.
40 Ibid., 2:480.

Trinity in our evangelical doxological participation in those events in the final point 7 of part 2 of that sermon:

> "That the Lord God might dwell in them." This refers to . . . his inward manifestation of himself. . . . By enabling us to believe in his name. For he is then inwardly manifest to us [the "pouring of Holy Spirit on the day of Pentecost" noted above] when we are enabled to say with confidence, "My Lord, and my God." . . . He both opens and enlightens the eyes of your understanding. . . . And then we see, not by a chain of *reasoning*, but by a kind of *intuition*, by a direct view, that "God was in Christ, reconciling the world to himself, not imputing to them their former trespasses," not imputing them to *me*. In that day "we know that we are of God," children of God by faith, "having redemption through the blood" of Christ.[41]

Notice that Wesley described this kind of knowledge of God not in terms of human cognitive deduction or induction but rather as a participatory spiritual/theological knowledge of God in Christ generated by the Spirit.

This inward manifestation is not simply forgiving human sin and restoration to God's favor through Christ. So at this point in his sermon "The End of Christ's Coming," Wesley expanded what is involved in this participatory knowledge of God and labeled it the very essence of "real religion": "Here then we see in the clearest, strongest light, what is real religion: a restoration of man . . . not only to favour, but likewise to the image of God; implying not barely deliverance from sin but the being filled with the fullness of God."[42]

It is easy to read this sentence and forget that Wesley told us earlier in the sermon exactly what he meant by this "being filled with the fullness of God" in explicit terms when he described humanity and the natural and moral image of God prior to the Fall. Here is what Wesley said a couple of pages earlier in the sermon about humanity's natural faculties that were all oriented toward "whatever was good" (the moral image): "In so doing [choosing the good] he was unspeakably happy, dwelling in God and God in him, having an uninterrupted fellowship with the Father and the Son through the eternal Spirit; and the continual testimony of his conscience that all his ways were good and acceptable to God." It is participatory "fellowship with the Father and the Son through the eternal Spirit," who unites us to Christ and through Christ with the Father, that restores the whole "moral image" of God: "righteousness and true holiness."[43] The essence of "real religion,"

41 Ibid., 2:480–81.

42 Ibid., 2:482.

43 Ibid., 2:475–76.

according to Wesley, is being filled with the fullness of God, understood in the explicit Trinitarian terms used by Wesley, that alone leads to righteousness and true holiness.

Wesley drove home this exact point in the sentence that follows his summary of true religion as not just deliverance from sin but being filled with the God's fullness: "It is plain, if we attend to the preceding considerations [everything Wesley said earlier in this sermon "The End of Christ's Coming"], that nothing short of this [being filled with the fullness of God] is Christian religion."[44] In fact, Wesley asserted, "Everything else, whether negative or external, is utterly wide the mark. . . . How little is it understood in the Christian world!"[45] These are illuminating statements by Wesley about the Trinitarian dimension at the center of genuine Christian faith.

At this juncture, Wesley made an astonishing admission of just how crucial this participatory, economic Trinitarian understanding of the gospel is to his vision of the very heart of Christian religion or "real religion" as portrayed in scripture: "And yet, if we believe the Bible, who can deny it? Who can doubt of it? It runs through the Bible from the beginning to the end, in one connected chain. And the agreement of every part of it with every other is properly the analogy of faith. Beware of taking anything else, or anything less than this for religion."[46] These are strong words from the father of Methodism about the participatory Trinitarian character of Christian religion that he associated explicitly with the "analogy of faith," or the interconnected central meaning of the Bible from beginning to end. Wesley read back into the Genesis account of humanity prior to the Fall this Trinitarian understanding of the humanity "dwelling in God and God in him, having an uninterrupted fellowship with the Father and the Son through the eternal Spirit; and the continual testimony of his conscience that all his ways were good and acceptable to God."[47] Wesley next recounted the Fall: this Trinitarian "life of God was extinguished in his soul. . . . He was unholy; he was unhappy; . . . full of sin, full of guilt."[48] The father of Methodism then interpreted "The End of Christ's Coming" in the participatory, economic Trinitarian terms and identified it as the very essence of "real religion": "Here then we see in the clearest, strongest light, what is real religion: a restoration of man . . . not only to favour, but

44 Ibid., 2:482–83.
45 Ibid., 2:483.
46 Ibid.
47 Ibid., 2:475–76.
48 Ibid., 2:475–77.

likewise to the image of God; implying not barely deliverance from sin but being filled with the fullness of God."[49]

Finally, Wesley labeled this whole participatory Trinitarian trajectory, which "runs through the Bible from beginning to end, in one connected chain" (from pre-Fall through the Fall to the restoration that happens in Christ's life, death, resurrection, and the outpouring of the Spirit), the *"analogy of faith."*[50] Wesley's analogy of faith was essentially identical with his

---

49 Ibid., 2:482.

50 Ibid., 2:482–83. In his "Sermon of the Mount, IV," Wesley provided the early Methodists with an exposition of the Lord's Prayer in Matthew 6. In that exposition, Wesley presented a participatory Trinitarian vision of the kingdom of God and eternal life that is nearly identical with how he described the heart or essence of Christian faith in his "New Birth" sermon and with his understanding of the analogy of faith.

Wesley's commented on the preface, "Our Father which art in heaven," followed the same pattern in his "Letter to a Roman Catholic," noting that "Father" refers to "our Creator" and "our Preserver," but

> above all, the Father of our Lord Jesus Christ, and of all that believe in him; who justifies us "freely by his grace, through the redemption that is in Jesus"; who hath "blotted out all our sins," "and healed all our infirmities"; "who hath received us for "his own children, by adoption and grace," "and because we are sons, hath sent forth the Spirit of his Son into our hearts, crying, Abba, Father"; "who hath begotten us again of incorruptible seed," "and created us anew in Christ Jesus" . . . therefore. . . . We pray, because we love. And "we love him, because he first loved us." . . . "God so loved the world, that he gave his only-begotten Son," even to death, that they "might not perish, but have everlasting life." (*Works*, 1:578–79)

Once again Wesley portrayed our coming into that family of God in Trinitarian terms. In the highest sense, Father and Son are an intra-Trinitarian relation that reaches out and embraces us when the Father, through the redemptive work of our Lord Jesus Christ, blots out our sins and receives us as children adopted in Christ so that we share in the filial relation between the Father and the Son and receive the Spirit of the Son into our hearts to assure that we are children of God the Father. It is easy to see the parallels between what Wesley said here in his exposition of the Lord's Prayer, what he said about the Trinitarian Christian faith in his "Letter to a Roman Catholic," and what he said in his "New Birth" sermon.

Two pages later in the sermon on the Lord's Prayer, Wesley connected our adoption into the family God with the eternal life and with the coming of the kingdom: "The Kingdom comes to a particular person when he 'repents and believes the gospel'; when he is taught of God not only to know himself but to Jesus Christ and him crucified" (*Works*, 1:578–79). Wesley then forged the deeper connection: "As 'this is eternal life, to know the only true God, and Jesus Christ whom he hath sent', so it is the kingdom of God begun below and set up in the believer's heart." In

understanding of the central message of scripture and his most basic summary of essence of "true Christian faith" or "vital religion," all conceived in the participatory, economic Trinitarian terms.

When we look at the "cure" for the disease of sin in Wesley's earlier 1759 sermon "Original Sin," it is, as we would expect, remarkably similar to what we find in his later sermon "The End of Christ's Coming." What is the nature of the religion of Jesus Christ through which God the great Physician heals us and restores our humanity corrupted in all its faculties? According to Wesley, in this earlier sermon "Original Sin," "God heals all our atheism by knowledge of himself, and of Jesus Christ whom he hath sent; by giving us faith, a divine evidence and conviction of God [by the Spirit] . . . in particular of this important truth: Christ loved *me* and gave himself for *me*."[51]

As we have seen, for Wesley, restoration to God's favor is not enough. As with his sermon "The End of Christ's Coming," so in the "Original Sin" sermon Wesley moved immediately to the renewal of our hearts in the image of God in "righteousness and true holiness," the same phrase he used in "The End of Christ's Coming." Indeed "all religion which does not answer this end . . . is no other than a poor farce and a mere mockery of God." In the final paragraph of the "Original Sin" sermon, Wesley summarized his message: "Know your disease! Know your cure! Ye were born in sin; therefore 'ye must be . . . born of God.' . . . 'In Adam ye died': in the second Adam, 'in Christ, ye all are made alive.' . . . He hath already given you a principle of life. . . . Now 'go on' 'from faith to faith,' until your whole sickness is healed."[52]

---

the next section, Wesley stated that, "Thy kingdom come," is a prayer "that this his kingdom, the kingdom of grace, may come quickly, and swallow up all the kingdoms of the earth." It is a prayer "for the coming his everlasting kingdom, the kingdom of glory in heaven, which is a continuation and perfection of the kingdom of grace on earth" (ibid., 1:582).

In this exposition of the Lord's Prayer, Wesley portrayed eternal life as God the Father adopting us in Christ and sending the Spirit of his Son into hearts to assure us that we are children of God. Wesley then identified this account of adoption and eternal life with the kingdom of God or the kingdom of grace, as Wesley also designated it, a foretaste of the kingdom of glory in heaven. The presence and activity of all three Trinitarian persons are involved together, as we have seen throughout Wesley's summaries of vital religion and true Christian faith examined thus far. For Wesley, the essence of Christian faith and the kingdom of God are nearly identical, and he conceptualized both in participatory, economic Trinitarian terms. The next chapter will deal with Wesley's Trinitarian vision of the New Creation or the kingdom of glory, as he named it here in his sermon on the Lord's Prayer.

51 Ibid., 1:184.

52 Ibid., 1:185.

This final exhortation served as a bridge to the sermon "The New Birth," where Wesley explicated the new birth in similar Trinitarian terms examined in the previous section of this chapter in the long quotation with its winsome image of evangelical and doxological Trinitarian spiritual respiration.

Through all three of these sermons, we find an impressive consistency regarding the Trinitarian categories Wesley utilized when he discussed the core of the gospel, the essence of Christian religion, and the analogy of faith. It is a consistency that extends to what Wesley said in his sermon "On the Trinity" about the Trinity being bound up with vital religion, and what he said about the participatory Trinitarian faith that Protestants and Catholics share in his "Letter to a Roman Catholic." The Trinitarian pattern throughout Wesley's various accounts of "vital religion" or the essence of Christian faith is becoming rather clear.

We turn now to several sermons that Wesley wrote immediately after his evangelical awakening in the spring of 1738. One would expect Wesley to be theologically careful when he constructed these sermons, since he delivered them at the University of Oxford in the presence of the university community, including its leaders and his former professors. These university sermons presented Wesley's theological perspective after his encounter with the Moravians at the beginning of Wesley's career as a leader in the revival that swept over the British Isles, leader of the people called Methodists who began to associate with the Wesley brothers during the years after 1738.

4. University Sermons after May 1738

Brief Trinitarian Summaries

By the early 1740s, Wesley saw the possibility of a career in the groundswell movement of revival sweeping across the British Isles. He had already become a pointed critic of his alma mater, Oxford University, after his theological and spiritual changes in the spring of 1738.[53] When it was time for him to serve as university preacher in July 1741, Wesley used the opportunity to present in sharp contrast the difference between nominal and real Christian faith. The application at the end of the sermon openly questioned whether many at Oxford had not even reached the point of being "almost a Christian."

Wesley concluded the sermon with a succinct Trinitarian summary of the essence of being altogether a Christian: "May we all thus experience what it is to be not almost only, but altogether Christians! Being justified freely by

---

53 See Outler's introduction to the university sermons in ibid., 1:110–11.

his grace, through the redemption that is in Jesus, knowing we have peace with God through Jesus Christ, rejoicing in hope of the glory of God, and having the love of God shed abroad in our hearts by the Holy Ghost given unto us!"[54] Here again is the basic participatory, economic Trinitarian pattern that we have seen in Wesley's sermon "On the Trinity," in his "Letter to a Roman Catholic," and in other sermons examined above: the love of God the Father is manifest in the grace of our Lord Jesus Christ, who redeems us and reconciles us to the God the Father as the Spirit of God sheds the love of God in Christ abroad in our hearts.

There is a similar Trinitarian summary of vital religion in the first sermon, entitled "Salvation by Faith," that Wesley preached at Oxford on June 11, 1738, only a few days after the Aldersgate event in May 1738. In part 1 of the sermon, Wesley described the true *faith* by which we are saved.

Part 2 answered the question, What is "salvation"? For Wesley, it was salvation from sin, "both from the guilt and the power of it."[55] He developed what this salvation from sin entails in participatory Trinitarian categories, like those we have seen above.

According to Wesley, we are saved "from the guilt of all past sin . . . through the redemption that is in Jesus Christ. Him God hath set forth to be a propitiation through faith in his blood." Christians are also "saved from fear . . . of punishment, from fear of the wrath of God, whom they now no longer regard as a severe master, but as an indulgent Father."[56] Indeed, Wesley pointed out that they receive "the Spirit of adoption, whereby they cry, Abba, Father: the Spirit itself also bearing witness with their spirit, that they are children of God. . . . Thus have they 'peace with God through our Lord Jesus Christ. . . . And the love of God is shed abroad in their hearts through the Holy Ghost.' "[57]

So for Wesley, we are justified and become beloved children of God the Father through adoption in Christ by the Spirit, who assures of God's love for us in Christ. This is what it means to be "saved from guilt." Wesley clearly understood our justification, adoption, and assurance as Christians as rooted in the activity of all three persons of the Trinity in the gospel.

Wesley provided a parallel account of sanctification (salvation "from the power of sin") in Trinitarian categories. A Christian "cannot sin, because he is born of God." Salvation includes "a deliverance from the power of sin,

54 Ibid., 1:141.
55 Ibid., 1:122.
56 Ibid., 1:123.
57 Ibid., 1:122–23.

through Christ 'formed in his heart.'. . . He is 'born again of the Spirit' unto a new 'life which is hid with Christ in God' . . . 'going on in the might of the Lord his God,' . . . 'from grace to grace,' 'until at length he comes unto . . . the measure of the stature of the fullness of Christ.'"[58]

Wesley interpreted sanctification, our being saved from the power of sin, in participatory Trinitarian terms. We are regenerated or born again by the Spirit, who unites us to Christ so that Christ is formed in our hearts as our lives are hid with Christ in God the Father. This participation in the Trinitarian life of God, this indwelling of our lives on the part of the Triune God, is the key to the spiritual and moral transformation that sanctification entails, which parallels Wesley's account of how being filled with the Trinitarian fullness of life leads to restoration of the moral image of God and righteousness and true holiness, examined in the previous section.

A Trinitarian Account of "the Mind of Christ" and "Walking as Christ Walked"

In his final university sermon, preached at St. Mary's, Oxford, in August 1744, Wesley was most critical of his alma mater, critical to the point that he doubted whether the officials would invite him to preach there again. In his journal, Wesley noted: "I preached, I suppose the last time at St. Mary's. Be it so I am now clear of the blood of these men. I have fully delivered my own soul."[59]

By this point the revival had spread, and there were Methodist Societies in various parts of England and Wales. Wesley's stinging critique represented his final turning away from a career at the university and his embracing what he perceived to be his true calling in life as a leader of this new movement of "Scriptural Christianity," the title of his sermon.[60] The sermon was a classic statement of Wesley's understanding of the true character of "Scriptural Christianity," presented as a pointed question of whether it was manifest in the lives of those in the university community.[61]

58 Ibid., 1:123–24.

59 See Wesley's journal entry for August 21, 1744, in *The Works of John Wesley*, ed. W. Reginald Ward and Richard P. Heitzenrater, vols. 18–24, *Journals and Diaries I–VII* (Nashville: Abingdon, 1988–2003), 20:36–37.

60 See Outler's introduction to the university sermons in *Works*, 1:111–15.

61 Benjamin Kennicott, an undergraduate student at the time, characterized the sermon as a "sacred censure," an address "fired . . . with . . . zeal and unbounded satire" (see ibid.).

The text for the sermon is Acts 4:31, which followed the early church's prayer for boldness for bearing witness to the gospel in the face of persecution: "And they were all filled with the Holy Ghost." Wesley opened the sermon by noting that the reason behind this filling with the Spirit was not to provide "*extraordinary* gifts of the Holy Spirit" but rather was "for a more excellent purpose than this."[62] According to Wesley, the outpouring of the Spirit in Acts 4 was to provide "what none can deny to be essential to all Christians in all ages" or " 'the mind that was in Christ,' those holy fruits of the Spirit which whosoever hath not 'is none of his.' " The goal was "to fill them with 'love, joy, peace, longsuffering, gentleness, goodness . . .'; to endue them with 'faith' . . . with 'meekness and temperance'; to enable them to 'crucify the flesh' . . . ; and, in consequence of that *inward change*, to fulfill all *outward* righteousness, 'to walk as Christ also walked.' "[63]

This is an interesting passage for it reveals that when Wesley utilized the phrases having "the mind that was in Christ" and "to walk as Christ walked," these were not random fragments of scripture inserted into Wesley's sermons, treatises, and other writings. These phrases appear many times throughout Wesley's publications. The two expressions function as theological stenography and are capsule summaries of a range of theological content within what Wesley called, in this sermon, "Scriptural Christianity."

On occasion, like at the beginning of this university sermon, Wesley provided summaries of the theological content he intended by these phrases. "It was given to them (what none can deny to be essential to all Christians in all ages) 'the mind which was in Christ,' " which according to the "Scriptural Christianity" sermon, was "those holy 'fruits of the Spirit' [love, joy, peace, etc.] . . . to enable them [Christians] to 'crucify the flesh with its affections and lusts,' its passions and desires," or the "*inward change*," that the love of God through the grace of Christ in the fellowship of the Spirit effects in us.[64]

---

62 Ibid., 1:160.

63 Ibid., 1:160–61.

64 Ibid., 1:160. Elsewhere Wesley said that the "mind which was also in Christ Jesus": was nothing "less than the 'perfect love of God,' constraining us to love every soul of man, even as Christ loved us" (ibid., 3:173). In his sermon "On Dress," Wesley associated the "mind which was in Christ Jesus" with "the whole nature of inward holiness" (ibid., 3:256). In Wesley's sermon "On God's Vineyard," he spoke of "an inward change, from all unholy to all holy tempers, from pride to humility, . . . from peevishness and discontent to patience and resignation—in a word, from an earthly, sensual, devilish mind to the mind that was in Christ Jesus" (ibid., 3:506). See also Wesley's essay "A Blow at the Root, of Christ Stabb'd in the House of His Friends," in Outler ed., *Wesley*, 379, 380, 382. There will be additional references to Wesley's

As the Spirit of God works in us, this "mind of Christ," as the love of God is shed abroad in our hearts and the inner fruit of the Spirit characterizes our affections and dispositions, "in consequence of that *inward change*" we also will "fulfill all *outward* righteousness" and "'walk as Christ also walked,' in the 'work of faith, the patience of hope, the labour of love.'" Having the mind of Christ and to walk as Christ also walked, Wesley stated, is "that great work of God . . . which we are used to express by one word, 'Christianity'; not as . . . a system of doctrine, but as it refers to men's hearts and lives."[65] Elsewhere Wesley called outward righteousness works of mercy and works of piety, or avoiding evil, doing good, and using the means of grace, the General Rules of the United Societies that Methodists agreed to follow. Here is the significance of the title "Scriptural Christianity," for Wesley was providing a summary of that great work of God in people's hearts (the *inward* change, the holy fruits of the Spirit, or having mind of Christ) and lives (the *outward* change, fulfilling righteousness, or to walk as Christ walked). According to Wesley, having the mind which was in Christ and to walk as Christ also walked together are this great work of God called Christianity. Wesley will describe it in detail in the remainder of his sermon "Scriptural Christianity" and apply it to the lives of Oxford University community.

What will become clear when we examine that sermon in detail is that "Scriptural Christianity" turns out to be another phrase for what Wesley called, in his sermon "On the Trinity," true Christian faith or vital religion rooted in participatory acquaintance with the three-one God. However, before investigating the participatory Trinitarian account of scriptural Christianity or having the mind of Christ and walking as Christ walked in Wesley's "Scriptural Christianity" sermon in the next section, the rest of this section will examine a similar summary of the mind of Christ and walking as Christ walked in another sermon dealing with zeal.

In Wesley's sermon "On Zeal," published in the *Arminian Magazine* in 1781, we find what Collins called a "peek into the throne room of his [Wesley's] entire theological and moral enterprise."[66] The sermon provided

use of these two phrases, "to have the mind that was in Christ" and "to walk as Christ also walked," at various points in the chapters that follow.

65 *Works*, 1:160–61. In his sermon "On Living without God," Wesley distinguished true Christian faith from morality and said that a true Christian is a new creature having "the whole mind of Christ" and being enabled to "walk as Christ walked" (ibid., 4:174). See also ibid., 2:543, where Wesley defines "real Christians" as "all in whom is the mind which was in Christ, and who walk as Christ also walked."

66 Collins, *Theology of John Wesley*, 228.

another summary of the content of "having the mind that was in Christ" and "to walk as Christ walked."

According to this sermon, "True Christian zeal is no other than *the fame of love.*" "*Love* sits upon the throne, which is erected in the inmost soul [of a Christian]; namely love of God and man, which fills the whole heart, and reigns without a rival." In close proximity in a circle around the throne, "are the *holy tempers*: long-suffering, gentleness, meekness, goodness, fidelity, temperance—and if any other is comprised in 'the mind which was in Christ Jesus.'"[67] Notice that Wesley described the mind of Christ in terms of the fruit of the Spirit, including considerable overlap in the very phrases he used in his sermon "Scriptural Christianity," though in the sermon "On Zeal," he called them holy tempers instead of the Spirit's fruit. When Wesley used the phrase "the mind that was in Christ," here again it was theological shorthand for the fruit of the Spirit, for the inward change or the "holy tempers" that "vital religion" or "Scriptural Christianity" works in us, a vital religion that entails a participatory Trinitarian dimension.

The parallel between the two sermons does not stop here. After defining "having the mind of Christ" in terms of the fruit of the Spirit or "holy tempers," in the sermon "On Zeal," Wesley moved immediately to an "exterior circle" around the holy tempers that surround love for God and humanity seated on the throne. In that outer circle "are all the *works of mercy*, whether to the souls or bodies of men" by which "we exercise all holy tempers . . . continually improve them, so that all these [the works of mercy] are real *means of grace*."[68] Outside these works of mercy, Wesley said, "are those that are usually termed *works of piety*," what we usually call means of grace, "reading and hearing the Word, public, family, private prayer, . . . the Lord's Supper, and fasting."[69] In other words, these "outward works" of mercy and piety "spring from *holy tempers*," as Wesley explicitly stated the point toward the end of the sermon.[70]

In the sermon "On Zeal," Wesley did not use the phrase "to walk as Christ also walked" to summarize this fulfilling of "outward righteous" via works of mercy and works of piety. It is clear, however, that he intended the same reality that he described in the sermon "Scriptural Christianity" as the outworking of this inward change that leads us to "fulfil all *outward* righteousness," or "to walk as Christ also walked."

---

67 *Works*, 3:313.

68 Ibid.

69 Ibid.

70 Ibid., 3:320.

What is of particular interest is the significance that Wesley attaches to his account of love for God and others on the throne in one's inmost soul working itself out through holy tempers or fruit of the Spirit or everything comprised in the mind of Christ to outward righteous or works of mercy that "exercise" the holy tempers and works of piety. "This is the entire, connected system of Christianity [the analogy of faith?]: and thus the several parts of it arise one above the other . . . to the highest, love enthroned on the heart," states Wesley. "This is that real religion which our Lord established upon earth, ever since the descent of the Holy Ghost." Our deepest zeal, for Wesley, "should be reserved for *love* itself, the end of the commandment, the fulfilling of the law. . . . Here then is the great object of Christian zeal. Let every true believer in Christ apply with all fervency of spirit to the God and Father of our Lord Jesus Christ, that his heart may be more and more enlarged in love to God and to all mankind."[71] According to Wesley, the essence of vital religion is a life "hid with Christ in God," as he characterized it in "The New Birth" sermon, the Spirit breathing Trinitarian life into our hearts and lives, filling us with love on the throne and all the fruit of the Spirit surrounding it, so that we have the "mind of Christ" and breathe love to the Triune God in worship and obedience and love toward others, "walking as Christ walked" in works of mercy and piety, the fulfillment of the law, or as Wesley said it in his sermon on "The New Birth" till we come to "the full measure of the stature of Christ."[72]

---

71 Ibid., 3:314–15.

72 See *Works*, 2:193. When Wesley used the throne-room image, with love at the center (actually a raised center) and several widening circles depicting other elements that are bound with Christian faith or vital faith, the last element he noted is the church: "Lastly, that his followers may the more effectually provoke one another to love, holy tempers, and good works, our blessed Lord has united them together in one—"*the church*" (see *Works*, 3:313). Wesley saw all of these various facets together as "the entire, connected system of Christianity: and thus the several parts of it rise one above another, from that lowest point, 'the assembling ourselves together', to the highest, love enthroned in the heart." This led Wesley to argue that zeal should be exercised or "*proportioned* to that good, to the degree of goodness that is in its object" (ibid., 314). So while Christians should be zealous for the church, they "should be more zealous for the *ordinances of Christ* than for the church itself," still more zealous for good works, more yet for holy tempers, and the "choicest zeal should be reserved for *love* itself; the end of the commandments, the fulfilling of the law" (ibid., 3:314–15).

When one begins to reflect theologically on the image of the throne room with circles of priorities moving upward to the raised throne of love in the center, one is immediately struck by the fact that "love" for Wesley is inherently relational: it is not

The parallel Trinitarian descriptions that Wesley used when he described "vital religion," "true Christian faith," "spiritual respiration" that sustains the life of God in the soul, "the analogy of faith," "Scriptural Christianity," and the "connected system of Christianity" summarized by the mind of Christ and walking as Christ walked are becoming clear. "The mind that was in Christ" is theological shorthand for the fruit of the Spirit, "holy tempers," or inward change that Trinitarian "vital religion" or "Scriptural Christianity" works in us. To "walk as Christ also walked" is the outworking of this inward change in works of mercy and piety or "fulfilling all *outward* righteousness" or avoiding evil, doing good, and using the means of grace.

A Trinitarian Understanding of "Scriptural Christianity"

We return now to "Scriptural Christianity," Wesley's 1744 sermon at Oxford University. Wesley made it clear that having the mind that was in Christ and walking as Christ also walked is the "great work of God" among people in every age that is "express[ed] by one word, 'Christianity.'"[73] Wesley went right to the heart of the matter in part 1.

---

merely an isolated affection and/or temper possessed by an individual and then expressed in other elements of inward character manifested in outward behavior. Christian love, as Wesley described it, arises on the throne at the center of our hearts and lives only via divine Trinitarian redemptive presence and activity. The love of God the Father through the grace of our Lord Jesus Christ in the fellowship of the Spirit in the gospel recreates the human heart and life and implants the Trinitarian life and fellowship that alone can generate and sustain Christian love by a kind of spiritual respiration, as Wesley described it in "The New Birth" sermon.

In addition, Wesley is very clear that this re-creation by the Spirit into fellowship with and love for the Father and the Son also creates love for and fellowship with others. Christian love, for Wesley, is inherently relational in a way that not only involves the Trinitarian Persons, but also human persons in fellowship or communion. This is what *koinonia* is: participatory fellowship, an interpersonal ontological sharing of life together both in relation to the Triune God and to one another.

The question that remains is why Wesley placed the church at the low end of his scale of proportional goodness in this sermon "On Zeal." It is clear that Wesley wanted to emphasize *zeal for love* over the kind of zeal for the church (or a particular branch of it) that could degenerate into "*bitterness* toward them that oppose us . . . *bigotry* of every sort, and above all the spirit of *persecution*," as Wesley said it later in the sermon (ibid., 3:315). We will return to Wesley's discussion of the church in his sermon "On Zeal" in chapter 4.

73 *Works*, 1:161.

By now we should anticipate that Wesley provided an explicit economic Trinitarian account of the "Scriptural Christianity," and this was precisely what he did:

> Suppose then one of those who heard the Apostle Peter preaching . . . was "pricked to the heart," was convinced of sin, repented, and then "believed in Jesus." By this "faith of the operation of God," . . . the demonstrative "evidence of invisible things," he instantly "received the Spirit of adoption, whereby he (now) cried Abba Father." . . . He could "call Jesus Lord, by the Holy Ghost", the Spirit itself bearing witness with his spirit that he was a child of God. . . . He could truly say, "I live not, but Christ liveth in me; and the life which I now live in the flesh I live by faith in the Son of God, who loved me and gave himself for me."
>
> This then was the very essence of his faith, a divine *elegxos* of the love of God the Father, through the Son of his love, to him a sinner, now "accepted in the beloved." And "being justified by faith, he had peace with God." . . .
>
> "His soul" therefore "magnified the Lord, and his spirit rejoiced in God his Saviour." He rejoiced in him "with joy unspeakable," who "had reconciled him to God, even the Father" "in whom he had redemption through his blood, the forgiveness of sins." He rejoiced in that "witness of God's Spirit with his spirit that he was a child of God"; and more abundantly "in hope of the glory of God"; . . . the full "renewal of his soul in righteousness and true holiness." . . .
>
> "The love of God" was also "shed abroad in his heart by the Holy Ghost which was given unto him." "Because he was a son, God had sent forth the Spirit of his Son into his heart, crying Abba, Father!" And that filial love of God was continually increased by the "witness he had in himself" of God's pardoning love to him. . . . So that God was the desire of his eyes, and the joy of his heart . . .
>
> He that thus "loved God" could not but "love his brother also"; and "not in word only, but in deed and in truth." "If God," said he, "so loved us, we ought also to love one another"; yea, every soul of man, as the "mercy" of God "is over all his works."[74]

Wesley continued his description of genuine Christianity, moving from the inward Trinitarian activity, rebirth, and transformation described in this long quotation, to the fulfilling of all outward righteousness, or walking as Christ walked. The Christian "who had this love" of God in Christ through

74 Ibid., 1:161–63.

the witness of the Spirit reigning "in his heart would 'work no evil to his neighbor.'" Likewise, the Christian "deeply sensible of the truth of that word, 'without me ye can do nothing,'" could not but continue "'daily' in all the ordinances of God, the stated channels of his grace to man." Nor could such a Christian be content "barely to abstain from doing evil. His soul was athirst to do good."[75] Notice how Wesley used the three main headings of the General Rules of the Methodist Societies (avoid evil, do good, and use the means of grace) to describe this "walking as Christ walked" in all outward righteous.

Wesley concluded his Trinitarian description of "Scriptural Christianity" in part 1 of the sermon: "Such was Christianity in its rise. Such was a Christian in ancient days."[76] By now the Trinitarian pattern of Wesley's depiction of the essence of vital religion or the core of Christian faith should be rather familiar from the examples examined in this chapter to this point. All three Trinitarian persons are involved each in their own particular manner in human salvation and its various facets from conviction of sin through reconciliation and rebirth in the Spirit into fellowship with the Triune God and love toward God and others, growing and working itself out in works of mercy and piety or restoration to the moral image of God in righteousness and true holiness, all by a kind Trinitarian spiritual respiration between God and humanity, as Wesley described it in "The New Birth" sermon.

Part 2 of Wesley's 1744 sermon at Oxford traced the spread of scriptural Christianity into the world, which led inexorably to persecution, even by "men of religion, so called, the men of *outside* religion," for the spread of scriptural Christianity convicts people of sin, and those who do not repent take offense.[77] In part 3, Wesley asked whether he and his hearers could expect to see even greater things than what he had described thus far, "a *Christian world.*" Wesley answered with a resounding yes.

One can guess where Wesley was going. He defined scriptural Christianity: its rise, its spread, and its final telos. What remained was the "plain practical application" to his audience at the university: "Where does this Christianity now exist?"[78] Not at Oxford! Part 4 consists of eleven paragraphs filled with Wesley's pointed interrogation as to whether those in his Oxford audience were in touch with "Scriptural Christianity."

---

75 Ibid., 1:164.
76 Ibid., 1:165.
77 Ibid., 1:167.
78 Ibid., 1:172.

Wesley questioned Oxford in the same kind of Trinitarian terms that he used to describe "Scriptural Christianity," in parts 1–3 of the sermon. The eleven paragraphs of part 4 of the sermon are a stinging criticism of Oxford, a questioning whether the scriptural Christianity that Wesley described could be found there.[79] It is easy to see why Wesley knew he would not be invited to preach there again. What is of importance for this study is the explicit characteristic Trinitarian dimension of "Scriptural Christianity," or the essence of the gospel, in this 1744 University sermon.

There are many additional Trinitarian summaries in Wesley's sermons beyond those examined so far.[80] Through all of them there is a consistent participatory, evangelical, doxological, Trinitarian pattern in the essence of Christian faith or vital religion from 1738 on in every period of his life.

5. Trinitarian Summaries in Tracts and Treatises

Does Wesley summarize the gospel in Trinitarian terms in other places in his voluminous writings? He does, and this section will examine a sampling of those Trinitarian summaries of the gospel.

In 1742, Wesley wrote a tract that went through nineteen English editions in his lifetime.[81] Later in life, Wesley said it was the first tract that he wrote on Christian perfection. He wrote it to defend Methodism by showing that Methodism was simply genuine Christian faith. In so doing, Wesley

---

79 See ibid., 1:172–80.

80 See, for example, in *Works*, vol. 1, 124 (II.7), 152–56 (III.1–9), 161–63 (I.1–4), 193 (III.6), 194 (IV.2), 208–9 (II.10–12), 223–24 (I.10–12), 237–38 (II.1–2), 249 (1), 273–75 (I.6–9), 284 (II.14), 286 (II.1), 309–10 (16), 312–13 (20), 320 (II.4), 349–50 (II.5–6), 383 (6), 405 (I.7), 424–25 (II.5), 425–26 (III.1–2), 433–34 (6–8), 458–59 (II.12–13), 481–82 (I.11–13), 497 (II.4), 513 (I.6), 538 (I.9), 578–79 (III.4), 613–15 (2–5), 642–4 (20–22), 662 (27) & 691–3 (II.1–3). There are thirty-three sermons in *Works*, volume 1, and more than twenty-five have Trinitarian summaries of the gospel or the essence of Christian faith.

Here is a sampling of references to Trinitarian summaries found in other sermons of Wesley: *Works*, 2:15–16 (IV.1–3), 100–101 (I.1–2), 158 (I.4), 192–93 (II.4), 410–11 (II.8–9), 425–26 (I.1–5), 598 (II.8), and 600 (II.10); *Works*, 3:89–90 (1–5), 119 (8), 147 (10), 173–4 (8–9), 201 (3–4), 283 (I.1), 497–8 (12), and 507–8 (I.9); *Works*, 4:31–2 (7), 49 (1–2), 53–54 (11–13), and 171–76 (8–16). This is a far from exhaustive list of Trinitarian summaries of the essence of true Christian faith in Wesley's sermons. Chapters 3, 4, and 5 will document additional Trinitarian summaries found in Wesley's sermons and other publications.

81 See Davies's introduction to the tract "The Character of a Methodist," in *The Works of John Wesley*, ed. Rupert Davies, vol. 9, *The Methodist Societies: History, Nature, and Design* (Nashville: Abingdon, 1989), 9:31–32.

defined what a Methodist is: a Christian living out vital Christian faith, pressing on toward scriptural Christian perfection.[82]

Wesley stated his goal for the tract from the beginning: "What are the *principles* and the *practice* . . . and . . . the *distinguishing marks* of this 'SECT' . . . "called 'Methodist'?" As one of the first to be known by the label "Methodist," Wesley believed he was "able to give the clearest account these things."[83]

Wesley began his delineation of the character of a Methodist by noting that what distinguishes a Methodist is "not his *opinions*" nor particular "*words* or *phrases*" placing "our religion, or any part of it, in being attached to any peculiar mode of speaking," nor even "by *actions*, *customs*, or *usages* of an *indifferent* nature." Indeed, a Methodist is not distinguished "by laying the *whole stress* of religion on any *single part* of it."[84]

What, then, are the distinguishing marks of a Methodist? Wesley developed them, as we should expect, in Trinitarian terms:

> A Methodist is one who has "the love of God shed abroad in his heart by the Holy Ghost given unto him." . . . God is the joy of his heart, and the desire of his soul, which is constantly crying out . . . My God and my all! . . .

---

82 Ibid.

83 Ibid. 9:32.

84 Ibid., 9:33–35. It is interesting that Wesley affirmed that there are *some* beliefs that go to the very center of Christian faith and are not merely "opinions." Wesley noted two of them. The first is that a Methodist affirmed that the scripture is the inspired "written Word of God" and "the *only* rule both of both Christian faith and practice." This distinguished Methodists from "Jews, Turks and infidels." The second is that Methodists "believe Christ to be the Eternal Supreme God," and this distinguished them from "the Socinians and Arians." Here we see Wesley's staunch affirmation of the deity of Christ, which is crucial to the doctrine of the Trinity (see ibid., 9:33–34).

In addition, even though Wesley affirmed that we are "*saved by faith alone*," he saw this as integrally connected to holiness of heart and life, for that is what "salvation" means. Wesley refused to follow the "solafideism" and "antinomianism" he perceived in some Protestant groups like the Moravians. It is interesting and characteristic that Wesley then excluded placing the whole of religion in doing no harm, in doing good, or in using the ordinances of God, the basic General Rules that Methodists agreed to follow in order to be a part of the movement (ibid., 9:35). Wesley made this same move throughout his publication, repeatedly warning the Methodists that the General Rules are merely the "form" of godliness through which Methodists seek and wait for the "power" of godliness that comes from the Triune God of the gospel (see ibid., 9:69).

> He is therefore happy in God . . . having in him "a well of water springing up into everlasting life.". . . He "rejoices in the Lord always," even "in God his Saviour"; and in the Father "through our Lord Jesus Christ by whom he hath now received the atonement.". . . He cannot but rejoice . . . "being justified freely," and "having peace with God through our Lord Jesus Christ." For "he that believeth hath the witness" of this "in himself"; being now "the son of God" by FAITH, "because he is a son, God hath sent forth the Spirit of his Son into his heart, crying out, Abba, Father." And "the Spirit itself beareth witness with his spirit that he is a child of God.". . .
>
> He who hath his "hope" . . . "in everything giveth thanks," as knowing that "this" . . . "is the will of God in Christ Jesus concerning him." . . .
>
> He "prays without ceasing.". . . Many times "the Spirit maketh intercession for him, with groans that cannot be uttered.". . . And this is true prayer, the lifting up the heart to God. This is the essence of prayer, and this alone. . . .
>
> And while he thus always exercises his love to God, by prayer without ceasing, rejoicing evermore, and in everything give thanks, this commandment is written in his heart, that "he who loveth God, loves his brother also." And he accordingly "loves his neighbor as himself."[85]

Here again we see the same participatory Trinitarian pattern that we saw in Wesley's summaries of the essence of Christian faith in his sermon "On The Trinity," in his "Letter to a Roman Catholic," in "The New Birth" sermon, in Wesley's description of the analogy of faith, and in "Scriptural Christianity."

In his tract entitled "The Character of a Methodist," Wesley then spelled out how this transformative participatory Trinitarian activity works itself out in the life of a Methodist. The love of God through Christ in the Spirit purifies the heart from "every unkind temper or malign affection" so that a Methodist does not love the world but desires the Triune God alone in all things. This desire to love God is the "one design" in the life of a Methodist so that her intention is to please God in all things.[86]

To this end of returning love to the Triune God who has so loved us, a Methodist keeps God's commands, and "his obedience is in proportion to his love, the source from whence it flows." A Methodist does not lay up treasures on earth or speak evil of neighbors but avoids evil and does good to all people. A Methodist's "one invariable rule is this: 'Whatsoever ye do in word or deed, do it all in the name of the Lord Jesus, giving thanks to God and the

85 Ibid., 9:35–37.
86 Ibid., 9:38–39.

Father by him.'"[87] Wesley already made it clear that a Methodist does this only in the fellowship of the Spirit, for the Spirit sheds the love of God abroad in our hearts. "These," Wesley concluded, "are the *principles* and *practices* of our SECT; these are the *marks* of a true Methodist."[88]

It is at this point that Wesley interjected a question illuminating how this Trinitarian vision of the essence of Christian faith works itself out using similar capsule phrases for true Christian faith that we have seen a number of times in Wesley's sermons. Wesley wrote, "If any man say, 'Why, these are only the common, fundamental principles of Christianity'—Thou hast said.' So I mean." Wesley went on to say that he "vehemently" refused to be distinguished from other people "by any but the common principles of Christianity—the plain, old Christianity I teach." Wesley noted that "whosoever *is* what I *preach* (let him be *called* what he will; for names change not the nature of things), he is a Christian, not in *name* only, but in *heart* and in *life*."[89]

At this point Wesley further stated what he meant by of the essence of Christianity using the same phrases or theological shorthand that we have seen elsewhere in his sermons above. A real "Methodist" is simply a scriptural Christian who "is inwardly and outwardly conformed to the will of God, as revealed in the written Word." Such a person's "soul is 'renewed after the image of God,' 'in righteousness and in all true holiness.'" Wesley continued, "And 'having the mind that was in Christ' he 'so walked as' Christ 'also walked.'"[90]

We see in this account of the character of the Methodist the same evangelical and doxological Trinitarian spiritual respiration that we saw in Wesley's "New Birth" sermon. The Love of God the Father comes to us through the grace of our Lord Jesus Christ in the communion of the Spirit and blots out

---

87 Ibid., 9:39–40.

88 Ibid., 9:41.

89 Ibid. Wesley's idea that reality or the nature of things is deeper than the linguistic symbols we use to designate them is reminiscent of Athanasius's well-known dictum, "Terms do not detract from his [God's] nature; rather does his nature draw terms to itself and transform them. For terms are not prior to beings, but beings are first and terms come second" (qtd. in Torrance, *Trinitarian Faith*, 129).

90 Davies, introduction to "The Character of a Methodist," 9:41. As we saw earlier in this chapter, Wesley used the phrases "having the mind of Christ" and "walking as Christ also walked" as summaries of a range of theological content that included his participatory Trinitarian understanding of the essence of Christian faith or scriptural Christianity or, in this tract, the character of a Methodist who embraces "plain, old Christianity."

our sin and guilt, assures us of the Triune God's acceptance and love, and frees us for response (the evangelical movement) so that in and through the Spirit we pray, rejoice, give thanks, and trust in this astonishing Trinitarian God who has loved us with the very love that God is (the doxological movement).

This kind of transformative encounter with the Trinitarian persons leads to changes in our tempers, affections, and other elements of our character or the inward change that Wesley labeled "the mind of Christ" or the fruit of the Spirit as described in his sermon "Scriptural Christianity." This inner transformation manifests itself in "works of mercy" and "works of piety," what Wesley also called "walking as Christ also walked," or "outward righteousness."

Together this inward transformation leading to outward righteousness, or this developing of "the mind of Christ" leading us "to walk as Christ also walked," is an obeying of the law, but always by grace through faith on the basis of this participatory Trinitarian matrix that initiates, surrounds, upholds, and sustains the character of a Methodist from beginning to end. The consistency between this tract and various Trinitarian summaries of the essence of Christian faith examined above is clear.

What is also interesting is that Wesley extended his reflection on this Trinitarian vision of the "Character of a Methodist" into ecclesiology. At the very end of the tract "The Character of a Methodist," Wesley stated, "By these *marks*, by these fruits of a living faith, do we labour to *distinguish* ourselves from the unbelieving world . . . but from real Christians, of whatsoever denomination they be, we earnestly desire not to be distinguished at all." Wesley did not even want to be differentiated from those "who sincerely follow after what they know they have not yet attained."[91]

According to Wesley, in "The Character of a Methodist," if "'thy heart is right, as my heart is with thine,' I ask no farther question . . . 'give me thy hand.'"[92] This verse in 2 Kings 14:20 was also Wesley's text for his sermon entitled "Catholic Spirit." Wesley made the Trinitarian dimension explicit in the final lines of this tract: "Dost thou love and serve God? It is enough. I give thee the right hand of fellowship. 'If there be any consolation in Christ . . . if any fellowship of the Spirit' . . . let us 'strive together for . . . the gospel.'" Wesley then turned to Ephesians 4:1-6: let us walk "'worthy of the vocation wherewith we are called . . . endeavouring to keep the unity of the Spirit . . .'; remembering 'there is one body and one Spirit . . . ; one Lord, one faith, one baptism; one God and Father of all, who is above all, and through all, and in

91 Ibid., 9:42.

92 Ibid.

you all!'"[93] Ephesians 4:1–6 is the very text Wesley used for his sermon "Of the Church," where he explicated his ecclesiology, as we will see in chapter 4.

The Trinitarian dimension of and basis for Christian fellowship could not be clearer in Wesley's closing remarks. It is the economic Trinitarian participatory "having the mind of Christ" and "walking as Christ also walked" that are the marks that distinguish Christians from the unbelieving world, while at the same time uniting Christians to one another as the Body of Christ. This Trinitarian essence of Christian faith is community-constituting and the basis for Christian fellowship.

So if these Trinitarian marks of a Methodist and of "plain, old Christianity" are the basis for fellowship and if Wesley were consistent in applying these marks in practice, we would expect to see application of these marks in the actual life of the Methodist movement. Do we find any indication of this kind of application? Once again, the answer is yes.

In December 1738, Wesley developed the "Rules for the Band Societies." This, of course, was before the actual emergence of distinctively "Methodist" Societies in London or Bristol. Yet these "Rules for the Bands Societies" were used in early Methodism in small groups for those who had come to the faith.

In his "A Plain Account of the People Called Methodists," Wesley told of those who had "found the pearl of great price," who, "being justified by faith . . . had peace with God, through our Lord Jesus Christ." Wesley noted that "These felt a more tender affection than before to those who were partakers of like precious faith," and so "these therefore wanted some means of closer union."[94] To this end, Wesley divided them into bands and gave them the "Rules" for bands.

When we examine the "Rules of the Band Societies" we see the outworking and application of the Trinitarian marks of the "character" of a true Methodist or plain, old Christianity. Wesley listed "some of the questions proposed to every one before *he* is admitted among us" in a band:

1. Have you forgiveness of your sins?
2. Have you peace with God, through our Lord Jesus Christ?
3. Have you the witness of God's Spirit with your spirit that you are a child of God?
4. Is the Love of God shed abroad in your heart?
5. Has no sin, inward or outward, dominion over you?[95]

---

93 Ibid.

94 Ibid., 266.

95 Ibid., 77.

Note that the first three questions follow the economic Trinitarian pattern of participatory involvement, the "root of vital religion" or our "fellowship with the Father and Son" through Spirit that is the basis of fellowship with other Christians. Question 4 aimed at this inward transformation of affections and tempers or the fruit of the Spirit that Wesley also called "the mind of Christ": "Is God's love shed abroad in your heart?" This inward transformation leads to "walking as Christ also walked." This is what question 5 focused on the keeping of the law or the outward manifestation of the transformation of affections and tempers in our thoughts, intentions, and actual practices: "Has no sin, inward or outward, dominion over you?"

These questions clearly intend the marks or essence of Christianity that was the ground of fellowship that we saw above in the tract "The Character of a Methodist." For Wesley, these marks were the basis for admission into the bands. Bands were for those who had come to faith and to fellowship with the Triune God and with one another that the Trinitarian transformation in the gospel entails. The bands provided the means to express and to nurture this closer union.

This more intimate fellowship that comes in and with the awakening of faith did not exclude those who were genuinely seeking this awakening, who were seekers "'flee[ing] from the wrath to come,'" to use the words of the General Rules of the United Societies.[96] Wesley had already made his mind up about this point in the tract "The Character of a Methodist," as noted above. Wesley was willing to include genuine seekers within the fold of Methodism and offer them a kind of fellowship-on-the-way toward the deeper *koinonia* with the Trinitarian God and others that comes in and with the Trinitarian awakening of faith. Wesley offered the "right hand of fellowship" to "any who sincerely follow after what they have not yet attained," biblical Christian faith with its Trinitarian dimension.

Thus, in the "General Rules of the United Societies," this "fellowship-on-the-way" was extended to real seekers under the "one only condition" for admission into these societies: "a desire to flee from the wrath to come, to be saved from their sins." Wesley was clear that when this desire was really present "it will be shown by its fruits"; that is, by avoiding evil, doing good, and using the means of grace.[97]

In order to show the consistency in Wesley's thinking about the marks of Methodism (plain, old Christianity) over time, we will examine one additional summary from late in Wesley's life in his tract "Thoughts upon

96 Ibid., 9:70.
97 Ibid., 9:70–72.

Methodism," published in 1786 in the *Arminian Magazine*. This brief essay reveals Wesley's growing fear that the Methodist revival of true religion produced "both industry and frugality" among the Methodists, which in turn produced riches. Wesley stated what he saw to be the consequences toward the end of the essay: "I fear, wherever riches have increased (exceedingly few are the exceptions) the essence of religion, the mind that was in Christ, has decreased in the same proportion."[98] Notice again that Wesley associated the mind that was in Christ with the essence of Christian faith.

Wesley began this 1786 tract by stating his fear not that the Methodists "should ever cease to exist" but that "they should only exist as a dead sect, having the form of religion without the power." He then noted that this would undoubtedly happen if they did not hold on to the "doctrine, spirit and discipline" of the Methodists.[99]

Wesley's crisp summary of Methodist doctrine, spirit, and discipline was remarkably similar to what he said in the 1742 tract "The Character of a Methodist." He again affirmed that the Bible is the sole rule of Christian faith for Methodists. From it they learned:

> That religion is an inward principle; that it is no other than the mind that was in Christ; or in other words, the renewal of the soul after the image of God, in righteousness and true holiness. [Note yet again the use of nearly the identical phrases that we have seen repeatedly, pointing to the transformation of our affections, etc. that leads to transformation of the rest of our lives.]
>
> That this can never be wrought in us but by the power of the Holy Ghost.
>
> That we receive this and every other blessing for the sake of Christ;
>
> That whosoever hath the mind that was in Christ, the same is our brother, and sister, and mother.[100] [Here again Wesley drew the link between the participatory Trinitarian essence of religion that restores us not simply to fellowship with God and simultaneously to fellowship with others in the Body of Christ.]

The consistency between the two tracts is not just between Wesley's ideas; it is a consistency in the very phrases he used and a consistency in the consequence he drew in both tracts, for life together in fellowship with the Triune God entails fellowship with others who have encountered, or who are

98 Ibid., 9:529.
99 Ibid., 9:527.
100 Ibid.

seeking, this fellowship with God, a fellowship that must be recognized and embodied in actual life together.

In Wesley's tracts and treatises we find examples of this participatory, evangelical, doxological, economic Trinitarian summary of the essence of Christianity or vital religion that are remarkably similar to those found in Wesley's sermons. What is noteworthy in this section is that Wesley actually began to work out this Trinitarian vision of the essence of Christian faith in his ecclesiology and in the embodiment of it in the life, community, and practice of early Methodism, subjects that will be developed further in chapters 4 and 5. What is noteworthy about all of the Trinitarian summaries of the essence of Christian faith in the sermons, tracts, and treatises is the profound connection Wesley saw between the Trinity and vibrant Christian faith, worship, life, and community, a connection noticeably absent in the explications of the Trinity by the defenders of the doctrine in the Trinitarian controversies examined in chapter 1.

We find similar Trinitarian summaries of vital religion in Wesley's *Notes on the New Testament*, in his letters, and in his journals.

6. *Trinitarian Summaries in* Notes on the New Testament

There are many, though often very brief, Trinitarian summaries of the essence of Christian faith in Wesley's *Notes on the New Testament*, reflecting the succinct character of the *Notes* themselves. For example, in his comments on Ephesians 2:18, Wesley noted that through Christ we have "liberty of approaching, *by* the guidance and aid of *the one Spirit to* God as our *Father*. Christ, the Spirit, and the Father, the Three-One God, stand frequently in the same order."[101]

In his comments on 1 John 5:20, Wesley summarized the essence of vital religion in yet another way: we are "in Jesus Christ, the eternal Son of God" "'as branches in the vine.' *This* Jesus *is the* only living and *true God*, together with the Father and the Spirit, and the original fountain of *eternal life*."[102] In fact, the whole series of Wesley's comments on 1 John 5:1–20 affirmed the deity of all three persons of the Trinity, affirmed the three-one character of the Triune God, as well as manifested the kind of Trinitarian understanding of the eternal life or true Christianity we have seen in so

101 John Wesley, *Explanatory Notes upon the New Testament*, 2 vols. (1754; repr., Kansas City: Beacon Hill Press, 1981), comment on Eph. 2:18.

102 Ibid., comment on 1 John 5:20.

many places in Wesley's publications.[103] There are other examples of Trinitarian summaries in Wesley's *Notes on the New Testament* as well.[104]

In addition to these economic Trinitarian summaries of the essence of Christian faith, Wesley's *Notes* reveal many insights into various aspects of his understanding of the Trinity and the Trinitarian character of Christian faith. In his note on 2 Corinthians 4:4, Wesley astutely observed that "he that sees the Son, sees the Father in the face of Christ. The Son exactly exhibits the Father to us." His comment on 2 Corinthians 5:19 noted that "the whole Godhead" was in Christ reconciling the world. The comment on 1 Corinthians 12:4 presented a Trinitarian reading of the gifts of the Spirit. Wesley's note on the Matthew 6:13 stated that the doxology (and the petitions) of the Lord's prayer "is threefold, and is directed to the Father, Son and Holy Ghost, distinctly; yet is the whole fully applicable both to every Person, and to the ever-blessed and undivided Trinity."[105]

Especially interesting is Wesley's comment on Luke 4:18, where Jesus read from Isaiah, "The Spirit of the Lord is upon me." In the note, Wesley exclaimed: "How is the doctrine of the every-blessed Trinity interwoven even in those scriptures where one would least expect it! How clear a declaration of the great Three-One is there in those very words!" The note on John 16:13 provided yet another illuminating comment: "It is universally allowed, that the Father, Son, and the Holy Ghost dwell in all believers."[106] This insight by Wesley was the theological root of his asking Methodist laypersons in a number of letters whether they had "a clear sense of the presence of the ever-blessed Trinity," something Wesley encountered in the Marquis de Renty.[107] For a time, Wesley thought that those who were perfected in love would encounter this clear sense of the ever-blessed Trinitarian persons.[108] We will return to this subject in chapter 3, when we examine Wesley's doctrine of Christian perfection.

---

103 See ibid., Wesley's comments on 1 John 5:1–20.

104 See ibid., Wesley's comments on 2 Corinthians 13:13, Ephesians 1:17–18, Philippians 4:7, Colossians 2:9–23, Hebrews 1:1–9, and Revelation 3:22, 4:8, and 5:7.

105 See ibid., Wesley's comments on each of these texts.

106 See ibid., Wesley's comments on each of these texts.

107 See Wesley's letter to Jane Bisson dated December 1787, in *The Works of John Wesley*, ed. Thomas Jackson, 14 vols., 3rd ed. (London: Wesleyan Methodist Book Room, 1872; reprint ed. Grand Rapids, MI: Baker Book House, 1986), 13:107. In at least seven of Wesley's letters, he asked the same question in various ways.

108 See Collins's helpful discussion of this in Collins, *Theology of John Wesley*, 147–48.

There are many other brief comments that deal with the Trinity in Wesley's *Notes on the New Testament*.[109] This sampling provides a window into how Wesley's Trinitarian understanding of the essence of Christian faith comes to expression in relation to particular texts in various books of New Testament. Sometimes Wesley's Trinitarian comments are predictable; other times he injected them in unexpected places.

III. Trinitarian Summaries in Letters and Journals and the Source of the Summaries

1. The Lack of Trinitarian Summaries in the Journals and Sermons before 1738

When we turn to Wesley's journals and diaries and his letters, what is particularly noteworthy is when the Trinitarian summaries of vital religion began to appear in these documents. Prior to 1738, there is virtually nothing like the kind of Trinitarian expression of the essence of Christian faith documented in this chapter thus far.

This is also true of Wesley's sermons prior to 1738. There are no robust participatory Trinitarian summaries of the gospel in those early sermons. This does not mean that Wesley did not affirm the doctrine of the Trinity prior to 1738. He was raised in an orthodox Christian home. His father was a High Church Anglican priest for whom the Trinity was a crucial doctrine affirmed in the Anglican Articles, a doctrine that many Anglicans leaders in the seventeenth and eighteenth centuries viewed as worth defending, as noted in chapter 1.

In fact, many of John Wesley's sermons prior to 1738 concluded with standard Anglican Trinitarian ascriptions of glory. His sermon "Death and Deliverance," written immediately after his ordination as a deacon in September 1725, ended with an ascription: "Now to the adorable and ever-blessed Trinity, the Father, the Son and the Holy Ghost, be ascribed, as is most due, all honour, majesty, and dominion, both now and for ever! Amen."[110]

Wesley's second sermon, "Seek First the Kingdom," written in November 1725, ended with a slight variation: "To which adorable and ever-blessed Trinity, Three Persons and one God, be ascribed, as is most due,

---

109 See *Explanatory Notes*, Wesley's comments on Matthew 3:17, John 8:18–19, 17:10, 20:17–18, Romans 1:7–8, 5:5–6, 9:4, and 1 Corinthians 2:8, 15:24, and 15:28 for other examples.

110 See *Works*, 4:214. See 4:204–5 for the historical occasion for the sermon.

all honour, majesty, and dominion, both now and for evermore! Amen!"[111] Some of the Trinitarian ascriptions are brief and sound perfunctory, like the one at the end of his sermon "On Mourning the Dead": "Now to God the Father, the Son, and the Holy Ghost be honour, majesty, and dominion, world without end!"[112]

There is one ascription, at the end of a 1733 manuscript sermon, "The Love of God," that is far more elaborate than the others, and it reflects the kind of economic Trinitarian understanding of the essence of Christian faith that we find in John Wesley's publications beginning in 1738: "Unto God the Father, who first loved us, and made us accepted in the Beloved; unto God the Son, who loved us, and washed us from our sins in his own blood; unto God the Holy Ghost, who sheddeth the love of God abroad in our hearts, be all love and glory for time and for eternity!"[113] In fact, this ascription sounds a lot more like Charles Wesley than John.

The only manuscript we have of this sermon and its elaborate ascription is one that Charles transcribed in September 1736 "from my brother's copy," as Charles noted in a postscript.[114] Did Charles add his own ascription when he copied John's sermon? Further evidence that this ascription may very well have been a later addition by Charles Wesley is the ascription to Charles's own seventh sermon that we know came from Charles himself, a sermon that reflected Charles's own developing Trinitarian understanding of the gospel: "Now to God the Father, who first loved us and made us accepted in the Beloved; to God the Son who loved us and washed us from our sins in his own blood; to God the Holy Ghost who sheddeth abroad the love of God in our hearts, be all praise and glory in time and in eternity."[115] Given how markedly similar the two ascriptions are, it appears that the more elaborate ascription in John's 1733 sermon "The Love of God" was likely a later addition by Charles. Whoever composed this particular ascription of glory, it is different than the other Trinitarian ascriptions in John Wesley's early sermons.

---

111 See ibid., 4:223. See 4:215–16 for the historical occasion for the sermon.

112 See ibid., 4:243.

113 Ibid., 4:345.

114 Ibid., 4:330.

115 See Kenneth G. C. Newport, ed., *Sermons of Charles Wesley: A Critical Edition, with Introduction and Notes* (Oxford: Oxford University Press, 2001), 210. See also Vickers, *Invocation and Assent*, 175–77, for Vickers's astute analysis of the developing economic Trinitarian understanding of Christian faith in this sermon. Vickers also noted that the economic Trinitarian dimension in Charles Wesley's theology developed after 1738. This provides indirect evidence for my suggestion about the source of the Trinitarian dimension in John Wesley's theology.

More than half of the early sermons of John Wesley prior to 1738 concluded with the kind of perfunctory Trinitarian ascriptions noted above, indicating that Wesley clearly affirmed the doctrine of the Trinity during that period.[116] However, it also seems clear by the sheer lack of substantive economic Trinitarian descriptions of the essence of Christian faith in Wesley's sermons and journals prior to 1738 that this Trinitarian dimension was not yet integral to Wesley's thinking prior to 1738, especially in light of the fact documented throughout this chapter that from 1738 on these economic Trinitarian summaries of the gospel appear dozens of times in Wesley's sermons and in more than half of his standard sermons, as well as in other places in his writings.

This raises the question as to why the Trinitarian summaries did not begin until 1738. That question, in turn, points up the issue of the sources of the participatory Trinitarian depiction of vital religion that became so prevalent during 1738 and thereafter. We find intimations of a solution to both questions in Wesley's journals and letters.

2. The Source of the Trinitarian Vision: The Journal Evidence

At the very end of Wesley's first published journal, *An Extract of the Rev. Mr. John Wesley's Journal from His Embarking for Georgia to His Return to London*, we find the first robust Trinitarian summary of vital religion in his journals and diaries.[117] The extract was not published until later, probably the summer of 1740.[118]

At the end of the first journal extract, on Wednesday, February 1, 1738, Wesley landed back at Deal after nearly two and a half years in Georgia. In a disheartened and self-reflective mood, Wesley noted, "I who went to

116 (See *Works,* 4:235, 289, 303, and 359 for additional Trinitarian ascriptions of glory.) The preponderance of Trinitarian ascriptions in the early sermons is in sharp contrast to how few Trinitarian ascriptions are found in Wesley's sermons from 1738 on. There is one at the end of his sermon "Salvation by Faith," preached at Oxford on June 11, 1738 (see *Works,* 1:130). There are only eight concluding Trinitarian ascriptions of glory in all of Wesley many sermons from June 1738 through the end of his life.

117 See *Works,* 18:120ff.

118 Ibid., 18:121–22. According to Frank Baker, Wesley published his journal to aid in vindicating himself from charges leveled against him during his stay in Savannah, Georgia (see Frank Baker, "The Birth of John Wesley's Journal," in *Methodist History* [1970], 8:25–32).

America to convert others, was never myself converted to God."[119] Wesley's dour reflection unfolded over the next two pages.

Toward the end, in the final paragraph of this melancholy self-examination, Wesley revealed the kind of faith that he longed for:

> The faith I want is, "a sure trust and confidence in God, that through the merits of Christ my sins are forgiven, and I reconciled to the favour of God." I want that faith which . . . enables everyone that hath it to cry out, "I live not, but Christ liveth in me. . . ." I want that faith which none can have without knowing that he hath it. . . . For whosoever hath it is "freed from sin." . . . He is freed from fear, "having peace with God through Christ. . . ." And he is freed from doubt, "having the love of God shed abroad in his heart through the Holy Ghost which is given unto him"; which "Spirit itself beareth witness with his spirit, that he is a child of God."[120]

Here we find again the key elements of Wesley's Trinitarian understanding of faith or vital religion evident in the many other Trinitarian summaries examined throughout this chapter. In this February 1, 1738, journal summary, all three persons of the Trinity are actively involved together in the gospel and our participation in it, as the Spirit of God sheds the love of God in Christ abroad in the human heart, leading to trust in God and Christ living in the Christian via the Spirit.

At the time he wrote the journal entry or when he published the extract (1740), looking back on that memorable day in early 1738, Wesley thought he was devoid of the kind of faith he described.[121] What is clear after a careful examination of the Wesley's second journal extract, *An Extract of the Rev. Mr. John Wesley's Journal from February 1, 1737–38. To his Return from Germany*, published not long after the first, is that his melancholy self-examination at the end of the first journal extract set the stage for his discovery of the faith he longed for in the months that followed, as recounted in the second journal extract.[122]

Only a few pages (and a couple of days) later, in his second extract, Wesley noted that Tuesday, February 7, was "[a day] much to be remembered," for Wesley met several Moravians, including Peter Böhler, who became a

119 *Works*, 18:214.

120 Ibid., 18:215–16.

121 In 1774, Wesley added various qualifications to these negative judgements about his spiritual condition upon returning from Georgia in errata (see ibid., 18:214–15).

122 Ibid., 18:217ff.

central figure in Wesley's journal narrative from February 7 through the May 24, 1738, Aldersgate event. Wesley stated that he helped Peter and his friends find lodging near Mr. Hutton's, where Wesley was staying, and added that "from this time I did not willingly lose any opportunity for conversing with them while I stayed in London."[123]

On Friday, February 17, Wesley went to Oxford in Peter Böhler's company and recorded that he conversed much with Böhler, "but I understood him not." By March 5, Böhler had convinced Wesley "of unbelief, of want of 'that faith whereby we are saved,' with full, Christian salvation." Wesley immediately thought he should stop preaching, but Böhler retorted that Wesley should, "Preach faith *till* you have it, and then, *because* you have it, you *will* preach it."[124]

So the next day, Wesley "began preaching this new doctrine" and "offered *salvation by faith alone* to a prisoner under the sentence of death."[125] From this point on in his journal account, Wesley preached the new doctrine of faith whenever he had the chance.[126] But what precisely was "this new doctrine" that Wesley said he received from Böhler and then preached this whole period of time in the spring of 1738 leading up to the Aldersgate event? Given the proliferation of the Trinitarian summaries of the essence of Christian faith we have examined throughout this chapter, including those in Wesley's University sermons from June 1738 into the early 1740s, could this Trinitarian vision of Christian faith be the "new doctrine" Böhler encouraged Wesley to preach? The evidence suggests that the answer is yes, since Wesley explicitly identified Peter Böhler as the source.

On Saturday, April 22, Wesley met with Böhler again. According to his journal entry for that date, Wesley now had

> no objection to what he [Böhler] said about the nature of faith, viz., that it is (to use the words of our Church), "A sure trust and confidence which a man hath in God, that through the merits of Christ *his* sins are forgiven, and *he* is reconciled to the favour of God." Neither could I deny either the happiness or holiness he described as fruits of this living faith. "The Spirit bearath witness with our spirit that we are the children of God" and "He that believeth hath this witness in himself," fully convinced me

123 Ibid., 18:223–24.

124 Ibid., 18:228.

125 Ibid.

126 Ibid., 18:230, 232, 233, 237, 239, and 241 (Sunday, March 19; Sunday, March 26; Sunday, April 2; Tuesday, April 25; Sunday, May 7; Tuesday, May 9; Sunday, May 14; and Sunday, May 21).

> of the former; as "Whatsoever is born of God doth not commit sin," and "Whosoever believeth is born of God," did of the latter. But I could not comprehend what he spoke of *an instantaneous work*. I could not understand how this faith should be given in a moment; how a man could at once be turned . . . from sin and misery to righteousness and joy in the Holy Ghost.[127]

Wesley searched the scriptures, particularly the book of Acts, and found repeated examples of this kind of conversion. On Sunday, April 23, Böhler brought living witnesses who told how God had wrought this kind of faith in their lives.

Whatever other sources and events influenced Wesley's assimilation of this "new faith," Wesley identified Böhler as the person who convinced him of the truthfulness and the desirability of this new faith.[128] In addition, the *content* of this new faith, according to Wesley's journal entry, included more than simply "justification by faith" in contrast to the understanding of religion that Wesley had encountered in the Holy Living Tradition and attempted to embody and live out for more than a decade from 1725 on.

What is important for this study of the Trinitarian dimension of Wesley's vision of Christian faith is that Wesley summarized the content of this "new faith" in that journal entry for April 22, 1738, in vibrant participatory Trinitarian terms: the Spirit assures us that we are reconciled to God through Christ.[129] The content of Wesley's journal entry is nearly identical to what Wesley said about the Trinity and "vital religion" in his sermon "On the Trinity."[130]

On Wednesday, May 3, John Wesley recorded in his journal that his brother, Charles, who had been "strongly averse from what he called 'the new faith,'" "had a long and particular conversation with Peter Böhler. And

---

127 Ibid., 18:233–34.

128 Wesley may have encountered this "new faith" in the Moravians on the ship on the way over to Georgia or in his conversations with them in Georgia. He undoubtedly read about it in Anglican sources like the Book of Homilies or the Book of Common Prayer, and in other theological writings as well, earlier in his theological education at Oxford.

129 Part of what was included in this "new faith," according to Böhler, was freedom from sin, righteousness, and joy in the Spirit. Böhler's account of instantaneous justification seemed to include instantaneous sanctification, which proved to be problematic for Wesley immediately after his Aldersgate awakening. Over time, Wesley clarified and shifted the relation between justification and sanctification away from the way Böhler portrayed it.

130 See *Works*, 2:385–86, for the parallel summary of vital religion in his sermon "On the Trinity."

it now pleased God to open his eyes, so that he also saw clearly what was the nature of that one, true living faith, whereby alone 'through grace we are saved.'"[131] The next day, Böhler left for Carolina, and Wesley's journal stated, "O what a work hath God begun since his coming into England!"[132] So it seems highly probable that Wesley attributed his embracing this "new faith" to the witness of Peter Böhler, even though Wesley likely encountered it elsewhere prior to meeting Böhler.[133]

What is undeniable is that (1) Wesley repeatedly summarized this "new faith" in his journals and in his letters during this period of time in the spring of 1938 in participatory, economic Trinitarian terms; (2) from the spring of 1738 and throughout the rest of his life, Wesley repeatedly summarized the essence of Christian faith in Trinitarian terms in his various publications; and (3) before the spring of 1738, there are virtually no Trinitarian summaries of vital religion in Wesley's publications.

3. Additional Evidence from Letters and Journal Entries in 1738

There is a classic example of this "new faith," expressed in Trinitarian terms, in Wesley's feisty letter to William Law on May 14, 1738. Wesley complained about "the first elements of the gospel of Christ" (according to the Holy Living Tradition) that he had learned from Law: "Under this heavy yoke I might have groaned till death had not an holy man [Peter Böhler?] to whom God lately directed me . . . answered at once: "Believe, and thou shalt be saved. . . . This faith, as well as the salvation it brings, is a free gift of God."[134]

Wesley then further defined what this new faith entailed: it is not a "speculative, notion, airy thing which lives in the head, not the heart." It is "the living, justifying faith in the blood of Jesus. . . . The faith that cleanseth from all sin, that gives up to have free access to the Father, to rejoice in the hope of the glory of God, to have the love of God shed abroad in our hearts by the Holy Ghost which dwelleth in us; and the Spirit itself bearing witness

---

131 *Works*, 18:236, 237.

132 Ibid., 18:237.

133 I am not suggesting that this participatory Trinitarian vision of vital religion was unique to Böhler and the Moravians. It is part of the Christian tradition from the beginning. It can be found in Wesley's own Anglican heritage. The issue here is how Wesley came to accept, to seek, and to fully embrace this participatory, economic Trinitarian vision of vital religion or the essence of Christian faith. The evidence points to the influence of Peter Böhler.

134 *The Works of John Wesley*, ed. Frank Baker, vols. 25–26, "Letters I–II" (New York: Oxford University Press, 1982), 25:540–41.

with our spirit, that we are children of God."[135] Wesley drove home his point: "I beseech you, sir, by the mercies of God, to consider deeply and impartially whether the true reason of your never pressing this upon me was not this, that you had it not yourself!"[136]

What is even more interesting and illuminating is Wesley's final paragraph, which linked what Wesley considered to be Law's lack of love and sour demeanor to Law's lack of this "new faith": "Once more, sir, let me beg you to consider whether your extreme roughness, I might say, sourness, of behaviour, at least on many occasions, can possibly be the fruits of a living faith in Christ."[137] Here we see again the kind of connection between vital, participatory Trinitarian faith and the transformation of human affections and life that flow from it as we saw in Wesley's sermons discussed earlier in this chapter, where he developed what is involved in "having the mind of Christ" and "walking as Christ also walked." Wesley's rather frank, if not uncharitable, letter received a pointed response from William Law.

What is important for our purposes is that the clarity of Wesley's Trinitarian description of this new faith is matched by his passionate frustration that a Christian thinker of William Law's stature had not given Wesley what Wesley now considered "the first elements of the gospel of Christ." Law's letter indicated that he had told Wesley a lot more about "living faith in Christ" than Wesley remembered.[138] Maybe Wesley simply had not been ready to hear it. There are other letters in the spring of 1738 from Wesley's pen with similar Trinitarian summaries of the essence of Christian faith.[139]

This brings us finally to Wesley's account of the Aldersgate event in the second journal extract. The account is familiar, so we will only examine how it confirms the Trinitarian account of the "new faith" Wesley said he received from Peter Böhler.[140]

---

135 Ibid., 25:541–42.

136 Ibid., 25:542. See Wesley's letter, probably to John Gambold, on the eve of the Aldersgate event, for a similar Trinitarian summary of the Christian faith (ibid., 25:550).

137 *Works*, 25:542.

138 See ibid., 25:543–46, for Law's letter.

139 See ibid., 25:669–71, Wesley's letter to Dr. Henry Stebbing; and *Works*, 26:110, for a brief Trinitarian summary in Wesley's letter to the Moravian Church.

140 There has been substantial scholarly conversation about the significance of the Aldersgate event for Wesley and for Methodism. For instance, see Randy L. Maddox, *Aldersgate Reconsidered* (Nashville: Abingdon, 1990). What I am interested in is whether the Trinitarian dimension of this "new faith" Wesley embraced is evident in Wesley's account.

Wesley began his journal account by noting, "What occurred on Wednesday 24, I think best to relate at large, after premising what may make it the better understood."[141] It is clear Wesley believed what happened that day and the events leading up to it were sufficiently significant to warrant a much longer journal account than was his normal practice. What followed is an extended spiritual/theological autobiography, including his encounter with the Holy Living Tradition and all the problems that developed when he tried to live out "the first elements of the gospel of Christ" he learned from William Law, among others.[142]

As Wesley concluded this whole narrative of spiritual/theological struggle leading up to Aldersgate, he noted that along the way he "had many sensible comforts, which are indeed no other than short anticipations of the life of faith." However, the problem was that he "was only 'striving with,' not 'freed from sin.' Neither had I 'the witness of the Spirit with my spirit.'"[143]

At this point, Wesley once again recounted his return to England from Georgia in January 1738 and his relationship with Böhler:

> In my return to England, January 1738, being in imminent danger of death, and very uneasy on that account, I was strongly convinced that the cause of that uneasiness was unbelief, and that the gaining a true, living faith, was the "one thing needful" for me. But I still fixed not this faith on its right object: I meant only faith in God, not faith in or through Christ [note the participatory character of this faith]. . . . So that when Peter Böhler, whom God prepared for me as soon as I came to London, affirmed of true faith in Christ (which is but one) that it had those two fruits inseparably attending it, "dominion over sin, and constant peace from a sense of forgiveness." I was quite amazed, and looked upon it as a new Gospel.[144]

Wesley noted that he had hard time accepting this "new Gospel" until he confirmed that it was in scripture and something we could "experience"

141 *Works*, 18:242.

142 Ibid., 18:243–47. A comparison of this section of Wesley's journal and his letter to William Law reveals a number of commonalities. For example, Wesley noted in the journal the same deep sense of burden in his attempt to live out this Holy Living scheme of "Gospel" that we saw in his letter to Law: "I dragged on heavily, finding no comfort or help therein" (ibid., 18:246).

143 Ibid., 18:247.

144 Ibid., 18:247–48.

(participate in) in the present.[145] So by God's grace, Wesley resolved to seek this "new Gospel" by renouncing any and all dependence on his own righteousness or works, and by using the means of grace and prayer so as to wait "for this very thing, justifying, saving faith, a full reliance on the blood of Christ shed for *me*; a trust in him as *my* Christ, as *my* sole justification, sanctification, and redemption."[146]

At this point in his journal account, Wesley turned to the events that transpired on May 24, beginning at five in the morning, when he opened his New Testament to 2 Peter 2:4, "There are given unto us exceeding great and precious promises, even that ye should be partakers of the divine nature." The text underscores the participatory character of this new gospel. That evening at the Moravian society on Aldersgate Street, where someone was reading Luther's Preface to his commentary on Romans, Wesley states: "About quarter before nine, while he was describing the change which God works in the hearts through faith in Christ, I felt my heart strangely warmed. I felt I did trust in Christ, Christ alone for salvation, and an assurance was given to me that he had taken away *my* sins, even *mine*, and saved *me* from the law of sin and death."[147]

The long journal account for May 24 points to Böhler as the source of this "new Gospel," or at least Böhler convinced Wesley that it was scriptural and that God could make it real in Wesley's own life. This new gospel entailed more than a transition from the Holy Living Tradition to a more Protestant understanding of justification by grace and faith or the incorporation of justification by grace and faith into the developing fabric of Wesley's understanding of Christian faith and the order or way of salvation. There is a deep participatory Trinitarian dimension to this "new faith": grace and faith are not simply *in* Christ but *through* Christ. The love of God that reaches out

145 Wesley discovered that it was in scripture, and Böhler produced Moravians who testified to the reality of this new faith in their lives: "They added with one mouth that this faith was the gift, the free gift of God, and that he would surely bestow it upon every soul who earnestly and perseveringly sought it. I was now thoroughly convinced" (ibid., 18:248).

146 Ibid., 18:248–49.

147 Ibid., 18:249–50. Wesley's preoccupation with his own "experience" made it clear rather quickly that Böhler's promise of "dominion over sin, and constant peace from a sense of forgiveness" was partial at best. See Maddox, *Responsible Grace*, 144–45; and Collins, *Theology of John Wesley*, 199–200 and 208–22, for analysis of Wesley's relation to Böhler and Wesley's disappointment at the lack of the full fruit Böhler's new gospel promised. What is important for our discussion is the Trinitarian dimension of this new gospel Wesley embraced.

to humanity through the grace of our Lord Jesus Christ is realized in human lives by a change that the Holy Spirit works in our hearts and lives so that we participate in the divine nature. The economic Trinity is the source and substance of this new gospel of salvation by grace and faith. The Trinitarian dimension to this "new Gospel" or "new faith" is evident in Wesley's journals and letters from the spring of 1738 on.

IV. Conclusion

Even though Wesley clearly affirmed the doctrine of the Trinity and included Trinitarian ascriptions of glory at the end of more than half of his early sermons prior to 1738, we do not find this participatory, economic Trinitarian dimension in his accounts of vital religion or the essence of Christian faith in his sermons, journals and diaries, and letters until the spring of 1738. However, after the spring of 1738 and throughout the remainder of his life in many of his publications, Wesley repeatedly summarized the essence of Christian faith in Trinitarian terms.

The sheer number of these Trinitarian summaries from 1738 on discloses how deeply the participatory, economic Trinitarian dimension of Wesley's theology is embedded in his vision of Christian faith and life. Wesley depicted this Trinitarian essence of Christian faith as entering into the "throne room" of the human heart, the root of all vital religion, and even labeled it the *analogy of faith* or summary of the central motif of the Bible.

These Trinitarian summaries of vital religion, and the central role they play in so many of Wesley's sermons and other publications, provide a significant body of evidence that Wesley understood the essence of Christian faith in evangelical, doxological, participatory, economic Trinitarian terms, so much so that I think it is fair to say that it is a fundamental characteristic of his theology.[148] In addition, Wesley's linking the doctrine of the Trinity so closely to the essence of Christian faith, life, discipleship, and worship provided a radically different way to think about the Trinity and the Trinitarian dimension

148 At times Wesley's summaries of vital religion focused on the soteriological outworking of the activity of the Trinitarian persons and do not contain a Trinitarian dimension. These soteriological summaries of vital religion do not undermine the argument of this chapter, since Wesley noted in his sermon "On the Trinity" that one does not have to always "advert" or be explicit about the Trinitarian dimension, because that dimension "is implied" in what a Christian believes (*Works*, 2:385). Wesley's many Trinitarian summaries of vital religion make clear that the Trinitarian dimension underlies and undergirds salvation even when he does not explicitly reference that dimension in his discussion of salvation.

of Christian faith than did the defenders of the Trinity who disconnected the Trinity from vital religion during the Trinitarian controversies and turned the doctrine of the Trinity into an esoteric intellectual artifact. Wesley reconnected the Trinity with vibrant Christian faith, worship, and discipleship and closed the gap between them opened up by the defenders of the doctrine.

What about the *ordo salutis*? Does Wesley understand not simply the essence of the gospel but the entire fabric or pattern of our salvation in Trinitarian terms? Chapter 3 will examine the Trinitarian dimension of the Wesley's understanding of the order or way of salvation.

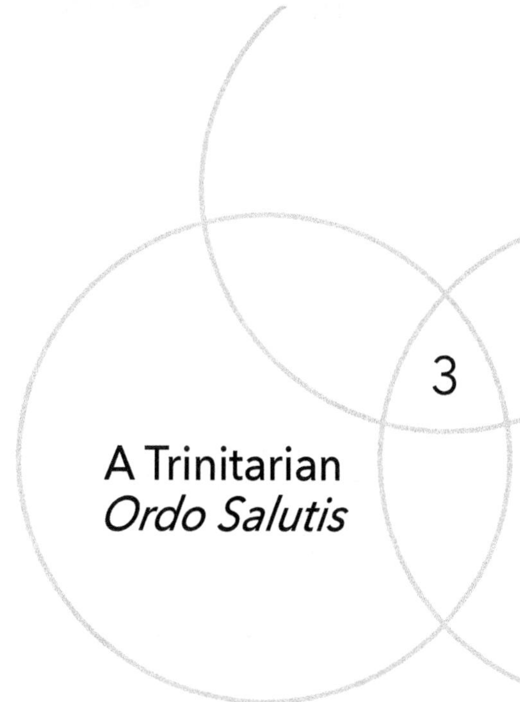

3

A Trinitarian *Ordo Salutis*

Introduction

The preceding chapter documented and analyzed Wesley's participatory Trinitarian summaries of the gospel throughout his sermons and in various other publications. The sheer preponderance and consistency of these summaries provide evidence that what Wesley said about the connection between "the Three-One God" and "vital religion" in his sermon "On the Trinity" reverberates throughout his understanding of Christian faith from the spring of 1738 on.[1] Our most basic encounter with the gospel always involves the presence and activity of all three persons of the Trinity. When someone encounters the Triune God in the gospel, according to Wesley, that person

> may be properly said *to live*: God having quickened him by his Spirit, he is alive to God through Jesus Christ. . . . God is continually breathing, as it were, upon his soul, and his soul is breathing unto God. Grace is descending into his heart, and prayer and praise ascending to heaven. And by this intercourse between God and humanity, this fellowship with the Father and the Son, as by a kind of spiritual respiration, the life of God

1 *The Works of John Wesley*, ed. Albert C. Outler, vols. 1–4, *Sermons* (Nashville: Abingdon, 1984–87), 2:385.

> in the soul is sustained: and the child of God grows up, till he comes to "the full measure of the stature of Christ."[2]

The Triune God breathes God's very life into us through the gospel so that we are set free to breathe back prayer, praise, and love to God, and love and fellowship toward those around us.

However, does Wesley understand not simply the essence of the gospel but the entire fabric or pattern of our salvation from beginning to end in Trinitarian terms? This chapter examines what Wesley said about the Trinitarian dimension of the order of salvation from prevenient grace to Wesley's vision of our eschatological destiny.

I. Wesley's Theological/Spiritual Struggle with the Holy Living Tradition

After years of reading and reflection, Wesley became convinced that there is a rich progressive pattern to the Christian life or the way God's grace transforms humanity in and through the gospel. Wesley found this progressive order in scripture, in the theology of the church, in the lives of the saints through the ages, and also in the lives of countless Methodists during his own lifetime, though there are all kinds of individual and communal variations to this unfolding pattern of God's grace in particular human lives.[3]

---

2 Ibid., 2:193.

3 There has been scholarly debate about whether to call Wesley's understanding of this unfolding pattern of activity on the part of the Triune God and the human soteriological transformation that results an *ordo* or a *via salutis*. Here I side with Kenneth Collins, who argues persuasively for retaining the language of *ordo salutis* over *via salutis* (see Kenneth J. Collins, *The Theology of John Wesley: Holy Love and the Shape of Grace* [Nashville: Abingdon, 2007], 307–12). Randy Maddox sees the *ordo* language as far more tied to Reformed Scholasticism than do I. The use of "*ordo*" does not have to connote a "set of abrupt transitions in status," or "discrete states," or deny or downplay the "possibility of regression," as Maddox contends (see Maddox, *Responsible Grace: John Wesley's Practical Theology* [Nashville: Kingwood Books, 1994], 157–58). The term *ordo* is more precise, and the content of what it means in relation to Wesley's vision of the unfolding pattern of God's grace in the Christian life must filled in by what Wesley actually said, not by whatever Scholastic overtones some might sense in the term. Theological language is malleable and defined by its use in relation to a particular theological figure.

I also agree with Collins that Wesley's understanding of the unfolding pattern of salvation was highly normed by scripture and the theological tradition of the church through the ages (Collins, *Theology of John Wesley*, 308–9). The pattern did not arise simply from "the pastoral needs" of the revival movement (see Maddox,

1. The Holy Living Tradition: Salvation as **Devotio**

Wesley's particular understanding of this pattern of grace arose out of a laborious and protracted spiritual and theological struggle in his own life that began in earnest in 1725, when he sensed a call into ministry and started to prepare for ordination. At that time, Wesley discovered the Holy Living Tradition found in Thomas à Kempis, Jeremy Taylor, and William Law. As Albert Outler astutely observed, despite "all their diversity, these three had actually taught him the same thing: that the Christian life is *devotio*, the consecration of the whole man in love to God and neighbor in the full round of life and death."[4]

Wesley's summary statement from his journal of what he learned from the Holy Living from his journal is revealing: "I saw that giving even *all my life* to God . . . would profit me nothing unless I gave my *heart*, yea, *all my heart* to him. . . . I determined, through his grace (the absolute necessity of which I was deeply sensible of) to be *all-devoted* to God: to give him *all* my soul, my body, and my substance."[5] In its simplest form, this understanding of the *ordo salutis* views the Christian faith and life as essentially the devotion of the whole person in love for God and for neighbor in all things, always only on the basis of grace.

We see the outworking of this set of ultimate beliefs in the trajectory of Wesley's life and ministry in the late 1720s and 1730s. He immersed himself in a flurry of activity, using all the means of grace, caring for widows, visiting prisons, sharing his faith, helping the poor, etc., until his life was a bit of a mess. In his "Aldersgate" journal entry for May 24, 1738, Wesley described this period of his life:

> I cried out to God for help and resolved not to prolong the time of obeying him, as I had never done before. And by my continued *endeavour to keep his whole law,* inward and outward, *to my utmost power,* I was persuaded that I should be accepted of him, and that I was even then in a state of salvation.

Responsible Grace, 158). In the end, despite all the individual variations, as well as the possibility of regression, Wesley saw a normative progressive pattern to the realization of God's transforming grace in human life from prevenient grace through Christian perfection and final glorification in our eschatological destiny.

4 See Outler's introduction in *John Wesley*, ed. A. C. Outler (New York: Oxford University Press, 1964), 7.

5 Ibid.

> In 1730 I began visiting prisons, assisting the poor and sick in town, and doing what other good I could by my presence or my little fortune to the bodies and souls of all me. To this end I abridged myself of all superfluities, and many that are called necessities of life. I soon became a "by-word" for doing so. . . . The next spring I began observing the Wednesday and Friday fasts commonly observed in the ancient church. . . . I diligently strove against all sin. . . . I carefully used . . . all the means of grace at all opportunities. I omitted no occasion for doing good. . . . And all this I knew to be nothing unless it was directed toward inward holiness. Accordingly this, the image of God, was what I aimed at in all, by doing his will, not my own. Yet when, after continuing some years in this course, I apprehended myself to be near death, I could not find that all this gave me any comfort, nor any assurance of acceptance with God. At this I was then not a little surprised.[6]

What is conspicuously missing in this quotation is any participatory Trinitarian primacy in Wesley's vision of devotion as the Christian way of salvation. There is nothing about fellowship with the Father and the Son through the Spirit creating a kind of spiritual respiration that sustains the life of God in the Christian pilgrimage that we find in Wesley's sermons and other writings after the spring of 1738, as documented and described in chapter 2.

Wesley's spiritual and theological perspective during these years leading up to 1738 drove him into frenzy of activity that left him often unsure of where he stood with God. His lackluster experience in America as a chaplain to the colony in Georgia and a missionary to the Native Americas in 1736–37 landed Wesley back in England in 1738 a deeply disillusioned and spiritually struggling man.

2. Wesley's Encounter with Peter Böhler: A Reordering of the Ordo Salutis

As noted in the last chapter, in the spring of 1738 Wesley embraced a rather different understanding of the vital religion through the influence of Peter Böhler, one that included a profound Trinitarian dimension. What Böhler taught Wesley was not simply that justification precedes sanctification as the basis upon which sanctification takes place but also that the essence of Christian faith is participatory and Trinitarian. Restoration to loving fellowship and union with the Triune God that entails justification and new birth

---

6 *The Works of John Wesley*, ed. W. Reginald Ward and Richard P. Heitzenrater, vols. 18–24, *Journals and Diaries I–VII* (Nashville: Abingdon, 1988–2003), 18:244–45.

is participatory, and it sustains the life of God in the human soul throughout the Christian life.

Moravian Pietism was Lutheran in its emphasis that we are justified and regenerated by grace, by faith, and by Christ alone. Collins correctly notes that the new faith Böhler communicated to Wesley included two fruits: (1) *happiness*, or peace through a profound realization of forgiveness, and (2) *holiness*, or power to overcome sin through union with Christ in the Spirit.[7] Wesley summarized it this way in his June 1738 university sermon "Salvation by Faith," examined in chapter 2: "Christian faith is then not only an assent to the whole gospel of Christ, but also a full reliance on the blood of Christ . . . a recumbency upon him as our atonement and our life, as *given for us*, and *living in us*."[8]

This new emphasis on faith as trust in Christ *given for us* and *living in us* shifted Wesley's understanding of the relation between justification and sanctification. In so doing, this shift changed the fundamental characteristic of the essence of Christian faith and life from *devotion* aspiring toward communion with God, as Wesley learned from the Holy Living Tradition, to *love* rooted in restored communion with Father and the Son in the Spirit, and to *gratitude* for the blessed Triune God's unstinting love for us in the gospel, though devotion remains as an expression of love.

So it is no coincidence that Wesley, in his sermon "On Zeal," placed *love* upon the throne, "which is erected in the inmost soul" and all the other holy tempers around love in a circle.[9] This shift to grateful love was also why Wesley repeatedly emphasized throughout his sermons and other publications that we simply cannot love without first being loved by the Triune God, who is a fellowship of love within God's own Trinitarian life. Wesley ended his sermon "On Zeal," "be most zealous for *love*, the queen of all graces, the highest perfection in earth or heaven, the very image of the invisible God. . . . For 'God is love; and he that dwelleth in love, dwelleth in God and God in him.'"[10]

---

7 Collins, *Theology of John Wesley*, 165–70, 199–200. Collins is also correct that Wesley drew upon a wider acquaintance with German Pietism. Wesley had read Johann Arndt's *True Christianity* after he arrived at the Colony in Georgia and later extracted it and included it in his *Christian Library* (ibid., 207–15). See John Wesley, ed., *A Christian Library: Consisting of Extracts from and Abridgements of the Choicest Pieces of Practical divinity which have been Published in the English Language*, 50 vols. (Bristol: Felix Farley, 1749–55).

8 See *Works*, 1:121.

9 *Works*, 3:313.

10 Ibid., 3:321.

This whole theological reorientation altered Wesley's pre-1738 understanding of the order of salvation and injected a deep Trinitarian dimension into it. We are first loved by God through Christ in the Spirit and reclaimed from guilt and sin by God's activity on our behalf in the gospel in justification. Our lives become radically grounded and reordered by this love of God in Christ shed abroad in our hearts by the Spirit so that we return love toward God and others in gratitude, worship, and thanksgiving, by a kind of spiritual respiration, breathing in Christ *given for us* and *living in us* and breathing back love of God and neighbor out of love at the center moving outward in all the other holy tempers to works of mercy and piety, or "having the mind of Christ" and "walking as Christ walked" as noted in chapter 2.

The whole series of events in the spring of 1738 had a profound effect upon Wesley spiritually, personally, and theologically, though it took some time for him to sort through all the issues involved. In the end, Wesley's sifting through these issues led him to break with the Moravians at crucial points. It is in his reordering of the various elements constituting the *ordo salutis* that Wesley made a significant contribution to the church and its theological reflection. What is noteworthy is that Wesley's reconceptualization of the *ordo salutis* was also profoundly Trinitarian, consistent with what he said about the Trinity in relation to vital religion and consistent with his many Trinitarian summaries of Christian faith examined in the previous chapter.

II. Wesley's Trinitarian Understanding of Grace

Wesley did not simply reject the Holy Living Tradition. Rather, in light of his "new faith" in Christ, he brought the best of what he had learned from it back into his reordered vision of the *ordo salutis*, but as the way we express our grateful response to God's love for us in Christ realized in our lives via the Holy Spirit. To put it into theological terms, Wesley now placed justification and regeneration before sanctification, as the necessary condition under which real sanctification takes place. He then reinterpreted the process of sanctification (and ministry) to be as fully by Christ, by grace, and by faith as justification itself, though always including our free human response in gratitude, love, devotion, and obedience, and always involving a deep Trinitarian dimension. Because God's Triune grace frees humanity for free response, Wesley made a place for "avoiding evil, doing good, and using the means of grace" on the basis of grace, even before justification/regeneration, as the best way to "wait" for the Triune God to lead people into the fullness of Christian faith and life.

Wesley developed his *ordo salutis* in terms of God's grace and its differentiated pattern in our lives. Yet when Wesley spoke of prevenient grace, convicting grace, justifying and regenerating grace, sanctifying grace, and perfecting grace, he did not mean that there are different *kinds* of grace mediated to Christians at different stages of the Christian life. All grace, for Wesley, is always and only the grace of our Lord Jesus Christ that flows from the love of God the Father and is realized in our lives through the communion of the Holy Spirit. The Trinitarian dimension embedded in Wesley's understanding of the *ordo salutis* strengthened and deepened the connection between the doctrine of the Trinity and vibrant Christian faith and life, which was lost for many in England in the course of the Trinitarian controversies that turned the doctrine of the Trinity into an esoteric intellectual artifact, as we saw in chapter 1. Wesley reconnected the Trinity with the order of salvation from the first dawning of prevenient grace through the Trinitarian eschatological destiny of all creation in union and communion with the Father and the Son through the Holy Spirit and provided the early Methodists with an all-encompassing vision of the Triune God as the Source, Active Agency, and Telos of the new creation.

Grace, for Wesley, is not merely God's favor, nor is it some kind of spiritual substance mediated to us through the church. Grace is the Triune God active on our behalf in the gospel. Grace, for Wesley, is Christocentric, pneumatological, and Trinitarian. It is constituted by the life, ministry, death, and resurrection of Jesus Christ, mediated to us through the Holy Spirit, but always involving all three Trinitarian persons throughout Jesus Christ's work and throughout our participation in it via the Holy Spirit.

Listen to Wesley's profound participatory and Christocentric definition of all grace from his tract *Thoughts on Christian Perfection*, published not long after the London Conference of 1759: "Christ does not give life to the soul separate from, but in and with, himself. Hence his words are equally true of all men, *in whatever state of grace they are* [my emphasis]: 'As the branch cannot bear fruit of itself, except it abide in the vine, no more can ye except ye abide in me. . . . [W]ithout,' or *separate* from, 'me, ye can do nothing.' Whatever grace we receive, it is a free gift from him. . . . We have this grace not *from* Christ but in him."[11] We are only "in Christ" through the fellowship of the Spirit who unites us not only to Christ but through Christ to the Father. For Wesley, there is no other grace than one that is identical with the Triune God's economic activity in the gospel.

It is true, as some secondary sources emphasize, that Wesley spoke on occasion of grace in pneumatological terms. However, when one examines

11 *The Works of John Wesley*, ed. Paul Wesley Chilcote and Kenneth J. Collins, vol. 13, *Doctrinal and Controversial Treatises II* (Nashville: Abingdon, 2013), 60.

the context in which Wesley referenced the Spirit in relation to grace and when one looks at what he said elsewhere, as in the text quoted above, it is clear that Wesley had a conception of grace that involves all three Trinitarian persons.[12]

For example, in his sermon "The Witness of Our Spirit," Wesley said that we could never gain simplicity and sincerity "but by the 'knowledge of Jesus Christ'; or 'by the grace of God' another expression of nearly the same import." Here Wesley closely associated Christ and God and grace. Wesley continued his definition of grace: "By 'the grace of God' is sometimes to be understood that free love, that unmerited mercy, by which I, a sinner, through the merits of Christ am now reconciled to God."[13] Here again we see the first and second persons of the Trinity associated with grace in this sense.

It is at this point that Wesley turned to the third person of the Trinity in relation to grace:

> But in this place it rather means the power of God the Holy Ghost which "worketh in us both to will and to do of his good pleasure." As soon as ever the grace of God (in the former sense, his pardoning love) is manifested in our soul, the grace of God (in the latter sense, the power of his Spirit) takes place therein. And now we can perform, through God, what to man was impossible.[14]

This sounds like Wesley at least distinguished one form of grace that is predominantly pneumatological.[15] But as is often the case, this is not all Wesley said even in the very paragraph in which the last quotation appeared. Listen to how Wesley continued his train of thought in the very next sentences

---

12 See Maddox, *Responsible Grace*, 84–86, for a discussion of grace as pneumatological power. Maddox is correct in much of what he wrote. Clearly Wesley wanted to combine (1) grace as pardon or unmerited love/forgiveness, and (2) grace as power that heals us and frees us for growth in love for God and others. Grace is the very presence and activity of the living God in our lives. Wesley does have a conception of "uncreated grace" similar to the Eastern Orthodox viewpoint, as Maddox rightly points out. But is it essentially pneumatological, as Maddox seems to think? Here I think Wesley's view is more fully Trinitarian, as will become clear by the end of this section.

13 *Works,* 1:309.

14 Ibid.

15 Maddox provides this very quotation as evidence for the uniting of grace as pardon and power and for viewing grace as power in pneumatological terms (see Maddox, *Responsible Grace*, 85).

after the pneumatological quotation above: "Now we can order our conversation aright. We can do all things in the light and power of that love, through Christ which strengtheneth us."[16] Here Wesley affirmed that the very same grace understood as "the power of the Spirit" is also Christological, for it is Christ who strengthens us in and through the Spirit who unites us to Christ! The only way to make sense of what Wesley said about grace when we examine the entire paragraph is that his understanding of grace involves perichoretic coactivity of Christ and the Spirit, and of the Father as well.[17]

Remember what Wesley said in his comments on John 16:13 from his *Notes on the New Testament*: "The Father, Son and the Holy Spirit dwell in all believers."[18] In his "Letter to a Roman Catholic," Wesley stated that the "eternal Spirit of God, equal with the Father and the Son," is "the *immediate cause* [my emphasis] of all holiness in us; enlightening our understandings, rectifying our wills and affections, renewing our natures, uniting our persons to Christ, assuring us of the adoption of sons, leading us in our actions, purifying and sanctifying our souls and bodies to a full and eternal enjoyment of God."[19] It seems clear that in naming the Father and the Son in this text along with the Spirit, Wesley's intent was to acknowledge that all three persons are involved.

In doing so, Wesley stressed the full deity of the Spirit, along with the Father and the Son, since it is the Spirit who immediately unites us to Christ and through Christ with the Father. Here Wesley followed the early church's emphasis that only God can save and that the Holy Spirit's integral presence and activity on our behalf in salvation implies the full deity of the Spirit, who, along with the Father and Son, is to be trusted and praised. There is nothing in this text indicating that grace as transforming power is the provenance only of the third person of the Trinity. Wesley did not use the term "perichoresis," but he clearly intended the Trinitarian "co-activity" designated by this theological term.[20]

There are many examples where Wesley interpreted grace as power in economic Trinitarian terms. In his sermon "The Repentance of Believers,"

---

16 *Works,* 1:309.

17 It makes one wonder whether the predilection toward a pneumatological reading of grace as the power of God in secondary sources on Wesley's theology betrays more the convictions of the writers of the secondary sources than an accurate portrayal of Wesley himself.

18 John Wesley, *Explanatory Notes upon the New Testament,* 2 vols. (1754; repr., Kansas City: Beacon Hill Press, 1981), vol 1., comment on John 16:13.

19 Outler, ed., *Wesley,* 495.

20 See Maddox, *Responsible Grace,* 139, 322.

Wesley said it this way: by "faith we feel the power of Christ every moment . . . whereby we are enabled to continue in spiritual life." Then Wesley concluded the paragraph by quoting from the Book of Common Prayer: "Thus doth he [God the Father] 'cleanse the thoughts of their hearts, by the inspiration of his Holy Spirit, that they may perfectly love him, and worthily magnify his holy name.'" In the paragraph that follows this one, Wesley summarized his whole point again in Christological terms: "By faith we receive the power of God in Christ, purifying our hearts and cleansing our hands. . . . Repentance says, 'Without him I can do nothing': faith says, 'I can do all things through Christ strengthening me.'"[21]

In his "Sermon on the Mount, IX," Wesley did not mention grace or power but rather spoke of the righteousness of God imparted (not simply imputed) to us in economic Trinitarian terms. Wesley was dealing with the Epistle to the Romans where Paul speaks of those ignorant of God's righteousness. Wesley wrote: "They were ignorant . . . not only of the righteousness of Christ, imputed to every believer. . . . [T]hey were ignorant of that inward righteousness, of that holiness of heart, which is with the utmost propriety termed 'God's righteousness,' as being both his own free gift through Christ, and his own work, by his almighty Spirit."[22]

Seldom do we find in Wesley statements about grace as power attributed solely to the third person of the Trinity. When we examine the entire context of even his pneumatological depictions of grace, we find that Wesley most often referenced the other Trinitarian persons as well.

Along similar lines, a number of secondary sources portray Wesley as associating justification with the second person of the Trinity and sanctification with the third person of the Trinity.[23] It is astonishing how often secondary sources lift out of Wesley's sermon "Justification by Faith" a single text to justify these associations. In that sermon, Wesley noted that justification is remitting the punishment our sins deserve and restoring us to God's favor. Then comes the oft-quoted text: justification "is not being made actually just and righteous. This is *sanctification*, which is indeed in some degree the immediate *fruit* of justification but nevertheless is a distinct gift of God and of a totally different nature. The one implies what God *does for us* through his Son; the other what he *works in us* by his Spirit."[24] After reading

---

21 *Works,* 1:349–50. See also the Trinitarian depiction of grace as power at the beginning of the section (ibid., 1:347).

22 Ibid., 1:643.

23 For one example, see Maddox, *Responsible Grace*, 84–86.

24 *Works,* 1:187.

this quotation many times in secondary sources, when I began my research into Wesley's theology and read through all of Wesley's sermons and other publications, I was surprised at how seldom Wesley made statements that associate justification with Christ and sanctification with the Spirit.

Indeed, Wesley's point in this text was not primarily about *which* person of the Trinity does *what* part of the *ordo salutis*. His point was to make a clear distinction between justification and sanctification and to underscore what is the right relation between the two, contra other Christian traditions that confuse justification and sanctification or collapse one into the other or make sanctification the basis for justification or turn justification into a substitute for sanctification, as the rest of the sermon made clear.

In fact, when we examine the rest of the sermon, we discover that Wesley associated the Father and the Son with sanctification and the Spirit with justification. Just two paragraphs before the oft-cited quotation noted above, Wesley said this: "For the sake of his well-beloved Son, of what he hath done and suffered for us [Wesley's theological shorthand for the active and passive obedience of Christ], God now vouchsafes . . . both to remit the punishment due to our sins [justification] . . . and to restore our dead souls to spiritual life [regeneration/sanctification]."[25] Here Wesley noted that the Father and Son are at work in sanctification, restoring our dead souls to spiritual life.

Several pages later in that same sermon Wesley dealt with the question, Who are those who are justified? His answer: the ungodly, who are incapable of pleasing God because they cannot do anything out of the real love for God. They are the ones who need to know the love of God in Christ that justifies us. Wesley continued: "This love cannot be in us till we receive the 'Spirit of adoption, crying in our hearts, Abba, Father.' If, therefore, God doth not 'justify the ungodly,' . . . then hath Christ died in vain."[26] Wesley noted the role of the Spirit in our justification whereby we are adopted in Christ into the family of God, transferred in status from guilty sinners to forgiven and pardoned children of God, a change in status and awareness that clearly involved the activity of all three persons of the Trinity.

At the beginning of Wesley's sermon "The New Birth," he provided a brief summary of the "doctrines within the whole compass of Christianity" that "may be properly termed fundamental," noting that "they are doubtless these two—the doctrine of justification, and that of the new birth." Wesley went on to use the phraseology that the one is what God does for us, the

---

25 Ibid., 1:186.
26 Ibid., 1:193.

other what God works in us. He linked the first with the redemption in Jesus and the second with the Spirit: "In the moment we are justified by the grace of God through the redemption that is in Jesus we are also "born of the Spirit."[27] Notice the economic Trinitarian trio of God, Jesus, and the Spirit.

However, when Wesley got into the theological and spiritual details, as he fleshed out what the new birth actually entails, he did so in a fully participatory Trinitarian manner: "And now he may properly be said *to live*: God having quickened him by his Spirit, he is alive to God through Jesus Christ. He lives . . . 'life' which 'is hid with Christ in God.'" Then Wesley launched into his account of grace as God "breathing" life into our souls, and our souls breathing back prayer and praise: fellowship with the Father and the Son via the Spirit is what sustains the life of God through sanctification toward Christian perfection."[28]

In his essay "A Blow at the Root, of Christ Stabb'd in the House of His Friends," Wesley said it this way: "'But ye are washed, but ye are sanctified,' as well as, 'justified in the name of the Lord Jesus and by the Spirit of our God.' You are really changed; you are not only *accounted* righteous, but actually *made, righteous.* . . . [T]he inward power . . . 'of the Spirit of life in Christ Jesus hath made *you* free.'"[29] This statement is noteworthy because of the close association of the Spirit of life *in* Christ Jesus and also because justification and sanctification both take place through the agency of the Christ and the Spirit.

While Wesley provided a few (very few) summaries that associate justification with the Son and sanctification with the Spirit, these terse statements cannot be cut off from the fuller Trinitarian accounts that Wesley provided when he developed the details of each of these doctrines. Often the Trinitarian dimension is present in the very places in his publications where, if one looks at the entire context, he associated justification with Christ and sanctification with the Spirit.

Indeed, very seldom do we find in Wesley statements linking justification to the second person of the Trinity and sanctification to the third person of the Trinity, without additional statements within a paragraph or two that implicate all three persons of the Trinity as involved in these facets of the *ordo salutis*. In fact, far more characteristic of Wesley is the kind of robust fully Trinitarian understanding of salvation and the entire *ordo salutis* documented throughout this monograph.

---

27 Ibid., 2:187.

28 Ibid., 2:193.

29 Outler, ed., *Wesley* 381.

In light of the many Trinitarian accounts of grace in general, of the essence of Christian faith, should we not interpret the few other statements that isolate one of the persons of the Trinity and make some aspect of grace the provenance of that particular person in light of Wesley's wider participatory, economic Trinitarian perspective? When we do so, Wesley's statements of grace as pneumatological power and justification as what Christ does for us become what I suspect they really are, simply another example of Wesley's theological shorthand that in no way indicates that Wesley had a serial or tag-team understanding of the Trinity rooted in systematic application of the law of appropriations.[30]

We will now examine what Wesley said about the various elements that comprise his understanding of the *ordo salutis*. For Wesley, the one grace of God in Christ our Lord that comes to us in the fellowship of the Holy Spirit works in a variety of ways in our lives at different stages in our Christian growth in discipleship. It was this pattern or order of God's grace that helped the early Methodists make sense of their spiritual pilgrimage of faith. The *ordo salutis* provided them with a vision of how the Christian life unfolded and developed. It enabled the early Methodists to discern where they were in their pilgrimage of faith and also created expectation and hope for what God still planned to do in and through them in the future. Wesley developed the order of salvation and communicated it to the Methodist movement for this very purpose. Furthermore, as will become clear in chapter 5, Wesley developed the mission, the ministries, and the polity of early Methodism in light of this pattern of grace that God longs to actualize in the lives of all people.

---

30 John Fletcher deployed the ideas associated with the law of appropriations and even spoke of three ages: the Old Testament being the age of the Father; the Gospels, or Jesus's earthly historical appearance in space and time, as the age of the Son; and the church as the age of the Spirit. One wonders whether Fletcher's influence on American Methodism is part of the reason why so many American Methodists have a predilection for this kind of serial understanding of the Trinity.

I fully agree with Thomas. F. Torrance, who argued that the law of appropriations was developed "by Latin theology to redress an unbalanced essentialist approach to the doctrine of the Trinity from the One Being of God, which obscured the evangelical approach from the economic Trinity" (see Torrance, *The Christian Doctrine of God: One Being Three Persons* [Edinburgh: T & T Clark, 1996], 200).

It is no coincidence that it has been primarily Latin theologians who have appealed to "analogies" to try to render the doctrine of the Trinity intelligible. Those who follow the Western essentialist approach, focused so heavily on the doctrine of the One God, have had recurrent difficulty differentiating the Trinitarian persons and therefore have repeatedly turned to the law of appropriations and analogies to render the Trinity intelligible.

We are now in a position to look at Wesley's mature Trinitarian conceptualization of the *ordo salutis*.

III. Wesley's Trinitarian Understanding of the *Ordo Salutis*

Wesley did not always speak of the *ordo salutis* in explicit Trinitarian terms. Neither does scripture, nor do other Trinitarian theologies. A theology does not need to explicitly identify the participatory, economic Trinitarian coactivity every time it treats an aspect of salvation for that theology to be Trinitarian. But there should be significant acknowledgment of the Trinitarian activity that is at the center of the themes that comprise the *ordo salutis*. That is precisely what we find in Wesley's publications: repeated expression of the economic Trinitarian dimension throughout the order of salvation.[31]

1. The Image of God and Sin

In chapter 2, we examined how, in his sermon "The End of Christ's Coming," Wesley developed a Trinitarian understanding of humanity's relation to the Triune God prior to the Fall. According to Wesley, "God created man, not only in his *natural*, but likewise in his own *moral* image. He created him not only *in knowledge*, but also in righteousness and true holiness. . . . As a free agent he steadily chose whatever was good, according to the direction of his understanding. In so doing he was unspeakably happy, dwelling in God and God in him, having an uninterrupted fellowship with the Father and the Son through the Spirit, and having a continual testimony of his conscience that all his ways were good and acceptable to God."[32] There is a similar account

31 See Maddox, *Responsible Grace*; and Collins, *Theology of John Wesley*. The two books are most helpful read together. I will not deal with every issue that arises in relation to the themes that compromise Wesley's *ordo salutis*, including shifts in his perspective between the early, middle, and later phases of his life and ministry. There are other outstanding and nearly exhaustive treatments of Wesley's understanding of the *ordo salutis*. There are many additional discussions of Wesley's understanding of sin, prevenient grace, justification, sanctification, etc. in Collins and especially in Maddox. Both interact with the secondary literature and provide bibliographic information regarding the secondary sources in the endnotes and selected bibliographies. Readers interested in various other themes and issues in relation to the order of salvation that I do not treat will find Maddox and Collins extremely helpful. The rest of this chapter will focus on what many secondary sources neglect, the Trinitarian dimension of Wesley's *ordo salutis*.

32 *Works*, 2:475–76.

of humanity prior to the Fall at the beginning of Wesley's sermon "The New Birth." Here Wesley's treatment included a tripartite concept of the *imago dei*. Humanity was created in the natural image of God, "a spiritual being endued with understanding, freedom of will, and various affections."[33] Affections are not emotions but rather, as Wesley said in his sermon "The End of Christ's Coming," "the will exerting itself various ways."[34]

Wesley also identified a political image of God in humanity wherein human beings are to govern the world of nature, of course with the kind of love and care that the Triune God manifests toward the creation. The third aspect Wesley called the moral image, which he defined in participatory Trinitarian terms as uninterrupted fellowship with the Father and Son through the Spirit, generating righteousness and true holiness, and a conscience void of offense in right relation to the Triune God.

In his sermon "The New Birth," Wesley delved more deeply into this moral image, identifying it not only with "righteousness and true holiness" but also with being "full of love" as "the sole principle of all his tempers, thoughts, words, and actions," because "God is love." Wesley added to his description of the moral image of God, "full of justice, mercy, and truth," for this, too, is the character of God. Original humanity was "pure from every sinful blot" because "God is spotless purity."[35]

There is no mention here in Wesley's immediate description of this tripartite *imago dei* of the Trinitarian dimension. But just a few lines before the description, Wesley began this long paragraph discussion of the image of God by stating that the foundation of the new birth lies nearly as deep as creation itself, for "in the scriptural account . . . we read, 'And God,' the three-one God, 'said, Let us make man in our image, after our likeness.'" In the paragraph immediately after his account of the tripartite image of God, Wesley explicitly identified the participatory basis of the moral image of God in the very life of God in his account of the Fall:

> He [original humanity] lost the life of God: he was separated from him in union with whom his spiritual life consisted. . . . And of this he gave

33 Ibid., 2:188.

34 Ibid., 2:474. See Maddox, *Responsible Grace*, 65–73; and Collins, *Theology of John Wesley*, 49–57, for helpful treatments of Wesley's anthropology. Wesley's anthropology is much more sophisticated than the popular North American vision of human beings as "mind, emotion, and will," a vision that conspicuously leaves out of the picture aspects of humanity that Wesley identified via affections, tempers, and other categories, though Wesley's own anthropology is also inadequate.

35 *Works,* 2:188.

> immediate proof; presently showing by his behaviour that the love of God was extinguished in his soul, which was now "alienated from the life of God." Instead of this he was now under the power of servile fear, so that he fled from the presence of the Lord. . . . So had he lost both the knowledge and the love of God, without which the image of God would not subsist. Of this therefore he was deprived at the same time and became unholy as well as unhappy. In the room of this he sunk into pride and self-will, the very image of the devil, and into sensual appetites and desires, the image of the beasts that perish.[36]

These are particularly illuminating passages, for they reveal that seldom are the participatory and Trinitarian dimensions missing from Wesley's reflections on so many theological topics if one takes care to read closely what Wesley wrote. It is clear that there is a Trinitarian relational theme in Wesley's depiction of original humanity and *imago dei*. Human beings were not created as individuals who possess humanity in isolated individuality. Human beings were created in the image of the Trinitarian God, whose own inner life as God is communion.[37]

According to Wesley, we have our true humanity and our true personhood and individuality only in loving relationship with the blessed Triune God (and other human beings), indeed only in a participation through the Spirit with the Father and the Son in the fellowship that God is. This participatory fellowship (union and communion) with the Triune God was the very

---

36 Ibid., 2:188–89.

37 It is interesting that while Collins acknowledges the relational character of the image of God in that God is love, nowhere in his discussion of the image of God does Collins develop the ontological ground of God being love in the loving relations that constitute the Trinitarian persons within God's own life and being as God. Indeed, Collins focuses more on the moral character of the one God as "holy love." So never once in his long and insightful six-page treatment of the image of God does Collins reference the participatory, Trinitarian, ontological ground of the moral image of God in humanity. In fact, at precisely the point in his discussion where he might have appealed to the participatory Trinitarian dimension in Wesley that could help tame the unbridled moralistic Methodist tendency, Collins appealed to what is one of the most problematic elements in Wesley whole theology: Wesley's Christological depiction of the moral law. Collins quotes Wesley's problematic conception of the moral law with approval: the moral law is "an incorruptible picture of the high and holy One that inhabiteth eternity," "a copy of the eternal mind, a transcript of the divine nature" (see Collins, *Theology of John Wesley*, 56; and Wesley himself in *Works*, 2:9–10, where the original quotation appears). We will return to this problem later in this chapter in the discussion of Christian perfection.

source of original humanity's spiritual life that sustained the image of God in humanity and without which that image could not exist. Wesley's *imago dei* is consistent with everything else we have seen about his doctrine of the Trinity being bound up with vital religion and his understanding of the essence of Christian faith as Trinitarian.

So it is no coincidence that Wesley discussed the Fall and human sin not simply in moral categories in terms of disobeying God's will or breaking God's law but also in terms of loss of fellowship with the Triune God, the fellowship that generated the image of God with its moral and social vibrancy of love, righteousness, holiness, justice, mercy, and truth, leading to loving relationships with our neighbors and loving concern and care for the rest of creation. When Wesley turned to the sinful fallen state of humanity after the Fall in his sermon "The New Birth," he spoke of it in the very same categories: "And 'in Adam all died,' all humankind . . . who were then in Adam's loins. The natural consequence of this is that everyone descended from him comes into the world spiritually dead, dead to God, wholly 'dead in sin' entirely void of the life of God, void of the image of God, of all that 'righteousness and holiness.' . . . This then is the foundation of the new birth—the entire corruption of our nature. Hence it is that 'born in sin' we 'must be born again.'"[38] Remember that Wesley began his discussion of the image of God in this "New Birth" sermon by stating that "the three-one God said, 'Let us make man in our image, after our likeness.'" For Wesley, sin included the loss of the Trinitarian dimension constitutive of true humanity because the *imago dei* with its strong moral resonance is relational and dynamic: the image of God, with its moral dimension, only "happens" within union through the Spirit with the Father and Son. Once union and communion with the Triune God are disrupted, so is the *imago dei*, including its moral dimension.

Loss of participatory fellowship with the Triune God, for Wesley, is the reason why we must be born again. It is the reason why Wesley said elsewhere that "his words are equally true of all men, *in whatever state of grace they are* [my emphasis]: 'As the branch cannot bear fruit of itself, except it abide in the vine, no more can ye except ye abide in me'. . . . We have this grace not from Christ but in him."[39] Only in and through restoration to union

---

38 *Works*, 2:190. For an insightful discussion of Wesley's perspective on how sin is transmitted after the Fall of humanity and how he ended up in a form of traducianism, see Maddox, *Responsible Grace*, 75–81.

39 Outler, ed., *Wesley*, 285–86.

and communion with the Triune God in the gospel are people able to be truly human, manifesting the image of God.

Since the focus of this study is the Trinitarian dimension of Wesley's theology, we will not rehearse the detailed consequences of sin, with its darkening of human cognitive faculties, searing of the conscience, loss of liberty to love and obey, and redirecting of human will/affection to the desires of the flesh, the desires of the eye, and the pride of life, that trio of actual sins that Wesley explicated time and time again throughout his sermons and other publications. For Wesley, human beings are born into the world debilitated and depraved, every faculty and power corrupted and compromised so that sinful thoughts, words, and actions flow freely from a thoroughly tainted source. The result is that human beings are entirely unable to save themselves.[40] Wesley's *ordo salutis* is an account of how the Triune God undertakes the great project of reclaiming, reconciling, and redeeming a tragically fallen and hopelessly lost creation.

2. Prevenient Grace

The late Albert Outler, who played a significant role in the reappraisal of Wesley as a serious theologian and, therefore, in the surge of interest in Wesley's theology during the last fifty years, once said, "If the Wesleyan theology had to be judged by a single essay, this one ["The Scripture Way of Salvation"] would do as well as any and better than most."[41] There is additional evidence supporting Outler's judgment in the fact that Wesley had preached on the text for this sermon, Ephesians 2:8, more times than any other passage of scripture. It is the same text that Wesley drew upon in his sermon that we examined in chapter 2, "Salvation by Faith," preached at Oxford on June 11, 1738, explicating the "new faith" Wesley learned from Peter Böhler. The content of the two sermons is similar.[42]

"The Scripture Way of Salvation" sermon opened with Wesley's complaint that while "religion" (including Christian religion) is complicated and difficult to grasp, the "genuine religion of Jesus Christ" is "plain and simple" and "easy to be understood." Indeed, "as described in the oracles of God," "the end is, in one word, salvation: the means to attain it, faith."[43] Wesley's sermon provided a classic summary of how he understood salvation by faith.

40 See Maddox, *Responsible Grace*, 81–83. See also Collins, *Theology of John Wesley*, 57–73, for an account of the Fall, sin, and the effects of sin.

41 See Outler's introduction to Wesley's sermon in Outler, ed., *Wesley*, 271.

42 See the introduction to Wesley's sermon in *Works,* 2:155.

43 Ibid., 2:155–56.

First, Wesley made clear that salvation in the Bible is not simply going to heaven, as many thought it to be: "It is a present thing, a blessing which, through the free mercy of God, ye are now in possession of." Wesley expanded his vision, stating that "the salvation which is here spoken of might be extended to the entire work of God, from the first dawning of grace in the soul till it is consummated in glory."[44] It ultimately included everything entailed in what we call the *ordo salutis*, though in this sermon Wesley focused on the two main themes of justification and sanctification.[45]

What is interesting in this sermon for our present purpose is what Wesley summarized before he launched into his discussion of justification and sanctification: a Trinitarian depiction of prevenient grace. Here is what Wesley said about the "first dawning of grace":

> It will include all that is wrought in the soul by what is frequently termed "natural conscience," but more properly, "preventing grace"; all the "drawings" of "the Father," the desires after God, which, if we yield to them, increase more and more; all that "light" wherewith the Son of God "enlighteneth everyone that cometh into the world," *showing* every man "to do justly, to love mercy, and to walk humbly with his God"; all the *convictions* which his Spirit from time to time works in every child of man. Although it is true the generality of men stifle them as soon as possible.[46]

This quotation reveals that prevenient grace is not some spiritual substance or an undifferentiated divine presence but actually the Triune God, the Father, Son, and Holy Spirit, always working together in a pattern of coactivity wherein the respective dimensions of each person's activity—the Father drawing, the Son enlightening, the Spirit convicting—coinhere and interpenetrate the activities of the other two. Geoffrey Wainwright astutely observed that Wesley ascribed "a role to each of the three Persons of the Trinity," and noted that Wesley understood this "in Johannine terms" as the Father who "draws" (John 6:44), the Son who "enlightens" (John 1:9), and the Holy Spirit who "convicts" (John 16:8).[47]

What is also interesting is that Wesley grounded "natural conscience" in this Trinitarian rendering of prevenient grace and not by an appeal to his high view of the moral law as "an incorruptible picture of the high and holy

---

44 Ibid., 2:156.

45 Ibid., 2:157.

46 Ibid., 2:156–57.

47 See Geoffrey Wainwright, "Wesley's Trinitarian Hermeneutics" in *Wesleyan Theological Journal* 36, no. 1 (Spring 2001): 17.

One," "coeval with his [humanity's] nature," and "the everlasting fitness of all things that are or ever were created."[48] However, Collins is correct that grace for Wesley is conceived in terms of the "normative value of the moral law,"[49] or, as Wesley said it, the moral law is "manifested to give and not to destroy life" so that people "may see God and live."[50] But this does not diminish the Trinitarian dimension in Wesley's account of natural conscience.

In another classic sermon, "On Working Out Our Own Salvation," based on Philippians 2:12–13, written in 1785, late in his career and reflecting his mature perspective, Wesley noted that "some great truths, as the being and attributes of God, and the difference between moral good and evil, were known in some measure to the heathen world; traces of them are to be found in all nations; . . . in . . . every child of man."[51] This sounds like a clear statement of general revelation and natural conscience. However, Wesley immediately gave this knowledge of God and morality a Christological basis by saying, God "has in some measure 'enlightened everyone that cometh into the world,'" a reference to Jesus Christ as the "true light" in John 1:9. Wesley qualified this "natural" knowledge of God and morality even further, as we will see in a moment.

After this opening point, Wesley moved to what "enlightened heathens" do not know, the "two grand heads of doctrine": "the eternal Son of God" "giving himself to be 'a propitiation for the sins of the world,'" and "the Spirit of God, renewing men in that image of God."[52] It should come as no surprise that Wesley developed these themes in Trinitarian terms on the very next page: "'God so loved the world' as to 'give his only Son, to the end that whosoever believeth on him should . . . have eternal life.'" Wesley added that "'God hath given us his Holy Spirit,' who 'worketh in us both to will and to do of his good pleasure.'" He then referred his readers to Philippians 2:5–6 and affirmed the "*fullness* and the supreme *height* of the Godhead" of Christ, who is "equal with God."[53] God the Father sent Christ, the eternal Son of God, to secure human salvation, and God sent the Holy Spirit to renew people in God's image.

Indeed, God gives the Spirit to work in us both "to will" and "to do." On the next page, Wesley wrote, "It is God that worketh in us, both to will and to

---

48 *Works,* 2:7, 9–10.

49 Collins, *Theology of John Wesley,* 56.

50 *Works,* 2:9.

51 *Works,* 3:199.

52 Ibid., 3:200.

53 Ibid., 3:201–2.

do." The former, "to will," Wesley said, entails the "whole of inward" religion, "including every good desire, whether relating to our tempers, words, or actions," or having the mind that was in Christ, as Wesley said it elsewhere. The latter, "to do," included "the whole of outward religion," or "every good word and work," or to walk as Christ walked, as Wesley often called it.[54] This was the first main point of the sermon.

The second point focused on the latter half of the Philippians text and our working out our own salvation. Here Wesley provided a capsule summary of the whole *ordo salutis* from "preventing grace" through "convincing grace" or repentance to "proper Christian salvation." Wesley summarized salvation again as "consisting of those two grand branches, justification and sanctification," a salvation that is "both instantaneous and gradual." What primarily concerns us here is what Wesley said about "preventing grace": "Salvation begins with what is usually termed (and very properly) 'preventing grace'; including the first wish to please God, the first dawn of light concerning his will, and the first slight, transient conviction of having sinned against him. All these imply some tendency toward life, some degree of salvation, the beginning of a deliverance from a blind, unfeeling heart, quite insensible of God and the things of God."[55]

Notice that Wesley's first three points in the first sentence directly parallel the Trinitarian conceptualization of prevenient grace from his sermon "The Scripture Way of Salvation" (the second quotation in each couplet below is from "The Scripture Way of Salvation" sermon): the "first wish to please God" or "the 'drawings' of 'the Father' "; "the first dawn of light concerning his will" or "that 'light' wherewith the Son of God 'enlighteneth everyone that cometh into the world' "; "the first slight, transient conviction of having sinned against him" or "the *convictions* which his Spirit from time to time works in every child of man."[56] It is obvious that Wesley's thinking about prevenient grace had become rather well-worn by 1785, so that in this later sermon, "On Working Out Our Own Salvation," he followed the identical path, noting the same points, as in the earlier sermon, "The Scripture Way of Salvation." Remember, Wesley had already established the Trinitarian context of salvation in the introduction to this later 1785 sermon, even if he did not make the Trinitarian dimension explicit in this brief tripartite summary of preventing grace that we just examined.

54 Ibid., 3:202–3.

55 Ibid., 3:203–4.

56 Compare ibid., 3:203 and 2:157.

It is also interesting that, according to Wesley in 1785, those who respond to prevenient grace do enter into "some degree of salvation," even if that is not yet "proper Christian salvation."[57] The question that remains is, What, precisely, does "some degree of salvation" involve? It is a point on which Wesley scholars do not agree.[58]

Later in the 1785 sermon "On Working Out Our Own Salvation," Wesley returned to prevenient grace and made the economic Trinitarian dimension explicit:

> Seeing all men are by nature . . . "dead in trespasses, and sins," it is not possible for them to do anything well till God raises them from the dead . . . till the Lord had given them life.
>
> Yet this is no excuse for those who continue to sin, and lay the blame upon their Maker by saying: "It is God only that must quicken us. . . ." For allowing that all the souls of men are dead in sin by *nature*, this excuses none, seeing there is no man that is in a state of mere nature; there is no man, unless he has quenched the Spirit, that is wholly void of the grace of God. No man living is entirely destitute of what is vulgarly called "natural conscience." But this is not natural; it is more properly termed "preventing grace.". . . So that no man sins because he has not grace, but because he does not use the grace which he hath.[59]

Once again Wesley identifies all three Trinitarian persons in this account of prevenient grace. God has to quicken people for them to respond. The Lord Jesus Christ has to give them life. The Spirit is also present and acting in this Trinitarian prevenient grace that goes out to everyone, unless they have quenched the Spirit.

Chapter 2 examined Wesley's "Letter to a Roman Catholic," where he said that "the infinite and eternal Spirit of God, equal with the Father and the Son, [was] not only perfectly holy in himself, but the immediate cause of all holiness in us," implying that the Father and the Son are also involved in the work of holiness in their own unique ways. According to Wesley, this Trinitarian activity extends throughout the *ordo salutis*, "enlightening our understandings" (prevenient grace); "rectifying our wills and affections" (convicting grace); "renewing our natures, uniting our persons to Christ"

---

57 Ibid., 3:204.

58 There is scholarly debate over what "some degree of salvation" involves. See Maddox, *Responsible Grace*, 87–93; and Collins, *Theology of John Wesley*, 73–82, for differing accounts of prevenient grace and its benefits.

59 *Works*, 3:206–7.

(justifying and regenerating grace); "purifying and sanctifying our bodies to a full and eternal enjoyment of God" (sanctifying and perfecting grace).[60]

For Wesley, no human is in a mere state of nature bereft of God's grace in Christ mediated to everyone through the Spirit. Prevenient grace is Trinitarian, involves the coactivity of the three divine persons, and initiates God's soteriological restoration of fallen humanity.

3. Convicting Grace

As people respond to prevenient grace, most often the one grace of God in Christ at some point takes the form of convicting grace, which, according to Wesley, brings even greater self-knowledge and further exposes human brokenness and sin that permeates all human life in a fallen world. Convicting grace shows us our need for the love of God the Father, the grace of our Lord Jesus Christ, and the fellowship of the Spirit. Wesley described it this way: "Salvation begins with what is usually termed . . . 'preventing grace.' . . . Salvation is carried on by 'convincing grace,' usually in scripture termed 'repentance,' which brings a larger measure of self-knowledge, a farther deliverance from the heart of stone."[61]

In his sermon entitled "The Spirit of Bondage and of Adoption," Wesley presented perhaps his clearest expression of the Trinitarian dimension of repentance:

> By some awful providence, or by his Word applied with the demonstration of his Spirit, God touches the heart of him that lay asleep in darkness and in the shadow of death. . . . Horrid light breaks in upon his soul [remember what we read earlier, that Christ is the true light that enlightens everyone]. . . . The inward, spiritual meaning of the law of God now begins to glare upon him. . . . God speaks in a thunder, "He that hateth his brother is a murderer"; he that saith to his brother, "Thou fool,' is obnoxious to hellfire."[62]

Notice that God the Father speaks his Word through the Holy Spirit. God speaks in a thunder, applying his Word via this demonstration of the Spirit through the mouth of Jesus Christ, "He that hates his brother is a murderer. He that says, 'you fool,' is in danger of hellfire." These are Jesus's words in the Sermon on the Mount in Matthew 5:21–22.

---

60 Outler, ed., *Wesley,* 495.

61 *Works,* 3:203–4.

62 *Works,* 1:255.

Kenneth Collins rightly notes the role of the Word and the Spirit in Wesley's vision of convicting or convincing grace. Prevenient grace awakens conscience and brokenly reinscribes the moral law in people's lives. But convicting grace, according to Collins, is "a conjunction of Word and Spirit to shed increasing light upon the conscience to reveal shafts of the righteousness and justice of God."[63] Wesley used rather dramatic Trinitarian language to speak of this heightening of conscience during conviction of sin: "The moment the Spirit of the Almighty strikes the heart of him that was till then without God in the world, it breaks the hardness of his heart, and creates all things new. The Sun of righteousness appears, and shines upon his soul, showing him the light of the glory of God in the face of Jesus Christ."[64]

What is especially interesting about Wesley on this point is the close connection he sees between the law and the gospel. In this work of convicting grace, both law and gospel are present in the conjunction of the Word and Spirit. In that same section of his sermon "The Spirit of Bondage and of Adoption," noted above, not only is the law of God glaring at the sinner through the words of Christ in the power of the Spirit but so is the gospel, which serves to heighten the distress of the sinner, somewhat as a person dying of thirst suffers all the more seeing water in the distance but being unable to reach it because of being so weak from dehydration.

Here is how Wesley stated it: "In every point he feels the Word of God 'quick and powerful, sharper than a two-edged sword.'. . . And so much the more because he is conscious *to himself* of having neglected so great a salvation; of having 'trodden under foot the Son of God' who would have saved him from his sins, and 'counted the blood of the covenant an unholy,' a common unsanctifying 'thing.'"[65] Wesley tersely stated the same point earlier in the sermon: the person under convicting grace "sees the loving, the merciful God is also 'a consuming fire.'"[66] So the Father speaks the Word (law and gospel) in the power of the Spirit to convict sinners of their sin, of their helplessness to save themselves, and of their failure to embrace God's solution in Christ, all of which serve to heighten the utter tragedy and folly of the human condition.

It is no coincidence that Wesley spent thirteen, or one-fourth, of his Standard Sermons expounding the spiritual meaning of the law provided by Christ in his Sermon on the Mount, thereby accentuating Christ's prophetic

---

63 Collins, *Theology of John Wesley,* 123.

64 *Works*, 4:172. See also Collins, *Theology of John Wesley,* 359n9.

65 *Works,* 1:256.

66 Ibid., 1:255.

office and turning the Sermon on the Mount into the great tract of scripture for convicting people of sin, as well as guiding Christians in discerning God's will for their lives.[67]

What exactly did Jesus Christ provide in the Sermon on the Mount? According to Wesley, Christ's design was "to lay down at once the whole plan of his religion, to give us a full prospect of Christianity, to describe at large the nature of that holiness without which no man shall see the Lord."[68] Nowhere else in scripture is there "a general view of the whole." Out of "amazing love," Wesley asserts, "does the Son of God here reveal his Father's will to man" for it is "the way of pleasantness; the path to calm, joyous peace."[69]

Thus, for Wesley, the Sermon on the Mount is not simply law; it is also gospel. It reveals the whole plan of religion or the nature of holiness, "a full prospect of Christianity." It is no coincidence that when Wesley actually exegeted and developed his expository comments on the beatitudes of Matthew 5:3–12, he saw the beatitudes as "the sum of true religion." Jesus's words in Matthew 5:3–5 (the first three beatitudes) dealt with hindrances: pride, removed by "poverty of spirit"; levity and thoughtlessness, removed by "holy *mourning*"; and impatience and discontent, removed by "Christian *meekness*." When these hindrances are gone, "the native appetite of a heaven-born spirit returns; it hungers and thirsts after righteousness."[70]

It is at this point that Wesley again returned to the character of vital religion, which he also defined in Trinitarian terms, as we will see in a moment. Someone who is "athirst for God, the living God," cannot be satisfied "with what the world accounts religion," Wesley noted. What is startling for some is that he defined the religion of the world in terms rather familiar to Methodists: "The religion of the world implies three things: first,

---

67 Many throughout the history of the church saw the Sermon on the Mount as primarily setting forth the way of life, the pattern of discipleship, for highly committed followers of Christ. In Wesley's words, "Many have supposed that other parts concerned only the apostles, or the first Christians, or the ministers of Christ; and were never designed for the generality of men." But "who told them this . . . ?" Wesley quips. "Has then our Lord himself taught us that some parts of his discourse do not concern all mankind? . . . But has he told us so? Where?" (see ibid., 1:472). Wesley's answer was a plain "no," and he added that neither the Apostles nor any of the writers of scripture say that Jesus's Sermon on the Mount was intended for any audience less than all of humanity.

68 Ibid., 1:473.

69 Ibid., 1:473–74.

70 Ibid., 1:495.

the doing no harm . . .; secondly, the doing good . . . ; thirdly, the using the means of grace."[71]

These three are the main divisions of the General Rules of the United Societies in early Methodism. Those who had encountered convicting grace were made aware of their profound need for God so that they were "fleeing the wrath to come."[72] If they wanted to be Methodists, they had to "evidence their desire for salvation" precisely by avoiding evil, doing good, and using the means of grace, which Wesley here in his "Sermon on the Mount, II" denounced as "religion of the world" that falls so far short of the real essence of Christian faith.

This initially sounds like an inconsistency or tension in what Wesley said in these two contexts. How can he require Methodists to keep the three General Rules and then denounce those same Rules as the religion of the world that entirely misses the mark? The apparent inconsistency vanishes when we read, at beginning of the General Rules of the United Societies, that "[s]uch a Society is no other than 'a company of men having the form, and seeking the power of godliness.'"[73] That "power of godliness" is the very center of Christian faith, a center that Wesley understood in Trinitarian terms. When anyone confused the form of godliness (the General Rules) with the (participatory Trinitarian) power of godliness, the Rules of Methodism degenerated into a form of religion that falls woefully short of the vibrant Trinitarian Christian faith and life.

In his "Sermon on the Mount, II," Wesley clarified the point in a remarkable passage that casts additional light on the General Rules of the United Societies and on the Sermon on the Mount as a great tract of scripture for convicting people of sin. One athirst for the living God because of convicting

---

71 Ibid., 1:496.

72 *The Works of John Wesley*, ed. Rupert Davies, vol. 9, *The Methodist Societies: History, Nature, and Design* (Nashville: Abingdon, 1989), 69–70. The only initial qualification necessary to be a Methodist was the desire to "flee the wrath to come," to be convicted of sin, and to be seeking God's grace. One could be a Methodist without being a person who had already come to faith in Christ. Early Methodism in this sense was a tremendously open, seeker-friendly movement. The Methodist societies and the small-group class meetings were open to anyone who was seeking God because if someone was a seeker, it could only mean that God's Trinitarian convicting grace was already at work in her life. But Wesley and the early Methodists had high expectations not only for those who had come into faith in, and fellowship with, the Triune God but also for seekers who needed to be watched over in love in community and held accountable for keeping the General Rules of the United Societies.

73 Ibid., 9:69.

grace does avoid evil, do good, and use the means of grace. But at the same time such a person recognizes that these General Rules of the United Societies are "only the outside of that religion which he insatiably hungers after. The knowledge of God in Christ Jesus; 'the life that is hid with Christ in God'; the being 'joined unto the Lord in one Spirit'; the having 'fellowship with the Father and the Son'; the 'walking in the light as God is in the light'; the being 'purified even as he is pure'—this is the religion, the righteousness he thirsts after. Nor can he rest till he thus rests in God."[74]

The Sermon on the Mount is law and gospel, and both simultaneously. The Sermon on the Mount can mediate convicting grace as law that makes people conscious that they are not only sinners but also have neglected so great a salvation, as Wesley said it in his sermon "The Spirit of Bondage and the Spirit of Adoption." Yet the reverse is also true for Wesley: the Sermon on the Mount, with all of its injunctions, indeed every other command in scripture, is also good news or gospel because, since as Wesley stated elsewhere, "Every command has the force of a promise, in virtue of those general promises: 'A new heart will I give you, and I will put my Spirit within you, and cause you to walk in my statutes.' "[75]

So convicting grace is Trinitarian: the Father speaks his Word through the mouth of Jesus Christ in words of scripture, like the Sermon on the Mount, or through preaching, as the Spirit applies it to peoples' lives. The Trinitarian persons are present and active in and through scripture, preaching, and the other means of grace. This is a crucial point for Wesley that many commentators on his theology have noted: God's Trinitarian presence can still be *immediate* even when it is *mediated* via various means of grace.[76]

In his sermon "The Means of Grace," Wesley noted that "there is a kind of order wherein God himself is generally pleased to use these means in bringing a sinner [via convicting grace] to salvation." Wesley then described that this convicting grace, as the Triune God personally present in and through, means:

---

74 *Works*, 1:497.

75 This quotation is found in Wesley's "A Plain Account of Genuine Christianity," which was a sixteen-page pamphlet published in 1753, though originally it was part of a much longer work arising out of a dispute with Dr. Conyers Middleton over the character of genuine Christianity (see Outler, ed., *Wesley*, 188, for the citation and 181–83 for Outler's introduction).

76 See Henry H. Knight III, *The Presence of God in the Christian Life: John Wesley and the Means of Grace* (Metuchen, NJ: Scarecrow, 1992), 191–96. See also Maddox, *Responsible Grace*, 192ff.

> A stupid, senseless wretch is going on in his own way, not having God in all his thoughts, when God comes upon him unawares, perhaps by an awakening sermon or conversation, perhaps by some awful providence; or it may be an immediate stroke of his convincing Spirit, without any outward means. . . . He [the senseless wretch] is amazed, and begins "searching the scriptures," whether these things are so. The more he *hears* and *reads*, the more convinced he is. . . . By all these means the arrows of conviction sink deeper into his soul. He begins also . . . to talk with God, to *pray* to him, although through fear and shame he scarce knows what to say. . . . He observes others go up to "the table of the Lord." He considers, Christ has said, "Do this." . . . After struggling with these scruples a while, he breaks through. And thus he continues in God's way—in hearing, reading meditating, praying and partaking of the Lord's Supper—till God, in the manner that pleases him, speaks to his heart, "Thy faith hath saved thee; go in peace."[77]

This is a wonderfully illuminating passage that clarifies Wesley's understanding of convicting grace and that the Triune God is immediately present at times without any outward means and at other times present in and through the means of grace used by those who are "fleeing the wrath to come" and are athirst for the living God.

Eventually those longing for and seeking God encounter the true religion they "thirst after," for the Triune God speaks, and the seeker is "joined unto the Lord in One Spirit," enters into "fellowship with the Father and the Son," and "thus rests in God," as Wesley said it in his "Sermon on the Mount, II." Trinitarian convicting grace makes those who have not yet come to what Wesley called "proper Christian salvation" aware of themselves, their brokenness, sin, and need for God, and begins to deliver them from a "heart of stone."[78]

In his sermon "The Spirit of Bondage and of Adoption," Wesley spoke of the profound and piercing effect of convicting grace this way: the sinner

> sees himself naked, stripped of all the fig-leaves which he had sewed together, of all his poor pretenses to religion or virtue, and his wretched excuses for sinning against God. . . . All within him stands confessed. His heart is laid bare, and he sees it is all sin, "deceitful above all things, desperately wicked . . . every motion thereof, every temper and thought, being only evil continually."

77 *Works,* 1:393–94.
78 Ibid., 3:204.

> And he not only sees, but feels in himself, by an emotion of soul which he cannot describe, that . . . he deserves to be cast into "the fire that never shall be quenched." . . . Here ends his pleasing dream, his delusive rest, his false peace, his vain security. . . . The fumes of those opiates being now dispelled, he feels the anguish of a wounded spirit. . . . He feels sorrow of heart from the blessings he has lost, and the curse which is come upon him; remorse for having thus destroyed himself, and despised his own mercies; fear, from a lively sense of the wrath of God, and of the consequences of his wrath. . . . Sometimes it may approach to the very brink of despair.[79]

Trinitarian convicting grace, for Wesley, is hostile to sin and everything destructive to humanity, everything destructive to love for God and neighbor, and everything that prevents people from entering into communion with the Triune God and one another. At the same time, Trinitarian convicting grace further transforms people from being sinners toward being forgiven and beloved children of God.[80]

---

79 *Works*, 1:256–57. This sermon was published in 1746, fairly early after the events and changes in Wesley's perspective surrounding Aldersgate. Maddox argues that Wesley came to downplay over time, and in the face of criticism, the role of intense fear, anxiety, and despair, and particularly prolonging it. Maddox says that Wesley, in his later sermons, stressed more positive elements of grace awakening sinners to their need for God in the gospel (see Maddox, *Responsible Grace*, 160–61).

80 There are other places in Wesley's publications where he developed a view of convicting grace involving all three Trinitarian persons. In his sermon "The Way of the Kingdom," Wesley described the Kingdom of God and the way into it. The first point of the sermon is a statement on "the nature of true religion" or "the kingdom of God." Wesley presented it in full participatory, economic Trinitarian terms similar to the many other summaries we have already examined (*Works,* 1:218–25).

In his second point, Wesley turned to convicting grace of the "first repentance, previous to faith, even conviction, or self-knowledge." He spent four pages developing what is involved in this repentance or self-knowledge that comes in and with convicting grace, making many of the same points that we saw above in the long quotation from his sermon "The Spirit of Bondage and of Adoption." In the process of coming to know one is a sinner, and "what manner of a sinner" one is, one comes to know that one has lived "contrary to the Spirit," one has departed "from the living God," one has grieved "the Holy One of Israel," "defiled" one's body "designed for a temple of the Holy Ghost" (ibid., 1:225–29). Such a sinner also feels "sorrow of heart for having despised [God's] own mercies; . . . fear of the wrath of God . . . and of the fiery indignation ready to devour those who forget God and obey not our Lord Jesus Christ" (ibid., 1:229). See also ibid., 1:477–79; and *Works*, 9:463.

4. *Justifying, Regenerating Grace, and Assurance*

After convicting grace comes what Wesley called "proper Christian salvation, whereby 'through grace' we 'are saved by faith,' consisting in those two grand branches, justification and sanctification."[81] In his sermon "The Scripture Way of Salvation," Wesley also stated that Christian salvation "consists of two general parts, justification and sanctification."[82]

We saw how Wesley, on occasion, made a firm distinction between justification and sanctification and said that sanctification "is a distinct gift of God, and of a totally different nature" than justification.[83] Statements like these, however, do not present the full picture of Wesley's theology on the relationship between justification and regeneration/sanctification.

Wesley stated emphatically that Christian faith is "a full reliance on the blood of Christ . . . a recumbency upon him as our atonement and our life, as *given for us*, and *living in us*."[84] Here Wesley made the Christological dimension of regeneration absolutely clear: Christ is the source of our new life in the Spirit. The Spirit regenerates by uniting us to Christ, who simultaneously lives his life through us in the power of the Spirit in obedience to and fellowship with the Father. As noted above, Wesley affirmed the participatory character of all forms of grace, including justification itself: "We have this grace not *from* Christ but in him."[85] This is as true of justification as it is of sanctification.

According to "The Scripture Way of Salvation" sermon, justification "is another word for pardon. It is the forgiveness of all our sins, and . . . our acceptance with God . . . procured for us (commonly termed the 'meritorious cause' of our justification)" by "the blood and righteousness of Christ, or . . . all that Christ has done and suffered for us."[86] Wesley then noted that when we are justified, "in that very moment, *sanctification* begins. In that instant we are 'born again,' . . . 'born of the Spirit'. . . renewed by the power of God."[87] Here we will distinguish between regeneration (being born again)

---

81 *Works,* 3:204.
82 Ibid., 3:157.
83 *Works*, 1:187.
84 Ibid., 1:121.
85 Outler, ed., *Wesley*, 285–86.
86 *Works,* 2:157–58. There is a lot of debate behind this little phrase "meritorious cause" that Wesley inserts here. It was a point of controversy with the Calvinists around predestination.
87 Ibid., 2:158.

that occurs the moment we are justified and the ongoing process of sanctification treated in the next section.

This emphasis on justifying and regenerating grace places Wesley close to the Protestant Reformers affirming that we are restored to a right relationship with God the Father through what Christ has done for us in his life, death, and resurrection, mediated to us freely and ungrudgingly through the activity of the Spirit. For Wesley, as for the Reformers, justification and regeneration are the beginning of sanctification. They occur simultaneously and are really two sides of a single participatory reality in which we are forgiven and restored to God's favor, as well as changed at the center of our being, indwelt by the Spirit of God as a deposit guaranteeing what is to come, set free for faith and new life in Christ.

Justification refers to God's pardon or forgiveness of our sins and our guilt because of the love of God the Father that comes to us through Christ's life, death, and resurrection and is made real in our lives by the Holy Spirit. Regeneration is another word for new birth or for the spiritual change that results because the Spirit of God now dwells in our hearts, simultaneously uniting us with Christ and through Christ with the Father.

This Trinitarian justifying and regenerating grace changes everything. For Wesley, it is what restores our relationship with the Triune God to love and fellowship because we are adopted into filial relation to God through union with the Son of God and into the Son's relationship to the Father. As children of God, sisters and brothers adopted in Christ into fellowship with God the Father and indwelt by the Spirit, this regeneration begins to work itself out, transforming our lives and our lives together so that we begin to become "Transcripts of the Trinity," to use Charles Wesley's wonderful phrase, whose relationships of deep fellowship and love with God and others reflect something of the love that God is, the love between the persons of the Trinity within God's own eternal being and life.[88]

Wesley's most characteristic way of speaking about justification and regeneration was to link them together, along with the witness of the Spirit or doctrine of assurance. In his 1746 sermon "The Spirit of Bondage and of Adoption," Wesley described a person coming to "proper Christian salvation" as one

> who has found "grace," or favour in the sight of God, even the Father [justification], and who has the "grace," or power of the Holy Ghost,

---

88 See Charles Wesley's Hymn #7 (1742), in *The Works of John Wesley*, ed. Franz Hildebrant and Oliver A. Beckerlegge, vol. 7, *A Collection of Hymns for the Use of the People Called Methodist* (New York: Oxford University Press, 1983), 88.

> reigning in his heart [regeneration]; who has received, in the language of the Apostle, "the Spirit of adoption, whereby he now cries, Abba Father" [assurance]. . . . Heavenly, healing light now breaks in upon his soul. . . . He sees "the light of the glorious love of God, in the face of Jesus Christ." . . . He hath a divine "evidence of things not seen" [one of Wesley's definitions of faith] . . . particularly of the love of God, of his pardoning love to him that believes in Jesus [justification]. . . . Here end both the guilt and power of sin [justification and regeneration/sanctification]. He can now say, "I am crucified with Christ. Nevertheless I live; yet not I, but Christ liveth in me [participation]."[89]

Here justification, regeneration, and assurance are closely linked and defined in participatory, economic Trinitarian terms.

In his sermon "The Scripture Way of Salvation," written twenty years later, in 1765, Wesley provided a full-orbed answer to the question, "What is 'that faith through which we are saved'?" In the second point of his famous sermon, Wesley defined faith this way:

> Faith . . . is . . . "an evidence," a divine "evidence and conviction" . . ."of things not seen"—not visible, not perceivable . . . by any . . . of the external sense. It implies both a supernatural *evidence* of God and of the things of God, . . . and a supernatural *sight* or perception thereof . . . "to give us the light of the knowledge of the glory of God in the face of Jesus Christ.". . . By this twofold operation of the Holy Spirit—having the eyes of our soul both *opened* and *enlightened*—we see . . . the invisible things of God.
>
> Taking the word in a more particular sense, faith is a divine evidence and conviction, not only that "God was in Christ, reconciling the world unto himself," but also that Christ "loved *me*, and gave himself for *me*." It is by this faith . . . that we "receive Christ"; that we receive him in all his office, as our Prophet, Priest and King. . . . And it is certain this faith necessarily implies an *assurance* (which is only another word for *evidence*). . . . For "he that believeth" with the true, living faith, "hath the witness in himself." "The Spirit witnesseth with his spirit that his is a child of God." "Because he is a son, God hath sent forth the Spirit of his Son into his heart, crying, Abba, Father"; giving him as assurance that he is so, and a childlike confidence.[90]

---

89 *Works,* 1:260–61.
90 *Works*, 2:160–62.

This long quotation demonstrates that Wesley viewed all these various dimensions of his Trinitarian conception of coming to faith in a holistic, inseparable, yet subtly differentiated manner. Living "faith" includes all of the economic activity of the Trinitarian persons interconnected in coactivity in Christ's life, death, resurrection, and ascension but also interconnected in coactivity bringing what God has done through Christ to bear upon our lives through the Spirit, awakening our spiritual senses (part of regeneration) to the presence of the Spirit of the Son, whom the Father sends to make real in us what the Triune God has done for us. This participatory coming to faith includes the assurance that we are forgiven and loved by God the Father in Christ (justification) and that Christ now dwells in our hearts via the Spirit (regeneration).

In his sermon "The Witness of the Spirit, II," Wesley, in a similar way, presented these various dimensions of "proper Christian salvation" by grace and by faith. "'This is the record' (the testimony, the sum of what God testifies in all the inspired writings), 'that God hath given unto us eternal life, and this life is in his Son.'"[91] After identifying the first and second persons of the Trinity, God the Father giving eternal life in Jesus Christ, Wesley turned to the topic indicated in the sermon title, the witness of the Spirit: "The testimony now under consideration is given by the Spirit of God to and with our spirit. He is the person . . . [who] testifies to us . . . 'that we are children of God.'"[92]

Then, over several pages, Wesley delineated various elements entailed in the witness of the Spirit. This witness is not by "any outward voice" nor "always by an inward voice." The Spirit "works upon the soul by his immediate influence, and by a strong though inexplicable operation." What the Spirit bears witness to, or makes real, is that Jesus Christ has "given himself for me," that "all my sins are blotted out," and that I "am reconciled to God."[93] According to Wesley, this witness is "*immediate* and *direct*," for "'God hath sent forth the Spirit of his Son into your hearts, crying Abba, Father.'"[94]

The holistic, inseparable, yet differentiated coming to faith in Wesley's theology becomes acutely clear in what he said about the relation between the witness of the Holy Spirit and the witness of our spirit. Wesley passionately maintained that there can be no "real testimony of the Spirit without the fruit of the Spirit." According to Wesley, "We assert, on the contrary, that

91 *Works*, 1:286.
92 Ibid.
93 Ibid., 1:287.
94 Ibid., 1:289.

the fruit of the Spirit immediately springs from this testimony."[95] For Wesley, the witness of the Spirit that we are children of God the Father through what Christ has done on our behalf is inseparably bound up with the spiritual transformation that occurs in our lives through the regenerative union with Christ via the Spirit. So interconnected are these two dimensions that we can only be sure that we are children of God when we have both the witness of the Holy Spirit and the fruit of the Spirit, which Wesley also described as the witness of our spirit.

Wesley defined the witness of our spirit this way: "Strictly speaking, it is a conclusion drawn partly from the Word of God, and partly from our own experience." Scripture makes clear that "everyone who has the fruit of the Spirit is a child of God. Experience, or inward consciousness, tells me that I have the fruit of the Spirit. And hence I rationally conclude: therefore I am a child of God."[96] Later in the sermon, Wesley stated that we have to be "holy in heart and life before we can be conscious that we are so. But we must love God before we can be holy at all, this being the root of all holiness. Now we cannot love God till we know he loves us."[97] In Wesley's mind, the witness of the Spirit is bound up with the entire transformative event of justification and regeneration that reconciles us in Christ to the God who has been reconciled to us through Christ and that simultaneously re-creates the core of our being so that we are fundamentally changed. We cannot but bear holy fruit in heart and life on the basis of this transformative event. Yet as we do bear fruit, in turn, this holy fruit (or witness of our spirit) confirms the witness of the Spirit that we are children of God, showing it to be authentic.

This emphasis on fruit is not a return to being justified by works. Wesley cleverly pounced on that very accusation later in the sermon and used it to drive home his point: "It supposes quite the reverse, namely, that they are sinners all over, sinners both in heart and life."[98] For Wesley, this is precisely what makes the fruit theologically, spiritually, and ethically significant: the fruit flows from justification and regeneration and appears precisely in the lives of those who *had been* sinners in heart and life and would have *continued to be* so were it not for the transformative power of grace. Therefore, fruit bears witness to the *reality* of the transformation that the blessed Triune God has affected in those whose lives bore a rather different witness to pervasive sin prior to that transformation.

---

95 Ibid., 1:288.
96 Ibid., 1:287–88.
97 Ibid., 1:290.
98 Ibid., 1:294.

In these texts dealing with the witness of the Spirit, Wesley focused on the noetic dimension of the Spirit of God awakening and enlightening us in the event of justification and regeneration by grace. But it is clear that the ontic dimension of regeneration and the resulting participation in Christ through the Spirit is implied and presupposed since, for Wesley, it is the root or basis of that change in heart that leads to holiness.

Nearly all of the quotations in chapter 2 dealing with Wesley's Trinitarian summaries of the essence of Christian faith refer to the witness of the Spirit, along with justification and regeneration, and conceive them in the kind of deeply interconnected participatory Trinitarian terms noted throughout this section.

In light of this discussion of the witness of the Spirit, it is easy to see why Wesley was absolutely clear that lack of assurance is not a desirable situation. For Wesley and the early Methodists, Trinitarian grace was utterly real and participatory: we can really enter it, or better, it can enter into us, and we can know it. Knowing it via the witness of the Holy Spirit and the witness of our spirit is crucial to the transformation that the Trinitarian God intends, for lack of assurance of God's love undermines our response in faith that works love toward God and neighbor. So Wesley ended that section describing faith in his sermon "The Scripture Way of Salvation" by noting that "in the very nature of the thing, the assurance goes before the confidence. For a man cannot have a childlike confidence in God till he knows he is a child of God."[99]

This is the whole purpose of there being two witnesses, the witness of the Holy Spirit and the witness of our spirit. Without the witness of the Holy Spirit, Wesley noted, "there is the danger lest our religion degenerate into mere formality": we have a form of godliness but deny the power of it that comes from Triune God. But without fruit, without the witness of our spirit, "we are liable to run into all the wildness of enthusiasm."[100] Together the witness of the Spirit and the witness of our spirit enable us to avoid both dangers and to enter into the confidence that is the privilege of God's children. Wesley said that this doctrine of assurance or witness of the Spirit is "one grand part of the testimony God has given them [the Methodists] to bear to all mankind," a "great evangelical truth" that "had been for many years wellnigh lost and forgotten."[101]

---

99 *Works*, 2:162.

100 *Works*, 1:285.

101 Ibid., 1:285–86.

5. *Sanctifying Grace*

For some Protestant traditions in North America, especially at the level of popular religious culture, the *ordo salutis* is almost over after justification/regeneration, except for heaven when we die. This certainly was not Wesley's view. He said that convicting grace was the porch of religion, that justifying and regenerating grace is the door, but this is all preparation for sanctifying grace, which is the house of religion itself. In Wesley's theology, for the blessed Triune God of the gospel to forgive us and assure us that we are beloved children of God and then leave us to ever fall back into sin again would be an inadequate and frustrating kind of salvation.

Wesley saw holiness as the point of Christian faith: the love of God through the grace of Christ in the fellowship of the Spirit forgives, regenerates, and assures us of God's love in order to transform us so that we can live lives of love for God and love for our neighbors because that is how the gospel expresses itself in fruit in the lives of Christians. Christian love for God and others is crucial to Christian witness in the world since others will know Christians by their love. In fact, many times, particularly toward the end of his life, Wesley noted that the great stumbling block to the conversion of the world to the gospel was the unholy lives of Christians.[102]

In Wesley's view of the *ordo salutis*, as soon as we encounter the justifying and regenerating Trinitarian grace of God, the one grace of God that we have only "in Christ," not simply "from Christ," continues the transformation process via sanctifying grace. In his sermon "On Working Out Our Own Salvation," Wesley provided a concise summary of sanctification: "By sanctification we are saved from the power and root of sin, and restored to the image of God."[103]

In his classic sermon "The Scripture Way of Salvation," Wesley's expansive summary of sanctification is particularly illuminating. The very moment we are justified, we are born again and sanctification begins:

> We are inwardly renewed by the power of God. We feel the "love of God shed abroad in our hearts by the Holy Ghost which is given unto us," producing love to all mankind, and more especially to the children of God; expelling the love of the world, the love of pleasure, of ease, of honour, of money; together with pride, anger, self-will, and every other

---

102 See, for instance, Wesley's sermon "The General Spread of the Gospel," *Works,* 2:495–96.

103 *Works*, 3:204.

> evil temper—in a word, changing the "earthly, sensual, devilish" mind into "the mind that was in Christ Jesus."
>
> We are enabled "by the Spirit" to "mortify the deeds of the body," of our evil nature. And as we are more and more dead to sin, we are more and more alive to God. We go on from grace to grace, while we are careful to "abstain from all appearance of evil," and are "zealous of good work," "as we have opportunity doing good to all men"; while we walk in all his ordinances blameless, therein worshipping him in spirit and in truth [walk as Christ walked?]; while we take up our cross and deny ourselves every pleasure that does not lead us to God. It is thus that we wait for entire sanctification.[104]

This text makes clear that sanctifying grace transforms our motives, reshapes our intentions, reorients our affections, and thereby moves us to love God and neighbor in gratitude, avoiding everything evil and unholy, denying ourselves, and living in joyful obedience to all of the Triune God's commands out of thanksgiving and praise for the transforming grace of God.

Wesley's summary is also Trinitarian. Sanctifying grace also always flows from God the Father through Christ in the Spirit to us so that sanctification is simply another dimension of our participation in the love of God through the grace of Christ via communion of the Spirit, a participation that enables and undergirds our response from beginning to end.

While Wesley referenced all three Trinitarian persons in his description of sanctification in "The Scripture Way of Salvation," the Trinitarian dimension is even more pronounced in his sermon "The Spirit of Bondage and of Adoption":

> And "where the Spirit of the Lord is, there is liberty"; liberty not only from guilt and fear, but from sin, from that heaviest of all yokes. . . . He [the Christian] not only strives, but likewise prevails; he not only fights, but conquers also. "Henceforth he doth not serve sin. . . . Sin doth not now reign, even in his mortal body." . . . Thus "having peace with God, through our Lord Jesus Christ," "rejoicing in hope of the glory of God," and having power over all sin, over every evil desire and temper, and word and work, he is a living witness of the "glorious liberty of the sons of God." . . . It is this Spirit which continually "worketh in them, both to will and to do of his good pleasure." It is he that sheds the love of God abroad in their hearts, and the love of all mankind; thereby purifying their hearts from the love of the world. . . . It is by him they are delivered from anger and

104 *Works*, 2:158–60.

> pride, from all vile and inordinate affections. In consequence, they are delivered from evil words and works, from all unholiness of conversation; doing no evil to any child of man, and being zealous of all good works.[105]

The liberty Christians have as children of God comes from the Father through the Lord Jesus Christ, who is the source of the peace with God and freedom from sin that is always mediated by the person and activity of the Holy Spirit. This Trinitarian activity sets us free from evil desires and inclinations, from vile and inordinate affections, and all the rest by shedding the love of God through Christ in the fellowship Spirit in the human heart that simultaneously dispels love of the world.

Late in his career, in 1789, Wesley composed a sermon entitled "The Unity of the Divine Being." It is an illuminating sermon for a variety of reasons. At the beginning of the sermon Wesley noted that "as there is one God, so there is one religion, and one happiness for all men." Wesley then treated many of the attributes of the one God in classic terms reflecting the Anglican tradition he had learned from a variety of sources.

Toward the end of this opening section, Wesley stated that God created everything "for himself," but not out of any kind of necessity as if God were under some kind of compulsion or need to create. Rather, God created all things, including human beings, in freedom, that they might all be happy in loving relation to the Creator.[106]

Ever the pastor, Wesley followed this up with sage advice to parents concerning how to inculcate this in children: "As soon as a child begins to talk or to run alone, say something of this kind: 'See! what is that which shines so over your head? That we call the sun. . . . Feel how it warms you. . . . But God made the sun. The sun could not shine, nor warm, nor do any good, without him.'. . . 'He made *you*; and he made you to be happy in him; and nothing else can make you happy.' "[107] Wesley said that "this should be pressed on every human creature, young and old, the more earnestly and diligently because so exceedingly few, even of those that are called Christians, seem to know anything about it."[108]

As we might expect, Wesley then moved into various rivals to God that vie for people's attention, love, and affection, including three false religions: "religion of opinions," "religion of forms," and "religion of works," or "in a word, a religion wherein 'God in Christ, reconciling the world unto

---

105 *Works*, 1:262–66.
106 *Works*, 4:62–64.
107 Ibid., 4:64.
108 Ibid.

himself' is not the Alpha and Omega, . . . the first and the last point." It is at this point that Wesley described true religion as "right tempers towards God and man" or "in two words . . . gratitude to our Creator . . . and benevolence to our fellow-creatures" or "loving God with all our heart, and our neighbor as ourselves."[109]

Here Wesley was talking about Christian salvation in general, but since sanctification is the real "house" of salvation, what he said here reflects his understanding of sanctification. He also noted that the foundation of true religion is found in God reconciling the world to himself in Christ and in our coming to know this forgiveness and love from God (justification/regeneration). This love of God for us is always the sole source that generates gratitude or love for God and benevolence or love for others (sanctification).

It is the profoundly Trinitarian dimension in Wesley's description of sanctification in terms of communion with the Father and Son through the Spirit in this sermon "The Unity of the Divine Being" that is of primary interest to us in this section:

> This is religion, and this is happiness, the happiness for which we were made. This begins when we begin to know God, by the teaching of his own Spirit. As soon as the Father of spirits reveals his Son in our hearts, and the Son reveals his Father, the love of God is shed abroad in our hearts; then, and not till then, are we happy. We are happy, first, in the consciousness of his favor, which indeed is better than the life itself [justification]; next, in the constant communion with the Father, and with his Son, Jesus Christ [participation]; then in all the heavenly tempers which he hath wrought in us by his Spirit; again, in the testimony of his Spirit that all our works please him; and lastly, in the testimony of our own spirit that "in simplicity and godly sincerity we have had our conversation in the world" [assurance]. Standing fast in this liberty from sin and sorrow, wherein Christ made them free, real Christians "rejoice evermore, pray without ceasing, and in everything give thanks" [sanctification]. And their happiness still increases as they "grow up into the measure of the stature of the fullness of Christ [Christian perfection]."[110]

This is a marvelous example of Wesley's participatory understanding of sanctification as constant communion with the Father and Son through the Spirit, which fills Christians' hearts with love toward God and toward others. In so doing, it transforms all our tempers and, in turn, all our conversation

---

109 Ibid., 4:66–67.
110 Ibid., 4:67.

with a world, a phrase with holistic intent that, according to Wesley, "is exceedingly broad, taking in our whole deportment, yea, every inward as well as outward circumstance, . . . every motion of our heart, of our tongue, of . . . our actions and . . . the employment of all our powers and faculties . . . with respect either to God or man."[111] In fact, one of Wesley's most common shorthand summaries of Christian salvation is "the faith that worketh love," echoing Galatians 5:6. The result is holiness and happiness, a growing into the fullness of Christ awaiting Christian perfection.[112]

In his "Sermon on the Mount, IX," Wesley provided a particularly clear statement that sanctification is affected by both Christ and the Spirit. Wesley here expounded Matthew 6:25, "Seek ye first the Kingdom of God and his righteousness." Wesley defined righteousness in familiar terms: "Righteousness is the fruit of God's reigning in the heart. And what is righteousness but love? The love of God and of all mankind flowing from faith in Jesus Christ, and producing . . . every right disposition of heart toward God and toward man. And by these it produces all holy actions."[113] This is a clear and consistent statement of sanctification, beginning with the Triune God's presence, love, and power in the inner sanctum of the soul, producing right dispositions of heart around love on the throne, and these dispositions working themselves out in holy action and works of love "acceptable to God and profitable to man," as Wesley expressed it.[114]

It is at this point that Wesley elaborated on what is involved in "His righteousness": "It is his own free *gift* to us, for the sake of Jesus Christ the

---

111 *Works*, 1:305.

112 Later in the sermon "The Unity of the Divine Being," Wesley made the same basic points:

> An unhappy man . . . cries out of the deep to him that is able to save. . . . It is not long before he finds "redemption in the blood of Jesus, even forgiveness of sins." Then "the Father reveals his Son" in his heart, and he "calls Jesus Lord by the Holy Ghost." And then the love of God is "shed abroad in his heart, by the Holy Spirit." . . . From this principle springs real, disinterested benevolence to all mankind. . . . This is religion, even the whole mind which was also in Christ Jesus [the transformation of our inner tempers leading to changed words and actions]. . . .
>
> There can be no doubt but from this love to God and man a suitable conversation will follow. . . . His actions will spring from the same source with his words, even from the abundance of a loving heart. (*Works*, 4:70)

113 *Works*, 1:642.

114 Ibid., 1:642–43.

righteous, through whom alone it is purchased for us." Here Wesley noted that this righteousness of heart and life comes as a gift *from* God, the Father, but a gift that comes to us *through* Jesus Christ, who secures it for us. Wesley continued, indicating the contribution of the third person of the Trinity: "And it is his *work*: it is he alone that worketh it in us by the inspiration of his Holy Spirit."[115] This is entirely consistent with what Wesley said in his "Letter to a Roman Catholic" about the role of the Spirit, the "immediate cause of all holiness in us."[116]

Wesley then turned to Romans 10:3, dealing with the "unbelieving Jews" "ignorant of God's righteousness." What is interesting here is that Wesley developed a fully Trinitarian conception of the righteousness of God:

> They [the unbelieving Jews] were "ignorant of God's righteousness," not only of the righteousness of Christ, imputed to every believer, whereby all his sins are blotted out, and he is reconciled to the favour of God [justification]; but . . . they were ignorant of that inward righteousness, of that holiness of heart, which is with the utmost propriety termed "God's righteousness," as being both his own free gift through Christ, and his own work, by his almighty Spirit [sanctification].[117]

In the next paragraph, Wesley defined this righteousness of God that comes through Christ and works in us by the Holy Spirit as "holiness of heart, the renewal of the soul in all its desires, tempers, and affections," which is another definition of sanctification.[118]

These many instances in Wesley's publications all present a clear yet theologically subtle conception of a participatory, economic Trinitarian understanding of sanctifying grace. The cumulative effect of these Trinitarian accounts of justification and sanctification, indeed of the entire *ordo salutis*, in Wesley's publications as documented through this chapter reveal that there is a deep Trinitarian dimension interwoven in Wesley's *soteriology*, or, as Wesley said in his sermon "On The Trinity," "Knowledge of the Three-One God is interwoven with all true Christian faith, with all vital religion."[119] This soteriological knowledge of the Triune God stands in stark contrast to the abstract and lifeless accounts of the Trinity by the defenders of the doctrine throughout the Trinitarian controversies and reveals the theological depth of

---

115 Ibid., 1: 643.
116 Outler, ed., *Wesley*, 495.
117 *Works*, 1:643.
118 Ibid., 1:644.
119 *Works*, 2:385.

Wesley's comment that the defenders "utterly lost their way" and "above all persons" profoundly hurt the cause they intended to promote.

There is one additional account of sanctification in Trinitarian terms in Wesley's sermons that we will examine, as it serves as a bridge to Wesley's Trinitarian account of Christian perfection. This one comes from his sermon "The Repentance of Believers" and reveals Wesley's carefully thought-out account of how sanctification in the Christian life proceeds.

In this sermon, Wesley dealt with in what "sense we are to *repent* after we are justified." Wesley adamantly argued for repentance after justification and stated that "till we do so we can go no farther. For till we are sensible of our disease it admits no cure." Even when we have been justified by grace and faith, we are to "repent" and "believe" in "a peculiar sense, different from that wherein we believed in order to justification."[120]

Wesley outlined several "branches" of this repentance on the part of those justified, including the "conviction of . . . sin *remaining* in their hearts" that "it *cleaves* to our words and actions," and "a conviction of their *utter helplessness* . . . to think one good thought, to form one good desire, to speak one good word, or to do one good work."[121] They can do all these things by the Triune God, "but it is not by *their own strength*."[122] This repentance or conviction of the sin that remains after justification and human powerlessness to overcome it sets the stage for believing the further good news of the gospel.

In the next section of the sermon, Wesley presented the startling scope of sanctification, indeed full sanctification, for we are called to believe that "he who is 'the brightness of his Father's glory, the express image of his person,' 'is able to save unto the uttermost all that come unto God through him.'. . . He is able to save you from all the sin that cleaves to all your words and actions."[123] Indeed, God is not only able is to save us, the Triune God is "*willing* to do this . . . willing to save you *today* . . . willing to save you *now*."[124]

Wesley summarized these two points (our powerlessness to save ourselves and the ability of the Triune God to do so) and the dialectic between them with particular clarity at the end of the second section of the sermon: "By repentance we feel the sin remaining in our hearts, and cleaving to our words and actions. By faith we receive the power of God in Christ, purifying

---

120 *Works*, 1:347.
121 Ibid., 1:341–45.
122 Ibid., 1:345.
123 Ibid., 1:347.
124 Ibid., 1:347–48.

our hearts and cleansing our hands. . . . Repentance says, 'Without him I can do nothing'; faith says, 'I can do all things through Christ strengthening me.'" At the end of this section, Wesley presented a full participatory Trinitarian account of sanctification, indeed full sanctification or Christian perfection:

> By the same faith we feel the power of Christ every moment resting upon us. . . . Leaning on our Beloved, even Christ in us the hope of glory, who dwelleth in our hearts by faith, who likewise is ever interceding for us at the right hand of God, we receive help from him to think and speak and act what is acceptable in his sight. Thus does he "prevent them that believe in all their doings, and further them with his continual help," so that all their designs, conversations, and actions are "begun, continued and ended in him." Thus doth he "cleanse the thoughts of their hearts, by the inspiration of his Holy Spirit, that they may perfectly love him, and worthily magnify his holy name." [125]

The two quotations that Wesley cited in this text are from the Book of Common Prayer. At God's "right hand," Christ intercedes to the Father on our behalf and simultaneously dwells in our hearts, bringing the efficacy of grace to bear upon our lives by the "inspiration" of the Spirit so that we love God and others in doxological refrain.

In the next and final paragraph of this section, Wesley reasserted that "Repentance says, 'Without him I can do nothing': faith says, 'I can do all things through Christ strengthening me.'" Then Wesley linked all that he has said thus far with full sanctification or Christian perfection: "Through him [Christ] I cannot only overcome, but expel all the enemies of my soul. . . . I can 'love the Lord my God with all my heart, mind, soul and strength' . . . and walk in holiness and righteousness before him all the days of my life."[126]

Wesley made his intention regarding Christian perfection clear in the next sentence, where he noted that his whole discussion of repentance in believers dispels the "mischievous" opinion "that we are *wholly* sanctified when we are justified; that our hearts are then cleansed from all sin."[127] The concluding sentences of the sermon drive home this intent: "We thus, as it were, go out of ourselves, in order to be swallowed up in him [a reference to the sheer depth of Wesley's vision of our union with Christ]; when we sink into nothing that he may be all in all. Then, his almighty grace having

---

125 Ibid., 1:349–50.

126 Ibid., 1:350.

127 Ibid.

abolished 'every high thing which exalted itself against' him, every temper, and thought, and word, and work is 'brought into the obedience of Christ.'"[128]

Wesley's account of sanctification follows the participatory, economic Trinitarian pattern that we have seen throughout his conceptualization of the *ordo salutis*. This is also true of his understanding of Christian perfection. The next section will summarize the Trinitarian dimension of Wesley's understanding of Christian perfection before dealing with his Trinitarian vision of our eschatological destiny.

6. Christian Perfection

So confident was Wesley in God's grace that comes to us through Christ in the power of the Holy Spirit that he affirmed a further development of Christian life called Christian perfection. This section will not delve deeply into all the details of Wesley's conception of being perfected in love. This is an area of Wesley's theology fraught with subtleties and, therefore, misunderstandings by both his followers and his critics. The secondary literature on the subject is voluminous. Those interested in a contemporary Trinitarian treatment of the subject should consult Thomas A. Noble's excellent work *Holy Trinity: Holy People, The Theology of Christian Perfection*, which includes a chapter entitled "Wesley's Doctrine of Christian Perfection."[129]

At its core, Wesley's doctrine of Christian perfection is rooted in his deep optimism about the power of the Triune God of the gospel to transform human life.[130] He believed that Christians can become so profoundly aware of, and transformed by, the love of God through Christ in the Spirit that Christians could live a life of love for God and for neighbor in all things. For Wesley, Christians perfected in love are not perfect in knowledge and, therefore, are ignorant of many things; nor are they free from infirmities like poor memory or impropriety of language. So those perfected in love still make mistakes and need Christ's forgiveness. They continue to grow in grace and

---

128 Ibid., 1:352.

129 Thomas A. Noble, *Holy Trinity: Holy People, The Theology of Christian Perfection* (Eugene, OR: Cascade Books, 2013). Noble's book is the printed form of the thirty-fourth *Didsbury Lectures* at Nazarene Theological College, Manchester, in October 2012. The work is a theologically rich restatement of the doctrine of Christian perfection from a Trinitarian perspective. See also the chapters on Christian perfection in Maddox, *Responsible Grace*, and Collins, *Theology of John Wesley*, for extremely helpful discussions, as well as references to the additional secondary literature on the subject.

130 See Albert Outler's insightful comments in his introduction in *John Wesley*, ed. Outler, 30–33.

in love so that "perfection" is not a static faultlessness, an unimprovable state from which Christians can no longer fall.[131]

Yet, Wesley believed that Christians can be so transformed by God's grace that all their affections, all their thoughts, all their words, all their actions are continually dominated by love for God and neighbor, though always only by grace through faith. Despite Wesley's careful stating of his position, including all of his nuancing and qualifying it, so as not be misunderstood, the Calvinists of Wesley's day were suspicious that this emphasis on "perfection" signified a reintroduction of some form of works-righteous into Christian faith and life. In his less careful moments, Wesley occasionally wrote things that contributed to the misunderstanding of his views.

The most famous participatory Trinitarian statement of Christian perfection quoted in nearly every treatment of Wesley on the Trinity is as brief as is it profound: "Constant communion with God the Father and Son *fills* their [Christians'] hearts with *humble love*. Now this is what I always did, and do now mean by [Christian] 'perfection.'"[132] In his "Letter to a Roman Catholic," Wesley stated that the Spirit is the immediate cause of communion with the Father and the Son. We hear echoes of the spiritual respiration imagery from "The New Birth" sermon of God breathing upon one's soul and one's soul breathing back a fellowship with the Father through the Son in the Spirit that sustains the life of God in the soul in his participatory vision of Christian perfection as constant communion with the Father and Son leading to hearts full of humble love.

The above quotation is not the only place where Wesley spoke of Christian perfection in terms of the Triune God dwelling in our lives in a fellowship that leads to the fullness of Christian freedom from sin and freedom for love. Toward the end of 1740, Wesley met with Bishop Edmund Gibson at Whitehall, where Gibson wanted an account of Wesley's teaching. Wesley told the bishop what he meant by Christian perfection "without any disguise or reserve." According to Wesley's account, the bishop responded by saying, "Mr. Wesley, if this be all you mean, publish it to all the world."[133] The result was Wesley's sermon "Christian Perfection," published in 1741.

After dealing with the various ways in which Christians are never perfect in this life, Wesley turned to his positive account of what Christian Perfection entailed. He began by noting that part of the underlying premise of

---

131 *Works,* 2:100–104.

132 *Works*, 21:245.

133 See Outler's introduction in *Works,* 2:97–98, for the account of the meeting with Bishop Gibson as the occasion for the sermon.

Christian perfection is "that there are several stages in Christian life as well as in natural"; there are "new-born babes," "young men," and "fathers" in the faith. Wesley then quoted from 1 John and inserted his understanding of the text: "'I write unto you, fathers, because ye have known him that is from the beginning.' Ye have known both the Father and the Son and the Spirit of Christ in your inmost soul." Wesley then linked this Trinitarian indwelling of a Christian's inmost soul with perfection: "Ye are 'perfect men, being grown up to the measure of the stature of the fullness of Christ.'"[134]

The sermon unpacked the stages of Christian life in relation to a growing liberty from the power of sin. Wesley maintained that all Christians, "even babes in Christ," "are made free from outward sin."[135] This is a bold statement, especially for a Protestant, so Wesley, in a rather amusing rhetorical flurry, dealt with common Protestant caveats around sin in the Christian life:

> Indeed it is said this means only, he sinneth not *wilfully*; or he doth not commit sin *habitually*; or, *not as other men do*; or *not as he did before*. But by whom is this said? By St. John? No. There is no such word in the text . . . nor in all this . . . . Why, then, the best way to answer a bold assertion is simply to deny it. And if any man can prove it from the Word of God, let him bring forth his strong reasons.[136]

Wesley then expended the next ten pages of the sermon defending his assertion. Wesley had a high view of the freedom of Christians, even new ones, from outward sin!

In the final pages of the sermon, Wesley moved on to the freedom of those who have grown up into the stature of the fullness of Christ. Here Wesley focused on the Christological participatory dimension of Christian perfection, stating that those who are mature are perfect so as

> to be freed from evil thoughts, . . . secondly, from evil tempers. . . . Every one of these can say with St. Paul, "I am crucified with Christ: nevertheless I live; yet not I but Christ liveth in me"—words that manifestly describe a deliverance from inward as well as from outward sin. . . . "I live not"—my evil nature, the body of sin, is destroyed—and . . . "Christ liveth in me"—and therefore all that is holy, and just, and good.[137]

---

134 Ibid., 2:105.
135 Ibid., 2:105–6.
136 Ibid., 2:107.
137 Ibid., 2:117–18.

Remember that Wesley noted the Trinitarian dimension of this stage of Christian maturity ("fathers" of the faith) at the beginning of the sermon: "Ye have known both the Father and the Son and the Spirit of Christ in your inmost soul. Ye are 'perfect men, being grown up to the measure of the stature of the fullness of Christ.'"[138]

In his *Plain Account of Christian Perfection, as Believed and Taught by the Reverend Mr. John Wesley, from the Year 1725, to the Year 1765*, Wesley not only noted various dimensions of Christian perfection, he identified the activity of the first and second persons of the Trinity involved in effecting perfection in our lives:

> In one view, it is purity of intention, dedicating all the life to God. It is the giving God all our heart; it is one desire and design ruling all our tempers. It is the devoting, not a part, but all our soul, body, and substance to God. In another view, it is all the mind which was in Christ, enabling us to walk as Christ walked. It is the circumcision of the heart from all filthiness, all inward as well as outward pollution. It is a renewal of the heart in the whole image of God, the full likeness of Him that created it. In yet another, it is the loving God with all our heart, and our neighbour as ourselves. Now, take it in which of these views you please, (for there is no material difference,) and this is the whole and sole perfection, as a train of writings prove to a demonstration, which I have believed and taught for these forty years, from the year 1725 to the year 1765.
>
> Now let this perfection appear in its native form, and who can speak one word against it? Will any dare to speak against loving the Lord our God with all our heart, and our neighbour as ourselves? Against a renewal of heart, not only in part, but in the whole image of God? Who is he that will open his mouth against being cleansed from all pollution both of flesh and spirit; or against having all the mind that was in Christ, and walking in all things as Christ walked?[139]

This statement on Christian perfection is particularly illuminating because it constituted one of Wesley's lively defenses of his teaching intended to disclose the consistency of his position over time. The focus of this statement was on the effect upon Christian life of this culmination of grace, not on the Trinitarian dimension, yet God and Christ are explicitly identified.

In his sermon "On Perfection," published in 1784, late in his career, Wesley provided yet another summary of various elements that comprise

138 *Works*, 2:105.
139 *Works*, 13:190.

his vision of being perfected in love, including the Trinitarian dimension. Wesley began his treatment by focusing on the predominant theme that we have seen throughout this discussion of Christian perfection: "This is the sum of Christian perfection: it is all comprised in that one word, love."[140]

The Trinitarian basis comes into focus as Wesley further defined Christian perfection in what is now a familiar manner as having the "mind that was in Christ," including "the whole disposition of his mind, all his affections, all his tempers, both toward God and man."[141] Wesley then conceptualized this "having the mind of Christ" in participatory Trinitarian terms.

Wesley first treated the pneumatological element: "Perfection in yet another view . . . is the one undivided 'fruit of the Spirit' . . . a glorious constellation of graces. . . . All these to be knit together in one . . . is Christian perfection."[142] Of course, the pneumatological fruit worked in us by the Spirit is in no way separate from the Christological grounding of Christian perfection in our re-creation that only occurs as the Spirit unites us to Christ.

As a result, Wesley referred his readers to Ephesians and Colossians, where Paul tells Christians to put "on the new man" and to be "renewed after the image of him that created him." "We can never recover" the "moral image of God," Wesley noted, "till we are 'created anew in Christ Jesus,' and this is perfection."[143] For Wesley, our participatory re-creation in Christ is simply the Christological element of Christian perfection, whereas the pneumatological element is the undivided fruit of the Spirit. It is clear that for Wesley these are simply facets of a unified whole and can only be understood in terms of the perichoretic presence and coactivity of the second and third persons of the Trinity in relation to Christian perfection.

Wesley did not neglect Christian perfection viewed from the perspective of the first person of the Trinity in this sermon. Here Wesley spoke of being holy and offering ourselves as living sacrifices to God. For Wesley, "perfection is another name for universal holiness—inward and outward righteousness—holiness of life arising from holiness of heart."[144] But what is this holiness of life arising from holiness of heart but an offering of ourselves "'a living sacrifice unto God' . . . 'acceptable to God through Jesus Christ.'" Wesley concluded: "If you have truly presented yourselves to God, you offer

140 *Works*, 3:74.
141 Ibid.
142 Ibid., 3:75.
143 Ibid.
144 Ibid., 3:75–76.

up to him continually all your thoughts, and words and actions, through the Son of his love, as a sacrifice of praise and thanksgiving."[145]

Thomas A. Noble argues that Wesley's vision of Christian perfection is not "primarily a negative, freedom or purification from sin," for "purification from 'inbred sin' . . . is only a means to an end: the end is that we should be filled with the love of God."[146] Wesley explicitly stated this point on occasion. In his comments on Ephesians 3:19 in his *Notes on the New Testament*, Wesley observed that "*That ye may be filled*—Which is the sum of all. *With all the fulness of God*—With all his light, love, wisdom, power and glory. A perfection far beyond a bare freedom from sin."[147]

Elsewhere, in his "Earnest Appeal to Men of Reason and Religion," Wesley said that love is what "real" religion is all about: "the loving God with all our heart and soul and strength, as having first loved us, as the fountain of all the good we have received, . . . and the loving . . . every man on earth, as our own soul." Wesley continued this line of thought in a moving vision of love:

> This love we believe to be the medicine of life, the never-failing remedy, for all the evils of a disordered world, for all the miseries and vices of men. Wherever this is, there are virtue and happiness, going hand in hand. . . . This is the religion we long to see established in the world, a religion of love and joy and peace, having its seat in the heart, in the inmost soul, but ever showing itself by its fruits, continually springing forth not only in all innocence—for "love worketh no ill to his neighbor"—but likewise in every kind of beneficence, in spreading virtue and happiness all around it.[148]

Wesley then told his readers that "the straight way to the religion of love" is "by faith," which he defined in Trinitarian terms: "Faith . . . is the eye of the new-born soul. . . . He seeth 'the light of the glory of God in the face of Jesus Christ' . . . 'what manner of Love the Father hath bestowed upon us' . . . who are born of the Spirit."[149]

---

145 Ibid., 3:76.

146 See Noble, *Holy Trinity: Holy People*, 86.

147 See Wesley's comment on Ephesians 3:19 in *Notes on the NT*, vol. 2.

148 See Wesley's 1743 "An Earnest Appeal to Men of Reason and Religion," in *The Works of John Wesley*, ed. Gerald Cragg, vol. 11, *The Appeals to Men of Reason and Religion and Certain Related and Open Letters* (Oxford: Clarendon, 1975), 45–46.

149 *Works*, 3:46–47

There is another side of Wesley's doctrine of Christian perfection, one that moved to the other end of the dialectic between love and the law. Love is the sum or fulfillment of the law, but, for Wesley, keeping the law at every point is what love has us do. Here is Wesley's rather pointed way of saying it: "Love is all in all . . . it is 'the fulfilling of the law,' 'the end of the commandment,' of every commandment of God. . . . It is true that without this whatever we do, whatever we suffer, profits us nothing. But it does not follow that love is all in such a sense as to supersede either faith or good works. It is 'the fulfilling of the law,' not by releasing us from but by constraining us to obey it."[150] As noted earlier in this chapter, Wesley saw no tension at all between the gospel/love and the law/obedience: "There is therefore the closest connection that can be conceived between the law and the gospel."[151]

Wesley's confidence in the love of God the Father through the grace of Christ in the power of the Spirit whose indwelling presence fills the hearts of those perfected in love led him to state the other side of this close connection between the gospel/love and the law/obedience with exacting precision: "The gospel continually leads us to a more exact fulfilling of the law."[152] Wesley followed the logic of his vision of keeping the law, asserting that "if these things be so, we cannot but be at a loss what to think of those who in all ages of the church have undertaken to change or supersede some commands of God." Wesley drove home his point, with passion and rigor: "Christianity . . . includes the whole moral law of God, both by way of injunction and of promise. . . . What God demands is an entire obedience; we are to have an eye to all his commandments; otherwise we lose all the labour we take in keeping some, and our poor souls for ever and ever."[153]

In light of these texts, it is clear that while Noble is correct that Wesley saw Christian perfection as freedom from sin so as to be fully in fellowship with the Father and Son through the Spirit filled with humble love, it is also true that this participatory Trinitarian embodiment of love, for Wesley, entails an absolutely rigorous keeping of every single command found in scripture. We should expect Wesley to develop his Trinitarian vision of Christian perfection precisely this way, given his estimation and portrayal of the moral law in Christological incarnational categories.

Wesley wrote his sermon "The Original, Nature, Properties, and Uses of the Law" in 1750 to safeguard the Methodists against the antinomianism

150 *Works*, 1:542.
151 Ibid., 1:554–55.
152 Ibid., 1:554.
153 Ibid., 1:555–56.

that Wesley detected first among the Moravians and then in the Calvinist branch of the revival. In this sermon, Wesley presented his vision of the moral law in Christological imagery:

> This law is an incorruptible picture of the high and holy One that inhabiteth eternity. . . . It is the face of God unveiled . . . to his creatures as they are able to bear it. . . . It is the heart of God disclosed to man. . . . The law of God . . . is a copy of the eternal mind, a transcript of the divine nature; yea, it is the fairest offspring of the everlasting Father, the brightest efflux of his essential wisdom, the visible beauty of the Most High. . . . It is indeed in the highest degree pure, chaste, clean, holy. Otherwise it could not be the immediate offspring, and much less the express resemblance of God, who is essential holiness.[154]

Wesley also described the moral law as "supreme, unchangeable reason; . . . unalterable rectitude; . . . the everlasting fitness of things that are or ever were created . . . the nature and fitness of things, and on their essential relations to each other . . . the work of his hands."[155]

Despite Wesley's candid admission (that he was "speaking after the manner of men" and was "sensible of what a shortness, and even impropriety, there is in these and all other human expressions, when we endeavor by these faint pictures to shadow out the deep things of God"), one cannot help but wonder whether this exalted vision of the moral law in incarnational categories is not the ultimate theological root of the rigorous moralism and legalism that has at times haunted the Wesleyan/Methodist tradition and its doctrine of Christian perfection. It is rather easy for a serious Methodist to shift the focus from the fullness of Trinitarian fellowship to a careful cataloguing of scriptural commands and a scrupulous legalistic conformity to every single one of them. This tendency is doubly reinforced by Wesley's assertion, "What God demands is an entire obedience; we are to have an eye to all his commandments; otherwise we lose all the labour we take in keeping some, and our poor souls for ever and ever."[156] The threat, in statements like this one, of what failure to embody exacting obedience includes is rather stark.[157]

---

154 *Works*, 2:9–11.

155 Ibid., 2:10, 13.

156 *Works*, 1:555–56.

157 There are multiple problems with Wesley's depiction of the law in Christological imagery. It drives a wedge between the moral character of the one God that comes to expression in the law and the character of the Triune God revealed preeminently in Jesus Christ, a knowledge of God actualized in us in the Holy Spirit. In so doing,

What is important for this discussion of Wesley's doctrine of Christian perfection is that this incarnational depiction of the moral law is the deep theological root of why Wesley thought that, when the love of God the Father through the grace of Christ in the fellowship of the Spirit fills our hearts and lives with the humble love for God and others, this fullness of Trinitarian fellowship expresses itself in a rigorous exact keeping of the moral law, all of the commands in scripture, and everything implied in those commands.[158]

---

this kind of depiction of the moral law separates the law from Christ and gives the law its own independent ontological status on par with Christ. The key theological root that Wesley did not grasp is that there is no hypostatic union between the moral law and the Word or Son of God, as there is in Jesus Christ in whom the very Word or Son of God has become incarnate. Jesus Christ alone forever hypostatically united the divine nature and human nature in his one person in an utterly unique manner unlike what we find in the moral law, either in nature, what Wesley calls the "eternal fitness of things," or in scripture. The hypostatic union in the incarnate Son must qualify all we think and say about the moral law and its character.

I see this to be the fundamental point in Collins's book signaled in the subtitle: *The Theology of John Wesley: Holy Love and the Shape of Grace*. Collins's predominant focus is not on the Triune God, and therefore the Trinitarian dimension of Wesley's theology does not really fully come into view throughout his book, despite the insightful treatment of the Trinity that Collins provides in his chapter on the Holy Spirit. The book focuses on the moral character of the one God as the key that unlocks the right nuancing of all aspects of Wesley's theology, but a nuancing at the expense of the Trinitarian dimension and what it has to contribute to understanding Wesley's theology.

What troubles me most about this is that it is this very aspect of Wesley's theology that so exalts the moral law in Christological imagery and status that is the theological root of the moralism and legalism that has always been the temptation of the Wesleyan/Methodist tradition, especially here in North America, where American individualism deformed Methodism nearly from the beginning and helped generate American Methodism's unhealthy intellectual fascination with the doctrine of the one God, the moral character of the one God, and a moralistic vision of the gospel and the church to go along with it, whether in terms of personal holiness or social holiness. What is missing is Wesley's Trinitarian vision of love that we come to know by participatory acquaintance with God's love in the gospel, a love that is the "medicine of life, the never-failing remedy" for a disordered world.

158 While theologically consistent within his doctrine of Christian perfection, this depiction of the moral law in incarnational categories points to a tension in Wesley's theology between his doctrine of the one God and the one God's attributes (especially the moral law as a "copy of the eternal mind," "a transcript of the divine nature," and "the fairest offspring" and "express resemblance of God") and his economic Trinitarian vision of Christian faith and the Triune God, whom we know by participatory "acquaintance." Remember how Wesley said it in his sermon on

Throughout this section it is clear that all the Trinitarian persons are present and coactively involved in Christian perfection along similar lines as with all the themes that comprise Wesley's understanding of the order of salvation. Indeed, this Trinitarian dimension of Christian perfection finds its final telos in our eschatological destiny, a destiny that Wesley also conceptualized in participatory terms.

7. Our Trinitarian Eschatological Destiny

The telos of Wesley's *ordo salutis* lies beyond the present age in the eschatological final destiny for human beings and all creation. According to Wesley, human beings (and all creation) will not simply be restored to the pristine condition of their pre-Fall original state, for the blessedness of the new age will far exceed that of the original creation.

Here Wesley affirmed the *felix culpa*, or "happy fault," tradition in which God permitted the Fall of humanity and all the evil consequences "that he may draw immense, eternal good out of this temporary evil."[159] What is of

original sin: "We had no acquaintance with him. As we know there is an emperor of China, whom yet we do not know, so we knew there was a King of all the earth; but yet we knew him not. For 'no one knoweth the Father but the Son, and he to whom the Son willeth to reveal him. And no one knoweth the Son but the Father, and he to whom the Father revealeth him" (*Works*, 2:177). Wesley saw no tension whatsoever between his doctrine of the one God and the doctrine of the Trinity. In fact, in his sermon "On the Trinity," Wesley admitted that how the one God and the three Trinitarian persons are related is a *mystery* we cannot know and about which we cannot speak: "I believe . . . that God is Three and One. But the *manner, how,* I do not comprehend; . . . in the *manner* lies the mystery . . . therefore I believe nothing about it" (ibid., 384). The appeal to mystery at precisely this crucial theological juncture absolves those like Wesley who appeal to it from inquiring into the Christian doctrine of God at precisely the point where the Trinitarian debates so damaged the doctrine and disconnected the Christian doctrine of God from vital vibrant Christian faith, life, and worship. While trying to show *how* the three could be one using various analogies that disconnected the Trinity from vital religion, the defenders of the Trinity turned the Christian doctrine of God into the esoteric intellectual artifact that moderns relegated to the rubbish heap of improbable and discredited ideas, as we saw in chapter 1. But is the appeal to mystery and, therefore, silence regarding this crucial point of the Christian doctrine of God the best or the only alternative to the unhelpful use of analogies on the part of those who tried to defend the doctrine? We will return to this question in the postscript to this work.

159 *Works,* 2:499. The "happy fault" tradition is theologically flawed, and there are better ways to incorporate a Trinitarian eschatological destiny that far exceeds that of original creation.

interest here is the way in which Wesley, in his sermon "God's Love to Fallen Man," interweaves the Trinitarian dimension into his position:

> Unless all the partakers of human nature had received that deadly wound in Adam it would not have been needful for the Son of God to take our nature upon him. . . . Was it not to remedy this very thing that "the Word was made flesh"? . . .
>
> What is the necessary consequence of this? It is this—there could then have been no such thing as faith in God, "thus loving the world," giving his only Son for us men and for our salvation. There could have been no such thing as faith in the Son of God, "as loving us and giving himself for us." There could have been no faith in the Spirit of God, as renewing the image of God in our hearts. . . .
>
> And the same grand blank . . . must likewise have been in our love. . . . We could not have loved him [God the Father] . . . as "delivering up his Son for us all." . . . We could not have loved him [the Son of God] as "bearing our sins in his own body on the tree." . . . We could not have loved the Holy Ghost as revealing to us the Father and the Son, as . . . sealing us unto the day of redemption.[160]

The eschatological vision Wesley had in mind was not simply disembodied saints contemplating the splendor, beauty, and glory of the God for all eternity. Wesley's theology of the new creation entails the renewal, the transformation of all creation, including all living creatures, indeed the entire universe, as Theodore Runyon emphasizes in his work *The New Creation: John Wesley's Theology for Today.*[161] In Wesley's own words, "We look for new heavens and a new earth—Raised as it were out of the ashes of the old."[162] Indeed, elsewhere Wesley stated that "universal restoration . . . is to succeed the universal destruction" when "the day of judgement and the destruction of ungodly men" take place.[163] In fact, "the whole brute creation

---

160 Ibid., 2:425–27.

161 Runyon, *The New Creation*, 7–12. See also the chapters on Wesley's eschatology in Maddox, *Responsible Grace*; and Collins, *Theology of John Wesley.*

162 See the note on 2 Peter 3:13 in Wesley, *Notes on the New Testament.*

163 *Works,* 2:502–3. Wesley affirmed a twofold final destiny of heaven and hell. His doctrine of hell is incredibly realistic, a lake of fire and unmitigated eternal punishment and suffering. In his sermon "Of Hell," Wesley said it this way:

> Let us consider the *peona damni,* the punishment of loss. This commences in that very moment wherein the soul is separated from the body; in that

will . . . undoubtedly be restored . . . to a far higher degree of each than they ever enjoyed [at their creation]."[164]

However, does Wesley understand the eschatological destiny of human beings and all creation in Trinitarian terms? Do we find a participatory Trinitarian dimension in Wesley's vision of the new creation? Of course! In his sermon "The General Spread of the Gospel," written for the *Arminian Magazine* in 1783, Wesley concluded his thoughts this way:

> All unprejudiced persons may see with their eyes that he is already renewing the face of the earth. And we have strong reason to hope that the work he hath begun he will carry on unto the day of his Lord Jesus; that he will never intermit this blessed work of his Spirit until he has fulfilled all his promises; until he hath put a period to sin and misery, and infirmity, and death; and re-established universal holiness and happiness, and caused all the inhabitants of the earth to sing together, "Hallelujah!". . . "Blessing, and glory, and wisdom, and honour, and power, and might be unto our God for ever and ever!"[165]

God the Father is carrying on the renewal of all things in Christ by the power of the Spirit until that day when the Lord Jesus returns in final victory and all creation will resound in praise and adoration to the Triune God. All three

---

> instant the soul loses all those pleasures. . . . There is . . . nothing new, but one unvaried scene of horror upon horror. . .
>
> If there be any fire it is unquestionably material. . . . Does not our Lord speak *as if* it were real fire? . . . Does he design to frighten his poor creatures? What with scarecrows? . . . O let not anyone think so!
>
> Nay, if . . . only one hand or one foot kept in a burning fiery furnace, would not a man meantime be much at ease? . . . Put your finger into that candle: can you bear it even for one minute? What then will it be to have the whole body plunged into a lake of fire burning with brimstone! (Works, 3:34, 37–40)

So the damned will not share in the restoration of all things that follows the final destruction and judgement. Given what Wesley said about God demanding a rigorous entire obedience to the law as an incorruptible transcript, the immediate offspring of a high and holy God, his doctrine of hell is no surprise at all. But it is this conception that turned hell into an unpreachable doctrine, as it should. A Christian doctrine of hell has to be related to the love of God that comes to us through Christ in the power of the Spirit, rather than merely correlated with attributes of the one God and the independent ontological status of the law.

164 *Works,* 2:445–46.

165 Ibid., 2:499.

Trinitarian persons are involved in this eschatological renewal that will come to final fruition with the return of Christ.

What about the final destiny itself? Will the blessed Trinity not only effect the eschatological renewal of all things but actually be the content of the end or telos of Wesley's vision of the new creation? In his sermon "The New Creation," he detailed the astonishing fullness of transformation, the new heaven and earth, that will one day be when God proclaims, "Behold, I make all things new."[166] All the elements, *fire*, *air*, *water*, and *earth*, will be renewed, "for all the earth shall be then a more beautiful paradise than Adam ever saw."[167] "The whole animated creation" will participate in this new creation.[168]

Yet, for Wesley, all of this is only a prelude to

> the most glorious of all . . . the change which then will take place on the poor, sinful, miserable children of men. . . . They shall "hear a great voice out of heaven, saying, Behold the tabernacle of God is with men, and he will dwell with them, and they shall be his people." . . . Hence will arise an unmixed state of holiness and happiness. . . . And to crown all, there will be a deep, an intimate, an uninterrupted union with God; a constant communion with the Father and his son Jesus Christ, through the Spirit; a continual enjoyment of the Three-One God, and of all the creatures in him![169]

It is hard to imagine a conclusion to Wesley's Trinitarian vision of the *ordo salutis* more entirely consistent with the participatory, economic Trinitarian fabric of the rest of Wesley's soteriology than Wesley's moving depiction of all God's children caught up together with one another and all creation in holiness and happiness that flow from uninterrupted union and communion with the Father and the Son through Spirit, continually enjoying the three-one God and all creation so that we are lost in wonder, love, and praise. It is also hard to imagine a Trinitarian vision as diametrically different from the arid intellectual artifacts that came from the pens of those who tried to defend the doctrine throughout the Trinitarian controversies in England in the seventeenth and eighteenth centuries.

In the words of Charles Wesley:

---

166 Ibid., 2:502.
167 Ibid., 2:504–8.
168 Ibid., 2:508–9.
169 Ibid., 2:509–10.

Finish then thy new creation,
  Pure and spotless let us be;
Let us see thy full salvation
  Perfectly restored in thee;
Changed from glory into glory,
  Till in heaven we take our place,
Till we cast our crowns before thee,
  Lost in wonder, love, and praise.[170]

IV. Conclusion

In light of the Trinitarian source, content, and goal of Wesley's *ordo salutis*, it should come as no surprise that the Wesley brothers referred to Christians as "Transcripts of the Trinity." In Charles Wesley's words:

And when we rise in love renew'd,
  Our souls resemble Thee
An image of the Triune God,
  To all eternity.[171]

It is also no coincidence that John Wesley, in his letters to various Methodist laypersons, at times asked them if they had "a clear sense of the presence of the ever-blessed Trinity,"[172] as noted in chapter 2. In a letter dated November 3, 1789, Wesley asked the question this way: "Do you still find deep and uninterrupted communion with God; with the Three-One God; with the Father, and the Son, through the Spirit?"[173] If Christians are to be transcripts of the Trinity, if the Triune God is the source, the active divine agency involving all three Trinitarian persons, and the goal of the *ordo salutis*, then Wesley's questioning the state of these Methodist laypersons' souls in explicitly Trinitarian terms is completely understandable because he thought that all true Christian faith, all vital religion, and the entire order of salvation has its origin, its agency, and its telos in the "Three-One" God.

170 *Works*, 9:547.

171 Charles Wesley, Hymn # LXXXVII, *Hymns on the Trinity* (repr.; Madison, NJ: Charles Wesley Society, 1998), 58.

172 See *The Works of John Wesley*, ed. Thomas Jackson, 14 vols., 3rd ed. (London: Wesleyan Methodist Book Room, 1872; reprint ed. Grand Rapids, MI: Baker Book House, 1986), 13:107.

173 Ibid., 13:110.

To be an early Methodist was to be on the royal road of salvation, a salvation free for all and free in all, a salvation that left no part of one's life untouched. It was first about the Triune God and the Triune God's grace at work in one's life, and then one's response to that Triune God.

That grace unfolds according to a pattern. This order of salvation created a wonderful road map of the Christian life for the early Methodists and a profound sense of what they could expect from the Triune God of the gospel in the course of their lives as Christians. While there are all kinds of individual variations to it, this order of salvation enabled the early Methodists to know something about where they were in their Christian lives and what the next step in their pilgrimage might be. It is a pattern of grace with a Trinitarian dimension from beginning to end because it is the Triune God who has taken up our cause, a three-one God who so loves us and does not want to be God without us. It was also a different way to be Trinitarian than the accounts of the Trinity that the defenders of the doctrine provided in England in the course of the Trinitarian controversies.

In addition, because the Trinitarian God of the gospel is communal, because God lives in a fellowship of love in God's own life, the grace of this Triune God or this Triune God in action for our salvation always moves us into community in love of God and for one another. Grace transforms our lives *together* in the Christian community that is the church, and not as separate individuals. The church is simply the communal dimension of salvation, just as salvation is the transformative dimension of the church. This is the subject of the next two chapters: Wesley's Trinitarian vision of the essence of the church (chapter 4) and the embodiment of this Trinitarian vision in the forms of life together and ministry in early British Methodism (chapter 5).

4
A Participatory Trinitarian Understanding of the Church

Introduction

This chapter focuses on another aspect of Wesley's theology neglected in some of the secondary literature surveying his thought: Wesley's vision of the essence of the church. Much has been written on various themes within Wesley's overall ecclesiology, like his understanding of the sacraments, his views on ministry, his understanding of the means of grace, and his relationship to the Church of England and to other Christian traditions. By comparison, less has been written on his core doctrine of the church, what is called the "ecclesiality" of the church or the church's *esse* or essence.

The previous two chapters showed that the Trinitarian dimension of Wesley's understanding of Christian faith is pervasive. Chapter 2 documented that Wesley understood the core of Christian faith in Trinitarian terms and demonstrated that Wesley's Trinitarian summaries of the essence of gospel are common in his publications from 1738 to the end of his life. Chapter 3 discussed Wesley's Trinitarian understanding of the order of salvation where the Triune God is the source, the active divine agent, and the goal of the entire *ordo salutis*. There is a Trinitarian dimension throughout the order of salvation in Wesley's theology.

If Wesley understood salvation in this kind of participatory Trinitarian manner, then we would expect Wesley to provide a Trinitarian account of the church. The previous two chapters noted intimations of a Trinitarian definition of the essence of the church like Wesley's short summary in his "Letter to a Roman Catholic": those "who have fellowship with God the Father, Son and Holy Ghost."[1]

Before documenting and discussing Wesley's Trinitarian essence of the church, the first section of this chapter examines what some of the secondary sources have to say about Wesley's ecclesiology. Once again, my intent is not to criticize the work of other scholars who have contributed to our understanding of Wesley's theology, particularly his ecclesiology, but to indicate where this book adds to the conversation.

I. Identifying Wesley's Ecclesiology

It is common for scholars writing on Wesley's ecclesiology to locate his understanding of the church within various ecclesial traditions that may have influenced him. Howard A. Snyder viewed Wesley's ecclesiology as influenced by the Catholic tradition mediated through the Anglican Church, but Snyder stressed the influence the Anabaptist or Believer's tradition in the spiritual dynamism of the small groups mediated to Wesley primarily through the Moranvians.[2] Frank Baker's important work *John Wesley and the Church of England* traces the development of Wesley's ecclesiology throughout his life, noting that Wesley was influenced by two different visions of the church, one as an institution with bishops and an ancient tradition, and the other a "church a fellowship of believers," "a faithful few with the mission to the world."[3]

Others, like Collin Williams, placed Wesley within Catholic, classical Protestant, Pietist, and Free Church expressions of the church.[4] Gwang Seok Oh, in his excellent monograph *John Wesley's Ecclesiology: A Study in Its Sources and Development*, also located Wesley's ecclesiology within the primitive and Catholic, Reformed Protestant, and Free Church (mediated through Pietism and Moravianism) traditions.[5] Although each of these

---

1 See Albert C. Outler, ed., *John Wesley* (New York: Oxford University Press, 1964), 495.

2 Howard A. Snyder, *The Radical Wesley and Patterns of Church Renewal* (Eugene, OR: Wipf and Stock, 1996).

3 See Frank Baker, *John Wesley and the Church of England* (Nashville: Abingdon, 1970), 137–39.

4 Colin Williams, *John Wesley's Theology for Today* (New York: Abingdon, 1960).

5 Gwang Seok Oh, *John Wesley's Ecclesiology: A Study in Its Sources and Development* (Lanham, MD: Scarecrow, 2008). This monograph is the most thorough study of the development of Wesley's ecclesiology, with special attention to the sources that shaped it.

studies provides valuable insights into the way Wesley's ecclesiology is situated in relation to the ecclesial streams that influenced his theology, none of these studies deals with the Trinitarian dimension at the heart of Wesley's vision of the essence of the church.

The opening section of chapter 2 noted how Ken Collins had no discussion of the Trinity in his book *The Scripture Way of Salvation*.[6] Likewise there is no discussion of the church. This may have been intentional on Collins's part, since only so much that can be covered within a single monograph. Nevertheless, given the tight connection between Wesley's soteriology and ecclesiology, we would expect some indication of the interrelation between Wesley's order of salvation and his vision of the church.

As noted in chapter 2, Randy Maddox's outstanding book *Responsible Grace: John Wesley's Practical Theology* provided a brief treatment of Wesley's doctrine of the Trinity at the end of his chapter on the Holy Spirit but did not identify or discuss the Trinitarian dimension of Wesley's order of salvation. What is more perplexing is that the work contains no chapter, not even a subsection, devoted to the church. The closest thing we find is a subsection on "The Reign of Grace in and through the Church" within a chapter entitled "The Triumph of Responsible Grace." In fact, Maddox stated that Wesley's ecclesiology has a "functional focus—he construed the essence of the church in terms of its contribution to God's redemptive purpose of transforming human life."[7]

It is certainly true that Wesley placed heavy emphasis on God's redemptive mission as a mark of the church, but as we will see, the church is missional because it is a community that exists and lives only in and out of union and communion with the Triune God who is a communion of other-directed love, the very other-directed love that is the ultimate reason for our creation and our redemption. So how could the church, those in communion with the Love of God through the Grace of our Lord Jesus Christ in the Fellowship of the Holy Spirit, not but live out new life together hidden with Christ in God in mission to all the world that the Triune God of the gospel has so loved? The redemptive mission is bound up with the church's communion with the Triune God and rooted in the primal essence of the church.

Yet according to Maddox, Wesley's "functional criterion" flows from Wesley's functionalist ecclesiology: Is not "the end of all ecclesiastical order . . .

---

6 Kenneth J. Collins, *The Scripture Way of Salvation: The Heart of John Wesley's Theology* (Nashville: Abingdon, 1997).

7 Randy L. Maddox, *Responsible Grace: John Wesley's Practical Theology* (Nashville: Kingswood Books, 1994), 241.

to bring souls . . . to God, and to build them up in his fear and love? Order, then, is so far valuable as it answers these ends: and if it answers them not, it is worth nothing."[8] The problem with Maddox's analysis is that for Wesley, church "order" is not part of the *esse* or ecclesiality of the church but rather the *bene esse*, or right functioning, of the church. As we will see, when Wesley discussed the *esse* of the church, that which constitutes the church, his vision is substantive and Trinitarian, not functionalist, in construing the church as merely a means of grace.

One has to be careful when reading Wesley's comments on the church to discern what aspect of the church he was discussing. As we will see, sometimes when Wesley spoke about the "church," he was referring to institutional expressions of the church or the "visible church." At other times he had in mind *the* church, the Body of Christ. Wesley did not separate the visible institutional expressions of the church from the church as Body of Christ, but he did distinguish between them.

In addition, Maddox saw Wesley's struggle to shepherd the Methodist movement of renewal within the Anglican Church as deeply influencing his ecclesiological reflection, which it certainly did.[9] Maddox concluded that the fruit of this for Wesley was a synthesis of Anglican and Moravian/pietist emphases: small intentional communities still linked to the larger Anglican Church (*ecclesiolae* in *ecclesia*).

This is a crucial point, and Maddox deepened and developed it by noting how this insight comports well with Wesley's understanding of ordinary or ordained and prudential means of grace. The Anglican mother church provided liturgical worship and the sacraments, whereas the smaller intentional Methodist Societies and their substructures like classes, bands, etc., included other means of grace beyond those ordained by scripture designed to nurture and incorporate accountability into the Methodist Societies.[10]

This Moravian/pietist stream comes to expression, according to Maddox, in Wesley's "informal definition of the church" as "the spiritual community of God's people."[11] Maddox here moved closer to Wesley's deepest reflection about the ecclesiality of the church. Yet, as we will see, whatever his sources,

---

8 Ibid. This quotation is from Wesley's letter to "John Smith" (June 25, 1746), in *The Works of John Wesley*, ed. Frank Baker, vols. 25–26, *Letters I–II* (New York: Oxford University Press, 1982), 26:206.

9 Maddox, *Responsible Grace*, 241.

10 Ibid. See also Henry H. Knight, *The Presence of God in the Christian Life: John Wesley and the Means of Grace* (Metuchen, NJ: Scarecrow, 1992). Knight's book is extremely insightful and the best treatment of this subject.

11 Maddox, *Responsible Grace*, 242.

Wesley's vision of the church was more substantially participatory and Trinitarian, focusing on communion (*koinonia*) with the Triune God and one another in the body of Christ. While Wesley's ecclesiology bears similarities to Catholic, Protestant, and Moravian/pietist traditions, what unifies the various emphases within Wesley's ecclesiology is the participatory, economic Trinitarian dimension at the core of his vision of the essence of the church.[12]

One further point in Maddox's discussion that is noteworthy is his assertion of "Wesley's unwillingness to define the church's holiness simply in terms of its relationship to Christ." According to Maddox, "the church must be holy in the fuller sense of nurturing—and expecting—the progressive holiness of its members."[13] Maddox is correct that Wesley expected that the members of the church would be holy. It is the "holy catholic church" not just because "Christ the head of it is holy" or "all its ordinances are designed to promote holiness" or even because "our Lord *intended* that all the members of the church should be holy," as Wesley himself said it in his sermon "Of the Church."[14]

Maddox also argued that holiness for Wesley is relational and does not isolate Christians or the church from the world but leads to love of God and love of others in and outside of the Christian community; though, because of his emphasis on the functional essence of Wesley's ecclesiology, Maddox did not mention the Trinitarian relational genesis and continuous dynamic that comes via participation in the love of God through Christ in the Spirit.[15] Later this chapter will return to Wesley's understanding of the specific kind of sociality bound up with the love that flows from union and communion with the Triune God in the gospel and awakens love for God and others along with the holy tempers that surround love.

Similar to Maddox, a number of secondary sources construe Wesley's ecclesiology as functionalist and/or practical. An example of this vision of the church is in the best explanation of United Methodist doctrine published to date, entitled *United Methodist Doctrine: The Extreme Center*,[16] by Scott J. Jones, a bishop in the United Methodist Church. Like Maddox's book, Jones's

---

12 See Williams, *John Wesley's Theology*, for an insightful discussion of Wesley's ecclesiology in light of the ecumenical movement in the mid-twentieth century that captures some of the subtlety of Wesley's vision of the church.

13 Maddox, *Responsible Grace*, 242.

14 *The Works of John Wesley*, ed. Albert C. Outler, vols. 1–4, *Sermons* (Nashville: Abingdon, 1984–87), 3:55.

15 Ibid., 3:56–57.

16 Scott J. Jones, *United Methodist Doctrine: The Extreme Center* (Nashville: Abingdon, 2002).

book has no chapter devoted to the church but rather subsumes the church under a chapter entitled "The Means of Grace."

Furthermore, Jones argued that the view of the church in the *Book of Discipline*, an understanding that he traced back to Wesley himself, is really, "a definition of the church that focuses on the church as a means of grace."[17] Jones concluded that "United Methodist ecclesiology and understanding of the means of grace is practical."[18]

Albert Outler, in his essay "Do Methodists Have a Doctrine of the Church?," seems to be the first scholar to argue that Wesley had a functionalist understanding of the church.[19] In the essay, Outler provided an insightful analysis of Methodist ecclesial self-understanding. Outler also stated that "Wesley defined the church as *act*, as mission, as the enterprise of saving and maturing souls in Christian life."[20]

In his essay "Salvation and the Church: The Ecclesiology of John Wesley," Clarence Bence argued that "Wesley combined the functionalist concept of the Church as *act*, with a substantial view of the Church as the new social order, breaking through from the eschatological future into the present age."[21] According to Bence's essay, Wesley saw the church as "the body of

---

17 Ibid., 244.

18 Ibid.

19 Albert C. Outler, "Do Methodists Have a Doctrine of the Church?" In *The Doctrine of the Church*, ed. Dow Kirkpatrick (New York: Abingdon, 1964), 11–28.

20 Ibid., 19. I agree with Outler that the mainstream of American Methodism had never fully thought through its ecclesiology. American Methodism has had significant problems in ecclesiological self-understanding from the very beginning. Methodism in England was originally a movement of renewal within the Church of England, and therefore Wesley never spoke of Methodist churches, but only Methodist societies. What is fascinating is that at the Christmas Conference in 1784, when American Methodists become the Methodist Episcopal Church, they immediately went on talking about members in Methodist "societies." They became a church without ever ceasing to be a connection of societies.

What is also illuminating about that whole course of events leading to the formation of the Methodist Episcopal Church is not that Wesley ordained Whatcoat and Vasey and appointed Coke and Asbury as "general superintendents" (bishops) but that Asbury refused to accept the "office" unless the American preachers elected him. His reasons for doing this were political, not theological, for he knew he would not be able to lead the Methodist Episcopal Church in this new democratic country without the American preachers' votes. So Asbury and the American Methodists effectively politicized the election of Methodist bishops in America from the beginning.

21 Clarence Bence, "Salvation and the Church: The Ecclesiology of John Wesley," in *The Church*, ed. Melvin E. Dieter and Daniel N. Berg (Anderson, IN: Warner, 1984), 314.

Christ, . . . the company of the redeemed and a visible manifestation of the kingdom of God . . . the foretaste of the eternal social order to come."[22] This is a significant improvement over the functionalist accounts of Wesley's vision of the church. What is missing in Bence, as well as in Jones and Outler, is the Trinitarian dimension, the participatory source of the church's being and life as the Body of Christ. The church as the Body of Christ is a foretaste of that deep, intimate, and "uninterrupted union with God" and "constant communion with the Father and his son Jesus Christ, through the Spirit; a continual enjoyment of the Three-One God, and of all the creatures in him" when Christ returns in final victory, as Wesley stated it in his sermon "The New Creation."[23] The participatory Trinitarian dimension of Wesley's ecclesiology documented in the following sections of this chapter deepens the missional character of the church by showing that the church's mission flows from its participatory Trinitarian essence.

Kenneth Collins's most recent book on Wesley, *The Theology of John Wesley*, has an entire chapter devoted to "The Church and the Means of Grace: The Community of Holy Love."[24] Collins realized that the church has a substantive place in Wesley's theological vision: "The realization of such animating and life-changing graces as justification and regeneration . . . presupposes a community of saints that not only bears the gospel story throughout history but also forms the primary context for the instantiation of holy love in the newly transformed." Indeed, "every Christian believer is and must be related to the church. . . . The very good news of the gospel that is believed and embraced is not the narrative of an individual but that of the church, the body of Christ." Collins concluded that according to Wesley "the church is the ark of salvation."[25] This is a profound vision of the church, but it is still not as robust as Wesley's own ecclesiology because it still subordinates the church to salvation rather than seeing the church as the *actual communal expression* of salvation, as it was for Wesley in those places where we find his deepest reflections and insights on the essence of the church.

Collins also rightly saw that Wesley affirmed the catholicity of the church as embracing all true believers, a "redeemed community" that transcends partisan visions of the church.[26] Part of the reason for Wesley's generous catholic spirit, Collins correctly noted, is Wesley's vision for the goal of religion

---

22 Ibid., 311.

23 *Works*, 2:509–10.

24 Kenneth J. Collins, *The Theology of John Wesley: Holy Love and the Shape of Grace* (Nashville: Abingdon, 2007), 241.

25 Ibid., 237.

26 Ibid., 238.

as holy love, even for those members confused or mistaken about beliefs and practices.[27]

As one might expect, this leads Collins to emphasize the holiness or sanctification of the church. Yet, like Maddox, he accentuated the holiness of the church and all its members without the crucial participatory Trinitarian source of this holiness we find in Wesley's own account of the church in his sermon "Of the Church," which we will examine in the next section.[28]

Following Outler, Snyder, and Maddox, Collins argued that the various elements in Wesley's definition of the church represent a blend of Anglican and the Believer's church (mediated through the Moravians/pietists) traditions or a "conjunction" of institutional and functionalist emphases. As we will see, Wesley's viewed the ecclesiality of the church in participatory Trinitarian terms, a vision that does not fit neatly into the Anglican definition of the church, nor does it really fit the Believer's or Free Church model either. It represents a different way of understanding the essence of the church. How Wesley dealt with (1) the Anglican Article on the church, and (2) how he understood holiness in relation to the Trinitarian essence of the church will help clarify this scholarly conversation about Wesley's ecclesiology.

After the first four pages of the Collins's chapter on Wesley's ecclesiology, where he comes closest to dealing with Wesley's understanding of the *esse* or ecclesiality of the church, Collins moved on to other topics within the broad theme of ecclesiology. He examined Wesley's "historiography" of the church, as essentially a history of institutional decline, particularly after Constantine heaped power, riches, and honor on the church, though a history with periodic movements of reform and renewal thereafter.[29] This sets the stage for viewing Methodism as a movement of reform and renewal, a vision that Wesley learned from German Pietism and Moravianism.[30] Collins's chapter then moves on to the structures of Methodism (like societies, classes, bands, conferences, preachers, etc.) and the means of grace (instituted and prudential).

While Collins's book included a chapter on the church as the community of holy love, there is little about the *esse* of the church in Wesley's theology. In Wesley's own theological reflections on the church we find a participatory Trinitarian dimension in the *esse* of the church far more pronounced than these scholars acknowledged in their discussions of Wesley's ecclesiology.

---

27 Ibid., 239.
28 Ibid.
29 Ibid., 240–44.
30 Ibid., 244–49.

For Wesley there is no Christian community apart from union and communion in the Spirit through the Son with the Father. There are no individual Christians apart from community or the church as the body of Christ. As will be clear by the end of the chapter, there is deep ecclesial and Trinitarian content in Wesley's often-quoted statement that "Christianity is essentially a social religion, and . . . to turn it into a solitary religion is indeed to destroy it."[31] If the church is the historical correlate of the salvific activity of the Triune God generating union and communion with the Triune God and one another, as Wesley saw it, then the church is more than a means of grace. We now turn our attention to Wesley's Trinitarian understanding of the ecclesiality of the church.

II. The Center of Wesley's Trinitarian Ecclesiology

1. Wesley's Sermon "Of the Church"

The Context of the Sermon

One of Wesley's main discussions of ecclesiology is his sermon entitled "Of the Church," the only sermon dedicated entirely to this subject. It was written toward the end of his life, so it represents his mature reflection on the subject. In fact, Wesley wrote it in 1785, the year after his ordinations of Whatcoat and Vasey for ministry in the new Methodist Episcopal Church in America, an act that many, including Charles Wesley, saw as a de facto break with the Church of England.

In his journal entry for Sunday, September 4, Wesley recounted, "Finding a report had been spread abroad that I was going to leave the Church, to satisfy those that were grieved concerning it, I openly declared in the evening that I had now no more thought of separating from the Church than I had forty years ago."[32] In the following weeks, Wesley composed his sermon "Of the Church," what Albert Outler calls "the first written summary of his ecclesiology."[33]

Wesley's text for the sermon is Ephesians 4:1–6, that wonderful Pauline passage encouraging Christians to "keep the unity of the Spirit in the bond of peace. There is one body, and one Spirit, even as ye are called in one hope of your calling; one Lord, one faith, one baptism; one God and Father of all, who is above all, and through all, and in you all."[34] In the introductory part of

---

31 *Works*, 1:553.

32 See Outler's introduction to the sermon, ibid., 3:45.

33 Again, see Outler's introduction to the sermon, ibid.

34 Ibid., 3:46.

the sermon, Wesley outlined the various points the New Testament makes about the church.[35]

In this early section Wesley stated that the New Testament never speaks of the church as a "building" set apart for public worship, but as "a body of people united together in the service of God."[36] These early Christians were at times divided into several congregations dispersed throughout a country or within a city like Jerusalem.

Sometimes in the Bible the word "church," according to Wesley, has "a still more extensive meaning" that includes "all the Christian congregations that are upon the face of the earth" or "all the Christians under heaven." Here "church" means "the catholic or universal church," and it is this understanding of the church that Paul defined in Ephesians 4:1–6, according to Wesley, "in the clearest and most decisive manner" as "all the Christians under heaven" and "instructs all the members of the church how to 'walk worthy of the vocation wherewith they are called.'"[37]

The Question of the "Ecclesiality" of the Church

This opening section of his sermon "Of the Church" is crucial to Wesley's ecclesiology, for here Wesley told his readers that the apostle Paul, in this text in Ephesians 4, (1) defines what the church *is*, and (2) instructs all the members of the church about how they are to *walk* (a comprehensive term that includes all of one's inner and outer life) worthy of their calling or how they are to live. It is precisely in light of these two points that scholars see Wesley as incorporating Anglican and Anabaptist or Free Church ecclesiologies. Wesley was a committed Anglican who embraced its episcopal form of order, even if he did not see bishops as a third order, and who wrote his sermon "Of the Church" to reassure those who feared he was leaving the Anglican fold. Yet, in the second half of the sermon, Wesley focused on the holiness of the members of the church, which seems to reflect the Anabaptist vision of the church. Indeed, the late Albert Outler stated the point in his introduction to Wesley's sermon in the recent critical edition of Wesley's works: "This is . . . an unstable blend of Anglican and Anabaptist

35 This is one example among many of Wesley's resolve to be a "*homo unius libri*" [a person of one book, the Bible] (see Wesley's "Preface" to his Standard Sermons in *Works*, 1:105).

36 *Works*, 3:46.

37 Ibid., 3:48.

ecclesiologies."[38] However, is this really what Wesley had in mind in this sermon "Of the Church"?

The very text that Wesley appealed to when he discussed the ecclesiality of the church is illuminating. Here "ecclesiality" refers to that which constitutes the church, that which is indispensable, the *esse*, or essence, of that church that undergirds and interpenetrates everything else.[39] Wesley did not appeal to the *loci classici* text of Anabaptist ecclesiology, Matthew 18:20, "Wherever two or three are gathered together in my name, there am I."[40] Nor did Wesley look to Matthew 16:15–20 ("Upon this rock I will build my church."), the text that is crucial to those who argue for an episcopal church standing in apostolic succession (understood in various ways). Rather, when Wesley decided to write on ecclesiology, particularly the essence of the church, he chose Ephesians 4:1–6.

The other main texts Wesley invoked when he talked about the church were Acts 2 and 4, where we find the writer of Acts describing the first Christian community that formed after the outpouring of the Spirit at Pentecost. As we will see in chapter 5, Acts 2 and 4 were Wesley's texts when he wanted to describe what a true "Gospel church" looked like. Wesley regularly appealed to these texts (Ephesians 4 and Acts 2 and 4) when he presented his understanding of the church in various contexts throughout his publications. So we see that already in his selection of scriptural warrant for understanding the ecclesiality of the church, Wesley was doing something different than we find in Anabaptist ecclesiology but also different from the mainstream of Protestantism and his own Anglican Church.[41]

---

38 Ibid., 3:46.

39 See Miroslav Volf, *After Our Likeness: The Church as the Image of the Trinity* (Grand Rapids, MI: Eerdmans, 1998), 127.

40 Ibid., 135–58.

41 I am not arguing that Wesley self-consciously selected Ephesians 4:1–6 to explicitly present his understanding of the essence of the church as unique and different for Anglican and Anabaptist visions of the essence of the church. Wesley provided no clues for his selection of the Ephesians text. There is no mention in his sermon "Of the Church" of questions or issues surrounding his ordinations of Vasey and Whatcoat and the formation of the Methodist Episcopal Church in America. The way Wesley defined the essence of the church in participatory Trinitarian terms and raised questions about the Anglican marks of the church provided a theological vision of the church compatible with his ordinations and his part in the formation of the Methodist Episcopal Church. Wesley's definition of schism in his sermon "On Schism," written about six months after his sermon "Of the Church," reflected the same Trinitarian understanding of the essence of the church developed in the sermon "Of the Church." What Wesley said about schism could be viewed as a theological

Here is it helpful to remember that churches have understood ecclesiality, in the words of Miroslav Volf, as "externally perceivable and simultaneously necessary *conditions or consequences* of the ecclesially constitutive presence of the Spirit of Christ."[42] In both Roman Catholic and Orthodox ecclesiologies, though each in their own way, the church is constituted via the sacraments, sacraments inextricably connected to the office of bishop standing in apostolic succession to guarantee the divine origin of these sacraments.[43]

Luther and Calvin had a different understanding of ecclesiality. Both affirmed that the pure preaching of the Word and the right administration of the sacraments are what constitute the church. These are also the marks of the true church found in the Anglican Articles of Religion. Notice, however, that the same pattern is evident in that the church is defined by externally perceivable and simultaneously necessary *conditions* (the pure Word and rightly administered sacraments) that constitute the church.

The Anabaptist tradition emphasized one or two additional necessary conditions in its understanding of ecclesiality. The first is obedience or particular forms of public confession. This is what drives the Anabaptist ecclesial tradition toward sectarianism: while not a church of the perfect, there still must be clear boundaries between true Christians/the true church and those who are not, though there is significant disagreement among Anabaptists about exactly what those boundaries are.

The Anabaptist church exists where "two or three gather in my [Christ's] name." So the church is an "assembling" into community of those who name Christ. This naming of Christ is crucial for it implies a *confessing* Christ that includes not simply acknowledging Christ as Savior and Lord but also a deep *performative* dimension, engaging in appropriate acts of righteousness, even in the face of persecution.[44] Some Anabaptists include the one

---

justification for not separating from the Anglican Church, either for himself or for others in Methodism. But nowhere in either sermon did Wesley make explicit any of these issues around his ordinations of Whatcoat and Vasey or around his role in the formation of the Methodist Episcopal Church or around the fears voiced by some that Wesley was going to separate from the Anglican Church. My interest is in how Wesley defined the essence of the church in participatory Trinitarian terms, not what motive he might have had for doing so after his ordinations and the concern some had that Wesley had effectively broken with, or planned to separate from, the Anglican Church.

42 Ibid., 130.

43 Ibid., 130–31.

44 Ibid., 145–54.

true scriptural organization as an additional condition of ecclesiality, one that does *not* include bishops![45] The question then is, Does Wesley end up with an unstable conception of the church that blends the Anglican vision of the church and the Anabaptist tradition, or is Wesley's view different from both?

Wesley's Definition of Ecclesiality

It should be clear from the introductory section of his sermon "Of the Church" that Wesley intended to provide his conception of the *esse* of the church. Wesley reinforced this intent at the beginning of the main body of the sermon, as he immediately moved to the two key questions: "Who are properly 'the church of God'? [and] What is the true meaning of that term?"[46]

The first half of the main body of the sermon explicated Wesley's vision of the church, answering those key questions with a fully Trinitarian understanding of his text in Ephesians 4, a Trinitarian conceptualization of the church consistent with everything we have learned so far concerning Wesley's understanding of the Trinity, of the Trinitarian character of Christian faith, and of his Trinitarian perspective on the *ordo salutis*. It is also a vision of the ecclesiality of the church that does not fit neatly into either Anglican or Anabaptist ecclesiologies.

What Wesley said at the beginning of his definition about "the saints . . . assembl[ing] themselves together" sounds Anabaptist, but when he developed what he meant by it, he defined the church in participatory Trinitarian terms:

> "The church at Ephesus," as the Apostle himself explains it, means "the saints," the holy persons, "that are in Ephesus, and there assemble themselves together to worship God the Father, and his Son Jesus Christ." . . . It is the church in general, the catholic or universal church, which the Apostle here considers as "one body"; comprehending not only . . . the Christians of one congregation, of one city, of one province or nation; but all the persons upon the face the earth who answer the character here given. The several particulars contained therein we may now more distinctly consider. [Wesley goes point by point through the list found in Ephesians that defines the universal church or body of Christ.]
>
> "There is one Spirit" who animates all these, all the living members of the church of God. . . And it is certain, "If any man have not the Spirit of Christ, he is none of his.". . .

45 Ibid., 131–33.
46 *Works*, 3:48.

"There is" in all those that have received this Spirit, "one hope."... They can cheerfully say, "Blessed be the God and Father of our Lord Jesus Christ, who, according to his abundant mercy, hath begotten us again unto a lively hope by the resurrection of Jesus Christ from the dead."...

"There is one Lord" who has now dominion over them, who has set up his kingdom in their hearts, and reigns over all those that are partakers of this hope. To obey him, to run the way of his commandments, is their glory and joy. And while they are doing this with a willing mind they, as it were, "sit in heavenly places with Christ Jesus."

"There is one faith," which is the free gift of God, and is the ground of their hope. This is not barely the faith of a heathen . . . that "there is a God."... But . . . it is the faith which enables every true Christian believer to testify . . . "The life I which now live, I live by faith in the Son of God, who loved me and gave himself for me."...

"There is one God and Father of all" that have the Spirit of adoption, which is "in their hearts, Abba, Father"; which "witnesseth" continually "with their spirits" that they are the children of God. . . . "And in you all"—in a peculiar manner living in you that are one body in one spirit:

Making your souls his loved abode,
The temples of indwelling God.

Here then is a clear unexceptionable answer to the question, What is the church?[47]

Notice that Wesley here defined the church in the very same participatory evangelical and doxological Trinitarian terms that Wesley used when he discussed the Trinity in his sermon "On the Trinity," and when he summarized vital religion or true Christian faith, as we saw in chapter 2. The church is all those persons everywhere throughout the world animated by the Spirit of Christ who bears witness in their hearts that they are children of God the Father through Jesus Christ their Lord and Savior. The church is all those persons who live by faith in Jesus Christ, who loved them and gave himself for them. The church is constituted by its evangelical encounter with the activity of all three persons of the Trinity in the gospel, bound up with the vital religion that is their life together in union and communion with the Triune God and one another.

Indeed, this encounter with the Triune God is participatory: the Spirit unites Christians to Christ as the body of Christ and through Christ with the

47 Ibid., 3:48–50.

Father so that they become the temple of this indwelling Triune God. God "in a peculiar manner" lives in Christians together as one body, and their life in the Spirit is hidden with Christ in God the Father. This participatory evangelical encounter with the Triune God in the gospel is doxological, for when the church comes to know the love that God is as Father, Son, and Holy Spirit, the church cannot but worship God the Father, Son, and Holy Spirit together, as Wesley said at the beginning of the quotation.[48]

Thus, in examining Wesley's sermon "Of the Church," it quickly becomes clear that he had a more substantial conception of the church than merely a functionalist definition of the church as a means of grace. In "Of the Church," where Wesley defined "what is the meaning of that term" in a "clear unexceptional" manner, there is nothing about a functionalist vision of the church as a means of grace.

In addition to selecting a text that comported well with his Trinitarian vision of the church and explicating the text in those terms, Wesley said nothing about the Anglican Articles and the classic Protestant marks of the church in his opening "clear unexceptionable answer to the question, What is the church?"[49] In contrast to the Anabaptist mark of the church as assembling in the name of Christ to confess Christ in word and deed, Wesley stated that "the catholic or universal church is all persons in the universe whom God hath so called out of the world as to entitle them to the preceding character," which Wesley then defined not first in terms of holiness (that comes later in the sermon) but "as to be 'one body,' united by 'one spirit'; having 'one faith, one hope, one baptism; one God and Father of all, who is above all, and through all, and in them all.'"[50] In other words, Wesley pointed to the participatory, economic Trinitarian vision of Christian faith as that which constitutes the essence of the church. Wesley's Trinitarian conception of the church is essentially identical with his Trinitarian understanding of the core of the gospel and of true religion, which is what we would expect if Wesley were theologically consistent in his conceptualization of the various core realities of Christian faith and life that always interpenetrate one another.

48 Here in his sermon "Of the Church," Wesley incorporated not only a Trinitarian dimension to his understanding of the church, he also provided an ecclesial dimension to his vision of Christian faith and salvation. Together all of these discussions provide the content for the terms used in this study to describe the Trinitarian dimension of Wesley's theology as evangelical, doxological, participatory, and economic. The content and meaning of these terms comes from Wesley's own pen. Documenting and describing that content is the goal of this book.

49 Ibid., 3:50.

50 Ibid.

There is deep Trinitarian theological consistency between Wesley's doctrine of Trinity, soteriology, and ecclesiology.

The Unity of Wesley's Ecclesiology, Soteriology, and Doctrine of the Trinity

There are other places in Wesley's writing where we see this tight connection between the Trinity, salvation, and the church. In the second sermon of his series on the Sermon on the Mount, Wesley warned that true religion is not found in avoiding evil, doing good, and attending all the ordinances of God: "this is only the outside of that religion," which cannot "satisfy . . . a soul that is athirst for God, the living God."[51] Such a person "wants a religion of a nobler kind, a religion higher and deeper than this."[52] To be sure, anyone seeking this higher and deeper genuine religion will "abstain from the very appearance of evil," will be "zealous of good works," and will attend "all the ordinances of God." Yet this is really not what he desires: "This is only the outside of that religion which he insatiably hungers after."[53]

Wesley summarized his understanding of the essence of this true religion: "The knowledge of God in Christ Jesus; 'the life that is hid with Christ in God'; the 'being joined unto the Lord in one Spirit'; the 'having fellowship with the Father and the Son'; the 'walking in the light as God is in the light'; the 'being purified even as he is pure'—this is the religion, the righteousness that he [we] thirsts after. Nor can he rest till he thus rests in God."[54] At the end of this section of the sermon, Wesley cautioned his readers: "Let nothing satisfy thee but the power of godliness, but a religion that is spirit and life; the dwelling in God and God in thee; . . . entering . . . 'within the veil,' and 'sitting in heavenly places with Christ Jesus.' "[55]

Wesley explained true religion in nearly the identical terms he used to define the church. The reason for the remarkable Trinitarian parallels between Wesley's description of the church as the Body of Christ and true religion is simple—they are facets of a unified whole. Both the church and true religion (the core of the gospel) are simply the result of the coactivity of the economic Trinity in history in the gospel for the salvation of the world. This means that for Wesley, the doctrine of the Trinity, soteriology, and

51 *Works*, 1:497, 496.
52 Ibid., 1:497.
53 Ibid.
54 Ibid.
55 Ibid., 1:498.

ecclesiology are finally inseparable and are all defined by the same participatory, economic Trinitarian activity and reality.

When Wesley developed his clear and explicit explanation of what is the essence of the church, he did not move in a functionalist direction of the church as a means of grace at all but instead provided a deeper understanding of the ontology of the church as communion with God and one another in vibrant Trinitarian terms, like what we saw when he discussed the Trinity and salvation. This is what we would expect in light of the Trinitarian dimension of Wesley's theology documented in the first three chapters.

In the very next sentence, at the beginning of part 3 of his "Sermon on the Mount, II," Wesley noted how the redemptive mission and missionary motive of the church flow from the participatory Trinitarian reality of the church/true religion/the gospel: "And the more they are filled with the life of God [as Wesley had described it in Trinitarian terms in the previous point examined above], the more tenderly will they be concerned for those who are still without God in the world, still dead in trespasses and sins."[56] The church is inherently missional and in this sense is a means of grace *because* its life is hidden with Christ in God, *because* it is a temple of this Trinitarian indwelling God who loves the world with the very love that God is. For Wesley, the mission of the church flows from the *esse* of the church as the body of Christ in the Spirit manifesting the love of God for the world. Wesley's theological consistency here is compelling.

Wesley's Reinterpretation of the Anglican Articles

Now what is also fascinating, and further reveals how seriously Wesley worked out this vision of the church in his sermon "Of the Church," is that he interpreted not simply the universal catholic church but every other part of the universal church, whether it be a "'national' church" or "the Christians that inhabit one city" or even "two or three Christian believers united together" (a reference to Matthew 18:20?) in the same participatory and Trinitarian manner: "But still, whether it be larger or smaller, the same idea is preserved. They are one body, and have one Spirit, one Lord, one hope, one faith, one baptism, one God and Father of all."[57] Notice that Wesley said nothing about "assembling for confession" or holiness of life, nothing about the Protestant marks of the church, and nothing that would indicate a functionalist vision of the church as a means of grace. The church always and everywhere is those united to the Lord in one Spirit, and in the communion

56 Ibid., 1:499.

57 *Works*, 3:50.

of the Spirit the church has fellowship with the Father and the Son and finds its life in the Spirit hidden with Christ in God.

Furthermore, Wesley reinterpreted the nineteenth Anglican Article dealing with the church in light of his Trinitarian vision of the essence of the church. The shifts in his language in this section are interesting and indicate that he was not afraid to challenge the Anglican Article if it conflicted with his core ecclesiological vision. Wesley asserted: "This account [the Trinitarian account examined above] is exactly agreeable to the nineteenth Article of our Church, the Church of England—only the Article includes a little more than the Apostle has expressed. 'The visible church of Christ is a congregation of faithful men, in which the pure word of God is preached, and the sacraments be duly administered.'"[58]

The Latin translation of "faithful men" in the Article, Wesley stated, was "*coetus credentium*," "plainly showing that . . . the compilers mean men endued with 'living faith.'" Note how Wesley's explanation shifted the intention of the Anglican Article toward his understanding of the Trinitarian root of the church: it is those who are "endued" with a kind of faith that Wesley said "is the free gift of God . . . the faith which enables every true Christian believer to testify . . . 'The life which I now live I live by faith in the Son of God, who loved me and gave himself for me'" so that God "in a peculiar manner" lives in those "that are one body by one spirit."[59]

Here, as throughout his sermon "Of the Church," Wesley placed the accent of his understanding of ecclesiality not primarily on the human response of faithfulness (which was, of course, very important to Wesley), as is characteristic of the Anabaptist tradition, but rather on a participatory ecclesiology where the economic Trinitarian activity is always the leading edge defining the characteristics of what makes the church the church. Wesley concluded that once we consider the character of this "living faith," it is easy to answer the question as to what is the Church of England: "The Church of England is that 'body' of men in England in whom 'there is one Spirit, one hope, one Lord, one faith,' which have 'one baptism,' and 'one God and Father of all.'" Wesley then drove home the point by adding, "This and this alone is the Church of England, according to the doctrine of the Apostle."[60] So Wesley, rather self-consciously, provided his readers with a very particular "reading" of the Anglican Article on the church that brought the article into line with his Trinitarian vision of the church.

---

58 Ibid., 3:51.
59 Ibid., 3:49–50.
60 Ibid., 3:52.

It is precisely at this point that Wesley added some revealing qualifications to the classic Protestant marks of the church, the pure preaching of the Word and sacraments duly administered, found in the Anglican Article. He expressed his discontent with the classic Protestant marks of the church at this point, saying, "But the definition of a church laid down in the Article includes not only this ["living faith" of the text of Ephesians 4, "there is one Spirit, one hope, one Lord"] but much more, by that remarkable addition, 'in which the pure Word of God is preached, and the sacraments are duly administered.'" Wesley then asserted that "According to this definition those congregations in which the pure Word of God (a strong expression) [note again Wesley's profound discontent] is not preached are no parts either of the Church of England or the church catholic."[61] Wesley then applied the same point to the right administration of the sacraments.

Before we examine Wesley's rejoinder to the Protestant marks, marks that he clearly did not fully approve, it is helpful to pause and reflect on the intention behind the Protestant marks. What was the point of Protestants adding those marks of "the pure preaching of the Word" and "right administration of the sacraments" to the classic marks of the church (one, holy, catholic, and apostolic) found in the Creeds in the early church? Those Protestant marks were added by the magisterial Reformers to distinguish the "true" Protestant church from false Roman Catholic and Anabaptist churches! The reason why pure preaching and the right administration of the sacraments were marks of the true church was because Luther and Calvin believed that those marks are constitutive of the church: Christ is efficaciously present creating the church where the pure Word is preached and sacraments are rightly administered. When the true Word and sacraments are not present, there is no church or at least no assurance that there is a church. The problem, however, is that this definition of ecclesiality subordinates the participatory Trinitarian dimension to these particular forms of the church or means of grace.[62]

The same was true of the Roman Catholic and Anabaptist ecclesiologies. They both also wanted to seize the ecclesiological high ground by defining the ecclesiality of the church in a way that either Roman Catholics or the Anabaptists were the one true church. Despite their differences,

---

61 Ibid.

62 It also reveals that on more than a few occasions in the history of the church, the whole question of the *esse* of the church has been dealt with within the context of fraternal fighting between Christian groups who want to claim the ecclesial high ground over against one another. This is not the most helpful way to approach this question of what is the essence of the church.

classic Protestant, Roman Catholic, and Anabaptist ecclesiologies all used certain perceivable and simultaneously constitutive signs or forms to define the ecclesiality of the church in order to identify which church was the true church: their own!

It is at this point in his sermon that Wesley reversed this order and subordinated these Protestant marks of the church to his Trinitarian understanding of the church as communion in the Spirit with the Son with the Father and one another:

> I will not undertake to defend the accuracy of this definition [found in the Protestant marks]. I dare not exclude from the church catholic all those congregations in which any unscriptural doctrines which cannot be affirmed to be the "pure Word of God" are sometimes, yea, frequently preached. Neither all those congregations in which the sacraments are not "duly administered." Certainly if these things are so the Church of Rome is not so much as a part of the catholic church; . . . *Whoever they are that have "one Spirit, one hope, one Lord, one faith, one God and Father of all"* [my emphasis], I can easily bear with their holding wrong opinions, yea, and superstitious modes of worship. Nor would I on these accounts scruple still to include them within the pale of the catholic church. Neither would I have any objection to receive them, if they desired it, as members of the Church of England [notice Wesley's distinction between the catholic church and the Church of England].[63]

In other words, for Wesley, the church is present wherever the constitutive participatory, economic Trinitarian relations are present, even if there are some wrong opinions expressed in preaching and the sacraments are not duly administered.

Here we see the seriousness of Wesley's resolve to think out his ecclesiology in terms of the constitutive relations that form the essence of the church. For Wesley, it is the participatory, economic Trinitarian relations in the gospel that constitute the church. These relations can and do exist in the midst of wrong opinions and superstitious modes of worship, where the pure Word is not always preached and the sacraments are not duly administered. Wesley would not exclude from the church as the body of Christ those (including Roman Catholics) who disagree with him about the sacraments and all manner of doctrinal issues that do not strike at the Trinitarian root of the gospel, Christian faith, and the essence of the church. "Whoever they are that have 'one Spirit, one hope, one Lord, one faith, one God and Father of

---

63 Ibid., 3:52.

all,'" Wesley would not "scruple still to include them within the pale of the catholic church."[64]

This is the deepest theological root of Wesley's "catholic spirit" that so remarkably distinguishes his ecclesiology from the Anabaptist and other ecclesial traditions with sectarian tendencies. In fact, there is a sense in which the drive of Wesley's ecclesiology is in the opposite direction than sectarian traditions on this particular point: real Christians or the true church as the body of Christ must remain within the institutional or State Church precisely to leaven the visible church. So in his tract *Reasons against a Separation from the Church of England*, which was a digest of a paper Wesley read at the lively debate at the 1755 Annual Conference after two lay preachers had administered the sacrament of Holy Communion the previous October, Wesley noted that "many witnesses of pure religion . . . lived and died . . . in the churches to which they belonged, notwithstanding the wickedness which overflowed both the teachers and the people therein, they spread the leaven of true religion far and wide."[65] But when true Christians "separated and founded distinct parties, their influence was more and more confined; they grew less and less useful to others, and generally lost the spirit of religion themselves in the spirit of controversy."[66]

It comes as no surprise that Wesley told the Methodists, some of whom wanted to abandon the Anglican Church, that to separate was to "act in direct contradiction to that very end for which we believe God hath raised us up": "to quicken our brethren . . . the lost sheep of the Church of England. Now would it not be a flat contradiction to this design to separate from the Church?"[67] On this point Wesley's vision is closer to that of Pietism with its

---

64 Ibid.

65 *The Works of John Wesley*, ed. Rupert Davies, vol. 9, *The Methodist Societies: History, Nature, and Design* (Nashville: Abingdon, 1989), 335.

66 Ibid. Wesley's point has implications for the factious conflicts in many churches today, including the United Methodist Church.

67 Ibid., 9:336. Wesley's "catholic spirit," his openness to those who hold differing opinions on doctrine and practice, was not without boundaries. Some interpreters of Wesley portray him as more open than he really was. There have to be boundaries in both faith and practice. What Wesley really said about this in his sermon "Catholic Spirit," made his commitment on this point rather clear:

> There is scarce any expression [the Catholic Spirit] which has been more grossly misunderstood and more dangerously misapplied than this. . . . For from hence we may learn, first, that a catholic spirit is not *speculative latitudinarianism*. It is not an indifference to all opinions. This is the spawn of hell, not the offspring of heaven. This unsettledness of thought . . . is a great curse,

ecclesiola in ecclesia idea of renewing and reforming the institutional or state church.[68] Later in this chapter we will see that Wesley had even deeper reasons for his arguments against separation or schism that go to the core of his Trinitarian vision of the church.

Theodore Runyon correctly noted that "Wesley's basic ecclesiology adheres neither to the state-church nor to the sectarian criteria. He intends a genuinely ecumenical renewal movement able to benefit all Christian bodies."[69] Wesley's understanding of the essence of the church is at the root of his ecumenicity. His vision of the church led him to reinterpret the Anglican Article on the subject in a way that is clearly in tension with the intent of the Protestant marks, a reinterpretation that also reveals that Wesley's view of ecclesiality does not comport so well with the Anabaptist and other visions of the church with sectarian tendencies, including the Moravians. Wesley was exceedingly clear on this point about his vision of the character

---

> not a blessing: an irreconcilable enemy, not a friend, to true catholicism. A man of a truly catholic spirit has not now his religion to seek. He is fixed as the sun in his judgement concerning the main branches of Christian doctrine. 'Tis true he is always ready to hear and weigh whatsoever can be offered against his principles. . . . Observe this, you who know not what spirit ye are of, who call yourselves men of a catholic spirit only because your mind is all in a mist; because you have no settled consistent principles, but are for jumbling all opinions together. Be convinced that you have quite missed your way . . . You think you are got into the very spirit of Christ, when in truth you are nearer the spirit of antichrist. Go first and learn the first elements of the gospel of Christ, and then shall you learn to be of a truly catholic spirit. (*Works,* 2:92–93)

What are those first elements of the gospel? Wesley made it abundantly clear throughout his writings, as we have seen in the course of the last two chapters: the first elements of the gospel are the participatory, economic Trinitarian relations at the heart of soteriology and ecclesiology. It is at precisely these points where Wesley is clear and consistent not only about the danger of schism around issues that do not go to the heart of the Trinitarian essence of the church but also about the need for clear boundaries around that Trinitarian center that Wesley's ecclesiology has something to contribute to the conversation within churches characterized by shrill divisive factions.

68 See Gwang Seok Oh, *John Wesley's Ecclesiology,* 89–124, for a discussion of the relationship of the Wesley and Pietism in the area of ecclesiology.

69 See Theodore Runyon, *The New Creation: John Wesley's Theology Today* (Nashville: Abingdon, 1998), 107. Runyon also has Wesley right when he notes that for Wesley, "It is the trinitarian God who calls it [the church] into existence. . . . Trinitarian spiritual energy not only constitutes the church but is its continuing dynamic" (ibid., 103).

of Methodism: "If it be said, he [God] could have made them a separate people like the Moravian Brethren, I answer, This would have been a direct contradiction to his whole design in raising them up; namely to spread scriptural religion throughout the land, among people of every denomination, leaving everyone to hold his own opinions and to follow his own mode of worship. This could only be done effectually by leaving these things as they were, and endeavouring to leaven the whole nation with that 'faith that worketh by love.'"[70]

It seems that, for Wesley, the Protestant and Anabaptist "marks" of the church are part of the *bene esse*, not the *esse*, of the church, or at least those marks are subordinate to the participatory, economic Trinitarian essence.[71]

---

70 *Works,* 3:511.

71 While Wesley did not systematically employ the theological distinction between the *esse* and *bene esse* of the church, he was familiar with the concept, and the basic idea is present in his thinking. He explicitly referenced the distinction in his "An Earnest Appeal to Men of Reason and Religion," where he said that "a visible Church (as our Article defines it) is 'a company of faithful (or believing) people: *coetus credentium*.' This is the essence of the Church" (see *The Works of John Wesley*, ed. Gerald Cragg, vol 11, *The Appeals to Men of Reason and Religion and Certain Related and Open Letters* [Oxford: Clarendon, 1975], 77). Wesley then asserted that the properties or marks of the church are the Protestant pure preaching of the Word of God and the right administration of the sacraments. On the next page, Wesley noted that without living faith, there can be no church at all, though as we saw in his sermon "Of the Church," "living faith" for Wesley entailed union and communion with the Triune God and one another. To place primary emphasis on the human response of faith is to misread what Wesley consistently said about the essence of the church, as we see in this Earnest Appeal and as we saw in his sermon "Of the Church."

It is at this point in the Appeal that Wesley employed the distinction between the *esse* and *bene esse* of the church in relation to sacraments as one of the two marks of the true church: "The third thing requisite, if not to the *being*, at least to the *well-being* of a Church, is the due administration of the sacraments" (ibid., 78). This is a rather telling statement, as it reveals not simply Wesley's knowledge of this important theological distinction between the *esse* and the *bene esse* of the church but also his questioning of whether the Protestant marks of the church are part of the essence of the church. This is exactly in keeping with what Wesley said about those marks in his sermon "Of the Church."

In addition, various statements underscore that for Wesley, it was the Trinitarian relations, the union and communion with the Father through the Son in the Spirit and one another at the heart of the people coming to faith, that define the essence of the church, not the Protestant marks nor the human response of faith as in the Anabaptist tradition. It also reveals, once again, that Wesley had an ontological Trinitarian understanding of the church, not a functionalist conception of the church as

Everything Wesley wrote in this part of his sermon "Of the Church" flows from the participatory, economic Trinitarian understanding of ecclesiality Wesley developed earlier in the sermon.

How Members of the Church Should Live

Only after he had defined the essence of the church in the first half of the sermon "Of the Church" and critiqued the classic Protestant marks of the church found in the Anglican Article, did Wesley turn to the other point of his text in Ephesians 4:1–6: instruction to all the members of the church about how they are to walk worthy of their calling or how they are to live. We have already noted that Wesley saw the New Testament conception of "walk" as including "all our inward and outward motions, all our thoughts, and words, and actions . . . not only everything we do, but everything we either speak or think," and doing it "in every instance in a manner worthy of our Christian calling."[72]

Ephesians 4 tells readers that they are "to walk, first, 'with all lowliness,'" which in characteristic fashion, Wesley defined as "to have that mind in us which was also in Christ Jesus."[73] This familiar theological shorthand points to the transformation of the human heart and its affections and tempers, as noted in chapter 2. For Wesley, this meant "to be deeply sensible of our own unworthiness . . . that we are not only sick but dead in trespasses and sins, till God breathes upon the dry bones, and creates life by the fruit of his lips." Indeed, "Who is able to think one good thought, or to form one good desire, unless by that Almighty power which worketh in us both to will and to do of his good pleasure?"[74] Wesley continued his exposition of Ephesians 4:1–6 by discussing the other phrases of the text dealing with "humility," "meekness," "long-suffering," and "forebearing one another in love" along similar lines. Wesley summarized this whole line of thought: "Let all our actions spring from this fountain; let all our words breathe this spirit; that all men may know that we have been with Jesus."[75]

The concluding section of Wesley's sermon "Of the Church" dealt with the unity of the church: "True members of the church of Christ 'endeavour,' with all possible diligence, with all care and pains, with unwearied patience

---

a means of grace, when he spoke of the essence of *the* church, rather than institutional expressions of the visible church that are part of the *bene esse* of the church.

72 *Works*, 3:53.

73 Ibid.

74 Ibid., 3:53–54.

75 Ibid., 3:53.

. . . 'to keep the unity of the Spirit in the bond of peace'; to preserve inviolate the same spirit of lowliness and meekness, of long-suffering, mutual forbearance and love." Wesley drove home his irenic, nonsectarian emphasis on unity, mutual forbearance, and love that was at the center of his plea that Methodists not leave the Church of England by stating, "Thus only can we be and continue living members of that church which is the body of Christ."[76] This profound irenic emphasis on the unity of the church is a prelude to Wesley's sermon "On Schism," which he wrote a few months after "Of the Church."

What is especially ironic about viewing Wesley's sermon "Of the Church" and his understanding of ecclesiality as having Anabaptist tendencies is that only after Wesley had defined the essence of the church in Trinitarian terms, only after he had made his third point that members of the church are to do everything in their power to "keep the unity of the Spirit," contra the sectarian tendencies of some in the Methodist movement who wanted to leave the Church of England, did Wesley get around to talking about holiness. Surely this is neither coincidental nor an oversight on Wesley's part. Is it not Wesley's way of keeping holiness in its proper place? Holiness is the *fruit* that grows only out of the participatory Trinitarian vine, where we are all beggars before the Triune God, spiritual paupers who cannot be arrogant, sectarian, or insular. In Wesley's view, the only holiness in us derives from the power of God's Trinitarian grace, and it is there to bear witness to the gospel as a leaven in the Anglican Church and the world, the exact point where Wesley ended his sermon.

"Does it not clearly appear from this whole account why," Wesley questioned his audience, the Apostles' Creed calls the universal church "the holy catholic church?"[77] Here Wesley took issue with those ecclesial traditions that lowered the standard of the church's holiness by saying that "the church is called holy because Christ the head of it is holy" or "our Lord *intended* that all the members of the church should be holy." In Wesley's view, the "plainest reason" and "only true one" was simply that "the church is called 'holy' because it is holy; because every member thereof is holy, though in different degrees, as he that called them is holy."[78]

Wesley already stated that holiness is not a human possibility, "unless we are every hour, yea, every moment, endued with power from on high."[79]

---

76 Ibid., 3:55.

77 Ibid.

78 Ibid., 3:55–56.

79 Ibid., 3:53–54.

This is a crucial point in Wesley's understanding of the ecclesiality of the church and how the holiness of the church and all its members is bound up with this essence. Listen to the forceful way Wesley stated this point:

> How clear is this! [that the members of the church are all holy in differing degrees] If the church, as to the very essence of it [notice Wesley's chosen language at this point], is a body of believers, no man that is not a Christian believer can be a member of it. If this whole body be animated by one spirit, and endued with one faith and one hope of their calling; then he who has not that spirit, and faith and hope, is no member of this body. . . in a word, none that is dead to God—can be a member of his church.[80]

In other words, for Wesley, those who are united to the Lord in one Spirit and are animated by the Spirit and find their lives in the Spirit hidden with Christ in God cannot but be "holy, though in different degrees, as he that called them is holy."[81] Those whose lives are caught up in the economic Trinitarian soteriological/ecclesiological activity are people whose lives are radically changed, rebirthed, redeemed, bound to Christ and, simultaneously, to one another in holy love.

Any holiness in our lives is only always a participation in Christ's holiness, but a participation that *does change* us and makes us *actually holy* in varying degrees. The holiness of the church, which includes real embodiment in our lives, is the result of our soteriological, personal, and ontological participation through the Spirit in Christ and thus in communion with the Triune God.

Holy to what end? Here again, what Wesley actually said is revealing:

> Let all those who are real members of the church see that they walk holy and unblameable in all things. "'Ye are the light of the world!' . . . 'O let your light shine before men!' Show them your faith by your works. . . . Let all your words and actions evidence the spirit whereby you are animated! Above all things let your love abound. Let it extend to every child of man; let it overflow to every child of God. By this all men know whose disciples ye are, because you love one another."[82]

Walking holy and blameless in all things evidences the Triune God who animates the church, particularly in the way the members of the church

---

80 Ibid., 3:56.
81 Ibid., 3:55–56.
82 Ibid., 3:57.

love one another so that nominal Christians and non-Christians alike might know what kind of Savior the church's Lord and Head actually is. This kind of participatory Trinitarian holiness cannot be sectarian, insular, or schismatic because holiness is to leaven the institutional churches and also enlighten the world. Separating and forming parties is antithetical to Wesley's vision of the Trinitarian ecclesiality of the church and to the church's mission that flows from it.

2. Other Trinitarian Definitions of the Church

Wesley's Trinitarian understanding of the essence of the church appears in various other places in his writings. One of Wesley's most profound discussions of it is found in his sermon "Spiritual Worship," based on 1 John but echoing Romans 12:1–2, where Paul says that we are to offer ourselves as living sacrifices, which is our spiritual act of worship.

This sermon is especially significant for it emphasized the exact same point that we just examined about the relationship of holiness, as a mark of the true catholic church, to the church's Trinitarian essence. The sermon also underscored the doxological dimension essential to Wesley's doctrine of the Trinity and his Trinitarian soteriology and ecclesiology. Wesley defined spiritual or true worship in Trinitarian terms.

The sermon begins by noting that 1 John is a tract dealing with "the whole Christian church in all succeeding ages." Then comes the telling point: it "does not treat directly of faith . . . neither of inward and outward holiness . . . but of *the foundation of all, the happy and holy communion which the faithful have with God the Father, Son and Holy Ghost* [my emphasis]."[83] Notice that, once again, Wesley made the participatory Trinitarian dimension the "foundation" or most basic relation constitutive of the church. It is this happy and holy communion which the faithful have with the Triune God and one another that *is* the church. In addition, Wesley said that this happy and holy Trinitarian communion is the *foundation* of everything else or has a theological priority over everything else, including faith, and inward and outward holiness, though all of these dimensions are finally inseparable.

In fact, Wesley interpreted all of 1 John in terms of participatory communion with the Triune God that is the core essence of the entire evangelical and doxological fabric of the church and the Christian life. 1 John treats:

83 Ibid., 3:89–90.

> First, severally, of communion with the Father, chapter one, verses 5–10; of communion with the Son, chapters two and three; of communion with the Spirit, chapter four.
>
> Secondly, conjointly, of the testimony of the Father, Son, and Holy Ghost, on which faith in Christ, the being born of God, love to God and his children, the keeping of his commandments, and victory over the world, are founded, chapter five, verses 1–12.
>
> The recapitulation begins, chapter five, verse 18: "We know that he who is born of God," who sees and loves God, "sinneth not," so long as this loving faith abideth in him. "We know that we are of God," children of God, by the witness and the fruit of the Spirit. . . . "We know that the Son of God is come" . . . "that we may know the true one," the faithful and true witness. "And we are in the true one," as branches in the vine. "This is the true God, and eternal life."[84]

Later in the sermon, Wesley summarized the entire Epistle:

> "This is" the sum of "the testimony which God hath" testified "of his Son, that God *hath* given us," not only a title to but the real beginning of "eternal life. And this life is" purchased by, and treasured up "in his Son," who has all the springs and the fullness of it in himself, to communicate to his body, the church.
>
> This eternal life then commences when it pleases the Father to reveal his Son in our hearts; when we first know Christ, being enabled to "call him Lord by the Holy Ghost"; when we can testify, our conscience bearing us witness in the Holy Ghost, "the life which I now live, I live by faith in the Son of God, who loved me and gave himself for me." And then it is that happiness begins—happiness real, solid, substantial. . . .
>
> As our knowledge and our love of him increase by the same degrees, and in the same proportion, the kingdom of an inward heaven must necessarily increase also; while we "grow up in all things into him who is our head." And when we are . . . "complete in him," . . . more properly when we are "filled with him"; when "Christ in us, the hope of glory," is our God and our all, when he has taken the full possession of our hearts; when he reigns therein, without a rival, the Lord of every motion there; when we dwell in Christ, and Christ in us, we are one with Christ and Christ with us; then we are completely happy; then we live all "the life that is hid with Christ in God." Then, and not till then, we properly experience what that

84 Ibid., 3:90.

> word meaneth, "God is love; and whosoever dwelleth in love, dwelleth in God, and God in him."[85]

This is an absolutely winsome and profound passage summarizing the Trinitarian themes we have seen throughout the last two chapters and in this one on the church. It is vintage Wesley, combining a tapestry of biblical texts within his Trinitarian vision of soteriology and ecclesiology.

Notice that for Wesley eternal life and the church as the body of Christ are inseparable, facets of a single differentiated reality. Eternal life refers to our communion in the Spirit with Christ and through Christ with the Father. The church refers to the reality of our being constituted members together in the body of Christ, inseparably bound in the Spirit through Christ with God and with one another in and through this very same communion.

The church as communion with the Triune God and one another is the actual form that eternal life takes both now in history and in the eschaton, as we saw at the end of the last chapter. The church as communion with the Triune God and one another is the foundation of faith and inward and outward holiness, as Wesley noted right at the beginning of the sermon. So the church is an ontological end in itself and not merely a functional means of grace. Notice once again the thoroughly participatory Trinitarian fabric of Wesley's interconnected understanding of ecclesiology and soteriology, as is clear throughout that long quotation in all the "we" and "our" language Wesley used. According to Wesley, the Son "has all the springs and the fullness of it [eternal life] in himself, to communicate to his body, the church."[86] Notice also the link Wesley saw between communion with the Triune God and "real, solid, and substantial" happiness and, of course, holiness. Notice also that there is no gap whatsoever between Wesley's understanding of the Trinity and vibrant Christian faith, community, and life, as there was in the abstract portrayals of the Trinity by the defenders of the doctrine in the Trinitarian controversies.

One other important point in this sermon is that Wesley forged the closest of links between the deity of Christ and Christ as the source of the eternal life, echoing the deep conviction at the heart of the Trinitarian debates leading to the Council of Nicea in the fourth century that only if Jesus Christ is as fully divine as God the Father, indeed *homoousios*, of one being, with the Father, can he be the Author of salvation and the Object of our worship. So the whole first point of the sermon is a deep and prolonged explication of the deity of Christ, affirming, in Wesley's words, that "He and the Father

---

85 Ibid., 3:96–97.
86 Ibid., 3:96.

are one," that he is "God of God, Light of Light, very God of very God; in glory equal with the Father."[87] The same is true of the Holy Spirit, the Lord, the giver of life.

What is also revealing is that throughout this section on the deity of Christ, Wesley stressed that Christ is "the only Cause, the sole Creator of all things," "the *Supporter* of all things," the *Preserver* of all things," "the *Governor* of all things," "the *End* of all things," and "the *Redeemer* of all the children of men."[88] Christ is all these things in a way that includes the involvement of the Father and the Spirit. These kinds of statements do not fit the model of those who suggest that Wesley followed the Western church's use of the law of appropriations, where creation is primarily the province of God the Father.

In the second half of the sermon "Spiritual Worship," Wesley returned to the link between participatory knowledge of, and communion with, the Triune God, and true religion and happiness: "We may learn hence . . . that this happy knowledge of the true God is only another name for *religion*; I mean *Christian religion*." Religion does not lie merely in a set of doctrines or duties or outward actions. Wesley strongly asserted: "No; it properly and directly consists in the knowledge and love of God, as manifested in the Son of his love, through the eternal Spirit. And this naturally leads to every heavenly temper, and to every good word and work."[89] Two pages later, at the end of the sermon, Wesley drove the point home a final time: "In this alone can you find the happiness you seek—in the union of your spirit with the Father of spirits; in the knowledge and love of him who is the fountain of happiness, sufficient for all the souls he has made."[90]

For Wesley, union and communion with the Trinitarian God is constitutive of the church and is also the foundation of faith and inward and outward holiness that alone and together finally lead to human flourishing and happiness. Eternal life is communion with the three-one God and with one another as members together in the one body of Christ that begins now and continues on in ever-greater fullness in the eschaton. It is a union and communion that generates faith and transforms us into holy people together, manifesting love toward God, toward one another, toward those who are yet outside the church, and toward all creation, and therein toward full flourishing

87 Ibid., 3:90–91.
88 Ibid., 3:91–95.
89 Ibid., 3:99.
90 Ibid., 3:101.

as children of God in right relation to the Triune God, to everyone else, and to all creation.

This is what it finally means to be "transcripts of the Trinity"; we are united by the Spirit with Christ who *is* our eternal life, who lives his life through us, so that our life is hidden with Christ in God. We live in communion with the three-one God, with one another, indeed with all of redeemed creation in everlasting doxology, overflowing thanksgiving and praise to the Triune God who has loved us to the uttermost, who loves us with the very love that God is. In Wesley's soteriology and ecclesiology we really participate in, and thereby know something of, the love of God the Father that surpasses all knowledge through the grace of our Lord Jesus Christ in the communion of the Holy Spirit.

Movement within the order of salvation from Trinitarian prevenient grace through Trinitarian convicting, justifying/regenerating, and sanctifying grace to Trinitarian perfecting grace is the *very same process* that Wesley describes ecclesiologically as the ever-increasing fullness of the eternal life of God "purchased by, and treasured up 'in his Son,' to communicate to his body, the church" in and through the communion of the Holy Spirit.[91]

Sondra Higgins Matthaei has this point right in her book *Making Disciples*, when she defines Wesley's order of salvation in terms of communion: "Growth in grace begins with an *invitation to communion* through the Creator God's prevenient grace. Repentance and pardon through the justifying grace of Jesus Christ initiates a *deepening communion* with the Three-One God through the perfecting work of the Holy Spirit, until *full communion* with God is reached in glory."[92] This means in Wesley's theology that soteriology,

91 Ibid., 3:96

92 Sondra Higgins Matthaei, *Making Disciples: Faith Formation in the Wesleyan Tradition* (Nashville: Abingdon, 2000), 61–62, emphasis in the original. Matthaei's account of Wesley's Trinitarian understanding of the order of salvation and the church is inadequate because she followed Maddox's account of the law of appropriations distinguishing the persons of the Trinity by assigning certain attributes or activities to each person of the Trinity, as noted above near the beginning of chapter 2. Matthaei missed the crucial point that for Wesley all three persons of the Trinity are always involved in every form that grace takes within the order of salvation. It is not characteristic of Wesley to associate prevenient grace with the Creator-God [notice also her reticence to name the first person of the Trinity, Father], justifying grace with Christ, and sanctifying and perfecting grace with the Spirit. As noted in chapter 3, Wesley saw that all grace in whatever form it takes comes to us not simply from Christ, but in Christ in the fully Trinitarian manner involving all the persons of the Trinity. What is interesting is that Matthaei referenced a number of texts where Wesley clearly stated that we enter into participatory union and communion with

ecclesiology, and the Trinity really are finally inseparable, as noted at various points in this monograph: the coactivity of the persons of the Trinity on our behalf is the source of our communal salvation that simultaneously restores us to communion with the Triune God and one another and constitutes us as the church, the body of Christ, the beginning of the kingdom of God that will one day encompass the whole world, indeed the entire universe.

III. A Trinitarian Perspective on Schism

If Wesley really had a Trinitarian understanding of the church as communion with the Triune God and others, then we would expect that Wesley's understanding of schism should reflect it as well. In other words, if the foundation or the *esse* of the church is the evangelical, doxological, participatory *"happy and holy communion which the faithful have with God the Father, Son, and*

the Father and the Son through the Spirit and know the Triune God where we know God face to face (ibid., 64–65).

I might add that Matthaei's serial account of the activity of the persons of the Trinity is theologically and ecclesiologically problematic. It all too easily degenerates into a conception of history as divided into three ages. The Old Testament is the age of the Father. The New Testament is the age of the Son. The subsequent history of the church becomes the age of the Spirit. This serial account of the activities of the persons of the Trinity, mediated to American Methodism through John Fletcher, has created theological problems for American Methodism ever since. It is part of the theological baggage that made American Methodism so susceptible to the Liberal Protestant temptation to jettison a high Christology in favor of a pneumatologically conceived vision of Christian faith, in which Jesus becomes the great example that we are to follow or emulate in our own day via the power and presence of the Spirit. Whenever the Spirit becomes preeminent and a high Christology fades away, not only is the doctrine of the Trinity and the Trinitarian dimension of Christian faith and life imperiled, almost always the "kingdom of God" becomes identified with the latest social project envisioned by those who appeal to the Spirit without a deep and abiding Christological criterion. Matthaei does not follow this pattern, but her serial account of the Trinity reopens the door for just the kind of problems that have been the bane of some segments of American Methodism from the second half of the nineteenth century right up to today.

Nevertheless, I am deeply encouraged to find a professor of Christian education thinking of spiritual formation or disciple-making within the framework of Wesley's Trinitarian vision of the order of salvation and the church. Matthaei's proposal could be enriched and deepened by incorporating the Trinitarian dimension of Wesley's understanding of the core of the gospel or Christian faith, the order of salvation, and the essence of the church and then consistently thinking through in her vision of disciple-making in light of it.

Holy Ghost," as Wesley said it, then did Wesley think out schism and separation in these terms as well? This is precisely what Wesley did.

Wesley opened his sermon "On Schism" by linking it to his sermon "Of the Church," noting that the word "schism" in England is "as ambiguous and indeterminate in its meaning as the 'church,'" and "nearly allied to it."[93] Here Wesley signaled that there is a close connection between "church" and "schism," and also between his two sermons. Wesley also noted that schism had been the subject of numerous books over several hundred years and "exceedingly little good has been done by all these controversies" because "they seldom agreed as to the meaning of the word concerning which they disputed."[94]

Wesley's sermon, then, focused on two points: (1) the nature of schism, and (2) the evil of it. Being a person of one book, Wesley turned to scripture to understand schism: any who "calmly consider the several texts wherein the word 'schism' occurs" will discover "that it is not a separation *from* any church (whether general or particular, whether the catholic or any national church) but a separation *in* a church."[95] Exegeting 1 Corinthians 1:10, Wesley noted that here schism means "not separations *from* but divisions *in* the church of Corinth."[96] In his comment on this text in his *Notes on the New Testament,* Wesley called it an "alienation of affection from each other."[97] In the schism sermon he stated that "union in mind and judgement was the direct opposite to the Corinthian schism."[98]

In fact, Wesley argued that schism is "a disunion in mind and judgment (perhaps also in affection) among those who, notwithstanding this, continued outwardly united as before." Moving on to the use of schism in Corinthians 11:18, Wesley added: "It seems in doing this they divided into little *parties,* which cherished anger and resentment one against another."[99]

The final text Wesley considered was 1 Corinthians 12:25. Here Wesley asserted, "We may easily observe that the word 'schism' here means the want of this tender care for each other." According to Wesley, schism "undoubtedly means an alienation of affection in any of them toward their brethren, a division of heart, and parties springing therefrom, though they

---

93 *Works,* 3:59.

94 Ibid., 3:59–60.

95 Ibid., 3:60.

96 Ibid., 3:61.

97 John Wesley, *Explanatory Notes upon the New Testament,* 2 vols. (1754; repr., Kansas City: Beacon Hill Press, 1981), comment on 1 Cor. 1:10.

98 *Works,* 3:61.

99 Ibid.

were still outwardly united together."[100] We see throughout his treatment of these texts that schism is the opposite of communion with the Triune God and one another that is the body of Christ. It is alienation, the disruption or dissolving of the fellowship at the core of who persons are: their affections [remember what Wesley said in his sermon "On Zeal" about love on the throne of the heart with the other affections and tempers surrounding it] no longer manifest the love that unites them, but rather the anger and resentment that divide them.

It, then, comes as no surprise that when Wesley recapitulated and unified "the whole tenor" of these texts, he defined schism/separation in the same Trinitarian terms that he used to define the church:

> To separate ourselves from a body of living Christians with whom were we before united is a grievous breach of the law of love. It is the nature of love to unite us together, and the greater the love the stricter the union. And while this continues in its strength nothing can divide those whom love has united. . . . The pretenses for separation may be innumerable, but want of love always is the real cause; otherwise they would still hold the unity of the spirit in the bond of peace. [Notice Wesley's return to Ephesians 4, the very text he used when he defined the *esse* of the Church in his sermon "Of the Church." He then referenced text after text that emphasize that Christians are called to love one another.] . . . This indeed is not so much consequence to *you* who are only a *nominal* Christian. For you are not now vitally united to any of the members of Christ. . . . But if you are a living member, if you live the life that is hid with Christ in God, then take care how you rend the body of Christ by separating from your brethren. It is a thing evil in itself.[101]

---

100 Ibid., 3:61, 63.

101 Ibid., 3:64, 68. In this sermon "On Schism," Wesley noted two instances in which schism or separation is not only permitted but "an absolute necessity": when remaining in a society, a congregation, or a national church requires "doing something which the Word of God forbids, or omitting something which the Word of God positively commands . . . you ought to separate" (ibid., 3:67). However, unless one or both of those conditions arise, Wesley was absolutely clear: "It is then my indispensable duty to continue therein [in a society, a congregation, or a national church]. And if I separate from it without such necessity I am justly chargeable . . . with all the evils consequent upon that separation" (ibid.). There is a correlation between what Wesley said here about the two conditions for separation and what Wesley said in his "Catholic Spirit" sermon about the need for boundaries (fixed as the sun around the central doctrines of Christian faith) as well as openness to differences in opinion around doctrine and practice.

This is an amazing quotation that solidifies the contention that Wesley understood (1) the church in participatory Trinitarian terms as union and communion with God and other Christians in the body of Christ; and (2) schism as the rupture of that communion, both rooted in the nature of persons whose affections are simultaneously person-constituting and community-constituting. The love of God through Christ in the Spirit unites us to God and other Christians and simultaneously forms Christians' personhood and the character of the relations between them in a particular way that is loving, holy, and happy.

It is clear from this text that, for Wesley, only the economic activity of the Triune God in the gospel can create this kind communion or bond of love in people in relation to God and to one another. Christian ecclesial identity is bound up with these person-constituting and simultaneous community-constituting affections and relations that make the church the communion of saints that it is. Schism, in Wesley's view, was a grievous breach of the law of love. It is a breaking of the actual living union and communion with Triune God and one another that is the body of Christ.

The consistency with which Wesley thought out the ecclesiality of the church in terms of this kind of Trinitarian communion and then applied it to

---

Wesley explicitly applied this to himself, noting that he was and had been a member of and a minister in the Church of England and that he had "no desire or design to separate until my soul separates from my body." But if remaining meant doing something scripture forbids or omitting something scripture commands Wesley said he would be under absolute necessity and he would not be guilty of the sin and evil of separation. If Wesley separated without such a necessity, he would be chargeable of the offense of schism (ibid.).

Wesley likely made this application to himself and the Church of England to answer rumors that he planned to separate in the aftermath of his ordination of Whatcoat and Vasey and his involvement in the formation of the Methodist Episcopal Church in America. But he also mentioned "societies" multiple times in his sermon on schism. When he described the unraveling of communion with the Triune God and one another that is the body of Christ that he and his readers had witnessed, what he described sounds more like what had happened within Methodism and the societies that comprised it. We will examine this unraveling next.

At the very end of the sermon, Wesley passionately warned about involvement in schism: "O beware, I will not say of *forming*, but of *countenancing* or *abetting* of any *parties* in a Christian society! . . . Follow peace with all men, without which you cannot effectually follow after holiness" (ibid., 3:68–69). I am no expert on the unpleasant subject of schism. I do fully agree that schism and separation have to be thought out in terms of disrupting the participatory, economic Trinitarian relations constitutive of the *esse* of the church.

schism, viewing schism in the exact same terms, reinforces that this really is Wesley's deepest conceptualization of the essence of the church. If this communion of love is ontological and constitutive of Christian identity in community at the core of a person's being-in-relations, rooted in the affections, we might expect that Wesley would deal with the consequences or out-working of a schism as a breach of this communion and love, from a center in the affections spreading to a person's thoughts, words, and actions along lines similar to his account in his sermon "On Zeal," where love on the throne works itself out in thoughts, words, and actions, as we saw in chapter 2.[102]

In that sermon "On Zeal," Wesley portrayed love on the throne in our "inmost soul; namely love for God and man, which fills the whole heart, and reigns without a rival."[103] Wesley then moved through several concentric circles of other aspects of what it means to be a person and a Christian. In close proximity to the affection of love on the throne, are "holy tempers" or the fruit of the Spirit, what Wesley also calls "the mind which was in Christ Jesus," his theological shorthand for the inward change effected in us by the economic Trinitarian activity of the gospel. Outside the holy tempers are "outward works" of mercy and of piety (means of grace) that "spring from *holy tempers*."[104] Wesley used the phrase "to walk as Christ walked" to describe this outward righteousness that flows from the inward change that occurs when our lives are hidden with Christ in God. Therefore, if there is congruity between Wesley's soteriological account of this "throne room" of the soul in his sermon "On Zeal," and Wesley's ecclesiological account of schism, we would expect to see an outworking of the breach of love, this alienation of affection that is the theological/ontological root of schism, along similar lines of concentric circles in the deformation of persons and disruption of community as schism works itself out through unholy tempers to unholy words and actions. This is exactly the process Wesley outlined in his treatment of schism.

In his second point in his sermon "On Schism," Wesley asserted, "As such a separation is evil in itself, being a breach of brotherly love, so it brings forth evil fruit." And what is that evil fruit? According to Wesley, schism as a breach of the affection of love on the throne "opens a door to all unkind tempers, both in ourselves and others. It leads directly to a whole train of evil surmisings . . . of each other. It gives occasion to offence, to anger, and

102 See Collins, *Theology of John Wesley*, 228.

103 *Works*, 3:313.

104 Ibid., 3:313–14, 320.

resentment, perhaps in ourselves as well as in our brethren."[105] Of course, if left to run its course, this alienation of affection, this rending of the very fabric of love and union and communion in Christ with God and one another, "may issue in bitterness, malice and settled hatred."[106]

Yet this is not the end of the schismatic unraveling of the union and communion of love that is the church, for Wesley immediately noted that "the ill consequences of even this species of schism do not terminate in the heart. Evil tempers cannot long remain within before they are productive of outward fruit." Those whose hearts are full of love speak in wisdom and kindness. "So he whose heart is full of prejudice, anger, suspicion, or any unkind temper, will surely open his mouth in a manner corresponding with the disposition of his mind. And hence will arise . . . bitter words . . . and evil speaking of every kind."[107]

Wesley's insightful chronicling of how a breach in love threatens to unravel the union and communion with the Triune God and one another in the body of Christ illumines Wesley's commentary on the vicious Trinitarian controversies as "an evil hour" when the defenders "lost their way" and "above all persons hurt the cause they intended to promote." For Wesley the doctrine of the Trinity has a close connection with vital religion where the Spirit of God unites us to Christ and through Christ with God the Father but also to one another in a fellowship of love that is the essence of the church. The Trinitarian controversies were twice wrong for Wesley because they disconnected the Trinity from vibrant Trinitarian Christian faith, life, and community by turning the doctrine into an esoteric intellectual puzzle and because the vitriolic character of the debates even between those who affirmed the Trinity was a breach of love that is at the heart of church.

By now the trajectory of the outworking of this breach of love, this rending of union and communion that is the body of Christ entailed in schism, is ever so clear. Wesley moved predictably to actions: "From evil words . . . how many evil works will naturally flow! Anger . . . wrong tempers of every kind, do not vent themselves merely in words, but push men continually to all kind of ungodly and unrighteous actions."[108]

Wesley noted how this outworking of schism as a breach of the law of love not only rends the fabric of communion and love that is the church but also destroys the power and then the form of godliness in those who are

105 Ibid., 3:65.
106 Ibid.
107 Ibid.
108 Ibid.

sucked into the swirling vortex of schism. In so doing, it also undermines the witness of the church to the world. Wesley added that "these consequences are not imaginary, are not built on mere conjectures, but on plain matter of fact. . . . These have been the fruits which we have seen over and over to be consequent on such separation."[109] Indeed, Wesley lamented, "Such is the complicated mischief which persons separating from a Christian church or society do, not only to themselves, but to that whole society, and to the world in general."[110]

So there is an undeniable parallel progression from the rending of love and communion at the center of persons and their relations to unholy tempers, then unholy words, and finally unholy actions in Wesley's account of schism. Schism, for Wesley, follows the same pattern he identified in his sermon "On Zeal," from love on the throne to holy tempers or having the mind of Christ to holy works of mercy and piety. But schism is the sinful deformation of the law of love that progresses along the same path but with a destructive trajectory.

Now that we have clarified the parallels between his account of schism as a rending of the communion that the church is and his account of the "throne room," we are in a position to better understand what Wesley said about the church in his sermon "On Zeal," where he spoke of the church being a means of grace, a crucial text for those who argue that Wesley had a functionalist vision of the church.

IV. A Functionalist Understanding of the Church as a Means of Grace?

There is no question that Wesley, in this sermon "On Zeal," subordinated the church to the means of grace and saw the church as constituted for preaching and the sacraments. What did Wesley actually say, and what did he mean? According to Wesley, "True zeal must be always proportioned to the degree of goodness which is in its object."[111] Wesley said that "all that fear God should be zealous for the *church*." Indeed they bear "a strong affection to it . . . earnestly desiring its prosperity and increase." But they "should be more zealous for the *ordinances of Christ* than for the church itself."[112] On the next page, Wesley told us why. We are to be more zealous for the

---

109 Ibid., 3:66.

110 Ibid.

111 Ibid., 3:318.

112 Ibid., 3:314, 318.

ordinances because it was "for the sake of which, in a great measure, the church itself was constituted."[113]

Here it appears that Wesley had an essentially functionalist understanding of the church as a means of grace. Indeed, to provide the ordinances is the church's primary raison d'être. Let us follow Wesley's train of thought on zeal to its conclusion and see if we can make sense of what he said about the church as a means of grace and its apparent inconsistency with what he said about the essence of church as union and communion with the Triune God and with one another in his sermon on the subject.

While Christians should be zealous for the church and even more for the ordinances, Christians should be still more zealous for works of mercy than for works of piety, even more zealous for holy tempers, "but most zealous of all for that which is the sum and the perfection of religion—the *love* of God and man."[114] This last statement creates a bit of a quandary because, if love for God and others is the sum and perfection of religion and worthy of our highest zeal, what about the fact that Wesley, in both his sermons "Of the Church" and "On Schism," as well as in other places, said that it is this very love (and the union and communion with Christ and one another within which love exists and is what it is) that is constitutive of the church and that rending this love creates the disunity that is schism? Did Wesley's views change between 1781 when he wrote the sermon "On Zeal" and 1785 when he wrote "Of the Church"?

One problem with this kind of explanation is that it is highly unlikely at this late stage in Wesley's life, after years of theological reflection, that he would have had this kind of radical change in his understanding of something so central to his theological vision as the leader of a movement of church renewal, with all the complicated ecclesiological issues Wesley had to deal with over a number of decades. One might argue that Wesley's ordinations and involvement in forming the Methodist Episcopal Church in America in the years in between the two sermons is reason enough for the shift. The problem with that kind of explanation is that Wesley described the church as union and communion with the Triune God multiple times in other publications prior to those ordinations, as noted above.

In fact, Wesley wrote his sermon "Spiritual Worship," with its understanding of the "foundation" of "inward and outward holiness" in "the happy and holy communion which the faithful have with God the Father, Son, and

113 Ibid., 3:319.
114 Ibid.

Holy Ghost,"[115] in December 1780, less than six months before he wrote the sermon "On Zeal." In the latter sermon, Wesley placed the church much lower on his list of "degrees of goodness," lower than inward and outward holiness, for the church is only a means of grace: its chief purpose is to provide the ordinances that serve the ends of inward and outward holiness. Here the church is certainly *not* viewed in terms of the happy and holy communion the faithful have with the Triune God that is the very *foundation* of all else, including inward and outward holiness, according to the sermon on spiritual worship.

The proximity of those two sermons and their rather different visions of the church require explanation. I think the key to relaxing the apparent contradiction between what Wesley said about the church in these two sermons lies in the nature of ordinances themselves and what this suggests about "which church" Wesley had in mind in his sermon "On Zeal," where he subordinated church to the ordinances.

For Wesley, the very presence and power of God can be immediately present in and through the ordinances of God or more broadly the means of grace. Wesley believed that the means of grace were "outward signs, words, or actions ordained of God, and appointed for this end—to be the *ordinary* channels whereby he might convey to men preventing, justifying, or sanctifying grace."[116] Wesley quoted the classic statement from the Book of Common Prayer, that a "sacrament is 'an outward sign of an inward *grace*, and a *means* whereby we receive the same.' "[117]

So the means of grace are earthly historical vessels through which the Triune God is pleased to communicate the participatory Trinitarian activity that is preventing, justifying, and sanctifying grace. While the outward creaturely form and the divine Trinitarian presence and activity are linked for Wesley, he was also equally clear "that all the outward means whatever, if separate from the Spirit of God, cannot profit at all, cannot conduce in any degree either to the knowledge or love of God." Indeed, according to Wesley, "whosoever therefore imagines there is any intrinsic *power* in any means whatsoever does greatly err . . . the whole power is of him, whereby through any of these there is any blessings conveyed to our soul."[118]

At the end of his sermon "The Means of Grace," Wesley instructed his readers "always to retain a lively sense that God is above all means." Indeed,

---

115 Ibid., 3:89–90.

116 This is from Wesley's sermon "Means of Grace" in *Works*, 1:381.

117 Ibid.

118 Ibid., 1:382.

"It is in itself a poor, dead, empty thing: separate from God, it is a dry leaf, a shadow." When we use the means of grace we must "seek God alone" and "look singly to the *power* of his Spirit and the *merits* of his Son."[119]

For Wesley there is a similar parallel between the outwardly earthly historical *form* of the church and the participatory, economic Trinitarian *reality* of the church as the body of Christ. Wesley distinguished, but never severed, the earthly historical form of the church from the divine/human reality of the body of Christ in a way that parallels what he said about the means of grace.

In his work entitled "The Nature, Design, and General Rules of the United Societies," Wesley said that "a Society is no other than a company of men having the form, and seeking the power of godliness."[120] As we have seen, Wesley said that avoiding evil, doing good, and using the means of grace, the three main divisions of the General Rules that govern these societies, are "only outward form of that religion [of a nobler kind] which he insatiably hungers after," as Wesley said it in his "Sermon on the Mount, II" examined above. The religion that we long for, and of which the societies are only the outward *form*, is "The knowledge of God in Christ Jesus; 'the life that is hid with Christ in God'; the being 'joined unto the Lord in one Spirit'; the having 'fellowship with the Father and the Son,'"[121] in short the soteriologically and ecclesiologically constitutive participatory Trinitarian *reality* of the gospel. Wesley had earlier come to the conclusion that issues of polity, like bishops and other forms of church government, belong to the right ordering or *bene esse* and not to the essence of the church.[122]

We see in Wesley this same distinction in relation to the church between (1) the outward earthly historical form (institutional and ministry structures of congregations, state churches, or denominations and all the informal elements that are bound up with them) with all their imperfections that we are all too aware of, and (2) the church as the body of Christ, the soteriological and ecclesiological reality constituted by the economic activity of the Trinitarian persons and the human participatory response in faith and love with its inward and outward holiness.[123] Which "church" or aspect of the church was Wesley talking about in his sermon "On Zeal" when he subordinated the

---

119 Ibid., 1:395–96.

120 *The Works of John Wesley*, ed. Rupert Davies, vol. 9, *The Methodist Societies: History, Nature, and Design* (Nashville: Abingdon, 1989) 9:69.

121 *Works*, 1:497.

122 See Outler's article, "Do Methodists Have a Doctrine of the Church," 11–28, for a discussion of Wesley's convictions about bishops and forms of church government.

123 There is an element of dualism in Wesley's theology. It is evident in his anthropology with the immaterial soul inhabiting a material body, indeed a body subject to

church to the means of grace and moved in the direction of a functionalist understanding of the church?

Wesley provided an indication of his intent at the end of the sermon in his final summary statement. He urged his readers to "take then the whole of religion together, just as God has revealed it in his Word . . . holding fast this one principle, 'The life I now live, I live by faith in the Son of God who loved *me*, and gave himself for *me*'; proportion your zeal to the value of its object." Then came Wesley's clarificatory statement: "Be calmly zealous therefore, first, for the *church*—'the whole state of Christ's church militant here on earth,' and in particular for that branch thereof with which you are more immediately connected."[124] Wesley said nearly the same thing earlier in the sermon: "Be zealous for *the church*; more especially for that particular branch thereof wherein your lot is cast. Study the welfare of this, and carefully observe all the rules of it, for conscience' sake."[125] In both places in the zeal sermon it is the earthly historical form of the church, in its various branches with its structures and rules, that Wesley clearly had in mind and not the church as the body of Christ or all those who are truly united in the Spirit to Christ and through Christ with the Father and with one another in whatever branch of the church militant they might be.

The idea that Wesley had the visible church militant in mind in his sermon "On Zeal" is reinforced when he made this point: "Be more zealous for all those *ordinances* which our blessed Lord hath appointed to continue therein [in the visible church militant] to the end of the world."[126] Wesley was clear that the ordinances are part of the earthly historical form of the church, and those ordinances, like the forms of the visible church itself (including the office of bishop), have their place only until Christ returns when they will cease to exist. They are part of the *bene esse* rather than the *esse* of the church. This point might also explain why Wesley added his qualifications to the classic Protestant marks of the church as noted above, since preaching and the sacraments will cease when Christ returns in final victory. But the church as the body of Christ in union and communion with the Triune God and one another does not cease to be when Christ returns because these participatory Trinitarian relations are the *esse* of the church and, therefore, they continue after Christ returns in the eschatological destiny for all creation,

---

the "cause and effect" structures of the Newtonian universe, an idea influential during Wesley's lifetime.

124 *Works*, 3:320.

125 Ibid., 3:319.

126 Ibid., 3:320.

as we saw in the last chapter in Wesley's sermon "The New Creation." In Wesley's own words: "And to crown all, there will be a deep, an intimate, an uninterrupted union with God; a constant communion with the Father and his son Jesus Christ, through the Spirit; a continual enjoyment of the Three-One God, and of all the creatures in him!"[127]

For Wesley, the earthly historical form of the church with its bishops, congregations, conferences, administrative meetings, and all the rest, including the ordinances, is the vessel and context to continue the means of grace through which the living Triune God has promised to be present and mediate life-giving Trinitarian presence and activity, which alone creates union and communion in the Spirit through the Son with the Father that both saves us and constitutes us together as Christ's body, the church. The earthly historical form of the church is crucial between the times. This is why Wesley was so adamant that early Methodism be a community that had the "form of godliness" while waiting for the participatory Trinitarian dimension that will fill the forms with the power of the gospel.

When Wesley talked about the church in "functionalist" terms as a means of grace, it seems clear that he was talking about the earthly historical form of the visible church militant. This dimension of the church is not part of the essence of the church but rather the *bene esse*, or right ordering, of the church between the times. When Wesley discussed the essence of the church as the body of Christ, he did so, not in functionalist categories but in the same participatory, economic Trinitarian way he spoke of the core of vital religion, the *ordo salutis*, and of the doctrine of the Trinity itself.

V. The Social/Ecclesial Character of Love and Holy Tempers

Wesley's sermon "On Zeal" raises the question of the essential character of love as the crucial affection on the very throne in the hearts of Christians and the character of the holy tempers (or fruit of the Spirit) that surround love in Wesley's depiction of what it means to be a Christian. It is easy to interpret affections and tempers individualistically, as something that the Triune God works in the lives of Christians as individuals, or even worse as merely a human project, the attempt to "craft holy virtues" on our own, to use Maddox's wonderful phrase.[128]

---

127 *Works*, 2:510.

128 Maddox, *Responsible Grace*, 201. Maddox has a helpful brief discussion of affections as motivating dispositions and tempers enduring or habituated dispositions

This individualist reading of the essential character of love and holy tempers is often part of what drives a functionalist vision of the church as a means of grace. The visible institutional church becomes one more provider of goods and services for individuals to consume in the great marketplace of America. Yet when we consider the fundamentally participatory Trinitarian character of love and holy tempers (or fruit of the Spirit) that arise out of the union and communion with the Triune God and one another, it seems that love and holy tempers are intrinsically and essentially relational: they exist only in, with, and out of participatory union and communion with the Triune God and one another, a union and communion that is simultaneously constitutive of the church as the body of Christ. So the question becomes, Is there anywhere in Wesley's writings where he developed this point, where he made the connection between love and other holy virtues or tempers and the essentially relational union and communion with Triune God and one another in which love and holy virtues exist?

This brings us to Wesley's crucial sermon "Upon our Lord's Sermon on the Mount, IV." Wesley's text is Matthew 5:13–16. This discourse follows three sermons all on the beatitudes or what Wesley called "the sum of all true religion."[129] At the beginning of "Sermons on the Mount, VI" (on Matthew 6) and "Sermon on the Mount, X" (on Matthew 7), Wesley provided nearly identical and illuminating summaries of Matthew chapter 5: "In the preceding chapter [Matthew 5] our Lord has described inward religion in its various branches." Indeed in Matthew 5, according to Wesley, Christ presents "those dispositions of soul which constitute real Christianity: the inward tempers contained in that holiness 'without which no man shall see the Lord'—the affections which, when flowing from their proper fountain, from a living faith in God through Christ Jesus, are intrinsically and essentially good, and acceptable to God."[130] This statement tells us that in his sermons on Matthew 5, Wesley dealt with the same affections and tempers that he talked about in his sermon "On Zeal." In addition, Wesley made clear that these affections and tempers flow via participation from an economic Trinitarian fountain, living faith in the love of God through the grace of Jesus Christ in the communion of the Spirit, the same living faith that is bound up with the essence of the church according to Wesley's sermon "Of the Church."

(see ibid., 68–69, 187–88, and the notes on 288–89). See also Kenneth J. Collins, "John Wesley's Topography of the Heart: Dispositions, Tempers and Affections," in *Methodist History* 36, no. 3 (1998): 162–75.

129 *Works*, 1:474.

130 Ibid., 1:572–73.

When Wesley began his "Sermon on the Mount, IV" with the following statement, he was referring to everything he had said in the previous three sermons (Sermon on the Mount, I, II, and III) on holy tempers and affections, the sum of all true Christian faith: "The beauty of holiness, of that inward man of the heart which is renewed after the image of God, cannot but strike every eye which God hath opened, every enlightened understanding." Wesley added, "This inward religion bears the shape of God so visibly impressed upon it that a soul must be wholly immersed in flesh and blood when he can doubt of its divine original."[131] The beauty of holiness bears witness to its divine Trinitarian source so that Christians become transcripts of the Trinity.

It is easy to guess where Wesley was headed in the sermon. His text was Matthew 5:13–26, "You are the salt of the earth, the light of the world." Wesley wanted to clarify the link that exists between inward holiness, love on the throne of our hearts and all the holy tempers encircling it, and all "our *doing* and *suffering*," which for Wesley was "theological shorthand" for all our active obedience (fulfilling all God's commands) and passive obedience (enduring God's providential will for us in everything that happens in life), what he elsewhere called our conversation with the world.[132]

What is of interest for this discussion of the Trinitarian dimension of Wesley's ecclesiology is that in demonstrating that tight connection between inward righteousness (love and all the holy tempers described in the beatitudes) and outward righteousness in all we say and do, Wesley also forged an equally tight connection between holy tempers and their essentially

---

131 Ibid., 1:531.

132 See Wesley's sermon "The Lord Our Righteousness" for his discussion of "doing and suffering" as active (fulfilling the law at every point) and passive (enduring everything that God's will or providence brings into our lives, with reference to Christ, particularly suffering death on the Cross) obedience in Christ (see ibid., 1:452–53). In "The Lord Our Righteousness" sermon, Wesley also dealt with Christ's "internal righteousness," which "is the image of God stamped on every power and faculty of his soul," or "love, reverence, resignation to his Father; humility, meekness, gentleness . . . and every other holy and heavenly temper" (ibid.). In fact, Christ's internal righteousness is nearly identical with Wesley's description of the character of the beatitudes in the first three of his sermons on the Sermon on the Mount. Wesley explicitly linked the beatitudes to Christ himself at the beginning of "Sermon on the Mount, IV," that we are examining in this section: "we may say of this, in a secondary sense, even as of the Son of God himself, that it is 'the brightness of his glory, the express image of his person' . . . 'the beaming forth of his' eternal 'glory'; and yet so tempered and softened that even the children of men may herein see God and live" (ibid., 1:531).

relational character (1) in the participatory union and communion with the Triune God, (2) in social and communal embodiment in the church as the body of Christ, and (3) beyond the church in Christian ministry and influence in the world. For Wesley, love, holy tempers, and all of the other Christian affections and dispositions or virtues are inherently soteriological, relational, ecclesial, and social with reference to their Trinitarian source and with reference to other people.

After summarizing the inward holiness of a heart renewed in love in the image of God discussed in his first three sermons on the beatitudes, Wesley turned to the question of outward religion or "*doing* and *suffering*." If Christian faith is rooted in the heart in a transformation of our affections and tempers through union and communion with God, "what need" is there "of loading it with *doing* and *suffering*?" Wesley quips: "Will it not suffice to worship God, who is a Spirit, with the spirit of our minds, without encumbering ourselves with outward things? . . . And that instead of busying ourselves at all about externals, we should only commune with God in our hearts?"[133]

Of course, Wesley would have nothing to do with this neglect of outward religion, calling it a "grand engine of hell against some of the most important truths of God."[134] At this point, Wesley turned to Matthew 5:13–16, where Christians are called to be salt and light and summarized the two key points of his sermon: "In order fully to explain and enforce these important words I shall endeavour to show, first, that Christianity is essentially a social religion, and that to turn it into a solitary one is to destroy it; secondly, that to conceal this religion is impossible."[135]

The first point, that Christianity is a social religion, is often quoted in secondary literature on Wesley's theology, but seldom is there a careful analysis of what Wesley actually meant by it. Nearly all reference Wesley's epigrammatic assertion: "Christianity is a social religion, and that to turn it into a solitary religion is to destroy it." Some even point to how Wesley clarified what he meant in the next paragraph of the sermon: "When I say this [Christianity] is essentially a social religion, I mean not only that it cannot subsist so well, but that it cannot subsist at all without society, without living and conversing with other men."[136] But Wesley said a lot more about the "sociality" of Christian religion in the rest of the sermon.

---

133 Ibid., 1:532.
134 Ibid.
135 Ibid., 1:533.
136 Ibid., 1:533–54.

Immediately after these texts, Wesley added that he will confine himself "*to those considerations which will arise* [my emphasis] from the very discourse [Sermon on the Mount] before us."[137] By stating that he will limit himself to the considerations that arise from the text, Wesley signaled that there is more to this subject of the sociality of Christian faith than what he will discuss in his sermon. Given the insightful observations Wesley did share, one cannot but wish that Wesley had written more on the subject. The piecemeal character of Wesley's reflections leaves his interpreters with the task of trying to figure out the other aspects of Wesley's vision of the sociality of Christian faith that he did not explicitly address in this sermon or elsewhere in his writings.

Being the astute and balanced thinker and practitioner of Christian faith that he was, Wesley began speaking of Christian sociality by making it clear that the social character of Christianity does not exclude "solitude or retirement from society." We can and should retire from the business of life in community "to converse with God, to commune more freely with our Father which is in secret." Yet we should not spend all our time this way because "this would be to destroy, not advance, true religion." Wesley added, "The religion described by our Lord in the foregoing words [the beatitudes] cannot subsist without society, without our living and conversing with other men."[138]

Here Wesley began to bring to light the connection between love and holy tempers and their essentially social, communal, participatory Trinitarian character in, with, and out of which love and holy tempers come to be and continue to exist. Wesley's point was that love, at the center and the other holy tempers surrounding it, cannot exist without particular kinds of relations with the Triune God and without social embodiment in relation to other people. Wesley realized that love is essentially social and communal for it signifies a "disposition of heart" that in its very essence only is what it is in particular kinds of relationships: we cannot love God or others until we come to know God's love through Christ in the Spirit via union and communion through the Spirit with the Father and the Son, as we have seen throughout this chapter. This Christian love is awakened by the participatory Trinitarian relations involving the presence and activity of the Trinitarian persons in the gospel. Christian love that arises in, with, and out of those relations is inherently directed toward others. For Wesley, Christian love is always oriented toward God in gratitude and toward other people in beneficence, as we saw in chapter 2.

---

137 Ibid., 1:534.
138 Ibid.

Wesley then directed attention to the sociality of the particular dispositions or virtues identified in Matthew 5: "There is no disposition, for instance, which is more essential to Christianity than meekness. Now although this, as it implies resignation to God, or patience in pain and sickness, may subsist in a desert, in a hermit's cell, in total solitude; yet as it implies (which it no less necessarily does) mildness, gentleness, and long-suffering, it cannot possibly have a being [note Wesley's choice of ontological language] . . . without an intercourse with other men. So that to attempt turning this into a solitary virtue is to destroy it from the face of the earth."[139] Here Wesley grasped a profound insight into the way in which our affections and our tempers (enduring dispositions or virtues) that arise out of union and communion with a Trinitarian God are inherently relational or social. They only are what they are, and continue to be what they are, within "society," "living and conversing" with other people, to use Wesley's words.

It is not only meekness that is inherently social or relational; so are the other Christian dispositions or virtues. Wesley quipped, "For will any man affirm that a solitary Christian (so called, though it is little less than a contradiction in terms) can be a merciful man—that is, one that takes every opportunity of doing good to all men?" Wesley forcefully drove home his point that sociality is inherent in "being" merciful such that "it cannot possibly have a being" without social embodiment: "What can be more plain than that this fundamental branch of the religion of Jesus Christ cannot possibly subsist without society, without our living and conversing with other men?"[140]

So for Wesley, these Christian affections and tempers or virtues have "being"—they are utterly real and also utterly social. They arise in, with, and out of relations of union and communion with the Triune God and are continually sustained by those relations. But they only exist in and with relations with other people so that they "cannot possibly have a being," as Wesley said it, without those relations. In addition, what Wesley said about the sociality of meekness and being merciful are simply examples of the social character of living Christian faith with its transformed affections and dispositions arising out of union and communion with the Triune God.

What comes into view when we consider everything Wesley said (1) about the Trinitarian essence of the church as union and communion with the Triune God and one another, and (2) about the sociality inherent in Christian love and Christian virtues, is that affections and virtues cannot

139 Ibid., 1:534.
140 Ibid., 1:535.

exist without being socially embedded and embodied. Wesley had a profound reciprocal understanding of Christian persons and Christian community, where the utterly real affections and virtues form who persons are as persons who have their being in utterly real relations with the Triune God and one another. These communal relations configure, and are configured by, Christian persons and their holy affections and dispositions. Wesley envisioned relations-embedded-in-affections/dispositions and affections/dispositions-embedded-in-relations all with special characteristics embodied in particular forms of sociality or community.

In addition, as we saw above in Wesley's treatment of schism, when the relational dynamics of a community or the dispositions of particular Christians are of an unholy character, these relations-embedded-in-dispositions and dispositions-embedded-in-relations create tensions, misunderstandings, and/or offense between Christians in community that poison both the persons involved and the community as well. Those persons encounter a disruption of Christian fellowship and love and a deformation of their dispositions. The deformed dispositions and destructive relational dynamics then further poison or even fracture the relations between the members of the body of Christ, leading to schism, that grievous deformation of love and the other Christian tempers, and corollary un-Christian thoughts, words, and actions.

What we see here is that for Wesley, the relations of love between Christians and the Triune God, as well as the relations between Christians within the body of Christ, "have being" or are ontological and utterly real. Those relations between human persons constitute and profoundly influence, mold, and shape the persons who are in those relations, at times in positive ways that both manifest and further love and holiness. Yet at other times those relations are sinful, and they can deform persons and their constitutive dispositions, create alienation, and can ultimately lead to schism.

As we have seen throughout this chapter and the previous two, holy dispositions of love and the tempers surrounding love in the hearts/souls of Christians are rooted in the participatory, economic Trinitarian activity that is constitutive of salvation and the church. Wesley made these Trinitarian relations explicit in two places in his "Sermon on the Mount, IV," where he dealt with Christian faith being a "social" religion. The first of these occurs in that part of the sermon where Wesley dealt with objections. Here he further reinforced the connection between love and holy tempers and their essentially soteriological, relational, social, communal, participatory, economic Trinitarian character in, with, and out of which they come to be and continue to exist not only (1) in union and communion with the Triune God, but also

(2) in society with others. This is one of the deepest and most insightful of all Wesley's discussions of the issues involved.

Wesley noted that "it has been often objected that religion does not lie in outward things but in the heart, in the inmost soul; that it is the union of the soul with God, and life of God in the soul of man." Wesley answered that objection this way: "It is most true that the root of religion lies in the heart, in the inmost soul; that this is the union of the soul with God, the life of God in the soul of man."[141] Of course, we have already seen that it is this union and communion with the Triune God that (1) generates not only our salvation (including the holy dispositions through which that salvation takes root in human life and begins to work itself out in thought, word, and deed), but also (2) simultaneously generates the church as the body of Christ.

At this point, Wesley added two deep and illuminating points. First, "If this root [union with the Triune God] be really in the heart it cannot but put forth branches." Union and communion with God generates holy affections and dispositions, generates love and all the tempers surrounding love on the throne of one's heart/soul. But since these dispositions are inherently social, since they have no "being" without "society," as Wesley noted earlier in the sermon, these dispositions inherently manifest themselves in "living and conversing with other men" and in "*doing* and *suffering*."[142]

Here, in answering this first objection, Wesley provided a second telling observation: "And these [the branches that come from the root] are the several instances of outward obedience, which partake of the same nature with the root, and consequently are not only *marks* or *signs*, but *substantial parts* of religion [my emphasis]."[143] This is another profound insight in Wesley's participatory Trinitarian theological vision of Christian faith: while Wesley distinguished between inward religion of dispositions in the heart and outward observances, works of mercy for instance, and assigned a certain priority to the life of the Triune God in the heart and the holy dispositions bound with union and communion with God, he in no way diminished the cruciality of those dispositions expressing themselves in our thoughts, words, and actions. In fact, he made that outworking, which is bound up with the inherently social and relational character of those holy dispositions, part of the "being" of their dispositional roots in union and communion with the Triune God. As he said it here, they "partake of the same nature with the root" and

141 Ibid., 1:541.
142 Ibid., 1:541, 532–34.
143 Ibid., 1:541–42.

"are not only marks or signs, but substantial parts of religion."[144] This is why Wesley emphasized the importance of holiness at the end of his sermon "Of the Church," stating that Christians are to walk worthy of their calling, manifesting meekness and long-suffering, forbearing one in love, in order to keep the unity of the Spirit in the bond of peace among the Methodists so that the sociality of these enduring affections and dispositions could be a renewing influence on the Church of England. To leave the church would frustrate the social dynamic of those affections and virtues.

Near the end of his "Sermon on the Mount, IV," Wesley concluded with the "practical application" he promised in his introduction and made nearly the same point that he did at the end of his sermon "Of the Church." Here he added an additional observation that sheds further light on this entire discussion of the sociality of holy dispositions, including their embeddedness in persons and in relations between persons. Wesley reminded his readers that our Lord tells them, "'Let your light shine'—your lowliness of heart, your gentleness, and meekness of wisdom . . . your earnest desire for universal holiness and full happiness in God."[145] Here Wesley identified the salt and light of his text with Matthew 5:13–16, with the holy dispositions in the beatitudes covered in his "Sermon on the Mount, I, II, III."

Wesley admonished his readers to not conceal these affections and dispositions but let them shine in "the whole tenor of your conversation" and "more eminently in your actions." Christians should not try to hide the light of the love and the holy tempers that arise out of union and communion with the Triune God. This admonition is exactly what we would expect from everything Wesley said about the inherently social and relation character of these holy affections and dispositions that makes their expression in word and deed not simply "signs" but "substantial parts" of true religion. According to Wesley, "Let it be your sole aim that all who see your good works may 'glorify your Father which is in heaven.'"[146]

In fact, for Wesley, this is "your one ultimate end in all things. With this view be plain, open, undisguised."[147] In Wesley's theology, participatory love on the throne of a Christian's heart and the holy dispositions surrounding it are not only inherently social, relational, and communicative, they are also soteriological and ecclesiological: they are meant to be expressed to a particular end, that the love, grace, and community that the Triune God is, and

144 Ibid., 1:542.
145 Ibid., 1:547.
146 Ibid., 1:547–48.
147 Ibid., 1:548.

that the Trinitarian persons communicate to Christians, might flow through Christians to others precisely to influence and transform them, leading others to respond in praise and glorify God.

At this point, Wesley turned attention once again to love itself on the throne of our hearts spreading its light, as it must, through all the dispositions, as well as our thoughts, words, and actions, manifesting itself in particular sociality, a particular communal embodiment and embeddedness, that is part of love's very being:

> Let your love be without dissimulation. Why should you hide fair, disinterested love? Let there be no guile in your mouth; let your words be the genuine picture of your heart. Let there be no darkness or reservedness in your conversation, no disguise in your behaviour. Leave this to those who have other designs in view—designs which will not bear the light. Be ye artless and simple to all mankind, that all may see the grace of God which is in you. And although some will harden their hearts [the sociality between persons is personal and can be resisted, deflected, or deformed], yet others will take knowledge that ye have been with Jesus, and by returning themselves "to the great Bishop of their souls" "glorify your Father which is in heaven."[148]

Here Wesley stated ever so forcefully the congruity that exists, or at least ought to exist, between (1) the love of God filling our hearts with love for God and others, and (2) our words and actions. According to Wesley, our words and actions should be transparent, a window into those holy dispositions in our hearts through which the love of God streams forth through the grace of Christ in the communion of the Spirit. There should be no pretense, no disguise, no facades, no speaking or acting in ways that are other than who and what we *are* as Christians united to the Trinitarian God and to another in the body of Christ. In other words, Wesley here promoted a theological vision of a Christian whose being (the particular character of being that Wesley calls "the sum of true religion" or holy dispositions that arise and are sustained only via a relation of union and communion with the Triune God) is in her acts (all thoughts, words, and deeds are expressions of love and the other tempers, as particular circumstances warrant) and whose acts (all thoughts, words, and deeds) are in her being. Even if Wesley was unaware of the theological concept of being-in-act and act-in-being, the basic idea of it is present here in his "Sermon on the Mount, IV."

148 Ibid.

The other place in Wesley's "Sermon on the Mount, IV" where he made explicit the participatory Trinitarian root of the love and the other tempers and their intrinsically social character also entails several crucial insights into the character of the sociality of those holy dispositions that have implications for Wesley's ecclesiology. After Wesley noted that Christianity is essentially a social religion because of the holy dispositions that have no "being" apart from "living and conversing" with others, Wesley raised a rather pointed ecclesiological question: "Is it not expedient, however (one might naturally ask), to converse only with good men? Only with those whom we to know to be . . . holy of heart and holy of life?"[149] Wesley here probed into the character of the sociality entailed in Christian dispositions. Does this fruit of the Spirit (love and the various tempers) thrive only in "Christian" sociality?

Wesley appealed to 1 Corinthians 5:9 and Paul's injunction to the Christians in Corinth not to have "company" with those who are sexually immoral. Because "dispositions" are inherently social for Wesley, they are contagious. Wesley said it this way: intimacy with immoral persons "must necessarily expose" a Christian "to an abundance of dangers and snares, out of which he can have no reasonable hope of deliverance."[150] So maybe the church is called to be sectarian at points, and Christians ought to stay within their own social matrix of holiness.

However, we already know that Wesley intended the Methodist brand of social Christianity "to spread scripture holiness throughout the land." So it comes as no surprise that Wesley immediately argued that this does not mean that Christians are forbidden "to have any intercourse at all, even with men that know not God." In Wesley's mind, we are to "break off all familiarity, all intimacy of acquaintance" with bold sinners, but "we are not to renounce all fellowship" with them.[151] This point is interesting in itself, as it reveals Wesley's insight into the subtlety of the sociality that is bound up with holy dispositions and the subtlety of the mutual influence that exists within deep relationships between persons. It seems that for Wesley, the deeper and more intimate the relationship, the more "person-constituting" the relationship is for those involved, for good or for ill.

Wesley concluded that "here is no advice to separate wholly, even from wicked men. Yea these very words teach us quite the contrary." In fact, Wesley argued that "some intercourse even with ungodly and unholy men is absolutely needful in order to the full exertion of every temper which he

149 Ibid., 1:535.

150 Ibid.

151 Ibid., 1:535–36.

[Jesus] has described as the way of the kingdom [the sum of true religion found in the beatitudes]." Even more to the point, according to Wesley, "It is indispensably necessary in order to the complete exercise of poverty of spirit, of mourning, and of every other disposition which has a place here in the genuine religion of Jesus Christ. Yea, it is necessary *to the very being* of several of them [my emphasis]." Wesley provided examples and then concluded, "All these, it is clear, could have no being were we to have no commerce with any but real Christians."[152]

The root soteriological and ecclesiological vision here in Wesley's understanding of the sociality of holy dispositions (love and all the tempers or fruit of the Spirit surrounding love) is rather incisive: when we come to know the love of God through the grace of Jesus Christ in the fellowship of the Holy Spirit, we simultaneously are incorporated into the body of Christ and the personal relations and communion with God and other Christians that entail changes in our affections and tempers. Wesley's argument throughout this sermon is that sociality is in the very "being" of these affections and holy dispositions such that to dispense with the sociality is to destroy the being of the affections and dispositions.

Wesley went a step further and said that there is another dimension to the sociality that is part of the very being of holy dispositions, a dimension that implicates precisely those who are not yet Christian, who are ungodly, unholy, and even wicked. For the church/Christians to dispense with sociality with ungodly and unholy people is once again to destroy the very being of the dispositions. The soteriological and ecclesiological upshot and implication of Wesley's point is that the church, as the body of Christ, with the Christian social embodiment that is part of the very being of these transformed dispositions is a social embodiment that is inherently missional: ecclesial sociality by necessity must in certain ways embrace the ungodly, unholy, and even wicked because sociality with them is also necessary to the very being of Christian affections and dispositions rooted in the union and communion with the Triune God of love and grace who loves and longs to redeem the world, especially the ungodly and wicked.

This is a rather deeper theological grounding of the mission of the church than simply because Jesus told his follows to preach the gospel and make disciples. Once again, according to Wesley, the mission of the church is rooted in the very being of the church as the body of Christ, bound up with the sociality of the dispositions, which only are what they are in these relations of love that extend beyond the church to all those who do not yet

152 Ibid., 1:536.

know the love of God in the grace of Christ through the fellowship of the Spirit that configures the soteriological sociality of the church in this way. This is why Wesley was so adamant that the lives of Christians who do not reflect this kind of loving sociality constitute the great stumbling block to the world ever believing in the Lord whose disciples Christians are supposed to be.

In addition, is it not patently clear, as we unpack what Wesley said, that this is why mission belongs to the essence of the church grounded in the gospel of the Triune God? This is why Wesley regularly said things like, "The more they [Christians] are filled with the life of God, the more tenderly will they be concerned for those who are still without God in the world, still dead in trespasses and sins."[153] He made nearly the same point, here in his "Sermon on the Mount, IV," in relation to sociality as bound up with the very being of holy dispositions: "It is your very nature to season whatever is round about you. It is the nature of the divine saviour which is in you to spread to whatsoever you touch; to diffuse itself on every side, to all those among whom you are." Wesley thought this is why the providence of God does not remove the Christian from the unholy world, but "mingled you together with other men, that whatever grace you have received of God may through you be communicated to others; that every holy temper, and word, and work of yours, may have an influence on them also."[154]

It is clear that there is a tight nexus between (1) Wesley's understanding of the Trinity as bound up with vital religion; (2) his Trinitarian understanding of vital religion or the essence of Christian faith; (3) his participatory Trinitarian understanding of all aspects of the entire order of salvation; (4) his understanding of love on the throne in our hearts with the holy tempers surrounding it as the "sum of all true religion" arising in, with and through union and communion with the Triune God; (5) his understanding of the church as union and communion with the Father and the Son in the Spirit, the church as a manifestation of the sociality that is part of the being of those holy affections and dispositions; and (6) the missional dimension of the Church, as a sociality reaching out to the ungodly world that is also part of the being of those holy affections and dispositions that arise in, with, and through union and communion with the Triune God. These aspects of Wesley theology are all parts of a multifaceted whole. It is a multifaceted whole that entails a Trinitarian dimension interpenetrating everything else. As I read and carefully reflect on what Wesley said about all these facets, and particularly how profoundly interconnected all of these are, I find that it

153 Ibid., 1:499.
154 Ibid., 1:537.

illumines so much of Wesley's theology in his various publications in a way that makes me more and more convinced that it really does represent his central theological vision with its Trinitarian dimension. My hope in writing the book is that others may see it as well.

It is tragic that Methodism often grasped various pieces of Wesley's theological vision but has seldom understood the full significance of the Trinitarian dimension and how the various facets of Wesley's soteriology and ecclesiology are bound up with it. The time is ripe for Methodism to reclaim Wesley's insights and develop them much further than Wesley had either time or inclination to pursue.

One final point Wesley made in this section of his "Sermon on the Mount, IV" reinforces that sociality is a profound part of the being of the holy dispositions and that, without the appropriate sociality, the holy dispositions can wither and disappear. Wesley stated, "That we may the more diligently labour to season all we can with every holy and heavenly temper, our Lord proceeds to show the desperate state of those who do not impart the religion they have received; which indeed they cannot possibly fail to do, so long as it remains in their own hearts."[155] Because sociality is bound up with the being of the affections and tempers, when this soteriological sociality is not expressed, the affections and tempers themselves begin to wither. This is how Wesley interpreted Jesus's warning in his text in Matthew 5:13–16, that salt can lose its saltiness.

In fact, this lack of sociality not only deforms the holy dispositions, but it also disrupts the union and communion with the Triune God out of which those dispositions arise and within which alone they continue to thrive and develop. Wesley directed the attention of his readers to John 15 and added his own interpretive comments: "'Every branch in me that beareth not fruit, he (the Father) taketh away. . . . He that abideth in me, and I in him, bringeth forth much fruit. . . . If a man abide not in me' (or, do not bring forth fruit) 'he is cast out as a branch, and withered.'"[156] For Wesley, union and communion in the Spirit with our Lord Jesus Christ and through Christ with the Father, a union and communion of the branches in the vine alone generates and sustains those dispositions, which "cannot but put forth" fruit in word and deed that "are not only . . . signs, but substantial parts of religion."[157] The reverse is equally true. The sociality involved in holy dispositions is indispensable to those dispositions. Loss of the appropriate soteriological sociality threatens

155 Ibid.
156 Ibid., 1:537.
157 Ibid., 1:541–42.

the dispositions. But as we noted above, for Wesley the sociality of those dispositions is also subtle. The sociality gets expressed in connection with others and involves utterly real relations between persons that bear upon one another in subtle ways that cannot be construed in causal or deterministic categories but only in terms of personal categories where influence, persuasion, and various other subtle forms and characteristics of personal relations are what are really in place. This is why "openness" to others and their influence, or "mistrust" toward them, so colors the characteristics of those relations.

What Wesley was driving at is that it is inherent in the very ontology of a Christian in fellowship with the Triune God, inherent in the very character of a "person" formed by this kind of relation with God, that a Christian's life becomes interconnected with others in particular kinds of relations. These "character relations," or tempers/virtues that only exist in relations with God and others, are relations with a particular configuration involving a distinctively Christian openness and intimacy that arise out of love between persons and a deeply united community that embodies and nurtures these Christian virtues. As Wesley noted in his sermon "On Schism," "It is of nature of love to unite us together, and the greater the love the stricter the union."[158]

These kinds of relations are really at the heart of what took place within the small groups in early Methodism and are evident in the character of questions that Wesley developed for the bands. Wesley directed those in bands "to speak, each of us in order, freely and plainly the true state of our souls." He said they were to ask one another, "Do you desire to be told all your faults, and that plain and home?" and "Is it your desire and design to be on this and all other occasions entirely open, so as to speak everything that is in your heart without disguise, and without reserve?"[159] We see in the bands, and the directions and questions Wesley provided for them, this particular kind of open and intimate sociality bound up with the holy dispositions that are the sum of Wesley's vision of true religion, an open and intimate sociality designed to both express and nurture the dispositions, for that kind of sociality is part of the very being of what the dispositions are meant to be. We will return to this subject in the next chapter.

The final section of this chapter provides documentation and discussion of the Trinitarian dimension of the means of grace and the sacraments in Wesley's ecclesiology.

---

158 Ibid., 3:64.

159 *Works*, 9:77–78.

VI. A Trinitarian Understanding of the Means of Grace

By this point in our study, it should be clear that there is a Trinitarian dimension to Wesley's understanding of the means of grace, including the sacraments, since we have seen that all grace in all its manifestations, from preventing to perfecting grace, involves that participatory, economic activity of the Trinitarian persons working together for human reconciliation and redemption. So the means of grace, those earthly historical structures or media through which the Trinitarian persons are still immediately present and active, are channels or means that the blessed Triune God has freely promised and graciously continues to work through for our salvation. Whatever formative function these creaturely structures or means of grace serve in and of themselves in the lives of those who use them, which Wesley would not deny, the transformative reality and power, for Wesley, finally resides in the Trinitarian persons who freely act on our behalf in and through these means of grace.

Since we examined quite a bit of Wesley's sermon "The Means of Grace" in the previous section, here we will simply draw attention to the explicit Trinitarian dimension Wesley incorporated into his theological account of the means of grace.

In the opening section, Wesley made clear that "in the apostolic church . . . the whole body of Christians . . . agreed that Christ had ordained certain outward means for conveying his grace unto the souls of men."[160] Wesley defined these means of grace as "outward signs, words, or actions ordained of God, and appointed for this end—to be the *ordinary* channels whereby he might convey to men preventing, justifying, or sanctifying grace."[161]

As sinful human beings are prone to abuse even the greatest of God's gifts, Wesley noted that this happens with the means of grace as well. Some mistake the *means* for the *end*. To counter this misunderstanding, Wesley emphasized that "all outward means whatever, if separate from the Spirit of God, cannot profit at all, cannot conduce in any degree either to the knowledge or love of God."[162] In these quotations from Wesley's sermon, we see the Trinitarian persons all involved in the efficacy of the means of grace. God the Father ordains the means of grace to be channels through which we encounter Christ, whose redemptive activity in his life, death, and resurrection is God's grace to us. This grace is realized in

---

160 *Works*, 1:378.
161 Ibid., 1:381.
162 Ibid., 1:382.

our lives only via the Spirit of God who works in and through the means of grace.

Later in the sermon, Wesley drove this point home about abusing the means rather forcefully. Wesley complained that "a large proportion of those who are called Christians do to this day abuse the means of grace," as "is doubtless the case with all those who rest content in the form of godliness without the power." Wesley said that they use the means of grace "idly dreaming" that "there is some kind of *power*" or "a sort of *merit*" in the means themselves.

Wesley retorted: "Little do they understand that great foundation of the whole Christian building, 'By grace ye are saved.' Ye are saved from your sins, for the guilt and power thereof, ye are restored to the favour and image of God . . . by the free *grace*, the mere mercy of God through the merits of his well-beloved Son. Ye are thus saved . . . merely through the grace or power of the Holy Ghost, which worketh all in all."[163] At the end of the sermon, Wesley told his readers that "in using all means" they should "seek God alone."[164]

When Wesley turned to the other danger or abuse of the means of grace, he again provided a Trinitarian corrective to the misunderstanding. This abuse was the denial of any value in the means of grace, indeed the denial of any means of grace at all. Thus some spoke "as if outward religion were *absolutely nothing*, as if it had *no* place in the religion of Christ."[165] Wesley appealed to scripture to refute this idea: "According to the decision of Holy Writ, all who desire the grace of God are to wait for it in the means which he hath ordained; in using, not in laying them aside."[166] Then Wesley examined various places in scripture where we are told to pray, search the scriptures, and partake of the Lord's Supper as the proper way to wait for God's grace.[167]

Wesley also appealed to the Trinitarian activity in his answer to this abuse of the means of grace. Some objected that Christ is the only means of grace. Wesley said that this is a "mere playing upon words," for when people say, "Christ is the only means of grace," they "understand the sole price and purchaser of it; or, that 'no man cometh unto the Father, but through him.' And who denies it? But this is utterly wide the question."[168] Wesley noted the presence and activity of Christ and the Father. The issue is when, where,

163 Ibid., 1:383.
164 Ibid., 1:396.
165 Ibid., 1:380.
166 Ibid., 1:384.
167 Ibid., 1:380–90.
168 Ibid., 1:391.

and how this grace of God comes to us through Christ alone in the Spirit and becomes effective in our lives.

Here Wesley turned to the *order* "wherein God himself is generally pleased to use these means in bringing a sinner to salvation." He provided a thick description of the freedom of the Spirit of God working in very person-specific and variable manner in the lives of particular persons: "The means into which different men are led, and in which they find the blessings of God, are varied, transposed, and combined together in a thousand different ways . . . whereby his free Spirit is pleased most to work in our heart. And . . . the sure and general rule for all who groan for the salvation of God is this—whenever opportunity serves, use all the means which God has ordained. For who knows in which God will meet thee with the grace that bringeth salvation."[169]

What is particularly illuminating and moving in this whole account is how clear and consistent Wesley was about the core participatory Trinitarian activity that is at the center of all vital religion, that is constitutive of the very essence of the church, and here is the crucial factor in the means of grace. It is always the love of God the Father through the grace of Christ in the fellowship of the Spirit that effects salvation, but this is accomplished in and through a highly variable, person-specific, and circumstantial plethora of "means" of grace, both ordinary or ordained by Christ in scripture, or extraordinary or prudential means that the Spirit of God freely chooses to work through.

We find a similar Trinitarian account of baptism in Wesley's short treatise "On Baptism," which is a dramatically abridged version of his father's "Short Discourse on Baptism."[170] Wesley followed his father and the Anglican Church and asserted that baptism must "be administered in the Name of the Trinity" and the person baptized is "thereby devoted to the ever-blessed Trinity."[171]

This administration in the Trinitarian name points to the deeper reality and efficacy of baptism grounded in the coactivity of the Trinitarian persons that makes the sacrament what it is. When Wesley turned to the "benefits" we receive from baptism, the participatory Trinitarian activity is ever at the center of what Wesley said.

Under his first point, Wesley recounted that the first benefit of baptism is "washing away of the guilt of original sin." According to Wesley: "He [Christ] gave himself for the church, that he might sanctify and cleanse it with the washing of water by the Word'—namely, in baptism, the ordinary instrument

169 Ibid., 1:393, 395.

170 See Outler's introduction in *Wesley*, 317–18.

171 Ibid., 1:318–19.

of our justification. Agreeable to this, our Church prays in the baptismal office that the person to be baptized may be 'washed and sanctified by the Holy Ghost, and, being delivered from God's wrath, receive remission of sins and enjoy the everlasting benediction of his heavenly washing.'"[172]

The third benefit of baptism is particularly interesting in this chapter on Wesley's Trinitarian ecclesiology, as Wesley argued that membership in the church is one of the benefits of baptism, and he interpreted this benefit in terms of union with Christ through the Spirit: "'For as many as are baptized into Christ,' . . . are mystically 'united to Christ,' and made *one* with him." Wesley also underscored the pneumatological activity in baptism: "For 'by one Spirit we are all baptized into one body'—namely, 'the Church, the body of Christ.'" He added a final clarificatory statement: "From which spiritual, vital union with him proceeds the influence of his grace on those that are baptized; as from our union with the Church, a share in all its privileges and in all the promises Christ has made to it."[173] Wesley made clear once again, not only that the participatory Trinitarian character of the divine activity is the real heart of baptism but also that this activity entails union and communion with Christ through the Holy Spirit so that we are united to Christ and one another, and thereby constitutes the church.

For Wesley, we are simultaneously regenerated or born again in baptism, and "herein a principle of grace is infused which will not be wholly taken away unless we quench the Holy Spirit of God by long-continued wickedness." Indeed, it was not "the *outward* washing, but . . . the *inward grace* which, added thereto, makes it a sacrament."[174] This is a remarkably strong statement of baptismal regeneration in economic Trinitarian terms. In addition, in the two final sections of "On Baptism," which constitute over half the entire treatise, Wesley argued that infants are the proper subjects of baptism. Wesley then answered nearly every conceivable objection to infant baptism.[175]

---

172 Ibid., 1:321.

173 Ibid., 1:322.

174 Ibid., 1:323.

175 There has been more than a little ambiguity in the theology and practice of baptism in the history of Methodism after Wesley, not in relation to the Trinitarian dimension but in relation to baptism and regeneration. Some of this ambiguity can be traced back to Wesley himself. The debate has generally centered on baptismal regeneration and the Wesleyan emphasis on the necessity of human response, though a response grounded in grace (see Gayle Felton, *The Gift of Water: The Practice and Theology of Baptism among Methodists in America* [Nashville: Abingdon, 1993]). See also Bishop Ole Borgen's book *John Wesley on the Sacraments* (Grand Rapids: Francis Asbury, 1985). Borgen makes Wesley's reflections a little

When we examine Wesley's sermon "On the Duty of Constant Communion," there is not much reference to the Trinitarian dimension because

---

too tidy, and his characterizations of later developments are rather polemical at points.

James Logan points out that Methodism's contemporary quandary concerning baptism is reflected in divergent interpretations of Wesley's understanding of baptism (see James C. Logan, "Baptism—The Ecumenical Sacrament and the Wesleyan Tradition," in *Wesleyan Theology Today*, ed. Theodore Runyon [Nashville: UM Publishing House, 1985], 325).

The central and perennial point is: Did Wesley consistently maintain a doctrine of baptismal regeneration? There is no question that this was, in fact, his position in the years prior to his Aldersgate experience. But with Aldersgate came the emphasis on the experience of new birth, something that Wesley continued to stress throughout the remainder of his career. It is clear that in 1756, when he published "On Baptism," he certainly affirmed baptismal regeneration. Although Wesley had a high doctrine of baptism, viewing it as the ordinary means by which God brings new life, Wesley did not see it as the exclusive means, for as he wrote to Gilbert Boyce in 1750, "If it were [the exclusive means], every Quaker must be damned, which I can in no wise believe" (*Works*, 26:425). Here Wesley affirmed the freedom of God, which cannot be limited even to the very means of grace that God has ordained, in spite of the fact that we are, in a sense, bound to these means of grace and need to continue utilizing them in the life of the church. This point is entirely consistent with what we saw above in relation to his sermon "Of the Church," where Wesley did not restrict the ecclesiality of the church to the pure preaching of the Word and the right administration of the sacraments.

The other document of critical significance to Wesley's view of baptism is his sermon, "The New Birth." What is particularly fascinating is that during the very same year that Wesley edited and published the treatise "On Baptism," according the Sermon Register, Wesley preached his "New Birth" sermon eleven times. In the three years either side of the year 1756, he preached that sermon a total of forty-seven times (see *John Wesley's Fifty-Three Sermons*, ed. Edward Sugden [Nashville: Abingdon, 1983], 567). The historical proximity of these two documents pleads for a reading of each in light of each other. In "The New Birth" sermon, Wesley seemed to call baptismal regeneration into question, for he plainly asserted, "Baptism is not the new birth: they are not one and the same thing . . . but indeed the reason of the thing is so clear and evident, as not to need any other authority. For what can be more plain than that the one is external, the other an internal work; That the one is a visible thing, the other an invisible thing, and therefore wholly different from each other: the one being an act of man . . . the other a change wrought by God in the soul" (see *Works*, 2:196–97).

From this distinction, Wesley moved a step further, arguing: "That as the new birth is not the same thing with baptism, so it does not always accompany baptism. . . . A man may possibly be 'born of water', and not yet be 'born of the Spirit' " (see ibid., 197). It appears that Wesley conclusively repudiated what he said about

Wesley was showing that it is the duty of Christians to receive the Lord's Supper as often as possible.[176] Wesley did note that "the design of this sacra-

---

baptism in the treatise we examined earlier. It is at this point that the differences in interpreting Wesley's view of baptism by various scholars become intense.

Two observations are in order. First, the sermon is clearly not addressing the question of the relation between new birth and infant baptism. Second, so far as adults are concerned, not all who are baptized are born again. Wesley gave his unequivocal explanation for his certainty on the matter: "The tree is known by its fruit." A person who is truly spiritually regenerated by the Holy Spirit cannot but produce the appropriate fruit of this new life in God. If no fruit is forthcoming, Wesley reasoned that there is no new life (see *Works*, 2:197).

The key point that enables one to render a fairly coherent construal of Wesley's doctrine of baptism lies at just this point. For Wesley, unlike Luther and Calvin, the grace of God does not work irresistibly but rather sets us free to receive or resist the continued working of grace. Wesley said that, "The question is not what you was made in baptism (do not evade!): but what you are now?" (*Works*, 1:428). Indeed, Wesley stated, "If you have been baptized, do not own it. For how highly does this aggravate your guilt! How much will it increase your damnation! . . . O, be ashamed! Blush! . . . You have already denied your baptism; and that in the most effectual manner" (see *Works*, 2:199–200).

Wesley simply did not affirm unconditional perseverance. Thus, whereas Wesley held the objective and the subjective aspects of the baptism and the new birth together in his emphasis that the transforming grace of God always issues forth in the fruits of new life, when it comes to the doctrine of assurance, Wesley related it to the present witness of the Spirit and to ethical fruit in our lives (the witness of our spirit). In contrast to Wesley, Luther appealed not only to the witness of the Spirit but pointed to his baptism as a ground for solace and assurance in times of great turmoil and doubt. For Wesley, to appeal to baptism without the present witness of the Spirit and the ethical fruit of the Spirit was to simply aggravate one's guilt.

Wesley believed it is possible to sin away the grace one has received. This is true of baptismal grace and this appears to be the unstated premise that underlies the final pages of Wesley's sermon where he attempted to drive his listeners from any easy appeal to the fact that they were baptized as a way to avoid facing their need for personal transformation that can only take place on the basis of a genuine new birth.

In fact, in the treatise on baptism that we examined earlier, Wesley forthrightly stated this point that in baptism "a principle of grace is infused which will not be wholly taken away unless we quench the Holy Spirit of God by long-continued wickedness" (see Outler, ed., *John Wesley*, 323). According to Wesley, it is possible to sin away one's baptism! It is for this reason that Wesley said, "Lean no more on the staff of that broken reed, that ye *were* born again in baptism. Who denies that ye were then made 'children of God, and heirs of heaven'? But not withstanding this, ye are now children of the devil; therefore, ye must be born again" (see *Works*, 1:430).

176 *Works*, 3:428.

ment is the continual remembrance of the death of Christ, by eating bread and drinking wine, which are the outward signs of the inward grace, the body and blood of Christ."[177]

Wesley did give explicit reference to the economic Trinitarian activity in the Lord's Supper in other places, like in his sermon "The Means of Grace," which we examined above. In the section that deals with what scripture says about using the means of grace, Wesley examined the Lord's Supper. He concluded with a Trinitarian summary of the divine efficacy of the sacrament. He quoted 1 Corinthians 10:16, where the cup of blessing and the breaking of the bread are a communion in the blood and body of Christ. Then Wesley asserted: "Is not the eating of that bread, and the drinking of that cup, the outward, the visible means whereby God conveys into our souls all that spiritual grace, that righteousness, and peace, and joy in the Holy Ghost, which were purchased by the body of Christ once broken and the blood of Christ once shed for us? Let all, therefore, who truly desire the grace of God, eat of that bread and drink of that cup."[178]

This examination of what Wesley said about the means of grace in general, and the sacraments in particular, reveals that the Trinitarian dimension that permeates the core of Wesley's understanding of the church is present in these other aspects of his ecclesiology as well.

VII. Embodiments of Trinitarian Ecclesiology in Ministry and Community?

Wesley had a participatory Trinitarian understanding of the *ordo salutis* and a parallel conceptualization of the essence of the church and the means of grace. But if Wesley's order of salvation and ecclesiology are *participatory*, if we together are actually to become transcripts of the Trinity, then does not this Trinitarian salvation and ecclesiology have to be actually embodied in the communal life and ministry of the church at all levels? Is there a Trinitarian dimension in the actual forms of life, community, polity, and ministry that embody Wesley's Trinitarian vision of the order of salvation and the church? This is the question we will answer in the next chapter.

177 Ibid., 3:430.
178 *Works*, 1:389–90.

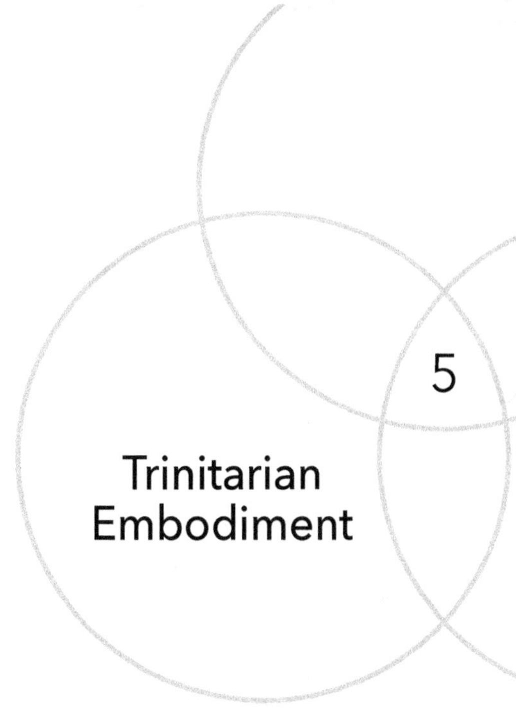

5

Trinitarian Embodiment

Introduction

According to Wesley, the Triune God's gracious activity in the gospel transforms human affections and tempers via union and communion with God, freeing humanity from guilt and the power of sin, and filling the human heart with the love of God so that love for God and for others becomes the characteristic of new life in Christ working itself out through holy virtues to holy thoughts, words, and acts. As we saw in chapter 4, this Trinitarian transformation of human affections and tempers is inherently soteriological, ecclesial, and social, so that only together, in union and communion with the Triune God and one another and in mission to the world, do we become transcripts of the Trinity. This participatory Trinitarian vision of salvation and the church has to be embodied in the communal life and ministry of the church and in the church's outreach to a lost world since the root of divine love in our hearts cannot but put forth branches that, in Wesley's words, "partake of the same nature with the root, and consequently are . . . substantial parts" of vital Christian faith and life.[1] This is where I find early Methodism especially fascinating and illuminating.

There are profound interconnections between Wesley's Trinitarian vision of Christian faith and the developing structures of life, community,

1 *Works of John Wesley*, ed. Albert C. Outler, vols. 1–4, *Sermons* (Nashville: Abingdon, 1984–87), 1:541–42.

and ministry in early Methodism. While I am interested in the Trinitarian dimension of Wesley's theological vision of salvation and the church, I am also concerned with how that vision was effectively communicated and embodied in the Methodist movement.[2] In every arena, human life is social and involves forms of life bound up with cognitive structures that are socially mediated. This is as true of scientific communities as it is of churches and religious movements.[3]

This chapter examines how the Trinitarian dimension of Wesley's understanding of the order of salvation and the church became embodied in the forms of life, community, and ministry in early Methodism. I will show that the Trinitarian character of Wesley's soteriology and ecclesiology found expression in early Methodism. In so doing, let it be clear that I am not arguing that Wesley and the Methodists always self-consciously embodied the Trinitarian character of Christian faith in their life together in Methodist movement, though at times they did, as in the case of Charles Wesley's two hymnals devoted to the Trinity. I am not suggesting that the early Methodists intentionally included an economic Trinitarian dimension in their deliberations, for instance, over what to teach, how to teach, and what to do? (doctrine, discipline, and practice), the three main points of the "agenda" for the famous 1744 London Conference.[4] Nor am I arguing that Wesley and

---

2 While I have no desire to repeat Wesley and the early Methodist experiment, I find this Trinitarian vision of soteriology and ecclesiology (and its embodiment in the life, community, and ministry) instructive and suggestive of a more comprehensively Trinitarian vision of Christian faith and life of the church in our day than we see in Methodism in America today.

3 See Thomas F. Torrance, *Reality and Scientific Theology* (Edinburgh: Scottish Academic Press, 1985); and Elmer M. Colyer, *How to Read T. F. Torrance: Understanding His Trinitarian and Scientific Theology* (Downers Grove, IL: InterVarsity, 2001), 55–69, 97–113, 322–72. See also Alister McGrath, *A Scientific Theology,* 3 vols. (Grand Rapids, MI: Eerdmans, 2001–3) for an account of theology that takes seriously sociology of knowledge while still maintaining a critical realist orientation.

Miroslav Volf's groundbreaking work *After Our Likeness: The Church as the Image of the Trinity* (Grand Rapids, MI: Eerdmans, 1998) is an example of a Trinitarian ecclesiology that takes seriously not only social factors that affect the transmitting and assimilating of Christianity in modern societies but also how particular theologies affect the life, community, and ministry of the church in relation to social factors that influence attracting and assimilating people into the church.

4 See *The Works of John Wesley,* ed. Henry D. Rack, vol. 10, *The Methodist Societies: The Minutes of Conference* (Nashville: Abingdon, 2011), 120–46. There are explicit economic Trinitarian references in the section on doctrine, where the Minutes describe coming to faith in Trinitarian terms (ibid., 10:126–27). There are also

the early Methodists embodied the Trinitarian character of salvation and the church comprehensively and consistently in all their forms of life, community, and ministry. What I intend to show is that there are interconnections between Wesley's participatory, economic Trinitarian understanding of salvation and the church and how this Trinitarian dimension actually became embodied in early Methodism.

I. Acts 2 and 4: The Dawn of a Proper Gospel Day and a Proper Christian Church

When Wesley wrote his sermon "Of the Church," where he presented his clearest and most developed understanding of the essence of the church as union and communion with the Triune God and one another, he appealed to Ephesians 4 as the crucial text for defining the church. When Wesley provided examples of what the ongoing life, community, and ministry of Christian community should be like, he often turned to Acts 2 and 4.[5] In fact, he spoke of Acts 2 and 4 as the "dawn" of a "proper gospel day" and a "proper Christian church."

In his sermon "The Mystery of Iniquity," Wesley opened with a narrative summary of the Christian story in familiar terms. God created human beings to be "perfectly holy and perfectly happy," but they rebelled and "lost the favour and the image of God." Wesley recounted the Triune God's great rescue operation: the "merciful Creator" "immediately appointed his Son, his well-beloved Son, 'who is the brightness of his glory, the express image of his person,'" . . . "to be the Saviour of men" . . . "the great Physician, who by his almighty Spirit should heal the sickness of their souls" and thus restore them both to "favour" and "the image of God."[6] At the outset of his sermon, Wesley made explicit the Trinitarian dimension of the God's answer to the mystery of iniquity. He then traced this "mystery of godliness" through the Old Testament from Abel and Noah through Abraham, noting how few were healed by the Son of God and how imperfect the healing was even for the few. Wesley linked this lack of godliness in a fallen world to the fact that the fullness of the Holy Spirit had not yet been poured out before Pentecost.[7]

Trinitarian resonances in the section entitled "What Is the Church of England?" and the section dealing with societies, classes, bands, and select bands (ibid., 10:133–34, 136–37).

5 So Acts 2 and 4 deal with *bene esse* or right functioning of the church.

6 *Works*, 2:452.

7 Ibid., 2:452–53.

With the ascension of the Christ, after his life, death, and resurrection, "'the promise of the Father' was fulfilled," and the Spirit came powerfully upon on the church at Pentecost. Here Wesley again incorporated the economic Trinitarian dimension into his narrative leading up to the "dawn" of a "proper gospel day" and a "proper Christian church." Wesley, then, turned to Acts 2 and 4 as a description of what the early church in the power of the Spirit looked like. The early Disciples were filled with the Spirit. Peter's sermon touched three thousand who were "restored to the favour and the image of God," "and the Lord added those that were saved daily to the church."[8] Wesley added a comment indicating the interconnection between soteriology and ecclesiology in the early chapters of Acts: "*they were saved* from the guilt and power of sin; then *they were added* to the assembly of the faithful."[9]

At this point, Wesley provided his description of the early Christian community of Acts 2 and 4 as the example, par excellence, of what happens when the love of God the Father though grace of God's beloved Son, Jesus Christ, is made real in the church by the fellowship of the Holy Spirit. Wesley asserted that "in order clearly to see how they were already saved we need only to observe the short account of them . . . in the latter part of the second and . . . fourth chapter."[10]

This is Wesley's account of the church in Acts 2 and 4:

> They were daily taught by the apostles, and had all things in common and received the Lord's Supper, and attended all the public service. "And all that believed were together, and had all things common; and sold their possessions, and parted them to all men, as every man had need." And again; "The multitude of them that believe," now greatly increased, "were of one heart and of one soul. Neither said any of them that ought of the things which he possessed was his own, but they had all things in common."
>
> But here a question will naturally occur. How came they to act thus, to have all things in common, seeing we do not read of any positive command to do this? I answer, there needed no outward command: the command was written on their hearts. It naturally and necessarily resulted from the degree of love which they enjoyed.[11]

8 Ibid., 2:454.
9 Ibid.
10 Ibid.
11 Ibid., 2:455.

Here again we see Wesley's central conviction about the inherently "social" transformation of our affections and tempers via union and communion with the Triune God, as we noted in chapter 4 in Wesley's account in his "Sermon on the Mount, IV." The sharing of possessions in community seems to be for Wesley "necessary to the very being" of love, for love "cannot possibly have a being" without that kind of sharing, to use Wesley's way of stating the essential ontological and communal character of affections and tempers in his "Sermon on the Mount, IV," examined in chapter 4.[12]

Wesley forcefully drove home that this common sharing of property flowed from Christians' hearts filled with the love of God through the grace of Christ in the fellowship of the Spirit: "Observe! 'They were of one heart and of one soul: and not so much as one' (so the words run) 'said' (they could not, while their hearts so overflowed with love) 'that any of the things which he possessed was his own.'" At this point, Wesley drew an important implication about this sharing of possessions that is part of the being of love awakened in the human heart by the redemptive presence of the Triune God: "And wheresoever the same cause shall prevail the same effect will naturally flow."[13] This idea that Christian sharing of possessions grows out of the Trinitarian root of love and partakes of the same nature as the root, as Wesley stated it in his "Sermon on the Mount, IV," will be important in the discussion of select bands in early Methodism later in this chapter.

Wesley, then, inserted his pointed soteriological and ecclesiological judgment about the particular ecclesial sociality of the Christian community in Acts 2 and 4: "Here was the dawn of the proper gospel day. Here was a proper Christian church. [Notice the tight connection between soteriology and ecclesiology.] It was now 'the Sun of righteousness' . . . did now 'save his people from their sins': he 'healed' all 'their sickness.' He not only taught that religion which is the true 'healing of the soul,' but effectually planted it in the earth; filling the souls of all that believed in him with *righteousness*, gratitude to God, and goodwill to man."[14] In this text we see so many of the key themes from Wesley's Trinitarian soteriology and ecclesiology discussed in the previous two chapters coming together. Salvation entails forgiveness (justification) and healing of our sin-sickness (regeneration and sanctification) and leads to gratitude toward God and love toward others, Wesley's way of summarizing the human response that flows from participation in the Trinitarian gospel.

12 *Works*, 1:531, 533, 534, 536.

13 *Works*, 2:455.

14 Ibid.

Salvation and ecclesiology are inseparable. We are united to the Triune God and to one another in the body of Christ but also oriented in love and compassion to those who do not yet know the love of God in Christ. With the dawning of the "proper gospel day," we find the dawning of "a proper Christian church." Elsewhere, Wesley described the church of Acts 2 and 4 this way: "In the fullness of time . . . God brought his first-begotten into the world. He then laid the foundation his church . . . a glorious church . . . 'filled with the Holy Ghost' . . . 'being of one heart and of one mind,' 'and continuing steadfastly in the apostles' doctrine, and in fellowship.' . . . 'In fellowship,' that is, having 'all things in common.'"[15] Notice the Trinitarian dimension involved in this formation of a glorious church that had all things in common.

In his sermon "The General Spread of the Gospel," Wesley again referenced Acts 2 and 4 when he described: "The grand Pentecost shall 'fully come' when 'devout men in every nation under heaven' will 'be filled with the Holy Ghost' and 'will continue steadfast in the apostles' doctrine and in the fellowship, and in the breaking of bread, and in prayers' . . . and they will be all 'of one heart and of one soul.'" Wesley then once again linked this future outpouring of the Spirit and the depth of fellowship that results with having all things in common: "The natural, necessary consequence of this will be the same as it was in the beginning of the Christian church. 'None of them will say that ought of things which he possess is his own, but they will have all things in common.'"[16] There are other places in Wesley's publications where he appealed to Acts 2 and 4 an example, par excellence, of what a right functioning church should look like.[17]

---

15 Ibid., 2:554. In many of his appeals to Acts 2 and 4 as an example of what the church should look like, Wesley followed with the account of Ananias and Sapphira and their "love of money" as an example of the "mystery of iniquity." Wesley saw the temptation toward love of money as a nearly universal temptation for genuine Christian faith, since real faith produces industry and frugality that leads to the accumulation of riches unless Christians give away everything but what they need for the necessities of life (see Wesley's sermons "The Use of Money," *Works*, 2:263–80; and "The Danger of Riches," *Works*, 3:227–46).

16 *Works*, 2:494. See also *Works*, 4:534.

17 See, for example, his final sermon at Oxford, "Scriptural Christianity," where he challenged the integrity of the university community around whether real "Christianity" is to be found. There he mixed in phrase after phrase from Acts 2 in his description of scriptural Christianity (see *Works*, 1:164–6, 171, 173, 174). See also ibid., 1:378, 630; 2:69–70; 3:469, 582; and 4:92 for other places where Wesley alludes to Acts 2 and 4 as an example of genuine Christian faith and/or Christian church. See also Wesley's notes on Acts 2 and 4 in his *Explanatory Notes upon the New Testament*, 2 vols. (1754; repr., Kansas City: Beacon Hill Press, 1981).

What we see here in Wesley's characterization of Acts 2 and 4 is an embodiment of the Trinitarian gospel in a particular kind of community, one where the love of the Triune God enacted in the grace of the Jesus Christ and made real by the fellowship of the Spirit transforms the throne-room of the saints' hearts so that love reigns supreme there. Because Wesley saw a profound ontological social dimension to love reigning in Christians' hearts, that love manifests itself in communal expression, where the saints are so "of one heart and soul" that they do not see themselves merely as individuals possessing life and property in isolation from others. Rather, they are bound together in a fellowship of love and community so deep that they hold all things, including their possessions, in common. Wesley included the economic Trinitarian dimension in his discussion of this gospel day and glorious church. He also made a clear connection between this kind of communal expression of love and fellowship that reflects, and is a participation in, the love and fellowship of the Triune God, in God's own Trinitarian life as God and in all activity of the Trinitarian persons in the gospel.

This vision of the right functioning of the church in union and communion with the Triune God is one where Christians together, because of the sociality of transformed affections, become an image of the Trinity—in Charles's poetic verse, "and when we rise in love renew'd, / our souls resemble Thee, / An image of the Tri-une God/ To all eternity."[18] Given what John Wesley said about Acts 2 and 4, as an example of what will happen whenever the love of God through the grace of Christ in the fellowship of Spirt prevails, we might expect to find allusions to Acts 2 and 4 in his account of the rise of Methodism as a genuine "dawn of a proper gospel day" and a "proper Christian church."

II. Acts 2 and 4 and Wesley's Account of the Rise of Methodism

In the winter of 1739–40, in the midst of growing tensions with the Moravians, Wesley purchased and refurbished an old cannon foundry. "The Foundry" became the headquarters for Methodism for forty years and Wesley's home as well. By 1775, the aging leader of Methodism was thinking of building a "New Foundry" as the center of Methodism for the future. In April 1777, Wesley laid the foundation for the new structure and preached a sermon, "On Laying the Foundation of the New Chapel," on

18 Hymn #LXXXVII, in Charles Wesley, *Hymns on the Trinity* (Bristol: William Pine, 1767; repr., Madison, NJ: Charles Wesley Society, 1998), 58.

the occasion. His message to the congregation emphasized Methodism's unique relationship to the Church of England and recounted the origins of the Methodist movement.[19]

Wesley's text was Numbers 23:23, "According to this time it shall be said, What hath God wrought!" He began the sermon by pointing out that some Christian leaders in his day saw no "remarkable work of God" (the dawn of a proper gospel day?) in the eighteenth century. Wesley, of course, disagreed.

The elder leader of Methodism took his audience on a tour of the history of Methodism. He located the rise of the movement in 1725, when "a young student at Oxford [Wesley, of course] was much affected by reading Kempis's *Christian Pattern*, and Bishop Taylor's *Rules of Holy Living and Dying*." Wesley developed an earnest desire to live according to those rules and to flee from the wrath to come. By 1729, a group had formed, and they gathered to pray, and read scripture, while "provoking one another to love and to good works."[20]

Wesley recounted that the "regularity" of the little coterie's behavior earned them the appellation "Methodists," an allusion to a group of physicians in Rome at the time of Nero, or so Wesley thought. By 1735, the group had grown to fourteen who "constantly met together." At this point in the sermon, Wesley provided a summary of the character of this rise of Methodism using various points and phrases drawn from Acts 2 and 4. (I include the phrases from Acts 2 and 4 and Wesley's comments on those texts in brackets.):

> They were all precisely of one judgement as well as of one soul [they were of one heart and of one soul]. . . . They were all orthodox at every point [they continued steadfastly in the apostles' doctrine]. . . . As to that practice of the apostolic church . . . the "having of all things in common," they had no rule, nor any formed design concerning it. But it was so, in effect, and it could not be otherwise; for none could want anything that another could spare [there needed no outward command, the command was written on their hearts . . . their hearts so overflowed with love]. This was the infancy of the work. They had no conception of anything that would follow.[21]

19 See *Works*, 3:577–79.

20 Ibid., 3:580–81.

21 Ibid., 3:581–82. See *Works*, 2:454–55 for the bracketed lines that come from Wesley's account of the dawn of the proper gospel day and a proper Christian church.

These are striking parallels between Wesley's account of the rise of Methodism and his commentary on Acts 2 and 4 as the dawn of a proper gospel day and a proper Christian church, an embodiment of his Trinitarian understanding of the essence of the church as union and communion with the Triune God leading to love for God and others socially embedded in fellowship and loving sharing of possessions.

Wesley's "New Chapel" sermon then moved quickly through the "rudiments of a Methodist Society" in the new colony in Georgia during his time there in 1735 through 1737 to 1738, when he was excluded from preaching in many Anglican churches. Because of this exclusion, Wesley "preached in the middle of Moorfields" to "thousands and thousands" who "were cut to the heart" and who came to Wesley "all in tears, inquiring with the utmost eagerness what they must do to be saved."[22] Notice Wesley's intentional allusion to Acts 2:14 and the following verses where Peter preached to the crowd at Pentecost and Acts 2:37, where those who heard were cut to the heart and asked Peter what they needed to do to be saved. This little group increased rapidly "to about a hundred" and "thus, without any previous plan or design, began the Methodist Society in England—a company of people associating together to help each other work out their own salvation"[23] (an allusion to Acts 2:44–47?).

The second point of the "New Chapel" sermon answered the question, "What is Methodism?" Given the character of the Methodist revival and Wesley's associating it with Acts 2, we would expect Wesley to answer the question with a Trinitarian account the essence of the gospel and the church similar what Wesley said about the dawning of a gospel day and Christian church in relation to Acts 2 and 4. This is what he did.

According to Wesley, Methodism was not some new religion: "Methodism, so called, is the old religion, the religion of the Bible, the religion of the primitive church, the religion of the Church of England." For Wesley, this old religion is "no other than love: love of God and of all mankind; the loving God with all our heart, and soul, and strength, as having first loved *us*, as the fountain of all the good we have received . . . and the loving every soul which God hath made, every man on earth." He added that "This love is the great medicine of life, the never-failing remedy for all the evils of a disordered world."[24]

---

22 Ibid., 3:582–84.

23 Ibid., 3:584.

24 Ibid., 3:585.

On the next page of the sermon, Wesley made explicit the participatory Trinitarian dimension of this "old religion" newly revived in the Methodist movement:

> Permit me to give a little fuller account, both of the progress and nature of this religion. . . . Many thousands gathered together to hear them [Wesley, his brother, and a few other preachers]. . . . Many were . . . deeply convinced of the . . . heinousness of their sins. . . . The whole form of their life was changed. They "ceased to do evil, and learned to do well.". . . But over and above this outward change, they began to experience *inward religion*. "The love of God was shed abroad in their hearts [by the Spirit],". . . and this love constrains them to love all mankind, and inspires them with every holy and heavenly temper, with the mind which was in Christ. Hence it is that they are now uniform in their behaviour, unblameable in all manner of conversation.[25]

In the sermon "On Laying the Foundation of the New Chapel," Wesley recounted the theological and spiritual foundation of the Methodist movement, linking it to the dawn of a proper gospel day and a proper Christian church, as exemplified in Acts 2 and 4. This embodiment involved human hearts transformed by the Trinitarian activity that is the very center of the vital religion, the old religion of the Bible, a transformation rooted in union and communion with God and one another, generating profound love of God and others, a love seated on the throne of Christians' hearts, a love that is inherently social, embracing others together in a community where Christians have all things in common, a love reaching out into the world in word and example. In so doing, they become transcripts of the Trinity.[26] What is becoming clear is that there are profound correlations between Wesley's participatory, economic Trinitarian understanding of the soteriology and ecclesiology and his account of the character of the life and community of the Methodist movement in the "New Chapel" sermon in 1777.[27]

---

25 Ibid., 3:586–7.

26 *The Works of John Wesley*, ed. Franz Hildebrant and Oliver A. Beckerlegge, vol. 7, *Collection of Hymns for the Use of the People Called Methodists* (New York, Oxford University Press, 1983), 88.

27 Wesley may have idealized what happened in the rise of Methodism. But what is significant for this study is not whether Methodism fully embodied Wesley's Trinitarian soteriology and ecclesiology. The question is did Wesley's vision of the proper embodiment include and reflect his participatory, economic Trinitarian account of soteriology and ecclesiology?

Wesley spent the latter part of the sermon challenging the Methodists to remain true to the origin and character of the Methodist movement and to stay in the Anglican Church, for that is how this religion of love, the great medicine of life, diffuses itself like salt and light into the Anglican Church and English society. The defenders of the Trinity in the seventeenth and eighteenth centuries turned the doctrine into an esoteric concept with little or no bearing on Christian faith, life, and witness. Wesley, however, offered an astonishing alternative Trinitarian vision of salvation and the church in which God's Triune love becomes the participatory source of a vibrant Christian community, a religion of love and the medicine to heal broken lives. This kind of social embodiment is bound up with the very "being" of love as it comes to us via participation in the love and life of the Triune God. Wesley concluded his sermon by reinforcing this point:

> First let our hearts be joined herein; let us unite our wishes and prayers; let our whole soul pant after a general revival of pure religion and undefiled, of the restoration of the image of God, pure love, in every child of man. Then let us endeavour to promote in our several stations this scriptural, primitive religion; let us with all diligence diffuse the religion of love among all we have any intercourse with; let us provoke all men, not to enmity and contention, but to love and to good works; always remembering those deep words (God engrave them on all out hearts!), "God is love; and he that dwelleth in love, dwelleth in God, and God in him."[28]

Wesley saw the Methodist movement, despite its flaws, as the dawn of a proper gospel day and a proper Christian church. We will now examine some of the concrete forms of life, community, and ministry in Methodism and how they reflected Wesley's Trinitarian understanding of salvation and the church.

III. Expressions of Trinitarian Community and Ministry in Early Methodism

1. The Rise of Societies

In this section dealing with various expressions of Christian community and ministry in early Methodism, we turn to another of Wesley's narratives recounting the rise and development of the Methodist movement. This one, "A Plain Account of the People Called Methodists," was published in 1749

28 *Works*, 3:592.

at the end of the first decade of Methodism, but there were nine editions during Wesley's lifetime, making it something of a standard fixture in Methodism. It provided the Methodist movement with a comprehensive vision of the theological convictions and the communal structures and forms of ministry for embodying and nurturing those convictions, all interwoven in a wonderful narrative tapestry portraying Methodism as the dawning of a proper gospel day and a proper Christian church.[29]

The "Plain Account" opened with Wesley noting that his friend, Rev. Vincent Perronet, had requested "an account of the *whole economy* of the people commonly called Methodists." Wesley's essay, of course, supplied it "that you [Perronet] may know not only their *practice* on every head, but likewise the *reasons* whereon it is grounded, the *occasion* of every step they have taken, and the *advantages* reaped thereby."[30] Wesley noted the Methodists had no idea that the movement would develop in the astonishing ways it did, since "they had no previous design or plan at all, but everything arose just as the occasion offered." They saw a pressing evil or an opportunity for good. They consulted "only *common sense* and *Scripture*—though they generally found, in looking back, something in *Christian antiquity*, likewise, very nearly parallel thereto."[31]

After these brief introductory remarks, Wesley described the heart of the movement. After their evangelical awakening in 1738, John and his brother Charles both began to preach what Wesley called a "new gospel" they learned from Peter Böhler, as discussed in chapter 2. Wesley stated: "We had no view therein but so far as we were able . . . to *convince* those who would hear what true Christianity was, and to *persuade* them to embrace it."

Wesley described this true Christianity in the same participatory, evangelical, doxological, and economic Trinitarian terms that we have seen throughout this study. It does not consist in "*orthodoxy*" or "*right opinions*"; neither is it "harmlessness," nor mere "*externals*," like doing good and using the means of grace. Rather, Wesley asserted:

> It is nothing short of or different from "the mind that was in Christ" [Wesley's theological short-hand for transformed affections and tempers],

---

29 See *The Works of John Wesley*, ed. Rupert E. Davies, vol. 9, *The Methodist Societies: History, Nature, and Design* (Nashville: Abingdon, 1989), 253, for Davies's introduction to the tract. See also Richard P. Heitzenrater, *Wesley and the People Called Methodists* (Nashville: Abingdon, 1995), 179–80, for his astute observations about this important account of the history and economy of the Methodist movement.

30 *Works*, 9:254.

31 Ibid.

> "the image of God" stamped upon the heart, inward "righteousness," attended with the "peace" of God, and "joy in the Holy Ghost.". . . The only way under heaven to this religion is . . . "repentance towards God, and faith in our Lord Jesus Christ.". . . By this faith, "he that worketh not . . ." is "justified freely by his grace, through the redemption which is in Jesus Christ." And . . . "being justified by faith," we taste of the heaven to which we are going; we are holy and happy; we . . . "sit in heavenly places with Christ Jesus."[32]

This Trinitarian understanding of true Christianity was the fontal source of the entire *ordo salutis* as well as the *esse* of the church, as we have seen in previous chapters. Here in the account of Methodism, Wesley maintained that this Trinitarian understanding of the genuine Christianity generated the Methodist movement.

At this point in his account, Wesley noted that upon hearing the Wesley brothers' preaching, "one and another and another came to us, asking what they should do, being distressed on every side."[33] Wesley encouraged them to meet together, encourage one another, and pray with and for one another, similar to Wesley's account of the genesis of Methodism in his sermon "On Laying the Foundation of the New Chapel," examined in the previous section.

These seekers wanted to meet with Wesley, but Wesley said, "They were too many for me to talk with severally," so they began to meet "every Thursday, in the evening."[34] "Thus arose," Wesley concluded, "without any previous design on either side, what was afterwards called a *Society*—a very innocent name . . . for any number of people *associating* themselves together." Their purpose in uniting was to "flee the wrath to come" and "to be saved from their sins" (the condition for admission into the Society), "to pray together, to receive the word of exhortation, and to watch over one another in love, that they might help each other to work out their salvation." Wesley pulled these statements right out of "The General Rules of the United Societies."[35] At this point in his "Plain Account" essay, Wesley listed the three "general rules" and some of the particular points under "doing no harm," "doing good," and "attending upon all the ordinances of God,"[36] providing his readers with the basic form of life at the heart of the Societies

32 Ibid., 9:254–55.
33 Ibid., 9:256.
34 Ibid.
35 Ibid., 9:256–57. See ibid., 9:69, for "The General Rules of the United Societies."
36 Ibid., 9:257.

as they sprung to life, since when Trinitarian grace stirs in peoples' hearts it manifests fruit in their lives.

2. Theological Rationale for Connection and Discipleship in Connection

The results of "uniting together" were swift and profound. Wesley noted that those who "were not united together, grew faint . . . and fell back into what they were before," whereas "those who were thus united together continued . . . to 'lay hold on eternal life.'"[37] As Wesley reflected on the changed lives of those who united together, he saw that "this is the very thing which was from the beginning of Christianity." As soon as people heard preaching of true Christianity, turned from sin, and sought God, the early Church "joined them together . . . advised them to watch over one another, and met with these *katecumenoi* (catechumens, as they were then called)" to disciple them.[38]

A few pages later in this "Plain Account" of the Methodists, Wesley went to the theological heart of the matter:

> Many now happily experienced that Christian fellowship of which they had not so much as an idea before. They began to "bear one another's burdens," and "naturally" to "care for each other." As they had daily a more intimate acquaintance with, so they had a more endeared affection for each other. And "speaking the truth in love, they grew up into him in all things with is the head, even Christ; from whom the whole body, fitly joined together, and compacted by that which every joint supplied, according to the effectual working in the measure of every part, increased unto the edifying itself in love." [This text is from Ephesians 4.][39]

It is noteworthy that when Wesley analyzed the impact of the early Methodists "uniting together," he recounted it in terms of Christian fellowship, growing intimacy, care and affection, and transparency of speaking the truth in love, which together parallel Wesley's account of the sociality of love and the other Christian dispositions that arise out union and communion with the Triune God in the gospel examined in chapter 4 above.

---

37 Ibid., 9:257–58.

38 Ibid., 9:258.

39 Ibid., 9:262. Wesley was referring to what happened in the lives of those who met in classes, but it is clear from what he said that this account of fellowship in small groups and the biblical/theological rationale for it applies to other expressions of union and communion with God and one another in early Methodism.

Elsewhere, Wesley developed even more fully his biblical and theological rationale for "connection" and discipleship in connection (the emphasis in the text is mine):

> It is only when we are *knit together* that we "have nourishment from Him, [Christ] and increase with the increase of God." Neither is there any time, when the weakest member can say to the strongest, or the strongest to the weakest, "I have no need of thee." Accordingly our blessed Lord, when his disciples were in the weakest state, sent them forth, not alone, but two by two. *When they were strengthened a little, not by solitude, but by abiding with him and one another, he commanded them to "wait," not separate, but "being assembled together," for "the promise of the Father." And "they were all with one accord in one place," when they received the gift of the Holy Ghost.* Express mention is made in the same chapter, that when "there were added unto them three thousand souls, all that believed were together, and continued steadfastly" not only "in the Apostles' doctrine," but also "in fellowship and in breaking of bread," and in praying "with one accord" [Acts 2]. Agreeable to which is the account the great Apostle gives of the manner which he had been taught of God, "for perfecting the saints, for the edifying of the body of Christ," even to the end of the world. And according to St. Paul, all who will ever come, in "the unity of the faith, unto the perfect man, unto the measure of the stature of the fullness of Christ," must "together grow up into Him: From whom the whole body fitly joined together and compacted" (or strengthened) "by that which every joint supplieth, according to the effectual working in the measure of every part, maketh increase of the body unto the edifying of itself in love" [Ephesians 4].[40]

Appealing yet again to Acts 2 and Ephesians 4, Wesley provided his biblical/theological rationale, including referencing all three persons of the Trinity, for discipleship in connection, for particular forms of life and ministry, for a set of relationships, communal structures, and practices, all reflecting his Trinitarian understanding of salvation and the church as invitation to communion, deepening communion, and full communion with the Triune God and one another.[41] The Triune God builds up the church toward full salvation in the context of *connection* or *koinonia* and mutual ministry in the Spirit

---

40 See Colin Williams, *John Wesley's Theology Today* (Nashville: Abingdon, 1960), 150–51, for this quotation from Wesley.

41 See Sondra Higgins Matthaei, *Making Disciples: Faith Formation in the Wesleyan Tradition* (Nashville: Abingdon, 2000), 61–62.

between the members of the body of Christ that leads to ever-deepening communion with the Triune God and one another.

When Wesley was charged with schism for "joining these people [the early Methodists] together" in this way, for *"gathering churches out of churches,"* his retort is revealing:

> I answer, That which never existed cannot be destroyed. . . . Who watched over them in love? Who marked their growth in grace? Who advised and exhorted them from time to time? Who prayed with them and for them, as they had need? This, and this alone is Christian fellowship. But alas! Where is it to be found? . . . name what parish you please. . . . What Christian connexion is there between them? What intercourse in spiritual things? What watching over each others' souls? What bearing one another's burdens? What a mere jest it is, then, to talk so gravely of *destroying* what never was! The real truth is the reverse of this: We *introduce* Christian fellowship where it was *utterly destroyed*. And the fruits of it have been peace, joy, love, and zeal for every good word and work.[42]

For Wesley, this kind of watching over one another in love, or discipleship in connection, is the very form of life and ministry, the very set of relationships, communal structures, and practices, that embodied his Trinitarian understanding of salvation and the church.[43]

Notice the profoundly communal phrases Wesley used to describe what "connexion" is: "intercourse in spiritual things," "bearing one another's burdens," "watching over them in love," "marking their growth in grace," "praying with them and for them." What Wesley intended by "connexion" is rather clear: an intimate, personal, participatory set of *relationships* with the Triune God and with one another. These relationships of love are deep, utterly real, and person-constituting so that one's very being as a Christian is being-in-communion with one another and the Triune God of the gospel. (Chapter 4 documented and described this in the discussion of the social and ecclesial character of love and the holy tempers.) "Connexion," for Wesley, seems to

---

42 *Works,* 9:259.

43 Wesley found precedent for this pattern of discipleship in connection in the early Church: "In the earliest times those whom God sent forth 'preached the gospel to every creature.' . . . But as soon as any of these were so convinced of the truth, as to forsake sin and seek the gospel salvation, they immediately joined them together . . . and met these . . . apart from the great congregation, that they might instruct, rebuke, exhort, and pray with them, and for them, according to their several necessities" (ibid., 9:258).

be synonymous with a participatory understanding of *koinonia*, as the particular character of the personal relations of love with Triune God and others constitutive of the church as the body of Christ. This kind of connection signals the dawning of a proper gospel day and a proper Christian church, and according to Wesley, is the context for discipleship and for discipline.

3. The Vision for Watching Over One Another in Love

Embodying connection in a movement of religious seekers who want to know more about Christian faith and life but have all kinds of personal issues and problems presented serious challenges. The problem was especially acute because of Wesley's highly moral vision of the Christian faith, where love is the fulfillment of the law.

For Wesley, "Love is the end of all the commandments of God. Love is the end, the sole end, of every dispensation of God, from the beginning of the world to the consummation of all things. . . . Love existed from eternity, in God, the great ocean of love."[44] So according to Wesley, faith "was originally designed of God to re-establish the law of love," "for there is no motive which so powerfully inclines us to love God as a sense of the love of God in Christ."[45] In addition, "from this principle of grateful love to God arises love to our brother also. Neither *can we avoid loving our neighbor*, if we truly believe the love wherewith God hath loved us."[46]

However, what does it mean to love? As we saw in chapter 3, Wesley understood the law as "a copy of the eternal mind," "a transcript of the divine nature."[47] Love does not abrogate this law but rather fulfills it. With remarkable clarity and consistency, Wesley insisted that "this love to man, grounded on faith and love to God, 'worketh no ill to our neighbor.'. . . It continually incites us to do good: as we have time and opportunity. . . . It [love] is therefore the fulfilling of the positive, likewise, as well as of the negative law of God."[48] In another sermon, Wesley drove home his point: "What then? Shall this evangelical principle of action be less powerful than the legal? Shall we be less obedient to God from filial love than we were from servile fear?"[49]

This is the theological root of the moral seriousness of early Methodism that finds embodiment in the General Rules of the United Societies and in

44 *Works*, 2:38–39.
45 Ibid., 2:40, 42.
46 Ibid., 2:42; my emphasis.
47 Ibid., 2:10.
48 Ibid., 2:42.
49 Ibid., 2:30.

the discipline characteristic of the early Methodist community. The General Rules made this moral seriousness explicit: wherever "a desire to flee the wrath to come, to be saved from their sins" "is really fixed in the soul it will be shown by its fruits." So the early Methodists were to avoid evil, do good, and use the means of grace "to evidence their desire for salvation."[50]

Furthermore, Wesley was not afraid to get specific. The convicting grace of God moves us to avoid uncharitable or unprofitable conversation and needless self-indulgence. It moves us to give food to the hungry, clothe the naked, and visit those who are sick or in prison. Why? Not because these things make us even one bit more loveable or loved by God. But because these acts are an expression of the community-forming grace of the Triune God, which always moves us outside of ourselves in love toward others. Furthermore, avoiding evil, doing good, and using the means of grace is where one is most likely to encounter more of God's grace. So keeping the General Rules in early Methodism was simultaneously an expression of the grace of the Triune God in one's life and a means of grace as well.

According to Wesley's "Plain Account," these General Rules, "all which we are taught of God to observe, even in his written Word," are "the sufficient rule, both of our faith and practice," for "all these we know his Spirit writes on every truly awakened heart." "Watching over one another in love," discipleship in connection, flows from the love rooted in union and communion with God and one another and comes to expression in all these social relations enshrined in the General Rules and applied to life via discipline, social relations that Wesley sees as bound up with the very "being" of love on the throne of our hearts. Christians care for one another enough to get involved in the messiness of Christian life while attempting to actually live out love, fulfilling the negative and positive law of God in the details of living. The Rules explicitly state, "If there be any among us . . . who habitually break any of them . . . we will admonish him of the error of his ways" and "bear with him for a season."[51]

In Wesley's "A Plain Account of the People Called Methodists," we find a classic example of the ideal of real love embodied in all the complexities of life, love that participates in and reflects the love of God that comes to us through the grace of Jesus Christ in the fellowship of the Spirit and affects a profound transformation of life. This kind of love, with a particular kind of sociality bound up with its very being, cannot but take this path of confrontation and discipline if it is to maintain the integrity of its being as a

50 *Works*, 9:70.
51 Ibid., 9:73.

participation in the love of God in Christ through the Spirit.[52] Wesley linked the purpose of classes in early Methodism to the embodiment of this morally serious love for one another.

4. Developing Structures of Community, Polity, and Ministry

It was to this end of discipleship in connection that Wesley gradually developed a highly evolved organization designed to nurture those awakened and lead them along the communal path of salvation, as well as propel them into ministry, for Christian faith always involves expressing Christian love for God and neighbor in ministry and service to others. Herein we see something of Wesley's true genius.

Classes: Connection and Discipline

To be an early Methodist, one did not have to be a Christian who had already come to faith in Christ. The Methodist Societies and the small-group class meetings were open to anyone who was "fleeing the wrath to come" and looking to the Triune God for grace, because if you were a seeker it could only mean that God's convicting grace was already at work in your life.

You could come to a Methodist class meeting with around ten others like yourself with all your struggles, your doubts, and your questions. The leader and the others would listen to you, pray for you and with you, help you to pray if you did not know how, and explain to you in simple terms the love of God in Christ and what Christian faith and life is all about. They continued to encourage, nurture, help you, and hold you accountable until you encountered the justifying and regenerating grace of the Triune God and therein found your way back to God.

These small groups in early Methodism were simultaneously an expression of Trinitarian communion with God and neighbor and also formation toward deeper communion with God and neighbor. It is no coincidence that many early Methodists encountered the love of God the Father through the justifying grace of our Lord Jesus Christ in the fellowship of the Holy Spirit in

---

52 In light of Wesley's understanding of watching over one another in love, the basic problem around discipline in the United Methodist Church is not that it does not always enforce its own *Book of Discipline*, the communally agreed practices for life together in Christian community and ministry. The more fundamental problem is that there is insufficient connection, as Wesley understood it, for discipline to really function the way it should in the context of fellowship, love, and trust.

those class meetings, though often only after they had been in the classes on average for more than two years.[53]

While open to anyone, early Methodist societies and classes had high expectations for those who became a part of the movement. If grace is the presence and power of the Triune God, how could it not transform human lives? That is its very purpose. The high expectations of early Methodism come to expression in discipline central to the connectional ethos of Methodism. The communal character of this discipline was expressed in the phrase "watching over one another in love," which, as we saw above, was at the core of the early Methodist understanding of what "connection" was really all about.

One cannot do any of these things apart from God's communion-forming grace. One does them out of gratitude, the first glimmer of love for God and for others, in response to the grace of the Triune God one has already received. The community held one accountable for avoiding evil, doing good, and using the means of grace because it really cared about and understood the importance of the kind of communal formation present in practices that faithfully embody the love and life of the Triune God.

The early Methodists viewed this kind of discipline as essentially positive. Living a careless life and avoiding the very means of grace that God has provided would simply impede one's progress. Listen to Wesley's own words: "I was more convinced than ever that the preaching like an apostle, without joining together those that are awakened and training them up in the ways of God, is only begetting children for the murderer. . . . How much preaching has there been for these twenty years all over Pembrokeshire! But no regular societies, no discipline, no order or connexion; and the consequence is that nine in ten of the once-awakened are now faster asleep than ever!"[54]

When Wesley described how the class meetings come into being in his "Plain Account" of Methodism, it is this necessity of discipline in connection where love expresses itself socially that comes to light. Wesley noted: "But

---

53 Thomas Albin's research into the spirituality of the early Methodist laity uncovered this fact (see Albin, "An Empirical Study of Early Methodist Spirituality," in *Wesleyan Theology Today*, ed. Theodore Runyon [Nashville: Kingswood Books, 1985], 278). Albin examined the spiritual autobiographies of more than five hundred early Methodist laypersons published in the *Arminian Magazine* and *Methodist Magazine*.

54 See A. Skevington Wood, *The Burning Heart: John Wesley, Evangelist* (Grand Rapids, MI: Eerdmans, 1967), 188, for this quotation from Wesley.

as much as we endeavoured to watch over each other, we soon found some who did not 'live the gospel.'. . Several grew cold, and gave way to the sins."[55]

There was no way that Wesley himself could deal with "several disorderly walkers" "scattered so wide in all parts of the town, from Wapping to Westminister." So Wesley and the early Methodists "groaned under these inconveniences long, before a remedy could be found."[56]

The story surrounding the development of classes is well-known. Wesley needed a way to pay off the debt associated with the building of the first New Room in Bristol in 1739. Captain Foy suggested collecting a penny a week from the members of the Society there and volunteered to contact the eleven poorest members and even pay their penny if they could not afford it.[57] But this venture quickly developed beyond its initial purpose since this collection process brought the leaders of the Bristol Society into close contact with the actual daily lives of the members. So Wesley expanded the vision of this ministry to include making "a particular inquiry into the behaviour of those whom he [the leader of these classes] saw weekly." The result was that "many disorderly walkers were detected. Some turned from the evil of their ways. Some were put away from us. Many saw it with fear, and rejoined unto God with reverence."[58] Wesley injected classes with leaders into Methodist Societies in London and elsewhere; though, since it was inconvenient for leaders to meet with members in their home, the classes soon became a weekly meeting of the entire group together in one place.

This development into weekly group meetings further expanded and transformed the character of the class meeting, which now became far more of a close-knit fellowship within which Christian formation took place. Here is how Wesley described the watching over one another in love that took place in classes: "Advice or reproof was given as need required, quarrels made up, misunderstandings removed. And after an hour or two spent in this labour

55 *Works*, 9:260. At this point, Wesley added a revealing observation: "We quickly perceived, there were many ill consequences of suffering these to remain among us. It was dangerous to others, inasmuch as all sin is of an infectious nature" (ibid.). Just as affections and tempers, transformed by the Triune God though the power of the gospel, are inherently social, so here Wesley indicated that sin, lodged in the affections and tempers, is also social and therefore infectious, as noted in chapter 4 above. In addition, open sin led to scandalizing the Methodist movement, which proved to be a stumbling block to others who were ready to "flee the wrath to come," and led at times violent persecution (ibid.).

56 Ibid.

57 Ibid.

58 Ibid., 9:261.

of love, they concluded with prayer and thanksgiving."[59] As Sandra Higgins Matthaei astutely observes, the class meetings were an "invitation to communion" with the Triune God and our neighbor, where "*communion*" or growth in relationship with God and one another, "*is both a means and an end of the Way of Salvation*."[60]

This kind of introduction into Christian community for those just beginning the process of "fleeing the wrath to come" could not have been without problems. Indeed, in his account of the rise of the classes, Wesley explicitly notes that "little misunderstandings and quarrels of various kinds frequently arose."[61] When Wesley explained his quarterly examination of society mem-

---

59 Ibid., 9:262.

60 See Higgins Matthaei, *Making Disciples*, 61–2, 133–4. The importance of maintaining this intimate fellowship and loving care for one another comes to expression in the way early Methodism accommodated those who wanted to visit a class meeting with the intent of joining. They could visit, but only twice, and then they either applied for membership or could not return. In addition, the classes were open to visitors only every other week to protect the fellowship and a depth of sharing that might be comprised if every meeting was flooded with visitors. D. Michael Henderson, *John Wesley's Class Meeting: A Model for Making Disciples* (Nappanee, IN, Evangel Publishing House, 1997), 107.

Wesley's clever way of handling admission into the classes (and meetings of the Society) was to issue tickets to those who were in good standing—and to withhold tickets from those whose behavior undermined their own spiritual progress or the integrity of the class. See Wesley's account of the use of tickets in *Works*, 9:265; and *Works*, 3:512. Early Methodism's sensitivity to small-group dynamics is remarkable, as is Methodism's intentionality around maintaining the particular kind of communal ethos that furthered the end of the classes.

61 *Works*, 9:261. Many of the early Methodist meetings of various kinds were segregated, so that in meetings of the society, the women sat on one side and the men on the other. But there were men and women in the class meetings. Indeed, the membership of classes could be rather diverse in terms of social class, educational background, age, economic situation, and spiritual maturity. See Higgins Matthaei, *Making Disciples*, 133–34; Collins, *The Theology of John Wesley*, 250–51; Davies introduction in *Works*, 9:11–12; and Henderson, *John Wesley's Class Meeting*, 93–112, for detailed descriptions of the classes.

Whether by design or by circumstance, this social/cultural diversity, often associated with barrier, prejudice, and offense, found itself confronted by Wesley and early Methodists' Trinitarian vision of Christian faith in which all persons, no matter who they are, no matter what their age, social or economic status, or level of education, were all sinners challenged by a Holy God, yet sinners equally embraced by the love of God through the grace of Christ in the fellowship of the Holy Spirit. Loved by a Trinitarian God they were being called to repent of sin, including turning away from prejudice, hatred, and suspicion of "others," to enter into communion with this

bers, he added the revealing comment, "At these seasons I likewise particularly inquire whether there be any misunderstandings or differences among them, that every hindrance of peace and brotherly love may be taken out of the way."[62] It is no coincidence that Wesley himself selected those who served as leaders of the classes and provided them with rules.

In spite of the significant diversity of those in classes and the petty squabbles that are always part of life together when those who are together are not yet perfected in love, what is amazing, as well as illuminating of Wesley's developing vision of connection and its actual practice in classes, is his comment about what actually happened in the classes: "Many now happily experienced that Christian fellowship of which they had not so much as an idea before. They began to 'bear one another's burdens,' and 'naturally' to 'care for each other' " and thus manifested "endeared affection for each other."[63] The sheer success of the classes points to the genuine community that those who attended found there. We see here Wesley's Trinitarian vision of salvation and the church as union and communion with the Triune God and one another coming to expression in the actual communal structure or polity and ministry of early Methodism even in the midst of social diversity and all kinds of interpersonal tensions.[64]

Trinitarian God and one another, and to manifest it all concretely in Christian fellowship that cut radically across these social barriers.

62 *Works,* 9:265. When reading through Wesley's Journals and diaries, one cannot help but be struck by how often he recounts having to deal with all manner of misunderstandings, differences, and quarrels between factions within various societies, and equally struck by his gift of diplomacy.

63 Ibid., 9:262. Wesley was referring to what happened in the lives of those who met in classes, but it is clear from what he said that this account of fellowship in small groups and the biblical/theological rationale for it applies to other expressions of union and communion with God and one another in early Methodism.

64 Some immediately objected to meeting in classes, as it was not part of the society structure and communal expectations when they joined. Wesley's responded that "'Tis pity but they had not been at first. But we knew not then either the need or the benefit of them." Wesley added that regularly changing the patterns and structures of discipleship in connection "is not a weakness or fault . . . but a peculiar advantage which we enjoy. By this means we declare them all to be merely prudential, not essential, not of divine institution." In addition, making changes helped prevent stagnation or "growing formal and dead" (ibid., 9:262–63).

However, when Wesley linked Christian fellowship, watching over one another in love, bearing one another's burdens, and caring for another so that "they had a more endeared affection for each other" with Ephesians 4 and the way the body of Christ builds itself up in love, were these small groups in which fellowship and discipline takes

Class meetings often began with a hymn, and then the leader recounted his or her spiritual life over the previous week, including growth in grace as

---

place merely "prudential"? Love, with its sociality that goes to its very being, must be concretely embodied, as we have seen throughout this section and in the previous chapter. In actual practice, in their results, and in Wesley's rationale for them, these small groups look a lot more like "equi–primordial" expressions of a proper Christian church arising out of a dawning of a proper gospel day rather than merely "prudential."

Wesley never affirmed this more robust theological vision of fellowship and discipline in small groups as being a primordial expression of the church. I suspect Wesley might say that the particular "form" of Christian fellowship Methodism developed in the classes (and the bands and other small groups) was "prudential," not a divine institution, even while the union and communion with the Triune God and one another that transpired in those small groups was of the very essence of the church. This is clearly consistent with what Wesley said about the essence of the church and with his questioning of marks of the church in the Anglican Articles.

Wesley made a similar point in answering those who objected that "there is no scripture for this, for classes." Wesley's answer was that "there is no scripture *against* it." In fact, "There is much scripture *for* it, even all those texts which enjoin the substance of those various duties, whereof this is only an indifferent circumstance." Wesley clarified the point further, noting that "Scripture, in most points, gives only *general* rules, and leaves the *particular* circumstances to be adjusted by the common sense of mankind" (ibid., 9:263).

All through this section of his "A Plain Account of the People Called Methodists," where he recounted the rise of classes, Wesley noted that many of the actual interpersonal activities and interactions that took place in the classes are enjoined in scripture, as is the communion or Christian fellowship that those practices concretely embody. So while "classes" per se are prudential, what took place in them, including entering into "Christian fellowship," bearing "one another's burdens," "caring for one another," and giving "advice or reproof," all seem to be expressions of the essence of the church.

It is interesting that throughout this section on classes in his "Plain Account," the one text of scripture that he quoted at length is Ephesians 4, the same chapter of Ephesians that he referenced when he discussed the essence of the church in his sermon "Of the Church." Ephesians 4:15–16 emphasized the importance of "speaking the truth in love"—recall what Wesley said about our words being a true picture of our hearts, as we saw in the previous chapter in relation to the sociality inherent in affections and tempers transformed by the love of God in Christ through the presence of the Spirit. Ephesians 4:15–16 continues this way: speaking the truth in love, Christians will grow "up into him [Christ]," "the head" of the church, and "the whole body, joined and held together by every supporting ligament, grows and builds itself up in love, as each part does its work" (see ibid., 9:262, and Ephesians 4:15–16 in the New International Version).

This description of Christian community in Ephesians 4:15–16 is not all that different from what actually happened in the classes, even if classes were not explicitly

well as honest sharing of temptation, failure, and sin. This practice allowed the class members to overhear the leader disclose something of the Christian life. The kind of intimate community in classes must have been contagious, as Henderson notes that members of classes often stayed in them for years and cultivated amazingly deep, intimate, and lasting relationships.[65] The kind of openness, intimacy, depth of fellowship, and trust created a particular kind of environment where advice and reproof played a crucial role. Discipline and accountability came from the very persons who sat across the table, who had confessed their struggles, failure, and sin, and who had asked for others' prayers and support.

As a result, discipline and accountability took place within the context of connection, love, and support. Discipline was enforced for primarily positive reasons and enforced in the context of loving fellowship. Discipleship and discipline within connection are the very form that real Christian love takes in communion with the Triune God of grace who loved us too much to leave us in our sin and guilt, for discipline is love saying, "We care too deeply about you not to uphold you and hold you accountable."

It is no surprise that attending a class meeting became mandatory. Wesley was blunt about this point: those who would not meet in classes could not remain in the Methodist movement. Why? Because failure to be a part of a loving and supportive small-group Christian fellowship that cares enough to hold one another accountable is failure to embody the love of God the Father manifested in the grace of our Lord Jesus Christ in the fellowship of the Holy Spirit. In order for the church to be the church it needs connection *and* discipline. Without discipline Christians always end up settling for a superficial form of community that does not care deeply enough to really get involved in one another's lives at a level where holding each other accountable is an act of profound love. Without connection Christians end up with a conflicted community in which various factions, no longer living in connection, struggle to impose their agendas on one another via parliamentary, political, juridical, or other avenues of power. While connection without discipline leads to superficial community, discipline without connection ends up in a divisive, conflicted, litigious community that resorts to coercive power to solve its problems.

---

enjoined in scripture. So when Wesley answered the objection that the classes are "all *man's inventions*," his response is, yes they are, "that is, they are methods which men have found . . . for the more effectually applying several scriptural rules, couched in general terms, to particular occasions" (ibid., 263).

65 Henderson, *John Wesley's Class Meeting*, 102.

Bands: Deepening Discipleship in Connection

Every Methodist in a society also had membership in a class, and admission did not require conscious faith or assurance of forgiveness, so seekers were welcome in both of these communal expressions of early Methodism. However, as soon as one encountered the justifying and regenerating grace of God, the one grace of God (in Jesus Christ flowing from the love of God the Father into one's heart and life via the Holy Spirit) led one into sanctification, what Wesley called the house of salvation. Sanctifying grace further transforms our motives, reshapes our intentions, and reorients our affections. Sanctifying grace is deepening communion with the Trinitarian God and leads to deepening communion with one another.

In his "Plain Account of the People Called Methodist," Wesley recounted that "by the blessing of God upon their endeavors to help one another, many . . . being justified by faith . . . had 'peace with God, through our Lord Jesus Christ.'" Those who came to faith "felt a more tender affection than before to those who were partakers of like precious faith." So it is no coincidence, Wesley noted, that "these therefore wanted some means of closer union: they wanted to pour out of their hearts without reserve, particularly with regard to the sin which did still 'easily beset' them."[66]

Once persons entered this stage of the Christian pilgrimage, Wesley provided another small group for them to be a part of, called a band. Wesley explained, "In compliance with their desire I divided them into smaller companies; putting married or single men, and married or single women together."[67] These bands were smaller and more intimate than the classes, often consisting of people in similar life situations. The activities of ministry in the bands were designed to help one grow in one's Christian faith, discipleship, and community.

The discipline or watching over one another in love became even more intense, more focused, more intimate. As people deepen in relationship with the Trinitarian God, they are propelled out of themselves into deeper relationships with one another as well. Listen to the stated design of the bands: "The design of our meeting is to obey the command of God, 'Confess your faults one to another, and pray one for another that ye may be healed.'"[68]

Once again, what is illuminating is not only the moral emphasis on obedience to God but also the communal way Wesley envisioned the process

66 *Works*, 9:266.
67 Ibid., 9:267.
68 Ibid. 9:77.

of sanctification: Christians do not simply confess their sins to the blessed Triune God, they do it *together*, in community with one another, *coram deo*, in union and communion with God. In so doing they simultaneously acknowledge and embody the profound sociality that is part of the "being" of transformed affections and tempers that sanctification entails.

There were questions posed to all who wanted to join a band: "Have you the forgiveness of your sins?" "Have you peace with God through our Lord Jesus Christ?" "Have you the witness of God's Spirit with your spirit that you are a child of God?" "Is the love of God shed abroad in your heart?"[69] As we saw above, in chapters 2 and 4, the participatory Trinitarian character of the questions precisely reflect Wesley's Trinitarian vision of vital religion, of salvation, and of the church.

Only after these questions (about "connection," union, and communion with God and one another) that go to the heart of the Christian faith, salvation, and ecclesiology had been answered did those in bands ask one another the probing questions that are at the heart of discipline or watching over one another in love: "Do you desire to be told your faults?" "Do you desire to be told of all your faults, and that plain and home?" "Consider! Do you desire we should tell you whatsoever we think, whatsoever we fear, whatsoever we hear, concerning you?" "Do you desire that in so doing this, we should come as close as possible, that we should cut to the quick, and search your heart to the bottom?" "Is it your desire and design to be on this and all other occasions entirely open, so as to speak everything that is in your heart?" These questions were not only asked of everyone who wanted to join a band, but Wesley's directions stipulated that they were to be asked "as often as occasion offers."[70]

Notice how these questions so closely parallel the phrases Wesley used to describe "connection" that we examined earlier. Wesley ended with a question aimed at allowing a Christian's words to be a picture of her heart, as we saw in the last chapter in relation to the sociality that is part of a Christian's transformed affections and tempers. Wesley further ensconced this open intimate communal intentionality in the Rules of the Band Societies: "4. [We intend] to speak, each to us in order, freely and plainly the true state of our souls, with the faults we have committed in thought, word, or deed, and the temptations we have felt since our last meeting."[71] The same

69 Ibid.
70 Ibid., 9:78.
71 Ibid., 9:77.

point came up yet again in the questions that Wesley required to be asked at every meeting: "5. Have you nothing you desire to keep in secret?"[72]

This was obviously rigorous communal discipleship in the early Methodism. The moral seriousness, the intentional fostering of open, intimate, and caring depth of fellowship with the Triune God and with one another in the bands, is both compelling as well as consistent with everything we have seen regarding (1) Wesley's Trinitarian vision of vital religion, (2) his Trinitarian vision of the salvation, including his progressive *ordo salutis* as growth in grace and community and in transformed affections and tempers that are inherently social, and (3) his Trinitarian vision of the church. The consistent Trinitarian dimension of early Methodist soteriology and ecclesiology, including embodiment traced in this chapter deepens what comes to mind when we read Charles Wesley's poetic verse, "And when we rise in love renew'd, / Our souls resemble Thee, / An image of the Tri-une God/ To all eternity."[73]

Another interesting dimension of the bands is that there were no assigned leaders. They selected their own leader, a rather telling fact given that John Wesley was Tory and not particularly fond of democracy.[74] Wesley viewed the bands as absolutely crucial if Methodism were to thrive, for he asserted that, "No circuit ever did, or ever will flourish, unless there are bands in the large Societies."[75] What is also illuminating is that the bands were voluntary. The upshot, much to Wesley's consternation, was that often only around 25 percent of the early Methodists were actually in bands.

One cannot help but wonder whether Wesley was acutely aware that the highest levels of intimacy, openness, and fellowship are in fact expressions of *love*, and love is a profound affection on the throne in Christians' hearts that cannot be coerced or compelled. A loving community of persons entails an element of liberty without which it cannot be what the Triune God intends it to be, even when love entails the moral seriousness of an exacting obedience to the law. The blessed Trinity, who lives in community and loves in freedom, comes to us with a love that frees us for free response in love in union and communion with God and one another. Was Wesley's keeping the bands voluntary his acknowledgment of this fundamental character of Christian love?

---

72 Ibid., 9:78.

73 C. Wesley, *Hymns on the Trinity*, hymn # LXXXVII, 58.

74 See Henry H. Knight III, *The Presence of God in the Christian Life: John Wesley and the Means of Grace* (Metuchen, NJ: Scarecrow, 1992), 101. Wesley had an aversion to the rigid supervision by the band monitors that was part of the Moravian use of bands.

75 See Henderson, *John Wesley's Class Meeting*, 119, for this quotation.

These bands met weekly, though Wesley also brought them together periodically for a "love-feast" where they shared bread and water and also praise, fellowship, and testimony to God's activity in the lives of these early Methodists. This joint meeting of the bands nurtured community among the bands.[76] Charles Wesley used his poetic gifts to draw these threads together in a hymn designed for the Love Feast:

> Let us join ('tis God commands),
> Let us join our hearts and hands;
> Help to gain our calling's hope,
> Build we each the other up.
> God his blessing shall dispense,
> God shall crown his ordinance,
> Meet in his appointed ways,
> Nourish us with social grace.[77]

In his "Plain Account of the People Called Methodist," examined throughout this section, Wesley recounted the profound impact of the bands upon those who participated in them: "Great and many are the advantages which have ever since flowed from this closer union of the believers with each other. They prayed for one another. . . . The chains were broken . . . and sin had no more dominion over them. . . . They were built up in our most holy faith. They rejoiced in the Lord more abundantly. They were strengthened in love, and more effectually provoked to abound in every good work."[78]

Penitential Bands for Backslidden Methodists

Despite the astonishing success of the classes and the bands, there were still some who fell back into sin and away from the small groups or were removed by Wesley. Wesley noted that "while most of these who were thus intimately joined together went on daily from faith to faith, some fell from the faith . . . by falling into known, willful sin, or . . . by giving way in what they called little things."[79]

Wesley discovered that the spiritual condition of these lapsed Methodists required a different small-group orientation than what was found in the classes and bands. So Wesley put these "penitents" in their own small

---

76 See Maddox, *Responsible Grace*, 210; Collins, *Theology of John Wesley*, 251; and Higgins Matthaei, *Making Disciples*, 135, 137.

77 *Works*, 7:698.

78 *Works*, 9:268.

79 Ibid., 9:268–69.

groups, which met on Saturday nights possibly to provide a healthy alternative to bars and gin. He provided "hymns, exhortations, and prayers . . . adapted to their circumstances" and "by applying both the threats and promises of God . . . we endeavoured to bring them back to the great Shepherd and Bishop of their souls."[80]

The amazing thing is that backslidden Methodists, who had forgotten that they are loved by the Triune God and set free for new life and had shipwrecked their faith by falling back into the various forms of human degradation, were often reclaimed via these penitential bands. Indeed Wesley noted: "Many of them soon recovered the ground they had lost. Yea, they rose even higher than before; being . . . more meek and lowly, as well as stronger in the faith that worketh by love."[81]

Select Bands: Fullness of Communion with the Trinitarian God and One Another

Wesley had a small group designed to aid the early Methodists in their growth in grace no matter where they were in their spiritual pilgrimage along the order of salvation. For those who were mature in their faith, having grown greatly in sanctifying grace and, therefore, on the threshold of perfecting grace and full communion with the Triune God and one another, Wesley developed select bands which were even more intense and searching.

In his "Plain Account of the People Called Methodists," Wesley told of some Methodists who "outran the greater part of their brethren, continually walking in the light of God, and having fellowship with the Father, and with his Son, Jesus Christ."[82] Notice that Wesley again associated growing in grace toward Christian perfection with communion with the Father and the Son in and through the Holy Spirit. This was the beginning of the select bands or select societies as they were also called.

Wesley said: "My design was . . . to direct them now to *press after perfection*; to exercise their every grace, and improve every talent they had received; and to incite them to love one another more, and to watch more carefully over each other. . . . They had no need of being encumbered with many rules having the best rule of all in their hearts [which, of course, is love]."[83] Notice again the same emphasis of deepening discipleship within the context of deepening connection or *koinonia*.

---

80 Ibid., 9:269.

81 Ibid.

82 Ibid.

83 Ibid., 9:269–70.

For those who have grown this far in grace and have this depth of communion with the Triune God and one another, there is still a profound need for community and accountability, but less of a need to be encumbered with as many rules as those just starting out in the pilgrimage of faith. This helped mitigate the legalism that was always a danger with Wesley's high moral vision of Christian faith. Wesley did ask that the select societies keep strict confidentiality and submit to their minister in things indifferent.[84]

Wesley was also clear that here, where Christians are nearing the point of being perfected in love, there is no longer a need for leaders. Wesley stated: "Everyone here has an equal liberty of speaking, there being none greater or less than another."[85] In addition, Wesley hoped that select bands would be a place where he could "unbosom" himself "on all occasions without reserve." He also hoped that these select societies would be "a pattern of love, of holiness and of all good works" for the rest of the Methodists.[86]

What is particularly interesting about this last point is that Wesley provided explicit directions for those in the select bands, stating that "every member will bring once a week all he can spare toward a common stock."[87] In the *Minutes of the 1744 London Conference*, which played a crucial role in the unfolding of the Methodist movement thereafter, on Thursday, June 28, this rule of the select societies read a little differently: "Every member, till we can have all things in common, will bring once a week, *bona fide*, all he can spare towards a common stock."[88]

Here the discussion comes full circle back to Acts 2 and 4 as the example of the dawning of a proper gospel day and a proper Christian church. The kind of union and communion with the Triune God and with one another led to the profoundest manifestation of love and community where Christians held all things in common is not due to an outward command but because it "was written on their hearts." They were so one in heart and soul that not a one claimed that any of his possessions were his own. Remember Wesley's parenthetical insert at this point in the sermon "The Mystery of Iniquity" that we examined above: "They could not while their hearts so overflowed with love."[89]

---

84 Ibid., 9:270.

85 Ibid.

86 Ibid.

87 Ibid.

88 See *Works*, 10:137.

89 See ibid., 2:455. Maybe we see here the intimation of an alternative to Wesley's vision of the law in Christological and incarnational language: the love of God that we come to know through the grace of our Lord Jesus Christ in the power of the

Christians holding all things in common seems to have been Wesley's vision for the Methodists at that 1744 London Conference, one that those in attendance endorsed, since the rule made it into the official Minutes. Wesley hoped that the level of union and communion with the Trinitarian God and one another in the select bands would in fact lead to a depth of community in those who were pressing toward Christian perfection that would, in turn, manifest itself in a common stock leading in time to the Methodists' holding all things in common.

This vision of Christian community may be part of the reason why Wesley became rather incensed toward the end of his life over the attitude and behavior of Methodists with regard to money. They gained all the money they could and saved all they could, following the advice of Wesley's first two points in his sermon "The Use of Money."[90] But the aged leader of Methodism perceived that his people were not even close to holding all things in common. Indeed, they did not even follow the advice of the third point of Wesley's sermon on money, "give all you can,"[91] despite Wesley's impassioned plea and warning that failure to give would be the undoing of the Methodist movement.[92]

What this entire set of small-group structures in early Methodism suggests is that Wesley's vision for the Christian community of early Methodism was that every Methodist at every stage of his or her Christian life ought to

---

Spirit leads to love so dominating and supreme in the lives of Christians in union and communion with God and one another that they need no outward command since the law is ever only an approximation that cannot capture the richness of love.

90 See ibid., 266–76.

91 Ibid., 276–80.

92 In Wesley's sermon "The Danger of Increasing Riches," he defined "rich" as "Whoever has the necessaries and conveniences of life for himself and his family, and a little to spare for them that have not, is properly a rich man" (*Works,* 4:179). Wesley asserted what he perceived to be the assumption of those who are rich: "'Nay, may I not do what I will with *my own*?" (ibid., 186). It is an assumption in stark contrast to the proper Christian church of Acts 2 and 4 that held all things in common! Wesley retorted: "Here lies the ground of your mistake. It is not your *own*" (ibid.). Indeed, in Wesley's view, Christians who are one in heart and soul, in real union and communion with the Triune God and one another, have written on their hearts a different vision of what it means to be a Christian person whose being is bound up with a particular kind of sociality that mirrors here on earth the love that is the being-in-communion of the Triune God. As Wesley said it when he outlined the dawn of a proper gospel day and a proper Christian church: "How came they to act thus, to have all things in common . . . ? I answer. . . . It naturally and necessarily resulted from the degree of love which they enjoyed" (*Works,* 2:455).

be a part of a small group suited to each Methodist's spiritual development. Why? Because, in Wesley's words, "Christianity is essentially a social religion, and that to turn it into a solitary one is to destroy it."[93] Our Christian telos is finally communal: union and communion in the Spirit with the Son and through the Son with God the Father, and communion with one another as well. We are together in community in our forms of life and ministry becoming transcripts of the Trinity, persons who find our being, hope, and joy in loving relations with God and one another.

Furthermore, these small groups provided a concrete and reproducible form of connection and discipline by which early Methodists could "watch over one another in love." One of the things that we learn from the history of renewal is that, while it is always and everywhere the Triune God who is the primal active agent in the renewal of the church, God's Trinitarian activity in renewal always finds expression in forms of community, life, and ministry. These forms become the means by which renewal moves out across the church, beyond it, and forward in history. Renewal and revival in the church are always a both/and affair involving a fresh, new movement of the Triune God of grace but are also the embodiment of that movement in appropriate forms of life, community, and ministry.

There seems to be a connection between (1) the congruity of the forms of life, community, and ministry with the evangelical doxological participatory Trinitarian relations constitutive of salvation and the essence of the church, and (2) the reproducibility of those forms of life, community, and ministry, which leads to (3) the effectiveness and growth of a movement of renewal. This point, illustrated in early Methodism, ought to guide reflection on the direction renewal of the church might take in the future.

Finally, when Wesley finished recounting the rise of societies, classes, bands, penitential bands, and select societies, along with watch-night services and love-feasts, and also the advantages that resulted from them in over seventeen pages of his "Plain Account of the People Called Methodists" in the latest edition of his collected works, Wesley stated that "this is the plainest and clearest account I can give of the *people* commonly called Methodists." He then added, "It remains only to give you a short account of those who *serve* their brethren in love. These are the *Leaders* of classes and bands, . . . *Assistants*, *Stewards*, *Visitors* of the sick, and *Schoolmasters*."[94]

It seems clear that for Wesley, Methodism was primarily the *people* called Methodists and the various configurations of union and communion

---

93 *Works*, 1:533.
94 *Works*, 9:270.

with the Triune God and one another in societies and small groups. The leaders "*serve* their brethren in love." Leadership in Christian community for Wesley seems to be part of the right functioning of the church, not its essence. There were other formal and informal expressions of community in early Methodism, including retreats, schools for educating children, homes for poor widows, etc. This section will not examine all of them but will end with one final expression of community: conferences.

Conferences in Early Methodism

It is interesting that, in his "Plain Account of the People Called Methodists," Wesley never mentioned conferences or conferencing. Nevertheless, conferences were a significant part of the life of early Methodism. A thorough discussion of the origins, history, and character of conferences in early Methodism would require a monograph of its own. For the purposes of this study, I simply want to demonstrate that there was a Trinitarian dimension in the origin and the practices of conferences in early Methodism.[95]

---

95 See Henry D. Rack's insightful introduction to conferences in early Methodism in *Works*, 10:1–109.

The origin of conferences in early Methodism was bound up with divisions that arose within the revival along lines of doctrine and practice. Profound theological differences manifested themselves in various ways along with personal tensions between the Wesley brothers and George Whitefield and the Calvinists, and August Spangenberg and the Moravians (see ibid., 6–11; and Heitzenrater, *Wesley and the People*, 141–44).

The details of the differences need not detain us. What is important is that this disunity between the key leaders and their followers presented fundamental soteriological and ecclesiological issues for Wesley. We saw in chapter 4 that Wesley's understanding of the essence of the church involves union and communion with the Triune God and with one another. In addition, as we saw in chapter 4, that the transformed affections and tempers are inherently social and that part of that sociality is to offer the right hand of fellowship to other Christians because we are only Christians together in the body of Christ. Schism, for Wesley, was a breaking of this union and communion between the saints.

Therein lay the problem. By the middle of 1740, Wesley and the "United Society" that met at the Foundry in London had broken from the Moravian Fetter Lane Society. In addition, the revival movement split into three different factions in the years that followed: Methodist, Calvinist, and Moravian.

These three groups manifested profound differences in theology and practice that led to further shattering of fellowship. It is clear that this pained Wesley. Given his profound theology of love and his ecclesiology rooted in union and communion with the Triune God and with other Christians, it is perfectly understandable that he

In his sermon "On God's Vineyard," written late in his life in 1787, Wesley reflected on the rise of conferences and provided his theological and biblical rationale. He noted, "In order to increase the union between the preachers . . . they were desired to meet all together in London, and, sometime later, a select number of them." Wesley then recounted the content of the conferences, which follows closely the agenda of the 1744 London meeting: "They spent a few days together in this general Conference in considering what might most conduce to the general good. The result was immediately signified to all their brethren."[96] According to the agenda of the 1744 London Conference, they were "to consider before God: 1. What to teach. 2. How to teach. 3. What to do? [i.e., doctrine, discipline, and practice]."[97]

In "On God's Vineyard," Wesley then provided a biblical theological rationale for this Methodist conferencing. One can almost guess by now what it will be, Ephesians 4: "They soon found that what St. Paul observes of the whole church may be in a measure applied to every part of it: 'The whole body being fitly framed together, and compacted by that which every joint supplieth, maketh increase of the body, to the edifying of itself in

---

felt a profound Christian responsibility to "unite" with the Moravians and Calvinists. So throughout the early 1740s, Wesley attempted to get the Calvinist and Moravian leaders together for a conference in order to sort through their differences. But the Calvinists and Moravians failed to appear at the 1743 conference that Wesley had called. Wesley reached out to Anglican clergy, who he thought would be sympathetic with the revival movement, and invited them to a conference, hoping for greater union with them (see *Works*, 10:6–11; and Heitzenrater, *Wesley and the People*, 141–44).

It is no coincidence that Wesley's written Agenda for the famous London Conference of June 25–29, 1744, placed this issue of uniting with others on the table: "Can we unite any farther with Mr. Whitefield? With the Moravians? Is any conference with either advisable?" (see *Works*, 10:122). See also ibid., 10:6–7. The actual minutes provide further insight into the situation: "Can we unite any farther with the Moravians? It seems not, were it only for this reason, they will not unite with us. Can we unite any farther with Mr. Whitefield? If he make any overtures towards it. Shall we propose a conference with either? With Mr. Whitefield, if he returns to London. The Moravians absolutely decline it. Shall we send them the most material of the preceding questions, and desire their answer? This can do no hurt, and may do good" (ibid., 10:146). See also ibid., 10:7. Wesley made further attempts in subsequent years to unite with the Calvinist Methodists and the evangelical clergy of the Anglican Church. Some conferences to that end actually took place, but little "uniting" actually occurred because of them (ibid., 10:7–8).

96 Ibid., 3:510.

97 *Works*, 10:120.

love.'"[98] Here Wesley linked the Methodist conference with the chapter in Ephesians to which he repeatedly appealed when he discussed the nature and function of the church as the Body of Christ. When we consider not simply the text from Ephesians 4, with its vision of the church as the Body of Christ profoundly united to Christ and to one another in relationship and mutual ministry, but the language Wesley used in relation to gathering in conference, to "unite" those who came, to "increase the union between the preachers," it seems clear that conferences were yet another way to embody Wesley's participatory Trinitarian understanding of "connexion," or uniting in Christian love.

Remember what Wesley said about the church in his sermon "Of the Church": The "universal church is all those persons . . . whom God had so called out of the world . . . united by 'one spirit'; having 'one faith, one baptism; one God and Father of all, who is above all, and through all, and in them all.'"[99] In his sermon on schism, Wesley stated, "It is the nature of love to unite us together, and the greater the love the stricter the union."[100] In light of what Wesley said about the church in these two sermons and detailed discussions in this chapter and the previous one about various aspects of the church, it seems clear that Wesley's vision for Methodist Conferences was that they would be a place where the lay preachers and Anglican clergy associated with Wesley would gather (1) to manifest and deepen union and communion with the Triune God and one another, and then, in the context of this kind of union and connection, (2) to conduct the business of the Methodist movement.

When we turn to the Minutes of the Conferences and what they tell us about the actual conferencing that took place, we see resonances of this vision. The Minutes from the first day of the 1744 London Conference, with seven Anglican clergy and four of lay preachers in attendance, began by recounting the basic assumptions and practices that were to characterize the Conference (and those thereafter):

> It is desired that all things may be considered as in the immediate presence of God; That we may meet with a single eye, and as little children which have everything to learn; . . . That every person may speak freely whatever is in his heart . . . The first preliminary question was then proposed, namely, How far does each of us agree to submit to the

98 *Works*, 3:510.
99 Ibid., 3:50.
100 Ibid., 3:64.

> unanimous judgment of the rest? . . . In speculative things each can only submit so far as his judgment shall be convinced: In every practical point so far as we can without wounding our several consciences.[101]

The group also agreed to confidentiality. "How far should any of us mention to others what may be mentioned here? It was replied, 'Not one word which may be here spoken of persons should be mentioned elsewhere.'"[102]

We see a similar pattern to what we found in the bands and select bands. All were free to speak candidly. The goal was consensus, and if someone did not agree, he was to submit to the judgment of the rest as far as possible. Even if Wesley pronounced the final word, it seems that what he said often reflected the consensus that had arisen out of the conversation of those who attended the conference, though at times it is clear that he dominated the trajectory of the conversation, which frustrated some of the lay preachers and his brother Charles.[103] While the subject matter was not identical with that of bands and select societies, it appears that what Wesley and the group envisioned concerning the character of the conferences as a form of "uniting" or "union" among those who attended the conferences was similar to the bands.

The Minutes of the 1746 Bristol Conference widened the scope of those who could attend and suggested something about the character of the conferences: "Who are the properest persons to be present at our conferences? 1.) As many of the preachers as conveniently can come; 2.) the most earnest and most sensible of the band-leaders; . . . and 3.) any pious and judicious stranger who may occasionally be in the place."[104]

Although is it evident from the content of the rest of the Minutes that conferences conducted all manner of business, these kinds of statements in the Minutes make it clear that Methodist conferences were intended to be expressions of union and communion with the Triune God and one another at the heart of Wesley's understanding of salvation and the church embodied in the character of the conferences and the way they conducted business. These conferences seem generally to have been times of profound fellowship and worship.

---

101 *Works*, 10:125.

102 Ibid.

103 See Gareth Lloyd, *Charles Wesley and the Struggle for the Methodist Identity* (Oxford: Oxford University Press, 2007).

104 *Works*, 10:169.

When the conferences took up questions of doctrine, Wesley's Trinitarian understanding of the gospel and the *ordo salutis* found its way into the deliberations and the minutes that resulted.[105] The same is true of the conversations about discipline and practice. We find brief summaries of the character of bands, select societies, and groups for penitents that parallel the accounts of them that we examined above.[106] This is exactly what we would expect to find in the minutes concerning the deliberations of Wesley and the Methodist leaders on these various subjects. What is clear is that the Methodist conferences also included a Trinitarian dimension that is consistent with, and a reflection of, what we have seen thus far throughout this chapter and this entire study.[107]

5. *Means of Grace*

We examined Wesley's Trinitarian understanding of the means of grace, including the sacraments, in the last chapter. All grace in all its manifestations, from preventing to perfecting grace, is the direct activity of the Trinitarian Persons working together for human reconciliation and redemption. As Wesley said: "Christ does not give life to the soul separate from, but in and with himself. . . . Whatever grace we receive . . . we have this grace not *from* Christ but in him."[108]

The means of grace, those earthly historical structures or media through which the Trinitarian persons are immediately present and active, are simply the channels or means through which the Triune God freely and graciously promises to work for our salvation. What is particularly illuminating is how clear and consistent Wesley was about the core participatory Trinitarian activity that is at the center of all vital religion also being the crucial factor in the means of grace. It is the love of the Father through the grace of Christ in the fellowship of the Spirit that is at work through of means of grace, both those ordained by Christ in scripture and prudential ones that the Methodists developed.

---

105 Ibid., 10:126–27.

106 Ibid., 10:136–27.

107 I am well aware (1) that the character of the annual conferences became more legislative as time went on; (2) that Wesley was often rather vigorous and dominant force in the "free" conversations that took place; and (3) that there were squabbles, disagreements, and strained relationship at the conferences. This is always the case in the church when Christians are far from perfected in love.

108 Outler, ed., *Wesley*, 285–86.

This section will examine some additional evidence of the Trinitarian dimension in Wesley's understanding of various means of grace and the actual practice of those means of grace in early Methodism. The section will follow Maddox's way of grouping the means of grace.[109]

---

109 Maddox, *Responsible Grace*, 205–15. This section will not consider baptism and the Lord's Supper, since they were treated in the previous chapter.

Wesley utilized several typologies to organize his accounts of the means of grace (see Knight, *The Presence of God*, 2–5; Maddox, *Responsible Grace*, 193–94 and Collins, *Theology of John Wesley*, 257–59, 266. Knight's treatment is the fullest. In the Minutes of the 1745 Bristol Conference, we find a distinction between "general" means of grace (which include those intentions and practices that are to permeate the entire Christian life, like universal obedience to God's commands, denying ourselves, and bearing our cross on a daily basis) and "particular" means of grace (which include prayer, searching the scripture, communion, and fasting) (*Works*, 10:155). See also Knight, *The Presence of God*, 3.

A second way of categorizing the means of grace that Wesley employed repeatedly throughout his sermons and elsewhere is "works of piety" and "works of mercy" (*Works*, 3:313–14, 319; and 1:166). See also Knight, *The Presence of God*, 3–4. Works of piety include such practices as "reading and hearing the Word, public, family, private prayer, receiving the Lord's Supper, fasting," and even attending Christian conference (*Works*, 3:313). See also Collins, *Theology of John Wesley*, 257–58, especially for his comment on Christian conferencing.

Works of mercy entail doing all manner of good "whether they relate to the bodies or the souls of men; such as feeding the hungry, clothing the naked, entertaining the stranger, . . . endeavouring to instruct the ignorant, to awaken the stupid sinner . . . or contribute in any manner to the saving of souls from death" (*Works*, 1:166). See also Knight, *The Presence of God*, 3–4. These works of mercy are a means of grace, but they are also an end of religion; for as we saw in chapter 4 when we examined the social dimension of affections and tempers, the love of God in Christ via the Spirit awakens Christian love for others expressing itself in works of mercy so that, according to Wesley, Christians are to be more zealous for them than for works of piety (*Works*, 3:313–14). See also Knight, *The Presence of God*, 4.

The final way of classifying the means of grace for Wesley was to distinguish between "instituted" or ordinary means of grace and "prudential" means of grace. The ordinary means are those instituted by Christ and practiced by the universal church through the ages. Prudential means of grace are not explicitly commanded in scripture but emerge as we consider *general* rules given in scripture and apply them to *particular* circumstances via "common sense" or "reason and experience" (*Works*, 9:263). See also Collins, *Theology of John Wesley*, 266; and Knight, *The Presence of God*, 3. Examples of prudential means of grace include classes, bands, love feasts, covenant renewal services, and reading devotional literature.

Corporate Worship

Given his high estimation of the participatory Trinitarian depth of baptism and the Lord's Supper (the "grand channel" of grace), Wesley was adamant that the early Methodists use these means of grace. This meant Wesley had to encourage (plead, if not cajole) the Methodists to attend Anglican worship for the sacrament and liturgy.

In Anglican worship, it was not just the sacraments that were Trinitarian. The liturgies throughout the Anglican Book of Common Prayer were richly Trinitarian. Wesley's encouraging the Methodists to attend Anglican worship was partly rooted in his deep appreciation of the Anglican liturgy. In his preface to the *Sunday Service*, his abridged version of the liturgy from the Book of Common Prayer, which he sent over to the American Methodists in 1783 on the eve of the formation of the Methodist Episcopal Church, he asserted that "I believe there is no Liturgy in the world, either in ancient or modern language, which breathes more of a solid, scriptural, rational piety, than the Common Prayer of the Church of England."[110]

The sacraments and the liturgy of Anglican worship were Trinitarian twice over. They not only mediated the very economic Trinitarian activity that is grace, but the liturgies themselves also cognitively reflect this Trinitarian vision of God, grace, the gospel, and the church in their very language and verbal patterns.[111]

Methodism had its own corporate worship in the Methodist societies.[112] That worship included robust Trinitarian hymns and lively preaching by John and Charles Wesley. Preaching occurred both within societies and in all kinds of other places, indoors and out. Charles and especially John itinerated

---

110 Qtd. in Knight, *The Presence of God*, 161.

111 The Book of Common Prayer included a lectionary guide for the reading of scripture in worship, a cycle of readings that exposed worshipers to the economic Trinitarian tapestry of texts in scripture. Wesley retained the Anglican lectionary for Sunday worship in his *Sunday Service*. Anglican worship was structured the church year worship around Advent, Easter, and Ascension/Pentecost, including Trinity Sunday, though it contained many "holy days" devoted to saints that Wesley was not particularly fond of (see Maddox, *Responsible Grace*, 205–8). These seasons of the church year in their own way bore witness to the Trinitarian character of Christian faith, focusing on the Father sending the beloved Son into the world to suffer and die before raising him from the dead and pouring the Holy Spirit out upon the church at Pentecost. This very narrative at the heart of Christian story and the liturgical pattern of the church year that followed it were Trinitarian.

112 See Knight, *The Presence of God*, 92–95, 130–48, 160–66; Maddox, *Responsible Grace*, 202–5; and Collins, *Theology of John Wesley*, 259–62.

throughout the Methodist connection so that the vast majority of Methodists had opportunity to hear them preach.

We have seen how consistently Trinitarian many of Wesley's written sermons were. Surely he reflected this Trinitarian dimension in his oral sermons as well. The same is true of Charles Wesley. Jason Vickers has traced the development of a Trinitarian understanding of the gospel, salvation, and Christian faith in Charles Wesley's theology beginning around the same time it developed in John's theology from 1738 on after.[113] The deeply Trinitarian content of John's and Charles's sermons was reinforced by Charles's hymns. The practice of singing hymns at the beginning and ending of nearly every significant gathering earned Wesley's followers a reputation for their lively singing.[114]

It was here that Charles Wesley made an astonishing contribution to Methodism and the greater church with his imaginative ability to put deep theology into poetic verse in hymnody. There were many hymnals published in early Methodism. Most of the hymns were written by Charles, but John often edited and published them, including two entire hymnals devoted to the doctrine of the Trinity, one in 1746 and the second in 1767.[115] The 1767 *Hymns on the Trinity* contains 136 hymns divided into four parts.

Charles often took prose he highly valued and transformed it into poetry using his lyrical genius to transpose theology into wonderful hymns. That is what happened with the 1767 hymnal. Charles took William Jones's book *The Catholic Doctrine of the Trinity* and transformed it into verse.

Hymns on the Trinity closely followed Jones's book, which was designed to vindicate the Trinity in the face of the Arianism and Socinianism in England in the middle of the eighteenth century, as noted in chapter 1. The hymnal includes hymns entitled "The Divinity of Christ," "The Divinity of the Spirit,"

---

113 See Jason Vickers, *Invocation and Assent: The Making and Remaking of Trinitarian Theology* (Grand Rapids, MI: Eerdmans, 2008); and Jason Vickers, "Charles Wesley and the Revival of the Doctrine of the Trinity: A Methodist Contribution to Modern Theology," in *Charles Wesley: Life, Literature & Legacy*, ed. Kenneth G. C. Newport and Ted A. Campbell (Peterborough, England: Epworth, 2007), 278–98.

114 See Maddox, *Responsible Grace*, 208. John Wesley was deeply impressed by the Moravian use of hymns on his trip to Georgia, and he soon published a *Collection of Psalms and Hymns* for worship in the congregation he served in the colony. It was originally published in 1737 but was reprinted in 1992 (Nashville, TN: United Methodist Publishing House, 1992) (see Maddox, *Responsible Grace*, 208). The Anglican Church used metrical psalms, so this was one of Wesley's early innovations.

115 Charles Wesley, *Hymns on the Trinity*; and Charles Wesley, *Gloria Patri, & c. or Hymns to the Trinity* (London: Strahan, 1746).

"The Plurality and Trinity of Persons," and "Trinity in Unity." Charles added his own section of "Hymns and Prayers to the Trinity," which is noteworthy as Charles incorporated a profound personal and doxological dimension that deeply connected the Trinity with adoration and devotion.

While Charles's hymns were a frontal assault on Arianism and Socinianism, the hymns also had critical things to say about those who turned the Trinity into an intellectual artifact. According to Charles, we know the Trinity by participation in the gospel, not by the arid intellectual reasoning. Charles said it this way:

> Full credence we give,
> And exult to believe
> What our reason in vain would aspire to conceive:
> Not *against*, but *above*
> Our reason we prove
> Three Persons reveal'd in the essence of love.[116]
>
> Not from Creeds alone
> The doctrine we receive:
> Jehovah Three in One
> *He* gives us to believe
> The God of truth Himself imparts,
> And writes His name upon our hearts.[117]

Here is one more example of Charles's pointed affirmation that we know the Triune God by evangelical and doxological participation:

> The Tri-une God we cannot know,
> Unless He doth the faith bestow,
> Faith which remove our mountain load,
> And brings us to a Pard'ning God:
>
> Sure evidence of things unseen,
> Which swallows up the Gulph between,
> The Light of Life Divine imparts,
> And forms Jehovah in our hearts.
>
> O that we might all thus believe,
> The truth in humble love receive,

---

116 C. Wesley, *Hymns on the Trinity*, 91.
117 Ibid., 93–94.

Author of faith our Saviour find,
In God the Father of mankind;

In Both the Holy Spirit know
(Who doth where'er he listeth blow)
And the whole Trinity receive
For ever in our hearts to live![118]

In place of the polemical tone of Jones's book defending the Trinity, Charles portrays the Trinity as vibrant and life-giving, the ever-present source and goal of our salvation, of the church, indeed of all creation. The hymns provided a robust Trinitarian theology, like that of John Wesley, but very much unlike what we find in the works of the Trinitarian defenders of the doctrine.[119]

The "Advertisement" for the 1767 collection of *Hymns on the Trinity* captured Charles's intention:

> He [Charles] has never lost sight of the experimental and practical bearings of that doctrine. Mr. Jones has an excellent paragraph at the conclusion of his argument, warning his readers that a sound belief without a holy life will not profit them. But our poet, true to the mission of Methodism . . . devotes an entire section of his work to "Hymns and Prayers to the Trinity," in which the doctrine is presented in the most intimate connection with his own spiritual interests, and those of his readers. Such a mode of treating it is the best answer to those who represent it as a mere metaphysical speculation devoid of practical interest. . . . The "higher Christian life" is thus shown to be dependent upon the highest revealed mysteries, and these in their turn to minister illumination, help, and comfort in the humblest believer who receives the testimony of God concerning His Son.[120]

118 Ibid., 101–2. See also ibid., 102–3, 112–13, 115–16, and 119–20.

119 Ibid., 114.

120 Ibid., xv. There is evidence that Charles really did intend that the Methodists sing the hymns in this final section entitled "Hymns and Prayers to the Trinity" of his 1767 hymnal on the Trinity. Charles wrote the first twenty-four of those hymns in meters identical to twenty-four tunes composed by John Lampe for earlier hymns written by Charles, and Charles specified the tune for each (see S. T. Kimbrough Jr., preface, ibid., v–vi). Since we examined some of the suggestive Trinitarian content of Charles's hymns in chapter 2 above, this section will not develop and document the Trinitarian theology of Charles's hymns any further.

Charles injected a profound evangelical, doxological, and participatory Trinitarian dimension into the worship of early Methodism through his two hymnals on the Trinity. In addition, nearly 25 percent of the hymns in the 1780 *Collection of Hymns for the Use of the People Called Methodist*, the closest thing early Methodism had to an official hymnal, are explicitly Trinitarian. We find that the Trinitarian understanding of the Christian faith and the doctrine of the Trinity bound up with vital religion permeated the hymnody of early Methodism.[121]

Additional Communal Support

The societies along with the General Rules, classes, bands, select bands, and conferences were all preeminent structures for communal support in early Methodism, and they include a Trinitarian dimension as noted above. Yet there were others as well.

We mentioned love feasts earlier in connection with bands that met together periodically for just that purpose. The section on the bands above described the deep participatory Trinitarian dimension at the center of the "closer union" provided via the bands and was ensconced in the questions used by the bands. The love feast served as a way to "unite" the bands and, and according to Wesley, "to increase in them a grateful sense of all his [the Triune God's] mercies."[122] The Methodists gathered to share unconsecrated bread and water but also for prayer, praise, and fellowship, with a growing emphasis on testimony and thanksgiving over time. But it seems that as Methodism developed, love feasts became a monthly phenomenon open to all society members and even some outside of Methodism who might benefit from it.

---

121 David Tripp published the interesting little study on the 1780 *Collection of Hymns for the Use of the People Called Methodist* and found that just under 25 percent of the *1780 Hymns* are explicitly Trinitarian. This fact is very telling, as it reveals how deeply the Trinity is embedded in theology of the Wesley brothers and permeates their piety and worship. David Tripp also analyzed the 1989 United Methodist Hymnal for its explicitly Trinitarian hymns and found a far lower percentage (see Tripp, "Methodism's Trinitarian Hymnody: A Sampling, 1780 and 1989, and Some Questions," *Quarterly Review* 14, no. 4 [Winter 1994–95]: 359–85). See also Barry E. Bryant, "Trinity and Hymnody: The Doctrine of the Trinity in the Hymns of Charles Wesley," *Wesleyan Theological Journal* 25, no. 2 (Fall 1990): 64–73.

122 *Works*, 9:267. See Maddox, *Responsible Grace*, 210; and Higgins Matthaei, *Making Disciples*, 137.

In his journal entry for Sunday, July 19, 1761, Wesley recounted his attending a love feast, and what he said gives insight into the character of this structure for communal support:

> I hastened back to the love-feast at Birstall. I was the first of the kind which had been there. Many were surprised when I told them, "The very design of a love-feast is a free and familiar conversation, in which every man, yea, and every woman, has liberty to speak whatever may be to the glory of God." Several then did speak, and not in vain: the flame ran from heart to heart. Especially while one was declaring with all simplicity the manner wherein God, during the morning sermon (on the words, "I will: be thou clean"), had set her soul at full liberty. Two men also spoke to the same effect, and two others who had found peace with God. We then joyfully poured out our souls before God and praised him for his marvelous works.[123]

All three Trinitarian persons are noted in Wesley's account: the words of the sermon text, "Be thou clean," are those of Christ from Matthew 8:3. Wesley identified the Spirit as "the flame" that ran from heart to heart. Together in response to the palpable presence of the Triune God in their midst these Methodists responded by praising God, so love feasts were profound times of fellowship with God and one another and of personal sharing of what the Triune God of the gospel was doing in people's lives.[124]

A final structure of communal support was the service of covenant renewal. Here Wesley drew upon the Puritan Richard Alleine and his *Vindiciae pietatis*, which Wesley included in his Christian Library. Alleine's work urged periodically renewing one's covenant with God. Wesley adapted portions of the work into covenant renewal service for the Methodists at the Spitalfields. This service soon became a New Year's Day practice and a tradition in Methodism.[125]

The basic liturgy for this early Methodist form of communal support can be found in the *United Methodist Book of Worship*. The liturgy focused on

---

123 *Works*, 21:336.

124 Another structure of communal support was Letter Days. These were similar to love feasts, though there was no partaking of bread and water but rather the sharing of "letters" from various persons connected with the Methodist movement containing news or accounts of how Triune God was at work in their lives. They were spiritual testimonies of encounters with the living God, similar to the sharing that took place at love feasts (Heitzenrater, *Wesley and the People*, 146).

125 See Maddox, *Responsible Grace*, 210–11; Heitzenrater, *Wesley and the People*, 98; and Higgins Matthaei, *Making Disciples*, 137.

the affirmation of God's forgiveness and faithfulness and on the renewal of people's commitment to God and to a life of discipleship. The entire service is deeply and pervasively Trinitarian. Here are some selections from the final covenant prayer that provide a sense of how Trinitarian the service was:

> I here acknowledge you as my Lord and God.
> I take you, Father, Son, and Holy Spirit for my portion,
> and vow to give up myself, body and soul, as your servant . . .
> I renounce my own wisdom and take you for my only guide . . .
> I do here willingly put my neck under your yoke, to carry your burden . . .
> I will strive to order my whole life according to your direction . . .
> And now, glory be to you, O God the Father,
> whom I from this day forward shall look upon as my God and Father.
> Glory be to you, O God the Son,
> who have loved me and washed me from my sins in your own blood,
> and now is my Savior and Redeemer.
> Glory be to you, O God the Holy Spirit,
> who by your almighty power have turned my heart from sin to God.
> O mighty God, the Lord Omnipotent, Father, Son, and Holy Spirit,
> you have now become my Covenant Friend.
> And I through your infinite grace, have become your covenant servant.
> So be it.
> And let the covenant I have made on earth be ratified in heaven.
> Amen.[126]

The depth of this prayer reflects a participatory Trinitarian understanding of the essence of Christian faith, and the prayer is the centerpiece of the culmination of the covenant renewal service.

Devotional Practices

In addition to communal support, Wesley provided a range of directions and resources for various devotional practices. He argued that "we have need daily to retire from the world, at least morning and evening to converse with God, to commune more freely with our Father."[127] This study has documented and described a wide range of Wesley's publications where he consistently stated that communing with the Father depends upon being

126 *The United Methodist Book of Worship* (Nashville: United Methodist Publishing House, 1992), 293–94.
127 *Works*, 1:534.

united to the Son of God in the fellowship of the Spirit. He encouraged the early Methodists to set aside time in the morning and evening for this kind of Trinitarian communion through reading scripture and edifying literature, and prayer.[128]

Wesley emphasized the importance of prayer, both in private and in various informal communal settings, like a family gathering for that purpose. In his sermon "The Means of Grace," Wesley listed prayer as the first means God has ordained whereby "all who desire the grace of God are to wait for it." Wesley reminded his readers of Christ's words in the Sermon on the Mount, "Ask, and it shall be given to you," for "here we are in the plainest manner directed to ask in order to, or as a *means* of, receiving; to seek in order to find the grace of God, the pearl of great price."[129]

In his tract "The Character of a Methodist," Wesley said that prayer is one of the marks of a Methodist. Wesley provided a remarkable Trinitarian vision of prayer in this tract:

> Indeed he "prays without ceasing." . . Not that he is always in the house of prayer. . . . Neither is he always on his knees. . . . Nor yet is he always crying aloud to God, or calling upon him in words. For many times "the Spirit maketh intercession for him, with groans that cannot be uttered." But at all times the language of his heart is this: "Thou brightness of the eternal glory [the Son], unto thee is my mouth, though without a voice, and my silence speaketh unto thee." And this is true prayer, the lifting up the heart to God. This is the essence of prayer, and this alone. But his heart is ever lifted up to God, at all times, and in all places . . . Whether he lie down or rise up, "God is in all his thoughts"; he "walks with God" continually, having the loving eye of his mind still fixed upon him.[130]

In order to aid the Methodists in their life of prayer, Wesley developed collections of written prayers for praying alone or in families. An example is *A Collection of Forms of Prayer for Every Day in the Week*. The work included morning and evening prayers for each day of the week. The opening prayer of the work for Sunday morning reads this way:

> Almighty God, Father of all Mercies, I thy unworthy Servant desire to present myself, with all humility, before Thee, to offer my morning sacrifice of love and thanksgiving! Glory be to Thee, O most adorable Father, who

128 See Maddox, *Responsible Grace*, 214.

129 *Works*, 1:384.

130 *Works*, 9:37. See Higgins Matthaei, *Making Disciples*, 153.

> after thou hadst finished the work of creation, entered into thy eternal rest. Glory to Thee, O Holy Jesus, who having thro' the Eternal Spirit offered Thyself a full, perfect, and sufficient sacrifice for the sins of the whole world, didst rise again the third day from the dead, and hadst all power given to Thee both in heaven and on earth. Glory be to Thee, O Blessed Spirit, who proceeding from the Father and the Son, didst come down with many tongues on the Apostles, on the first day of the week, and didst enable them to preach the Glad Tidings of Salvation to a sinful world, and hast ever since been moving on the faces of Men's souls, as thou didst once on the Face of the great deep, bringing them out of the dark chaos in which they were involved. Glory to thee, O Holy Undivided Trinity, for jointly concurring in the great work of our Redemption, and the restoring us again to the glorious liberty of the sons of God.[131]

This is a profound prayer, with deep Trinitarian theological content. Especially noteworthy is Wesley clear linking of the Holy Spirit to the life, death, and resurrection of the Incarnate Son, Jesus Christ. According to the prayer, Christ's entire sacrificial work took place only in and through the Holy Spirit echoing Hebrews 9:14. This point is reinforced when Wesley spoke of the Trinitarian persons "concurring" in the great work of human redemption, providing further evidence that the concept of "perichoresis" is part of Wesley's Trinitarian theology.

It is clear that Wesley was not timid about incorporating this kind of deep Trinitarian theology and piety into the prayer life of the early Methodists. The question that immediately comes to mind is whether or not this Trinitarian dimension made it into the lives and piety of the Methodist laity.

The Trinitarian Piety of the Early Methodist Laity

Thomas Albin, an expert on Charles Wesley and on spirituality in early Methodism, pointed out to me that the letters and journals of the early Methodist laity, mostly unpublished, contain many references to the Trinity in relation to their Christian lives and piety. I found this rather intriguing, and it was one of the early motivations for writing this book. The fact that Wesley's Trinitarian vision of Christian faith found its way into the piety of the early Methodists discloses another facet of how the Trinitarian dimension was actually embodied in the Wesleyan movement.

131 John Wesley, *A Collection of Forms of Prayer for Every Day in the Week* (Newcastle upon Tyne: John Gooding, 1743), 2.

In his letters to various Methodist laypersons, as noted in chapters 2 and 3, John Wesley on occasion asked them if they have "a clear sense of the presence of the ever-blessed Trinity."[132] The intention of Wesley's question is clear from all that we have seen thus far in the study: he was asking about the "knowledge of the Three-One God . . . interwoven with all true Christian faith, with all vital religion."[133] Wesley was questioning the state of this Methodist layperson's soul in explicitly Trinitarian terms because he thought that all true Christian faith, all vital religion, has its origin and its telos in the three-one God.

At least some of the early Methodist laity picked up this Trinitarian dimension and spoke of it as well. When we read the unpublished letters and journals of the early Methodist laity, we find that some of them expressed and interpreted their Christian faith and lives in Trinitarian categories like those we have seen throughout this study. What follows are examples of what is in the letters and journals of the laity.

In a letter dated in early 1777 to Hetty (Hester Anne Roe), a Methodist laywoman, John Wesley quoted from the papers of a Methodist layperson who recounted his evangelical and doxological encounter with the Trinitarian God:

> Just after my uniting with the Methodists, the Father was revealed to me the first time; soon after, the whole Trinity. I beheld the distinct Persons of the Godhead, and worshipped one undivided Jehovah, and each Person separately. . . . When I approach Jesus, the Father and the Spirit commune with me.
>
> Whatever I receive now, centres in taking leave of earth, and hasting to another place. I am as one that is no more. I stand and look on what God has done; his calls, helps, mercies, forbearances, deliverances from sorrows, rescues out of evils; and I adore and devote myself to Him with new ardour. If it be asked how, or in what manner, I beheld the Triune God, it is above all description. . . . I was overwhelmed with it; body and soul were penetrated through with the rays of Deity.[134]

132 See Wesley's letter to Jane Bisson dated December 1787 in John Wesley, *The Works of John Wesley*, ed. Thomas Jackson, 14 vols., 3rd ed. (London: Wesleyan Methodist Book Room, 1872; reprint ed. Grand Rapids, MI: Baker Book House, 1986), 13:107.

133 *Works*, 2:385

134 *Works* (Jackson), 13:79–80.

The Trinitarian piety of this early Methodist is remarkable, although he could have benefited from knowing how to use the Trinitarian symbols with a bit more theological precision.

Another example is Ann Cutler, who said that she daily renewed her covenant with the Triune God: "I have union with the Trinity thus. I see the Son through the Spirit, I find the Father through the Son, and God is my all in all."[135] This statement of Ann Cutler is even more interesting since it bears even greater similarity to the participatory, economic Trinitarian perspective we find in both John and Charles Wesley.

Here is one final example by an anonymous person who wrote to Wesley in 1790 and provided the following account of what seems to have happened during the celebration of the Lord's Supper: "The Father, Son and Holy Ghost encompassed about me. I felt surrounded with Deity . . . swallowed up, I would almost say, in the beatific vision."[136]

There is evidence that Wesley at one point associated some kind of conscious awareness of union and communion with all three Trinitarian Persons with Christian perfection, though later he seemed to change his mind on the matter. In June 1777, he wrote to Hannah Ball and said, "I have lately made diligent inquiry into the experiences of many that are perfected in love. And I find very few of them who have had a clear revelation of the several Persons of the ever-blessed Trinity. It therefore appears that this is by no means essential to Christian Perfection."[137]

In a later letter to Lady Maxwell, Wesley made the same point that this kind of Trinitarian encounter was not the experience of everyone perfected in love but adds that it is a "wonderful instance of divine mercy."[138] The very fact that Wesley questioned whether "a clear revelation of the several Persons of the ever-blessed Trinity" might be included in Christian perfection reveals how crucial the Trinitarian dimension was, not only in Wesley's theology but in his vision of how the Trinitarian God was present in the lives of the laity in a recognizable manner.

---

135 William Bramwell, *A Short Account of the Life and Death of Ann Cutler* (Sheffield, 1796), 18. See Henry C. Rack, "Early Methodist Visions of the Trinity," in *Proceedings of the Wesley Historical Society* 46 (1987–88): 40–41.

136 See Rack, "Early Methodist Visions of the Trinity," 42, for this quotation, which originally appeared in the *Arminian Magazine* in 1790, 247.

137 See Rack, "Early Methodist Visions of the Trinity," 43, for this quotation, which can be found in *The Letters of the Rev. John Wesley, A.M.*, ed. John Telford, vols. 1–8, (London: Epworth Press, 1931), 6:43:266.

138 See Rack, "Early Methodist Visions of the Trinity," 44, for this quotation, which can be found in *The Letters of the Rev. John Wesley*, 7:392.

Whatever we make of these amazing accounts, it is noteworthy that some of the Methodist laypersons thought and talked about their Christian faith and piety in such vivid Trinitarian language. It seems that the Trinitarian dimension of Wesley's vision of Christian faith, of the *ordo salutis*, and of the church found its way into the Christian faith, piety, and conversation of the Methodist laity. What makes this point even more noteworthy is that John and Charles Wesley effectively mediated this vibrant Trinitarian vision of Christian faith and life to the Methodist laity in the aftermath of the Trinitarian controversies when the defenders detached the Trinity from vital Christian faith, worship, piety, and life by turning the doctrine into an abstract intellectual puzzle.

Works of Mercy

We have already examined works of mercy in several other contexts, including the sociality that is part of the very being of the holy affections and tempers at the center of Wesley's vision of how the Triune God transforms our lives together in union and communion with God and one another, as described in chapter 4. Wesley asserted that mercy "cannot possibly have a being" without social embodiment, for mercy only arises in, with, and out of soteriological relations of union and communion with the Triune God and exists in and with relations with other people. While works of mercy flow from and are inherently bound up with the being of transformed affections and tempers, they are also, according to Wesley, real means of grace.[139]

Anyone who has been involved in ministry knows that loving and serving others is a channel of God's grace not only for those are ministered to but also for the person used by God to serve and bless others. This was a crucial insight that helped move the Methodists from viewing works of mercy in a unidirectional fashion from the doers to the recipients, to a more fully communal, interpersonal, two-way interaction in which both giver and receiver are caught up in an event where the Triune God's presence and activity encompasses giver and receiver both blessed and bound together in fellowship in the event that is a "work of mercy." It is not coincidental that Wesley told the Methodists that they are not simply to care for the poor in

139 *Works*, 1:535. As Wesley expressed it in his sermon "On Zeal," which we examined at some length in chapter 3: "In an exterior circle [around holy tempers with love on the throne in the center] are all the *works of mercy* . . . . By these we exercise all holy tempers; by these we continually improve them, so that all these are real *means of grace* (ibid., 3:313).

various ways, providing them with food and clothing, but personally embrace them, interact with them, and befriend them.

For Wesley, works of mercy were extraordinarily far-reaching, encompassing all the ways we can relieve the distress of our neighbors or in any other way serve them, whether spiritually or materially. Because of this profound vision of works of mercy as being Trinitarian means of grace, early Methodism manifested an equally robust vision and embodiment of the priesthood of all believers in which every Methodist was invited to be involved in ministry.

6. Nurtured in Community for Ministry

Since the goal of all grace is faith expressing itself through community in love for God and neighbor, Wesley realized that every Christian needed to be involved in ministry. To deny the laity the opportunity to be in ministry to others is to bottle up the grace of the Triune God in their lives, frustrate its intention, and prevent it from finding its natural expression in concrete acts of love toward God and others. Even people who had experienced only prevenient and convicting grace needed to respond to God's Trinitarian grace by avoiding evil and doing good to others. Consequently it comes as no surprise that after his plain and clear "account of the *people* commonly called Methodists is his "A Plain Account of the People Called Methodists," Wesley provided "a short account [five pages] of those who *serve* their brethren in love. These are the *Leaders* of classes and bands . . . *Assistants, Stewards, Visitors* of the sick, and *Schoolmasters*."[140] Wesley added an additional five pages of various ministries of mercy in early Methodism to the poor, the sick, widows, orphaned children, children needing educating and clothing, and those needing short-term loans.

Works of mercy and ministry in the broadest sense of the word turn out to be nearly synonymous. Everything noted about the inherent sociality of transformed affections and tempers, where expressions of love in works of mercy are bound up with transformed affections and the Trinitarian matrix of union and communion with God and one another in which they exist, also applies to ministry.

Early Methodism was able to develop such an astonishing array of ministries because Wesley and the Methodists embodied the priesthood of all believers by which the body of Christ expresses itself in community, building itself up in love, and extending that love to a hurting and broken world, not because this is a good thing to do or even because it is enjoined in Scripture,

140 *Works*, 9:270.

but because ministry is bound up with the inherent Trinitarian sociality of the transformed affections and tempers.

Wesley and the Methodist traveling lay preachers moved across the landscape of England using a scandalous method of evangelism called "field preaching," employed by George Whitefield, the great Calvinist evangelist. It was an efficacious way to initially reach those outside the Anglican Church in Wesley's day. We have already noted that this profound missional intentionality on the part of Wesley and the early Methodists was rooted in that same sociality inherent of the transformed affections and tempers, a sociality that by its very character reaches out beyond the body of Christ toward all those persons who are objects of the Love of God the Father through the grace of Jesus Christ in the communion of the Spirit.[141] Wesley and his lay preachers went out in the highways and byways of England, preaching the gospel to those who had not yet embraced the love of God in Christ.

In the second half of his "Plain Account of the People Called Methodists," Wesley identified a number of the different offices or officers in Methodism, including *Leaders* of classes and bands, *Assistants, Stewards, Visitors* of the sick, and *Schoolmasters*.[142] Wesley provided training for persons serving in these capacities, including developing lists of their responsibilities and "rules" concerning how they should conduct themselves. We see some of Wesley's practical administrative genius in his ability to create these kinds of structures for ministry and its oversight, along with providing training and resources so that those who stepped into these positions might flourish and succeed.[143]

With regard to Wesley's *Assistants* or *Lay Assistants* or lay preachers, what is illuminating in terms of the Trinitarian dimension in Wesley's view of ministry is the process for entering this form of ministry and the questions used to examine candidates. At the Newcastle Conference in 1749, Wesley and the Conference put in place a five-step method for receiving a new "Helper": (1) be "recommended" "by the Assistant to whose Society he belongs"; (2) "read and carefully weigh" the doctrine and discipline recorded in the Minutes and, of course, agreement is presupposed; (3) accept the position of "Probationer" and receive the copy of the Minutes, with a note indicating that the Probationer was on "probation" and needed to "make

141 As Wesley pointed out, "The more they [Christians] are filled with the life of God, the more tenderly will they be concerned for those who are still without God in the world, still dead in trespasses and sins" (*Works*, 1:499).

142 *Works*, 9:270.

143 See ibid., 9:270–80 for Wesley's account of these offices and ministries in Methodism.

full proof that God has called you hereto"; (4) after a year, be "received as a Helper" and accept a new copy of the Minutes with an inscription stating that "So long as you freely consent and earnestly endeavour to walk according to the following rules, we rejoice to go on with you hand in hand"; (5) know that "this full acceptance as a helper is renewable yearly and that a new copy of the Minutes would be given and the old one returned at each annual conference.[144]

Candidates who hoped to serve as lay preachers or helpers or assistants, as they were variously called, had to read and assent to the Conference Minutes, including Methodist doctrine and discipline with their Trinitarian dimension documented in the section on Conferences above. They also had to "make full proof" that the Triune God had called them to the office. This brings us to the examination of candidates.

At the 1746 Conference in Bristol, Wesley and the Conference developed careful guidelines for examining those who believed they were called to serve as lay preachers. The Minutes read: "How shall we try those who believe they are moved by the Holy Ghost and called of God to preach?"[145] At this point in the study, the reader should be able to guess what the response will be. If Christian faith, if the church, if the means of grace, if ministry are all participatory and Trinitarian, then should not a lay preacher be a person caught up in this Trinitarian activity?

This is how the Minutes stated it: "Do they know in whom they have believed? Have they the love of God in their hearts? Do they desire to seek nothing but God? And are they holy in all manner of conversation?"[146] Here we see again a participatory understanding of Christian faith with its inherent Trinitarian dimension documented in chapters 2–4 above where Wesley repeatedly explicitly stated that it is the love of God in Christ that is shed abroad in their hearts by the Holy Spirit. The Methodists wanted preachers who really *knew* the love of God the Father through the grace of the Lord Jesus Christ in the fellowship of the Holy Spirit and who lived sufficiently in union and communion with the Triune God that their affections and tempers were transformed and they therefore manifested holiness in all manner of their conversation.[147]

---

144 See *Works,* 10:235–36. See also Heitzenrater, *Wesley and the People*, 174–75.

145 Ibid., 10:177.

146 Ibid. Conversation for Wesley and the early Methodists implied all conduct, in word and deed.

147 *Works*, 1:305.

In addition to knowing whom they believed, they needed gifts and grace for the work. This included, according to the Minutes, "a clear sound *understanding*," "a right judgement in the things of God," and "a just conception of *salvation by faith*."[148] But it is the third qualification that we find in the Minutes that is especially illuminating: "Have they success? Do they not only so speak as generally to convince or affect the heart? But have any received remission of sins under their preaching? A clear and lasting sense of the love of God?"[149] The intent is clear. If lay preachers were really called by the Spirit of God to the ministry, peoples' lives will be transformed by the Triune God through their ministries. Others will encounter the participatory, economic activity of the Trinitarian persons in and through their preaching and wider ministry. The minutes concluded by saying that when all three of these marks "undeniably concur in any, we *allow* him to be called."[150]

It is clear that the Triune God is free to work through human vessels with varying degrees of unworthiness. But the point of the three marks is deeper. What is the blessed Triune God's preferred way to work? Is it not through those who actually participate in the Trinitarian verities that make the gospel what it is? And should not a movement of renewal like early Methodism be concerned with the integrity of the minister as well as the ministry? Here the spiritual and moral rigor of Wesley's Trinitarian vision of the power of the gospel to transform human life was evident in application to ministry and in those called to serve as lay preachers.

Since the Triune God's love extended to the whole person, so did the love of Wesley and the early Methodists, who developed an astonishing range of ministries to care for all the needs of the whole person: schools, poor widows' homes, and orphanages, as well as providing clothing and food for those who needed it. Remember that this kind of concrete embodiment of love in personal works of mercy, caring for others' spiritual and physical well-being is bound up with the sociality of the transformed affections and tempers that occurs in union and communion with the Triune God and one another. Wesley and the early Methodists believed that ministry to the whole person, including physical well-being, is integral to the pilgrimage of faith, the order of salvation, and the church as the body of Christ. For Wesley, to fail to love is a violation of the very being and nature of love in persons restored to the image of a Trinitarian God.

---

148 *Works*, 10:177.

149 Ibid., 10:178.

150 Ibid.

It is no coincidence that Wesley recounted in his "Plain Account of the People Called Methodists," "I was still in pain for many of the poor that were sick . . . I saw the poor people pining away, and several families ruined, and that without remedy."[151] A few pages later, Wesley said, "A year or two ago I observed among many a distress of another kind. They frequently wanted, perhaps in order to carry on their business, a present supply of money. They scrupled to make use of a *pawnbroker*." In response, Wesley "begged" for resources, raised fifty pounds, and set up a lending stock so that those who needed it could procure twenty shillings to be repaid in three months (250 loans in the first year). A few lines later he added, "Will not God put it into the heart of some lover of mankind to increase this little stock?"[152] Wesley wrote his *Primitive Physic* to provide affordable health care to the thousands of poor throughout England who had no access to doctors.[153] The Trinitarian taproot of these ministries lies deep in the sociality of love and transformed holy affections and tempers that takes place in, with, and out of union and communion with Triune God in the gospel and in the Trinitarian dimension of Wesley's soteriology and ecclesiology.

We conclude this section with Wesley's account of the "Poorhouse" he and the Methodists developed to care for feeble aged widows and orphans:

> In this . . . "Poorhouse" we have now nine widows, a blind woman, two poor children, two upper servants, a maid and a man. I might add, four or five preachers. For I myself, as well as the other preachers who are in town, diet with the poor on the same food and at the same table. And we rejoice therein as a comfortable earnest of our eating bread together in our Father's kingdom. I have blessed God for this house ever since it began; but even lately much more than ever . . . I can now say to all the World, "Come, and see how these Christians love one another!"[154]

We see Wesley's understanding of the dawn of the proper gospel day and a proper Christian church in the practices of these early Methodists who developed a remarkable range of ministries arising out of the sociality of Trinitarian love.[155]

---

151 *Works*, 9:275.

152 Ibid., 9:279.

153 John Wesley, *Primitive Physic: An Easy and Natural Method of Curing Most Diseases*, Library of Methodist Classics (Nashville: United Methodist Publishing House, 1992).

154 Ibid., 277.

155 *Works*, 2:455.

IV. Conclusion

What the reader should not miss is the coinherence of Wesley's evangelical, doxological, participatory Trinitarian vision of (1) salvation and (2) the church. But also the embodiment of that Trinitarian vision in (3) discipleship in connection, including discipline in the context of connection, that came to expression in (4) the organized forms of community, life, ministry, and mission that reflect Trinitarian vision and that were reproducible. The Trinitarian dimension of Wesley's spiritual/theological vision of God, salvation, and the church, along with disciplined discipleship in connection, and forms of ministry, polity, community, and life developed in early Methodism were profoundly interconnected and mutually reinforcing.

Despite the foibles of Wesley (and there were more than a few) and the nearly continuous problems in the Methodist movement that threatened its unity and its integrity (connection is always imperfect this side of the eschaton), this kind of comprehensive embodiment of a participatory, economic Trinitarian vision of Christian faith is remarkable. I am not suggesting that Wesley and the early Methodists consciously incorporated a Trinitarian dimension into the communal structures and practices of Methodism. Nor am I arguing Wesley and the early Methodists were fully cognizant of the way the Trinitarian dimension found its way into the various facets of Methodism. Wesley made it clear in his sermon on the Trinity that the Trinitarian dimension of Christian faith is far deeper and more subtle—even if Christians are not always consciously aware of, and explicit about, the participatory, economic, Trinitarian presence and activity, "if you ask any of them a few questions you will easily find it is implied in what he believes."[156] This chapter documented, explained, and described this Trinitarian dimension that found its way into the developing structures of life, community, and ministry in early Methodism in a significant manner consistent with Wesley's doctrine of the Trinity bound up with vital piety and with the Trinitarian dimension of Wesley's understanding of essence of Christian faith, soteriology, and ecclesiology.

---

156 Ibid., 3:385–86.

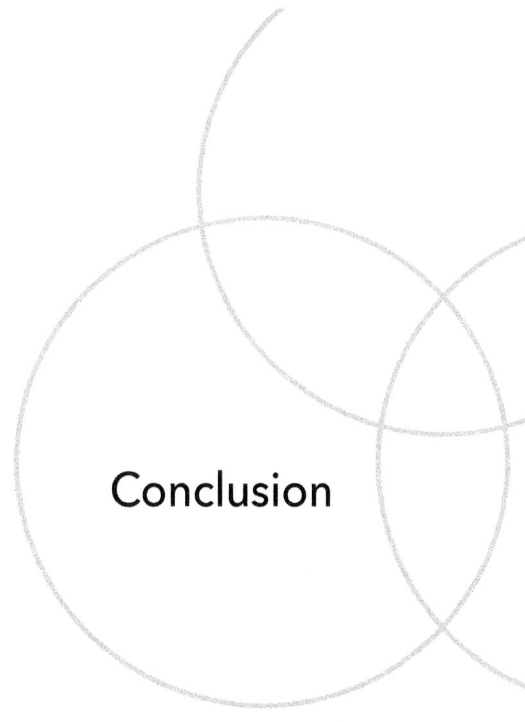

Conclusion

The purpose of this book has been to identify, document, and describe the Trinitarian dimension of Wesley's theology. For Wesley, the Trinity is not merely an intellectual artifact affirmed by the church through the ages but rather the divine source, agency, and telos of Christian faith, life, community, and ministry. Wesley believed that the gospel and human participation in it arise out the patterned activity of the Trinitarian persons. John and Charles Wesley retrieved this Trinitarian vision of Christian faith and life and injected it into early Methodism during the era that witnessed the demise of the doctrine of the Trinity for many in England and beyond.

Chapter 1 documented the Trinitarian controversies in the seventeenth and eighteenth centuries that swept over the British Isles in wave after wave and embroiled many of the greatest intellects of that era in deep and bitter debate. Those controversies were part of a wider intellectual and cultural turmoil and transition that generated modern Western culture. From the inroads of Socinianism in the early seventeenth century, through debates in which the defenders of the Trinity turned the doctrine into an esoteric intellectual puzzle, to the formation of the first openly Unitarian congregation in 1774, chapter 1 chronicled the unraveling of the doctrine of the Trinity, including the loss of its significance for Christian faith and life. It was in the midst of this unraveling that the Wesley brothers provided an alternative way to be Trinitarian and placed the Trinity at the center of vibrant Christian faith and life.

In his sermon "On the Trinity," Wesley distanced himself from defenders of the doctrine in the Trinitarian debates and argued that the Trinity "enters into the very heart of Christianity" so that it is impossible to be Christian without being Trinitarian as well. According to Wesley, "Knowledge of the Three-One God is interwoven with all true Christian faith, with all vital religion." "I know not how anyone can be a Christian believer," Wesley argued, "till God the Holy Ghost witnesses that God the Father has accepted him through the merits of God the Son—and having this witness he honours the Son and the blessed Spirit 'even as he honours the Father.'"[1] For Wesley, all three persons of the Trinity are involved in the gospel and our participation in the pattern of God the Father's reconciling activity through the incarnate Son, Jesus Christ, and his life, death, and resurrection, a reconciliation realized in Christians' lives through the fellowship of the Holy Spirit.

It is a pattern of personal presence and activity through which the Trinitarian persons mutually mediate and reveal one another. In Wesley's words:

> Happiness undoubtedly begins when we begin to know him [God] by the teaching of his own Spirit; when it pleases the Father to reveal his Son in our heart, so that we can humbly say, "My Lord and my God"; and when the Son is pleased to reveal his Father in us, "by the Spirit of adoption, crying in our hearts, Abba Father," bearing his testimony to our spirits, that we are children of God. Then it is that "the love of God" also "is shed abroad in our hearts." And according to the degree of our love is the degree of our happiness.[2]

This is the *evangelical* movement of Trinitarian divine agency toward us in our salvation that restores us to union and communion with the Father through the Son in the Spirit and frees our human agency for a free, full, and joyous response that Wesley described as a holiness and happiness.

The *doxological* movement of our response to this encounter with the Trinitarian persons in the gospel is shaped by what we come to know of this Trinitarian God in the gospel and our participation in it. Wesley stated the essential point forcefully: "We are to 'honour the Son even as we honour the Father.' We are to pay him the same worship as we pay to the Father. We are to love him with all our heart and soul; and to consecrate all we have and are, all we think, speak, and do to the Three-One God, Father, Son and

---

1 *The Works of John Wesley*, ed. Albert C. Outler, vols. 1–4, *Sermons* (Nashville: Abingdon, 1984–87), 2:385.

2 *Works*, 3:283

Spirit, world without end!"[3] Implicit in Wesley's account of the presence and activity of all three Trinitarian persons in the gospel, in our encounter with the gospel, and in our response is that deep soteriological and doxological conviction concerning the divinity of Christ and the Holy Spirit found in early church: only God can save, and only God is worthy of our worship.

Wesley realized that not every Christian is focally aware of the robust Trinitarian content of this evangelical, doxological, participatory encounter with the Triune God in the gospel: "Not that every Christian believer *adverts* to this; perhaps at first not one in twenty; but if you ask any of them a few questions you will easily find it is implied in what he believes. Therefore I do not see how it is possible for any to have vital religion who denies that these three are one."[4] What we come to know of the Triune God in our encounter with the gospel entails a tacit dimension of theologically rich Trinitarian content that can become explicit: God the Holy Spirit witnesses that God the Father loves and accepts us through the merits of God the Son's life, death, and resurrection. For Wesley, this is how we come to know the Triune God as three-in-one and one-in-three or "Trinity in Unity and Unity in Trinity."[5] It is what Wesley meant when he said that "knowledge of the Three-One God is interwoven with all true Christian faith, with all vital religion."[6] This evangelical, doxological, participatory, economic Trinitarian pattern is characteristic of all that John Wesley had to say about the Trinity, and this pattern is the Trinitarian dimension of his theology.

Chapter 2 identified, documented, and explained Wesley's characteristic way of summarizing the essence of Christian faith in participatory, economic Trinitarian categories throughout his sermons and other publications from the spring of 1738 on after Peter Böhler introduced Wesley to this "new faith." There are striking similarities between these Trinitarian summaries and what Wesley said about the Trinity in his sermon. Wesley saw the Trinity as bound up with our basic evangelical and doxological encounter with the gospel, and he summarized the essence of Christian faith in the same Trinitarian terms of our participatory encounter with the presence and activity of the Trinitarian persons in the gospel.

Wesley depicted the Trinitarian essence of Christian faith as a kind of spiritual respiration:

---

3 *Works*, 4:106.

4 *Works*, 2:385–86.

5 *Works*, 1:581.

6 *Works*, 2:385.

> And now he may properly be said *to live*: God having quickened him by his Spirit, he is alive to God through Jesus Christ. . . God is continually breathing, as it were, upon his soul, and his soul is breathing unto God. Grace is descending into his heart, and prayer and praise ascending to heaven. And by this intercourse between God and man, this fellowship with the Father and the Son, as by a kind of spiritual respiration, the life of God in the soul is sustained: and the child of God grows up, till he comes to "the full measure of the stature of Christ."[7]

This text from Wesley's sermon "The New Birth" epitomizes what I mean when I characterize his theology as evangelical, doxological, participatory, economic, and Trinitarian. The theological content of these terms comes progressively into view by attending to what Wesley said about the Trinity and the Trinitarian dimension documented throughout the chapters of this book.

Wesley not only understood the center of Christian faith in Trinitarian categories, this Trinitarian wellspring of the New Creation was spiritually and theologically central to Wesley's soteriology and ecclesiology. There is Trinitarian dimension in Wesley's entire soteriology, including grace and the *ordo salutis* from prevenient through perfecting grace, as chapter 3 made clear. All three persons of the Trinity are present in a pattern of co-activity throughout the order of salvation. According to Wesley, even our eschatological destiny involves "a deep, an intimate, an uninterrupted union with God; a constant communion with the Father and his son Jesus Christ, through the Spirit; a continual enjoyment of the Three-One God, and of all the creatures in him!"[8] It is no coincidence that Charles Wesley wrote hymns so that the early Methodists could sing their Trinitarian faith and salvation: "And when we rise in love renew'd, / Our souls resemble Thee, / An image of the Triune God, / To all eternity," and "You whom he ordained to be Transcripts of the Trinity."[9] The Triune God is the source, the divine agent, and the goal of Wesley's *ordo salutis*.

The robust Trinitarian dimension of Wesley's soteriology also found its way into his classic definition of the church in his "Letter to a Roman Catholic"

---

7 Ibid., 2:192–94.

8 Ibid., 2:510.

9 See Charles Wesley, hymn # LXXXVII, in *Hymns on the Trinity*, (repr., Madison, NJ: Charles Wesley Society, 1998), 58; and *The Works of John Wesley*, ed. Franz Hildebrant and Oliver A. Beckerlegge, vol. 7, *A Collection of Hymns for the Use of the People Called Methodists* (New York: Oxford University Press, 1983), 88.

as those "who have fellowship with God the Father, Son and Holy Ghost."[10] Chapter 4 documented that Wesley repeatedly defined the essence of the church in same participatory Trinitarian terms he used when he summarized the gospel and discussed various themes throughout the *ordo salutis*. The church is constituted by its evangelical encounter with the activity of all three persons of the Trinity in the gospel, where Spirit of Christ bears witness in their hearts that they are children of God the Father through Jesus Christ their Lord and Savior, and they enter the union and communion with the Triune God and one another that *is* the essence of the church.

Wesley added a parallel account of schism that begins as a breach of love between those who disagree, leading to unholy tempers, and then to unholy words and acts by groups that splinter into factions and eventually rend the fabric of the church. According to Wesley's definition, the real core of schism is the disunion of mind and heart, the disruption of fellowship with one another and with the Triune God, that leads to mistrust, loss of love, ill-will, and finally bitter words and acts on the part of groups alienated from one another even if they have managed to remain outwardly united. The accuracy of Wesley's depiction of this pattern of schism is all too evident in the subsequent history of Methodism right up to the present day.

The chapter also noted the ecclesial and social character of love for God and others arising out of a participatory encounter with God's love in the gospel, a love that works itself out through holy tempers to holy loving thoughts, words, and acts. For Wesley, the sociality and ecclesial nature of the love and the holy dispositions are relationally contagious and communicative: they are to be expressed to their particular end, that the love and communion the Triune God is and that the Trinitarian persons communicate to members of the body of Christ flow through members to one another and to world: "It is the nature of the divine saviour which is in you to spread to whatsoever you touch; to diffuse itself in every side, to all those among whom you are . . . that whatever grace you have received of God may through you get communicated to others."[11] Love and the holy dispositions, with their inherently relational, soteriological, and ecclesial character, were at the heart of small groups in early Methodism and are evident in the questions Wesley developed for the bands, as noted in chapter 4. Wesley's soteriology and ecclesiology are intertwined and are simply different dimensions

10 John Wesley, "Letter to a Roman Catholic," in *John Wesley*, ed. A. C. Outler (New York: Oxford University Press, 1964).

11 *Works*, 1:537.

of a single reality within his participatory, economic Trinitarian understanding of Christian faith.

Since there is a Trinitarian dimension in Wesley's soteriology and ecclesiology, because Christian faith, salvation, and the church are constituted by the activity of the Trinitarian persons in the gospel, then other aspects of Christian life, worship, discipleship, community, and ministry should bear the imprint of their Trinitarian source, agency, and telos. Chapter 5 documented and described the Trinitarian dimension in Wesley's descriptions of various forms of life, worship, discipleship, community, and ministry in early Methodism. When Wesley described the Trinitarian essence of the church as union and communion with the Triune God and one another in his sermon "Of the Church," he appealed to Ephesians 4. When Wesley provided examples of the *bene esse* of the church (what the ongoing life, community, discipleship, and ministry should be like), he often looked to Acts 2 and 4 and what resulted after Christ's life, death, resurrection, and ascension back to God the Father, and the outpouring of the Holy Spirit at Pentecost. Wesley saw the rise of a Methodist movement as the "dawning of a proper gospel day" and "a proper Christian church," similar to Acts 2 and 4. Wesley's Trinitarian vision of salvation and the church found its way into his discussions of many aspects of the Methodist movement, which further documents and explains the significance of Trinitarian dimension of Wesley's theology.

Whether readers find these chapters that identify and describe the Trinitarian dimension of John Wesley's theology convincing will depend on how well the chapters *together* illumine the pervasive Trinitarian pattern found in a variety of theological themes across a wide spectrum of Wesley's publications from 1738 to the end of his life. It may even require a rereading of Wesley's publications with the Trinitarian dimension as a pair of spectacles bringing Wesley's theology into focus in a new way.

Finally, a personal word. Writing this monograph has been a joyous journey of discovery and appreciation of the Trinitarian dimension of John Wesley's theology that he (along with Charles) injected into early Methodism at precisely the time when the doctrine of the Trinity was in the process of unraveling for many in England and throughout Western culture. I am grateful for all I have learned from the secondary sources cited throughout this work and for the work of scholars who wrote them even when I challenge their reading of Wesley at points. I hope the book illumines the Trinitarian dimension of Wesley's theology for others, and I hope it will encourage Wesleyans and Methodists to appreciate and appropriate Wesley's insights into the Trinitarian character of Christian faith, thought, life, community, and ministry.

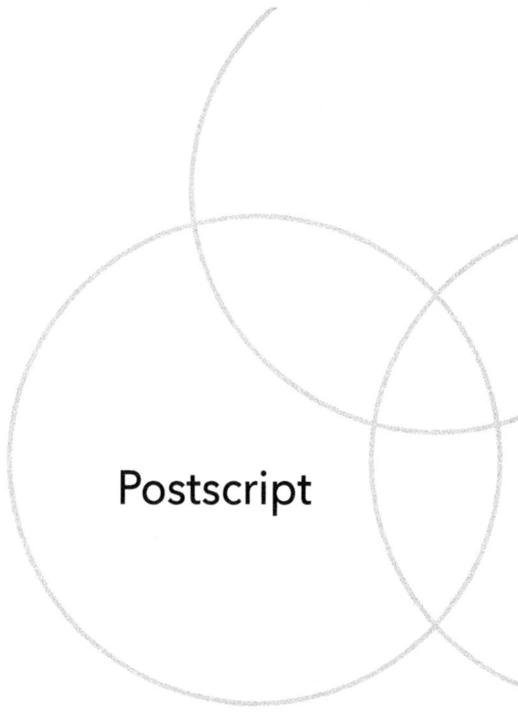

Postscript

The Trinitarian dimension of Wesley's vision of the center of Christian faith, the order of salvation, the essence of the church, and the societies, classes, bands, conferences, worship, devotional practices, and ministry documented and described in the chapters of this book intimate a more comprehensive Trinitarian expression of Wesleyan Christian faith than we have seen to date. This postscript is intentionally provocative in developing this point.

Until the recent resurgent interest in the Trinity and the Trinitarian dimension of all Christian faith and life over the past decades, the intellectual history of the Trinity in American Methodism after Wesley has been one of affirmation and neglect, and sometimes outright rejection. By the late nineteenth and into the twentieth century, scholars and pastors in one stream of American Methodism dismissed the doctrine of the Trinity as a relic of premodern Christianity, no longer viable after the discoveries of modern science and after critical historiography dissected the New Testament in ways that isolated its documents and undermined a holistic canonical theological approach to reading and interpreting this witness of the early church to Triune God of the gospel.

Methodism's focus on the personality of the one God from Asa Shinn through Daniel Whedon to Borden Parker Bowne proved to be incompatible with a Trinitarian understanding of personhood and made it difficult for Methodists to make sense of the doctrine of the Trinity. John Cobb illustrates the culmination of this tradition in his own unsuccessful attempt to incorporate a Trinitarian dimension into his theological perspective.[1] Even systematic theologians from Richard Watson through John Miley to others in the early twentieth century marginalized the Trinity within the dogmatic structure of their theologies so that the Trinitarian dimension of all of Christian faith, thought, and life got lost.

This opposition and neglect fostered a parallel marginalization of the Trinity in Wesleyan/Methodist churches right up to the present day.[2] How many pastors and laypersons today think and speak about their Christian faith and life in the kind of Trinitarian terms we see in Charles Wesley's hymns and in the early Methodists' accounts of their spiritual lives? Church talk about God today often sounds rather generic and more in tune with American monotheism or panentheism than with the Trinitarian Christian doctrine of God.

Recent interest in the Trinity and the Trinitarian dimension of Christian faith, thought, and practice in scholarly circles is a welcome relief from American's Methodism unhelpful monotheistic focus on the personhood of the one God and hopeful sign for the future of the Wesleyan/Methodist tradition.[3] The renaissance of Trinitarian Christian faith in Methodism today needs to continue and find its way into the life of churches.

My underlying interest in writing this book goes beyond providing a Trinitarian reading of Wesley's theology and documenting and describing the depth and breadth of the Trinitarian dimension in his theology. I hope the book encourages dialogue about Wesley that will help Methodism correct its vision and practice of Trinitarian Christian faith today. If the Wesleyan/Methodist tradition is to become more fully Trinitarian, it will require an appropriation and extension of the Trinitarian insights of the Wesley brothers and early Methodism. There is more work to be done on Wesley's doctrine of the Trinity, the Trinitarian character of his theology, and the Trinitarian dimension of the early Methodist experiment.

While Wesleyan/Methodism tradition can learn from Wesley's practical theological activity and produce its own Trinitarian materials for Christian formation, worship, community, ministry, and witness, Methodism also needs its own rigorous form of Trinitarian theology. Wesley did not provide his children with an *Institutes* or *Summa* where the Methodist body

1 See Elmer M. Colyer, "The Trinity," in *The Oxford Handbook of Methodist Studies*, ed. William J. Abraham and James E. Kirby (Oxford: Oxford University Press, 2009), 505–21.

2 Ibid.

3 Ibid.

of divinity that frames and interpenetrates Christian faith, life, and practice comes to careful, comprehensive, and architectonically rigorous expression, disclosing its distinctive Trinitarian patterns in praise of the Triune God of the gospel.[4] In fact, Wesley's theology created additional problems for those in the Wesleyan/Methodist tradition who want to learn from and develop his Trinitarian insights.

Chapter 3 noted one of these problems in relation to the quasi-Christological and incarnational language Wesley used to describe the moral law as a "transcript of the divine nature" and the "fairest offspring of the Father."[5] Wesley also gave the moral law a platonic spin as "supreme, unchangeable reason; . . . the everlasting fitness of things that are or ever were created . . . the nature and fitness of things, and on their essential relations to each other."[6] This vision of the law undermines the contingent character of creation, its creaturely freedom, and its intelligible order called into existence out of nothing by the Triune creator in freedom out of love, including the contingent character of the human mind and its ability to discover the order of creation and bring it to articulation in praise of Trinitarian God.

Wesley's vision of the law in Christological and platonic categories drives a wedge between (1) the character of God coming to expression in the law as a transcript of the divine nature, and (2) the Triune God revealed through Jesus Christ via the Spirit, and gives the moral law with its own independent ontological status separate from Christ. The crucial theological point that Wesley missed is that there is no hypostatic union between Word/Son of God and the moral law.[7] Only in Jesus Christ do we find the very Word/Son of God incarnate via the hypostatic union between the divine and human natures within the one person of Jesus Christ, a redemptive hypostatic union throughout the life, ministry, death, resurrection, and ascension where Christ as Savior and Lord continues to be the incarnate Son of God and sole source for the reconciliation and re-creation of humanity and the entire universe.

It is here in Wesley's vision of the moral law as a "transcript of the divine nature" and "the everlasting fitness of things that are or ever were created"

---

4 Ibid.

5 *The Works of John Wesley*, ed. Albert C. Outler, vols. 1–4, *Sermons* (Nashville: Abingdon, 1984), 2:9–11.

6 Ibid., 2:10, 13.

7 This same problem is the source of Wesley's biblicism that was mediated to American Methodism. There is no hypostatic union between the Word/Son of God and the Bible, giving Scripture an independent ontological status apart from the incarnation and the hypostatic union between the divine and human natures in Jesus Christ.

that we find the theological root of the moralism and legalism that have at times plagued the Wesleyan/Methodist tradition from Wesley on. In Wesley's vision, the moral law displaces the vicarious humanity of Christ in the nexus between Christology and soteriology, including the moral dimension of soteriology.

Some streams of theology, particularly in the Western tradition, view the Son of God assuming a neutral sinless humanity different from our own fallen, diseased, and dying humanity tragically enmeshed in sin and alienated from God, as does Wesley in various places in his publications. The question becomes how Christ's sinless humanity in his life, death, resurrection, and ascension is soteriologically related to our sinful humanity. Most often these traditions see Christ's sinless humanity as preparatory for him dying in our place, and his death on the cross becomes a forensic juridical transaction where the sinless Christ bears the punishment for human sin and guilt so that we can be forgiven and our status in relation to God changed from guilty sinners to God's children. But the question then becomes what about our sinful human nature? How is this aspect of the human predicament overcome, since Christ's humanity is sinless and only provides for our forgiveness and change in status? Wesley has a far more robust understanding of how all grace including justification and sanctification comes to us not *from* Christ but *in* Christ. We will return to this question in a moment.

It is precisely at this point that the crucial character of Christ's vicarious humanity comes into view. The Son/Word of God assumed our actual sinful, broken, diseased, and dying humanity in order to enter fully into the human predicament and overcome our sin, guilt, alienation, ignorance, and death. The incarnate Son did this in order to sanctify, perfect, and bend our wayward humanity that he assumed from us in the incarnation back to perfect obedience to God at every single point throughout Christ's life, ministry, death, and resurrection. The fully incarnate Son ascended to God the Father with that vicariously perfected humanity still intact. The incarnation is not an episode that ended with the empty tomb. Christ is still the incarnate Son of God and our faithful, fully human high priest at the right hand of the Father within the Trinitarian life and communion of God.

The Son of God assumed our actual sinful humanity to be made like us in every way and tempted in every way just as we are (Hebrews 2:14–18 & 4:14–16). Far from ever sinning, our elder brother Jesus overcame our temptation and sin, reconciling our humanity, including the alienated human mind, realizing within his human mind genuine knowledge of God. Christ redeemed our sinful humanity that he vicariously assumed from us and restored that humanity to participation in the love of God the Father through fellowship of the Spirit of God, the Spirit that Christ received into our humanity on our behalf and in our place at his baptism by John the Baptist at the onset of Jesus's earthly ministry. When the Holy Spirit comes upon the church at Pentecost and ever after, the Spirit comes as the Spirit of Jesus who unites us to the vicarious redeemed humanity of our elder brother Jesus Christ, our savior and Lord, and through Christ with God the Father. The Spirit unites us to Christ and, in so doing, mediates Christ's vicarious humanity to our fallen, broken, and sinful humanity, effecting our reconciling and redemption, our justification and sanctification, including the moral dimension of soteriology.

In Christ's vicarious humanity, substitution and representation are intertwined in the reconciling and redeeming incarnational union of the Son of God with our actual sinful humanity. Jesus Christ lives and acts in our place, on our behalf, and in our stead from his birth, through life, ministry, death, resurrection, and ascension in a true, faithful, and perfect human response of faith, prayer and praise, morality, ministry, and everything else, the self-offering of Jesus Christ to God the Father with which the Father is well pleased.[8]

This means that Christian faith, life, ministry, and morality are always participatory via union with Christ and his vicarious humanity through the Spirit. Wesley understood this crucial point about participation via union with Christ: "Christ does not give life to the soul separate from, but in and with, himself. Hence his words are equally true of all men, in whatever state of grace they are: 'As the branch cannot bear fruit of itself, except it abide in the vine, no more can ye except ye abide in me . . . without,' or *separate* from, 'me, ye can do nothing.' 'Whatever grace we receive, it is a free gift from him. . . . We have this grace not *from* Christ but in him."[9] But the question is whether Wesley's Christology can support his participatory "in Christ" understanding of soteriology expressed is this text without incorporating an account of the role of Christ's vicarious humanity, especially in relation to the Christ's fulfilling of the moral law. There are several places in Wesley's writings that point in the right direction. This lack of a clear account of the vicarious humanity of Christ is also a theological root of Methodism's tendency to associate justification with what Christ does for us and sanctification with what the Spirit works in us.

---

8 See Elmer M. Colyer, *How to Read T. F. Torrance: Understanding His Trinitarian and Scientific Theology* (Downers Grove, IL: InterVarsity, 2001), chapters 2 and 3 for an account of the mediation of Christ along these lines.

9 *The Works of John Wesley*, ed. Paul Wesley Chilcote and Kenneth J. Collins, vol. 13, *Doctrinal and Controversial Treatises II* (Nashville: Abingdon, 2013), 60.

Without a robust doctrine of the vicarious humanity of Christ and our participation via the Spirit in that humanity, Wesley's portrayal of the moral law in Christological imagery as the "face of God unveiled," "a transcript of the divine nature," and " the fairest offspring of the Father" comes to the forefront in our human response as the absolute standard of faithfulness, and the Christian life becomes life in the Spirit aiding us in an exact keeping of the law in life, discipleship, and ministry.[10] For too many of Wesley's followers, Christ who provides our justification fades into the background, and sanctification easily becomes the province of the Spirit with an exalted vision of moral law as the exacting standard by which we live out our sanctification and in light of which we and will be judged. Those who follow Wesley on this point are then faced with a strict cataloguing of moral laws and scrupulous conformity to every single one of them in community, discipleship, and ministry. Remember Wesley's own terse way of stating it: "What God demands is an entire obedience; we are to have an eye to all his commandments; otherwise we lose all the labour we take in keeping some, and our poor souls for ever and ever."[11] The threat of failure to enact stringent legalistic conformity to the moral law is rather stark, despite Wesley's insight that every command is a promise of what Christ will work in us.[12]

---

10 *Works*, 2:9–10.

11 *Works*, 1:555–56.

12 It is at precisely this point that the Wesleyan/Methodist tradition often falls prey to the fallacy of false alternatives between monergism and synergism in the relationship between divine and human agency in salvation. Wesley's followers repeatedly embrace some form of synergism where agency is apportioned to God and the human person in a zero-sum game where human agency contributes to the soteriological synergy by living holy lives meticulously keeping the moral law. This misunderstanding leads inexorably to a grim kind of Christian faith and life where some aspect of humanity agency parceled out via synergism becomes the weak link in the soteriological chain no longer fully "in Christ" from beginning to end, and it leads to fear and the loss of faith, love, and hope.

Here those in the Wesleyan/Methodist tradition can benefit from the anhypostatis/enhypostatis couplet developed by T. F. Torrance, among others. The anhypostatis/enhypostatis couplet expresses the inner character of grace in which all of grace (full divine agency) includes all of humanity (full human agency), first in the Incarnate Son of God, Jesus Christ, and his vicarious humanity/human agency, and then in us and our full agenic response that is always a participation via the Spirit in Christ and his vicarious humanity. Our humanity was and is personalized and humanized, our agency is transformed, upheld, and intensified first in Christ's vicarious humanity and then in our humanity in all areas of faith, life, community, discipleship, and ministry (see Colyer, *How to Read T. F. Torrance*, 117–23, 176–80).

Over the past thirty-seven years as a pastor and seminary professor, I have repeatedly encountered this kind of moralism and legalism and its destructive consequences in the lives of faithful Methodists who have lost any sense of what Wesley called "the happy and holy communion which the faithful have with God the Father, Son and Holy Ghost"[13] and who have found themselves continuously imperiled by the law as a transcript of the divine nature rather than comforted by Jesus our great high priest and elder brother, who is at the right hand of God the Father, who is able to empathize with us in our weakness because he became like us in every way and was tempted as we are, as we see in Hebrews 2 and 4. There is a place for the moral law in the Christian life, but not for a moral law with its own independent ontological status separate from Christ and exalted as "a transcript of the divine nature" and a stringent legalistic conformity to the moral law that flows from it. The Christian life has to be understood as a participation in Christ's vicarious humanity overcoming our sin, our guilt, our broken and sinful nature, in his obedience to God the Father in our place and on our behalf, restoring our humanity to holy and happy union and communion with the Triune God and one another, a participation realized in our lives via the personal presence and agency of the Spirit. Only within that context do we think about the place of the moral law in the Christian life. In other words, there is and must be a robust participatory Trinitarian dimension in how we think about the moral law in relation to the Christian life.

There are intimations of a better way forward in Wesley's insight into the dawning of a proper gospel day and a proper Christian church in Acts 2 and 4. His sermon "The Mystery of Iniquity" provided an alternative account to careful cataloguing of moral laws and scrupulous conformity to them:

> They were daily taught by the apostles, and had all things in common and received the Lord's Supper, and attended all the public service. "And all that believed were together, and had all things common; and sold their possessions, and parted them to all men, as every man had need." And again; "The multitude of them that believe," now greatly increased, "were of one heart and of one soul. Neither said any of them that ought of the things which he possessed was his own, but they had all things in common."
>
> But here a question will naturally occur. How came they to act thus, to have all things in common, seeing we do not read of any positive command to do this? I answer, there needed no outward command:

13 *Works*, 3:89–90.

> the command was written on their hearts. It naturally and necessarily resulted from the degree of love which they enjoyed.[14]

Wesley stated with deep theological insight that when Christians' hearts are filled with the love of God through the grace of Christ in the fellowship of the Spirit they need no moral command to share all things: "Observe! 'They were of one heart and of one soul: and not so much as one' (so the words run) 'said' (they could not, while their hearts so overflowed with love) 'that any of the things which he possessed was his own.'" Wesley noted that whenever this love awakened in the human heart by the redemptive presence of the Triune God, we should expect the same kind of results: "And wheresoever the same cause shall prevail the same effect will naturally flow."[15]

This is a robust Trinitarian alternative to Wesley's vision of the law in Christological and incarnational language: the love of God that we come to know through the grace of our Lord Jesus Christ in the power of the Spirit leads to love so supreme in the lives of Christians in union and communion with God and one another that they need no outward command. The moral law is an approximation that cannot capture the richness of Trinitarian love, and the love for God and one another that flow from it. A strict cataloging of moral laws and a scrupulous conformity to every single one of them (as the exacting standard for Christian life and community) have often become antithetical and an impediment to a life of love for God and for one another and for the character of the community that results. The moral law has its proper place and is crucial for restraining evil, for convicting people of sin, and for guiding Christian life. But the ultimate vision of the New Creation is Trinitarian love, love that is holy, but not a love or a holiness defined as a careful cataloguing of moral laws and scrupulous conformity to them.

It is not only legalism/moralism that emerges from this lack of a clear account of the vicarious humanity of Christ and the tendency to associate justification with Christology and sanctification with pneumatology. When modern American Methodism lost its vision of the deity of Christ, it was theologically easy for Methodists to move into some form of panentheism where the dynamism of a pneumatically conceived divine presence already present in all people displaces the high Christology of historic Christian faith clearly present in Wesley's theology as the constitutive source of grace. The result can take the form of an individualist religion where people already possess a spark of the divine and their own potentiality (novel possibilities) and simply need to be awakened to it, a religion that comports well with

14 *Works*, 2:455.
15 Ibid.

American culture. Or it can take the form of a morally driven expression of religion that attempts to create the kingdom of God on earth as the latest social project realized by human ingenuity and persuasion and/or by power and coercion. Both versions lead to an anthropocentric Christian religion devoid of the participatory Trinitarian dynamism that characterized the Wesley brothers' vision of Christian faith, life, community, and mission, and its embodiment in early Methodism. The inability of these anthropocentric versions of Christian religion to revitalize the church and its mission is only all too evident in Methodism in America today.

The other problem Wesley passed on to the Wesleyan/Methodist tradition is the lack of an account of the relation between (1) Wesley's the doctrine of the Trinity and the Trinitarian dimension of soteriology and ecclesiology, and (2) his understanding of the one God, God's attributes, and a doctrine of providence that comes close to divine determinism. Wesley stated, "If God presides *universis tanquam singulis, et singulis tanquam universis* . . . what is it (except only our own sins [the misuse of the grace we receive]) which we are not to ascribe to the providence of God?"[16] Wesley here reflected ideas present in eighteenth-century Anglicanism. Yet he passed the problem on to his followers. We find his doctrine of the one God and God's attributes, including his vision of providence, affirmed and embraced in some segments of American Methodism right up to the present day, though we find many Wesleyan/Methodist scholars and some pastors are turning to various forms of process panentheism in an attempt to redress the relation of providence to the problem of evil at the center of the theodicy debate and to move beyond Wesley's inadequate formulation of it.[17]

Nowhere in Wesley's writings did he provide a discussion of the relationship between the Triune God known via participatory "acquaintance" in the gospel, and his doctrine of the one God, God's attributes, and God's providence. In fact, in a few places, Wesley placed this doctrine of the one God and Triune God in proximity with one another within the same sermon.[18] There is a theological reason for this separation of the doctrine of the Trinity and the doctrine of the one God and the influence of that separation in other areas of Wesley's theology.

The key is in Wesley's sermon "On the Trinity." It arises, at least in part, over Wesley's dissatisfaction with those who defended the doctrine of the

16 Ibid., 2:56–57.

17 See Colyer, "The Trinity," 15–17.

18 *Works,* 1:572–89, compare 1:588–89 with 1:580–81.

Trinity throughout the Trinitarians controversies. Remember that in his sermon "On The Trinity," Wesley stated that no "well-judging man would attempt to explain them [how the three are one] at all."[19] Here Wesley appealed to Jonathan Swift's criticism of those Trinitarian defenders: "Herein [Swift] shows that all who endeavoured to explain it [the Trinity, how the three are one] at all have utterly lost their way; have above all other persons hurt the cause which they intended to promote."[20]

Later in the sermon, Wesley argued that "the Bible barely requires you to believe . . . the *fact* [*that* the three are one], but . . . the *manner, how* [*how* the three are one] I do not comprehend. . . . It is no object of my faith; I believe just so much as God has revealed and no more."[21] According to Wesley, Christians are to believe in the doctrine of the Trinity without ever inquiring further into how the three are one. Nothing can be known about relation between the one being and three persons of the Trinity, though Wesley said more about the relation than he realized or admitted. One cannot but remember the ridicule of Stephen Nye aimed at those who appealed to mystery around the relation between the one being and three persons: "They deny all Explications: we must say therefore 'tis Samaritanism for . . . they worship they know not what."[22]

This is precisely part of what allows the doctrine of the one God and the doctrine of the Trinity to drift apart theologically. In Wesley's own reflections, as documented throughout this book, he discussed the doctrine of the Trinity and the Trinitarian dimension of soteriology and ecclesiology in various places. At other points he dealt with the doctrine of the one God and the attributes and providence of the one God, but he never incorporated a corresponding Trinitarian dimension into those discussions.

The question immediately is how can this be, since there is no one being apart from the Trinitarian persons and no Trinitarian persons apart from God's one being? Wesley here simply reflected the discussions of the doctrine of the one God, God's attributes, and doctrine of providence in eighteenth-century Anglicanism and elsewhere in the history of Christian

19 *Works*, 2:376–77.

20 Ibid., 2:377.

21 Ibid., 2:383–84.

22 Stephen Nye, *Considerations on the Explications of the Doctrine of the Trinity by Dr. Wallis, Dr. Sherlock, Dr. S___th, Dr. Cudworth and Mr. Hooker; and also of the Account given by those who say, the Trinity is an Unconceivable and Inexplicable Mystery* (n.p., 1693), 32. See also Philip Dixon, *Nice and Hot Disputes: The Doctrine of the Trinity in the Seventeenth Century* (London: T & T Clark, 2003), 129.

thought,[23] even as his retrieved a Trinitarian vision of Christian faith and life and injected it into early Methodism during the period in England that witnessed the demise of the doctrine of the Trinity for many in Western culture. Only after many failed attempts to restate Christian faith and the Christian doctrine of God without a Trinitarian dimension throughout the modern period after the Trinitarian controversies did Karl Barth and Karl Rahner return to the doctrine of the Trinity and integrate the Trinitarian dimension back into Christian faith and thought in the twentieth century while providing more satisfactory accounts of the relation between the one God and the Trinitarian persons.

The separation and unrelieved tension between the doctrine of the one God and the doctrine of the Trinity in Wesley and in the Wesleyan/Methodist intellectual history is theologically problematic and needs to be challenged.[24] There is no one being of God separated from the Trinitarian persons and vice versa. That separation needs to be overcome so that the doctrine of God, God's attributes, and other doctrines like providence are developed in a fully Trinitarian manner. There are intimations of a more theologically adequate Trinitarian solution to this tension in the content of some of Charles Wesley's hymns and in a few places in John's theological reflections.

Chapter 2 noted how in "The End of Christ's Coming" sermon, Wesley read what he learned of the Triune character of God and the character of God's participatory Trinitarian relation with us established and revealed in the gospel back into the Genesis narrative, back into God's relationship with humanity prior to the Fall, indeed, as we saw in his "Letter to a Roman Catholic," ultimately back into God's own Trinitarian life as God. In fact, Wesley explicitly stated that this participatory Trinitarian character of Christian faith "runs through the Bible from the beginning to the end, in one connected chain. And the agreement of every part of it with every other is properly the analogy of faith. Beware of taking anything else, or anything less than this for religion."[25]

If we take Wesley's point about the economic, participatory Trinitarian character of the analogy of faith seriously, including Wesley's example of reading it back into the Genesis narrative and into humanity's relationship

23 There are plenty of examples in the history of Christian thought of the separation and isolation of the doctrine of the one God and the doctrine of the Trinity within theology, as we see in Thomas Aquinas's *Summa theologiae* or the Westminster Confession of Faith.

24 See Colyer, "The Trinity," 514–17.

25 *Works*, 2:483.

with the Triune God prior to the Fall, why would we not read the Trinitarian dimension into the doctrine of providence and God's attributes, and rethink what we can say about relation between the one being and three persons and how the three are one? Wesley's followers today can also learn from the renaissance in Trinitarian theology in other Christian traditions, as many Methodist scholars are already doing, and move beyond this separation between the one being of God and the Trinitarian persons in the Wesleyan/ Methodist tradition.[26]

Thomas Langford, at the end of his book *Practical Divinity: Theology in the Wesleyan Tradition*, raised the question of whether Wesleyan/Methodist theological tradition has run its course and should simply merge back into the broader Christian tradition out of which it arose as a movement of renewal.[27] I am not convinced that this should happen, because I believe that Wesleyan/Methodist tradition has unrealized potentiality. For Methodism to become a dynamic revitalizing movement again, it needs to learn from John Wesley and early Methodism and devote more attention to the Trinitarian dimension of all Christian faith, thought, and practice, and to the Trinitarian God of the New Creation who is always the source, the divine agent, and the goal of Christian faith and life, of the renewal of the church, and of the transformation of the world. I hope this monograph will further that end.

26 Colyer, "The Trinity," 517–19.
27 Thomas A. Langford, *Practical Divinity: Theology in the Wesleyan Tradition*, rev. ed. (Nashville: Abingdon, 1998), 256.

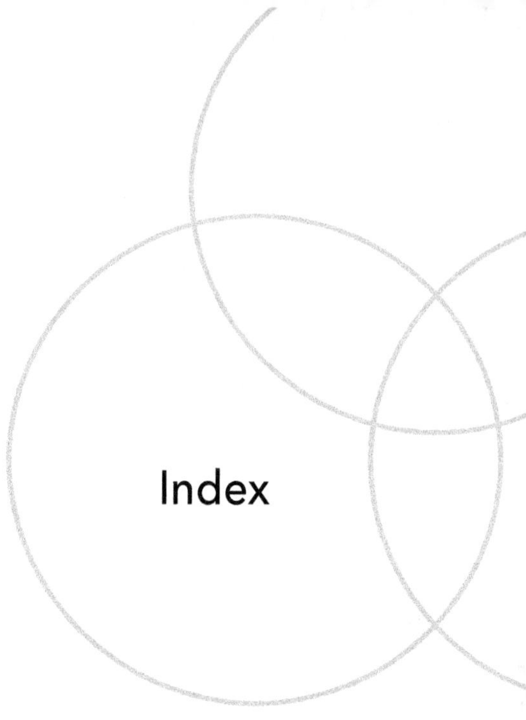

Index

Titles of works are by John Wesley unless otherwise noted.

www.ingramcontent.com/pod-product-compliance
Lightning Source LLC
LaVergne TN
LVHW020527100826
845148LV00010B/1377

* 9 7 9 8 3 8 5 2 7 6 7 3 8 *